THE
DIVIDED
METROPOLIS

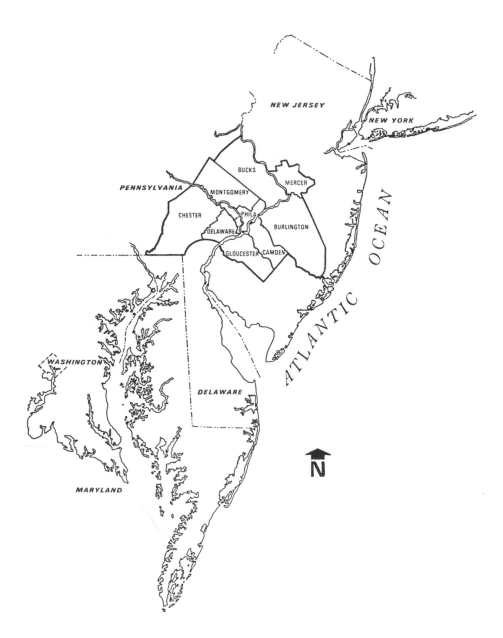

Philadelphia in Its Regional Context. *Courtesy of the Delaware Valley Regional Planning Commission.*

THE DIVIDED METROPOLIS

Social and Spatial Dimensions
of Philadelphia, 1800 -1975

Edited by
WILLIAM W. CUTLER, III
and
HOWARD GILLETTE, Jr.

CONTRIBUTIONS IN AMERICAN HISTORY, NUMBER 85

 GREENWOOD PRESS
WESTPORT, CONNECTICUT • LONDON, ENGLAND

Library of Congress Cataloging in Publication Data

Main entry under title:

The Divided metropolis.

(Contributions in American history ; no. 85
ISSN 0084-9219)
"Evolved out of the Bicentennial meeting of the
American Studies Association, held in Philadelphia in
April 1976."
Bibliography: p.
Includes index.
1. Philadelphia—Social conditions—Addresses,
essays, lectures. 2. Land use, Urban—Pennsylvania—
Philadelphia—Addresses, essays, lectures. 3. Philadelphia
metropolitan area—Social conditions—Addresses, essays,
lectures. I. Cutler, William W. II. Gillette, Howard.
HN80.P5D58   309.1'748'11   79-7729
ISBN 0-313-21351-8

Library of Congress Catalog Card Number: 79-7729
ISBN: 0-313-21351-8
ISSN: 0084-9219

First published in 1980

Greenwood Press
A division of Congressional Information Service, Inc.
51 Riverside Avenue, Westport, Connecticut 06880

Printed in the United States of America

10 9 8 7 6 5 4 3 2 1

Contents

Illustrations

Figures

Maps

Tables

70. Wister
71. Morton
72. East Mount Airy
73. West Mount Airy
74. Chestnut Hill
75. Cedarbrook
76. West Oak Lane
77. Logan
78. East Oak Lane
79. Olney
80. Lawncrest
81. Summerdale
82. Northwood
83. Frankford
84. Wissinoming
85. Tacony
86. Mayfair
87. Oxford Circle
88. Burholme
89. Fox Chase
90. Rhawnhurst
91. Lexington Park
92. Holmesburg
93. Upper Holmesburg
94. Torresdale
95. Academy Garden
96. Ashton-Woodenbridge
97. Pennypack Woods
98. Winchester Park
99. Pennypack
100. Bustleton
101. West Torresdale
102. Morrell Park
103. Crestmont Farms
104. Millbrook
105. Modena Park
106. Parkwood Manor
107. Mechanicsville
108. Byberry
109. Somerton

39. Spring Garden
40. Poplar
41. Northern Liberties
42. Francisville
43. Fairmount
44. Olde Kensington
45. Ludlow
46. Yorktown
47. North Central
48. Sharswood
49. Brewerytown
50. Strawberry Mansion
51. Stanton
52. Hartranft
53. Franklinville
54. Nicetown-Tioga
55. Allegheny West
56. Hunting Park
57. Fishtown
58. Kensington
59. West Kensington
60. Feltonville
61. Juniata
62. Richmond
63. Bridesburg
64. Andorra
65. Upper Roxborough
66. Roxborough
67. Manayunk
68. East Falls
69. Germantown

1. Logan Circle
2. Chinatown
3. Old City
4. Society Hill
5. Washington Square
6. Rittenhouse
7. Schuylkill
8. Southwest Center City
9. Hawthorne
10. Bell Vista
11. Queen Village
12. Pennsport
13. Wharton
14. Point Breeze
15. Grays Ferry
16. Girard Estate
17. Packer Park
18. Whitman
19. Eastwick

20. Elmwood
21. Paschall
22. Kingsessing
23. Southwest Schuylkill
24. Cobbs Creek
25. Garden Court
26. Cedar Park
27. Spruce Hill
28. University City
29. Powelton
30. Mantua
31. Belmont
32. Mill Creek
33. Haddington
34. Overbrook
35. Carroll Park
36. Parkside
37. Wynnefield
38. Wynnefield Heights

The Neighborhoods of Philadelphia. *Map and key courtesy of the Philadelphia City Planning Commission.*

Preface

WILLIAM W. CUTLER, III, and
HOWARD GILLETTE, JR.

Contemporary observers generally agree that the modern metropolis is socially and physically divided. Such division is associated with the deterioration of urban life, and its most often cited faults include the breakdown of central government, the separation of work from residence, the subsequent differentiation of residential neighborhoods by income and ethnicity, and the concentration of city dwellers in mutually exclusive clubs and associations. The cost of these patterns, according to Sam Bass Warner in his prize-winning study of Philadelphia, *The Private City*, has been nothing less than "the total loss of control over the metropolitan environment."[1] If the compact pedestrian city of the preindustrial era once operated on the basis of shared community goals, metropolitan growth has upset this balance, bringing instead demographic dispersal and eventually segregation. "From first to last," Warner concluded in 1968, "the structure of Philadelphia has been such that, with the exception of the brief and creative union of equalitarian goals and business leadership in the early nineteenth century, no powerful group" was fashioned "which understood the city as a whole and . . . wanted to deal with it as a public environment of a democratic society."[2]

Most scholars, including Warner, have placed the full emergence of such social and physical division in the twentieth century, most notably because of the effects of the private automobile. "The industrial metropolis was not just the nineteenth-century big city grown larger," Warner wrote, "it had a unique social and spatial organization." The modern metropolis, Hans Blumenthal has added, "is no longer a larger version of the traditional city but a new and different form of human settlement."[3] Such stress on recent changes in urban structures can be deceiving, however, for as Kenneth Jackson has persuasively argued, the central feature of metropolitanization—population dispersal—can be traced well back into the nineteenth century. So impressive is this continuity that Jackson has concluded that:

Although suburbs now contain more people than central cities, although urban densities are now lower and more even, although metropolitan sprawl now infests thousands rather than dozens of square miles, although the poor and disadvantaged are now present in larger proportions toward the center, and although a journey to work is now more common and longer, these differences are largely quantitative rather than qualitative.[4]

Jackson's evidence is compelling enough to justify a reassessment of the prevailing perceptions of metropolitan growth. Before passing judgment on his conclusions, however, more systematic study is needed. As a case study, Philadelphia offers a particularly good opportunity for such a reappraisal because of the early inception and long duration of its drive to metropolitan status. Here the nature of the changes associated with population dispersal and social and physical differentiation can be carefully traced over a substantial span of time and space. While this collection of essays necessarily relies on selected examples of the process, it considers nevertheless the kinds of links which Jackson envisioned between the nineteenth and twentieth centuries. At the same time it suggests the importance of distinguishing among different stages of urban decentralization. Although the process appears continuous, it should be viewed as having at least three intervals, each with its own set of distinctive qualities.

In the first wave of suburbanization artisans and manual workers moved to the periphery when they were no longer able to find space for their homes and shops in the urban core.[5] At this stage in its development before the Civil War, Philadelphia's social and financial elite still aspired to national leadership, and the removal of many of its craftsmen from the heart of the city underscored their relegation to the fringe of the socioeconomic system. With the growth of industry and the extension of markets in the second half of the nineteenth century, a new spatial arrangement emerged. Factories appeared in the working-class suburbs while transportation innovations induced white-collar workers to move their homes to more exclusive areas in a new outer ring of settlement. As Samuel P. Hays has pointed out, it was at this stage of suburbanization that specialized land use was greatly advanced,[6] and by the 1880s the modern pattern of differentiation between a downtown dominated by government, finance, and commerce and its suburbs, both blue- and white-collar, industrial and residential, had begun to take shape. Meanwhile, the professionalization of architecture further contributed to the social and spatial fragmentation of the city, making possible distinctive designs for more and more residences, businesses, and churches, which helped distinguish one part of the city from another. Finally, in the twentieth century a third wave of suburbanization occurred. Associated with the popularization of the automobile, it gave rise to the almost unrestricted decentralization of both jobs and population. More highways, cars, and trucks together with improved communications systems diminished demand for in-town locations and speeded up the centrifugal movement of business and people over a vastly expanded metropolitan area.

Despite these distinctions among different phases of suburbanization, the problems associated with dispersal have remained remarkably constant over time. Urban governments, for example, have long had to extend themselves to provide services required by metropolitan expansion. As inherited from the eighteenth century, privatism may have prevented cities from responding adequately to these demands, as Warner maintains, but at each stage in the process of metropolitanization, governmental growth has occurred. In the nineteenth century, cities attempted to exert control over their suburban hinterlands by annexing surrounding territory. When resistance to such incorporation peaked in the twentieth century, cities resurrected an innovation first introduced 100 years before—the limited service organization, formed to supply such essentials as water and transportation to a vast area. Indeed, throughout the history of metropolitan growth governmental expansion has been closely linked with social and spatial differentiation. If people were increasingly isolated in their places of work and residence or in their associational activity, they were nonetheless tied to one another through a growing web of public restraints emanating from centralized bureaucracies.

The application of power, then, as well as its extent became a critical factor in shaping the structure of the modern metropolis. Michael B. Katz, for example, has pointed out that the first stage of metropolitan growth was marked by an important shift from voluntary to formal institutions as the means for solving social problems in what Katz calls the triumph of incipient bureaucracy. Amateurs and later experts organized schools, hospitals, and other social welfare institutions ostensibly to expand opportunity, but, Katz argues, such efforts were biased in favor of assisting those already advantaged while imposing controls on those whose values and experiences placed them outside the mainstream.[7]

Whether by design or not, the results of governmental activism in the nineteenth and the twentieth centuries have often been selective. In housing, where privatism has long been entrenched, the expanding influence of government has served to confine rather than to overcome the practice of discrimination. Urban and regional planners have tried to think comprehensively about metropolitan areas, but at the same time they have enhanced specialized land use through such tools as zoning because, as one member of the American Institute of Planners put it, "a reasonable [amount of] segregation is normal, inevitable and desirable."[8]

Among current urban problems none has received more attention than social, economic, and racial segregation, typified in metropolitan regions by the contrast between white residential suburbs and black inner-city ghettos. Because earlier generations of immigrants to cities were never so fully isolated by residence as those in today's black districts, it is thought that such social confinement developed rather recently. But a review of Philadelphia's modern history suggests not only that the differentiation of residential areas first appeared well over a century ago but also that even within mixed communities powerful forces have long operated to divide one social group from another. For the Irish who settled in the Rittenhouse neighborhood in the mid-nineteenth century or the working-class whites who lived in the Franklinville section of East Mount Airy, roles and expectations were tightly prescribed, just as they are in the contemporary ghetto. Given the constraints imposed by the available housing stock, the inescapable trend in modern urban life has been toward residential homogeneity. But it should not be imagined that heterogeneity has ever assured either personal interaction or mutual respect, as the violent clashes between Philadelphia's native-born and immigrant workers demonstrated in the 1840s. A significant element of spatial structure, then, has been and continues to be the degree to which activity within that particular sphere is further defined and restricted.

Associated with the question of residential segregation has been the added separation of urban Americans into exclusive, private organizations such as clubs, fraternal and beneficial orders, parishes, and other similar groups. In *The Private City,* Warner, like other historians, traced this phenomenon back to the industrial stage of urbanization when formerly open organizations like the volunteer fire companies polarized according to race, ethnicity, or life-style. While he recognized that such institutions provided a necessary and wholesome service to first-generation city dwellers, he also argued that "an adaptation which served the interests of individual citizens did not when repeated a thousandfold create a good public result." A city of "closed social cells," he said, "could not imitate the open, easy neighborhood life of the town, nor could it establish a sufficiently inclusive system to maintain order against the stresses of industrialization."[9]

During the twentieth century local organizations based on ethnicity or socioeconomic status have often given way to residential associations which, according to their advocates, have provided the advantage of bringing different people together in an increasingly specialized world.[10] Yet as urban neighborhoods have grown increasingly homogeneous and as patterns of high residential turnover have worked their way into every part of most metropolitan areas, the benefits of such association have become limited. Neighborhood groups have occasionally transcended their localized interests to form coalitions, banding together, for example, to stop plans for disruptive highways or commercial developments. But for the most part they have confined their efforts to narrow fields of interest, making them no less parochial in their own way than the exclusively ethnic or class groups which preceded them.

These essays suggest, then, a process of evolution in which the immediate context may change but in which the long-term issues associated with social and spatial differentiation have remained remarkably consistent over more than a century of metropolitan development. Generations of planners, government officials, and social commentators have sought to achieve greater social and civic unity for cities. In many instances significant reforms have been accomplished, but the pieces of the whole remain in tension—a relationship which is sometimes healthy, sometimes not. For all Americans the challenge continues to be what it has been for the past century, to deal with the complex realities inherent in the divided metropolis.

□□□

This book evolved out of the Bicentennial Meeting of the American Studies Association, held in Philadelphia in April 1976. Since being offered the opportunity to build upon the papers read at that meeting, the editors have added a number of new topics while omitting others presented in 1976 as less fitting to the final goals of this volume. To both those whose papers we have included and those whose work we have not, we are grateful for the productive insights and contributions which they made to the ultimate form and content of this book.

In any anthology, with its several contributors, there are bound to be more scholarly debts to be acknowledged in public than in most monographs or texts. Individual authors in this volume have expressed their personal thanks to a number of people in the footnotes to their respective chapters. But special recognition is warranted here for Jon Wakelyn, the editor of the Greenwood Press series in American history, who encouraged us to undertake this project in the first place; Theodore Hershberg and his staff at the Philadelphia Social History Project, whose materials are invaluable to the study of Philadelphia in the nineteenth century; and Frederic M. Miller and his associates in the Urban Archives of Paley Library at Temple University where several of our contributors did research.

William W. Cutler, III
Howard Gillette, Jr.

Brookline, Massachusetts
December 1978

Notes

1. Sam Bass Warner, Jr., *The Private City: Philadelphia in Three Periods of Its Growth* (Philadelphia: University of Pennsylvania Press, 1968), p. 173.

2. Ibid., p. 223.

3. Ibid., p. 161. While Blumenthal notes that decentralization away from the core city has gone on for more than a century, he gives special emphasis to the effect of the automobile and the truck, writing that "with the acquisition of these aids to communication and mobility the city burst its eggshell and emerged as a metropolis." Hans Blumenthal, "The Modern Metropolis," *Scientific American* 213 (September 1965): 67. Urban historians Charles N. Glaab and A. Theodore Brown strike a similar chord, quoting the sociologist Roderick D. McKenzie's 1933 study, *The Metropolitan Community,* which said that the emerging metropolis ought to be considered "practically a new social and economic entity." *A History of Urban America,* 2d ed. (New York: Macmillan Publishing Co., 1976), p. 247.

4. Kenneth T. Jackson, "Urban Deconcentration in the Nineteenth Century: A Statistical Inquiry," in *The New Urban History: Quantitative Explorations by American Historians,* ed. Leo F. Schnore (Princeton, N.J.: Princeton University Press, 1975), p. 140.

5. Tracing the development of suburbs back to the early formation of towns in Western Civilization, Fernand Braudel notes that traditionally "to reach the suburbs was always to take a step downwards" in social status. *Capitalism and Material Life, 1400-1800,* trans. Miriam Kochan (New York: Harper & Row, 1973), p. 391.

6. Samuel P. Hays, "The Changing Political Structure of the City in Industrial America," *Journal of Urban History* 1 (November 1974): 9-11.

7. Michael B. Katz, "The Origins of Public Education: A Reassessment," *History of Education Quarterly* 16 (Winter 1976): 385-6; see also Michael B. Katz, *Class, Bureaucracy, and Schools: The Illusion of Educational Change in America* (New York: Praeger Publishers, 1971), pp. xiii, 28-48.

8. Robert Whitten, "Zoning and Living Conditions," *Proceedings of the Thirteenth National Conference on City Planning,* 28, quoted in Mel Scott, *American City Planning Since 1890* (Berkeley and Los Angeles: University of California Press, 1971), p. 198.

9. Warner, *The Private City,* p. 62. For an account of the polarization of fire companies along ethnic lines see Bruce Laurie, "Fire Companies and Gangs in Southwark: The 1840s," in *The Peoples of Philadelphia: A History of Ethnic Groups and Lower-Class Life, 1790-1940,* ed. Allen F. Davis and Mark H. Haller (Philadelphia: Temple University Press, 1973), pp. 71-87.

10. Among the earliest and most eloquent advocates of this position was Mary Parker Follett who wrote in 1918, "Some of us are looking for the remedy of our fatal isolation in a worthy and purposeful neighborhood life." To the charge that such association was too narrow, she retorted that cosmopolitans, grouped together by narrow interests, tended to be all alike. "I go to the medical association to meet doctors, I go to my neighborhood club to meet men." *The New State, Group Organization the Solution of Popular Government* (New York: Longmans, Green & Co., 1918), pp. 191-92, 196.

THE
DIVIDED
METROPOLIS

CHAPTER 1 The Emergence of the Modern Metropolis: Philadelphia in the Age of Its Consolidation[1]

HOWARD GILLETTE, JR.

The confluence of social and economic developments that made the process of urbanization in nineteenth-century American cities so dramatic—massive immigration, industrialization, and rapid population growth—has focused scholarly attention on the more divisive aspects of urban transformation. Class conflict and instability, the clash between different cultures and values, and the painful adjustment to changing employment conditions have offered great inducement for historical analysis. Such work has been well read for the possible insights it might offer into contemporary urban problems, but it has obscured a countervailing movement toward urban rationalization which marks the single closest link between the Victorian city and our own. Instead of responding passively to the changes at hand, city governments developed a range of measures designed to restore order to their communities. These innovations, primarily of an institutional nature, did not eliminate division, but taken together they signaled a dramatic change which set the modern city apart from previous urban forms.

In Philadelphia the crucial event proved to be the consolidation of the city with its county in 1854. Originally conceived as a relatively narrow measure for imposing greater social control over an increasingly heterogeneous population, consolidation ultimately achieved no less an effect than the transformation of the compact mercantile city as founded by William Penn into the modern metropolis. Although the goal of this reform was to substitute civic unity for social and political friction, the ultimate result was more complex and contradictory. Not only were the principles and influence of bureaucratic government developed and extended, but the basis for existing social and spatial divisions was also broadened, thus assuring the city's fate as a divided metropolis.

The Divided City before Consolidation

By any account preconsolidation Philadelphia was a divided city. While population stretched north and south along the Delaware River in a virtually unbroken stream of development, social as well as psychological differences separated the people of the adjacent suburbs from those in the city itself. The bulk of Philadelphia's residents congregating in the mercantile core of the old city east of Seventh Street found employment in white-collar or proprietary positions; the remaining portions of the city and its suburbs contained skilled and semiskilled workers who could not find space for their homes or shops in the urban core. Class distinctions between the city and its suburbs were manifest in average property valuations, which reached a peak in the central city wards fronting the Delaware but dropped rapidly in proportion to their distance from the heart of the city.[2] Such social distinctions were underscored by political differences which pitted the Democratic suburbs against the heavily Whig city.

Social differences also assumed physical dimensions in public and private building practices. Elaborately embellished buildings in the downtown stirred the pride of the many publishers of guidebooks for visitors. Although several of the built-up suburbs constructed substantial meeting halls for their local governments, they remained modest by comparison to Independence Hall, the Merchant's Exchange, or any number of other public buildings in the city's core. Banks and churches, which help anchor the physical identity of any place, took on a much more modest appearance in the working-class suburbs than in the city, where the patronage of the nation's outstanding architects, including Benjamin Latrobe and William Strickland, was a matter of civic pride. The majestic Bank of the United States, located in the heart of the mercantile district, stood as a symbol of Philadelphia's former preeminence in national affairs, serving as well to remind working-class Democrats of their dependence on the financial power concentrated in the city. When in the 1840s Whigs pursued plans to erect a grand, classical building to house the school willed by Stephen Girard, Democrats hastened to attack both its cost and pretentious architectural style as undemocratic.[3]

Such differences inevitably coalesced into institutional tensions among the different parts of the built-up city, not the least of which revolved around the provision of basic urban services. Despite their identity as independent political jurisdictions and their size in 1850, which placed them among the largest cities in Pennsylvania, Philadelphia's five built-up suburbs—Southwark and Moyamensing to the south and Kensington, Northern Liberties, and Spring Garden to the north (see Map 1-1 and Table 1-1)—were forced to rely on Philadelphia for such crucial services as water, which was pumped by the city from a central station at the Fairmount Falls. Such assistance from the city grated on suburban political leaders, ultimately encouraging

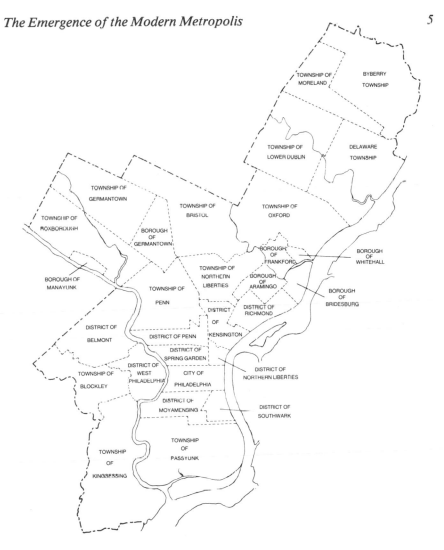

Map 1-1. The Jurisdictions of Philadelphia at the Time of Its Consolidation, 1854.
Courtesy of the Philadelphia City Planning Commission.

them to seek greater independence. With considerable pride, then, Spring Garden and Northern Liberties combined to build their own pumping station. But it was no accident that only Democrats appeared at the dedication ceremonies in 1844, since working-class sentiment for independence was ritually directed against what was termed the monopolistic tendencies of Philadelphia's city government.[4] As Elizabeth Geffen has written about the frequent outbreaks of violence in the city and its suburbs, "The parent city . . . often evinced an illiberal policy toward her surrounding children, which they, . . . more than requited by a spirit of retaliation."[5]

TABLE 1-1   Philadelphia County Jurisdictions and Their Populations, 1850

Area of County, and Minor Civil Divisions	Total Population 1850	Area of County, and Minor Civil Divisions	Total Population 1850
"Center City" (29.7%)		"West" (3.2%)	13,265
City of Philadelphia	121,376	Blockley Township	5,916
		West Philadelphia District	5,571
"South" (16.5%)	67,385	Belmont District	—
Southwark District	38,799	Kinsessing Township	1,778
Moyamensing District	26,979		
Passyunk Township	1,607	"Northwest" (4.7%)	19,384
		Roxborough Township	2,660
"Kensington" (25.3%)	103,294	Manayunk Borough	6,158
Northern Liberties Twp.	2,632	Germantown Township	2,127
Northern Liberties Dist.	47,223	Germantown Borough	6,209
Kensington District	46,774	Bristol Township	2,230
Richmond District	5,750		
Bridesburg Borough	915	"Northeast" (3.3%)	13,538
Aramingo Borough	—	Oxford Township	2,276
		Frankford Borough	5,346
"North" (17.3%)	70,520	White Hall Borough	—
Penn Township	2,687	Lower Dublin Township	4,294
Spring Garden District	58,894	Delaware Township	—
Penn District	8,939	Moreland Township	492
		Byberry Township	1,130

SOURCE: John Daly and Allen Weinberg, *Genealogy of Philadelphia County Subdivisions* 2d ed. (Philadelphia: Philadelphia Department of Records, 1966).

The massive immigration of Irish and Germans in the early 1840s interjected a volatile new element into an already unstable social situation. To the traditional class antagonisms between artisans and merchants were added ethnic and religious differences which served to separate many workers further from one another. Moreover, the flow of immigrants into working-class neighborhoods and manual jobs heightened the tensions already present in the city's economy as it changed from a regional to a national basis. A challenge from Francis P. Kenrick, the Catholic bishop of Philadelphia, to the practice of reading the Protestant Bible in the public schools as well as the increased visibility and power of Irish politicans fueled antagonisms which finally ignited in devastating riots between natives and immigrants in 1844. The emergence thereafter of a militantly nativist American Republican Party created an additional burden for authorities attempting to cope with the effects of social and economic change.[6]

To its credit, the city's Democratic paper, *The Pennsylvanian,* appealed to all workingpeople to honor a tradition of individual liberty within the party by extending civil and political rights to the new arrivals.[7] Enough workers remained unmoved by the appeal, however, to fill the ranks of the American Republicans who insisted instead that immigrants adopt the standard of right behavior prescribed by Protestant morality. Nativist politicians called not only for a 21-year naturalization period but also for a common standard of piety which included the practice of temperance, the observance of the Sabbath, and the retention of daily readings from the Protestant Bible in the public schools.[8]

The politicization of these ethno-cultural differences was apparently substantial enough to effect the designation of all new ward divisions in Philadelphia in the decade following the 1844 riots. In 1846 Cedar Ward in the city proper was divided into three new wards to accommodate a 39 percent concentration of blacks in the midst of Irish concentrations of 30 and 45 percent on either side. A year later the old Third Ward in Kensington, where the first riots of 1844 had broken out, was split into two wards of unequal population in recognition of an Irish Democratic concentration in the western portion and Protestant Irish and native strength in the east. In the same year ward lines were rearranged in Spring Garden to carve out an enclave to the west along the Schuylkill River for the only concentration of Irish in the district. In 1848 the boundaries for Moyamensing and Passyunk townships were altered dramatically to replace a north-south frontier with one running from east to west which established Moyamensing as an Irish and Democratic stronghold.[9] Thus while a similar nativist surge in New York City quickly dissipated, ethnically charged issues remained preeminent in Philadelphia politics into the 1850s.

The immediate response to the social turmoil which continued to plague the city after 1844 was not just to professionalize the police, which had been thoroughly discredited by the riots, but to embrace the more radical step of strengthening all governments in the county through consolidation. Judge Joel Jones voiced this view in his charge to the grand jury investigating the causes of the riots. The old system of limited government, he argued, no longer suited the needs of the nearly 300,000 people in the area. "This is enough for the country townships, where the old American reverence for the laws preserves the constable's staff as it once was everywhere on American soil. But a special system, less flattering to our patriotism, but more practically efficient is required for a great city, with its hoards of desperate vagabonds and its hosts of foreigners."[10]

Although a series of grand juries affirmed the desirability of consolidation, traditional rivalries between Philadelphia and its suburbs prevented any immediate action. On the one hand, many business and professional men

located in the city proper feared the loss of their political power, a fact which
one of their number, Sydney George Fisher, put bluntly in his diary after
joining their protest in December 1844:

The chief objection to the proposed plan is one that cannot be insisted on publicly,
that the city is conservative, the districts are radical. . . . If the city be merged in the
districts, the radicals will have the majority in the new corporation. The city in short
would be governed by the mob of the districts . . . its property would be applied to
the improvements of the districts, its patronage & revenue be placed in the hands of
demagogues & partisans of the lowest stamp.[11]

Suburban politicians, on the other hand, clung to their own independence
from the city. The Germantown *Telegraph,* for instance, openly opposed
consolidation, stating emphatically in one 1850 editorial, "We wish no closer
union with the city—no participation in her burthensome taxes. We can
take care of our own streets and highways, [and] are unwilling to help pay
for the paving of the streets of the city—lighting of the city—to say nothing
of the expensive police system from which we could derive no direct benefit
in any point of view."[12] The *Telegraph* took pride not just in Germantown's
independence but in that of other suburban areas as well. When Kensington
announced plans to build a new waterworks in 1849, the *Telegraph* claimed
that "in a little while each of the 'districts' will have its own waterworks,
and those at Fairmount will be reserved exclusively for the city."[13]

Suburban politicians could be so jealous of their own prerogatives as to
ignore the interests not only of Philadelphia but of other suburban jurisdictions as well. Moyamensing was frequently criticized for failing to discipline
its fire companies for attacking other companies in adjoining Southwark
or Philadelphia. A proposal designed to reduce such friction by establishing
separate fire jurisdictions for the city and the built-up suburbs to the north
and south quickly disintegrated when the different suburban governments
refused to work with one another.[14]

As has often been done in metropolitan areas recently, advocates of consolidation settled for a compromise in the form of a unified police district
for the city and its five built-up suburbs, a provision which took effect in
1850. The election that year of John S. Keyser, a nativist from Spring Garden,
as the first police commissioner appeared to blunt the drive for further
consolidation, but a change in goals among nativists kept the issue alive.
Finding the traditional means of moral suasion inadequate to their goal of
converting immigrants to temperate piety, the nativists turned increasingly
to government for help. Joining with a newly formed Prohibition Party, the
nativists helped elect an independent consolidation slate to the Pennsylvania
legislature in 1853 whose members pledged to use expanded government
power to root out the evils of intemperate behavior. With the passage of the

consolidation act in February 1854, the nativists elected as the first mayor of the consolidated city Robert T. Conrad, who had campaigned for prohibition and the enforcement of laws protecting the observance of the Sabbath.

The triumph of the militant nativist faction in 1854 has contributed to the belief that consolidation offered virtually no relief for the city's serious social cleavages. Sam Bass Warner has gone so far as to argue that the new law not only confirmed past localisms but actually institutionalized those divisions. By reinforcing the ethnically charged basis of local politics, it opened the way to professional bossism and, in his words, the institutionalization of "the expression of conflicts which formerly could seek only fragmentary, irregular, and violent expression."[15]

This interpretation stresses the conservative nature of consolidation as the enforcer of inherited traditions through public controls. In the hands of pietists, the new law was invoked to defend a rapidly disappearing form of community, which might be described as the urban village, where everyone had social knowledge of one another and where social relations were direct and personal.[16] In a compact area where virtually all the population was crowded into a few square miles, immigrants became increasingly visible; their customs, their dress, and often their work habits provoked suspicion and hostility, and stronger government power was seized upon to shore up the cultural status quo. But just as important, consolidation introduced a whole new set of arrangements which pointed the city toward the future, not the past, and embraced the modern form of the metropolis quite self-consciously as a desirable substitute for the urban village. The values of the village would continue to attract support, but with consolidation the structure of the city and ultimately its values gravitated in another direction.

The Modernist Thrust for Consolidation

In addition to the pietistic drive for consolidation there emerged quite a different basis of support which was secular where the nativists were religious and cosmopolitan where the nativists were parochial. Associated with the mercantile interests concentrated in the core city, this viewpoint focused not on the problem of immigrants flooding neighborhoods but on the restoration of Philadelphia to the top of the hierarchy of American cities. Capitivated as it was by the prospect of rapid industrial growth, this movement strove for the attainment of metropolitan status for Philadelphia through accelerated urban development.

The exemplary figure in this movement was Eli K. Price, a lawyer, often called the father of consolidation. With the help of the Prohibition Party, Price was elected to the state Senate in 1853 as an independent consolidation candidate, but he infuriated his pietistic supporters by casting the decisive vote against a prohibition law for the city in the following year. Revealing that his secular and cosmopolitan concerns were greater than those for piety, Price presented the case for consolidation in terms of enhancing Philadelphia's urban standing. In an age when urban supremacy was measured by statistics of trade and population, he seized upon consolidation as a means of improving Philadelphia's position in both categories. Recognizing the incipient pattern of land specialization whereby dwellings in the core city were being converted into stores and warehouses while the suburbs were attracting a growing proportion of residences, Price suggested a new partnership. Through consolidation, he said, "the strength, the unity and prestige of the city" would be extended in the form of vital services—surveys, grading, culverting, and the like—to the suburbs, which he described as "too weak of themselves advantageously to develop, but indispensable as the foundation of a great city." By harnessing the growing pool of manpower located in the suburbs to the sources of capital in the city, Price argued, consolidation would ultimately "enable Philadelphia to sustain the rivalry of other cities seeking to absorb her trade, wealth, and population."[17]

This support for expanded city services closely paralleled mercantile support for internal improvements to keep prosperity in Philadelphia and Pennsylvania. Significantly, however, Price's allies in the mercantile press wanted to emulate New York not just for its superiority in trade but also, as the Philadelphia *North American* put it, for its standing as "one grand municipality." As long as the county's different jurisdictions remained divided against themselves, the paper claimed, "they cannot hope to become anything more than they have been or are—a cluster of overgrown villages, having in exterior form the aspect of a great metropolis, without its large soul and concentrated vitality." Philadelphia, the *Sunday Dispatch* claimed, would become "what we are already termed, a mere village in comparison with New York, unless we avert it by consolidation."[18] Indeed, as the mercantile campaign for consolidation matured, it gained strength and coherence by emphasizing the need to sweep away any last vestiges of village-like patterns in a stream of urban progress.

As early as 1844, for instance, the *North American* described the practice of providing fire and police protection on a volunteer basis as more suitable to a country town than a great city.[19] Of special concern was not just the protection of private property but the desire to interject the rule of law where once the small-town pressures of custom and habit had been sufficient to maintain order. Significantly, these critics counted among their causes the adoption of a uniformed police. Traditionally officers had been identified only by wearing a badge, which by accident or design was often hidden from view. As long as policemen and private citizens were known to each other, sharp distinctions between them remained unnecessary. But the growing heterogeneity of the city's population prevented such familiarity and sparked interest in formalizing social relations.[20] By finally requiring the police to wear readily identifiable uniforms, Philadelphia took an important step away from the village-like ways of the preindustrial city.

The same interests which sought to rationalize social relations were just as anxious to formalize city space. During the 1850s a number of newspapers including the nativist *Sun* and mercantile *Sunday Dispatch* began to complain about the haphazard arrangement of city streets. Despite the highly rationalized grid system of the core city, which was so regular that citizens counted by "squares" instead of by "blocks," Philadelphia had no uniform system of street names or addresses. Not only did numerous streets possess the same name, but it was also common to find odd and even numbers on the same side of the same street, two houses with exactly the same address on the same block, or a repeated sequence of numbers in adjacent blocks.[21] Such irregular practices were not considered worthy of a modern city, as the *North American* revealed when it urged city councils to adopt the changes in street names pending before it. "The select council should remember that they legislate not for some sequestered village, where ancient customs reign supreme," an 1853 editorial charged, "but for a commercial metropolis, visited by thousands of strangers, whose convenience must be consulted." Ultimately, the codification of street names and addresses adopted in 1858 affected 960 different streets, a dramatic imposition of centrally directed order over indigenous customs.[22]

The effect of these changes was not just to embrace economic or urban development but, as Michael Frisch has said of the transition from town to city, to shift from a community experienced directly and informally to one that was perceived as a formal abstraction.[23] Nowhere was this more evident than in the pattern of ward designations adopted for the consolidated city. Instead of just accommodating past localisms, as Warner has argued, consolidation obscured once strong local identities, whether defined informally by the concentration of distinct ethnic groups or more formally in established independent governments. The ethnically inspired boundaries established for Cedar Ward, Spring Garden, and Kensington in the 1840s were all obliterated under the new act as these divisions were reconstituted as the new 7th, 15th, and 17th wards respectively. Despite proposals to carve new wards out of existing jurisdictions,[24] the new Second, Third, and Fourth wards each combined sections of Moyamensing with Southwark in apparent indifference to the intense political rivalry stemming from their respective concentrations of Irish and native Americans. Kensington was divided into four wards, one of which incorporated a portion of Northern Liberties and another of which included the previously separate jurisdiction of Richmond. Townships in the rural areas of the county were lumped together without

regard to special features of local character. The end result was the standardization of political representation out of respect for the impersonal factor of
population count rather than the conservation of established identities.

In the end, consolidation effected a dramatic shift of power from local to
central authority. Not only were the once largely voluntary services associated
with law enforcement and urban development codified and equalized for
the previously separate jurisdictions but they were also brought under the
control of a centralized bureaucracy, a fact which would be dramatized
annually with the publication of a mayor's report running to hundreds of
pages. Philadelphia's new wards retained control over a few services, notably
through the election of tax assessors and representatives to the boards of
health and public education. But these functions were eventually absorbed
by the central government, along with the volunteer fire companies, which
having been granted some independence under consolidation, were finally
incorporated into the city on a paid professional basis in 1871.[25] Such changes
were gladly accepted by the mercantile press in the name of order and efficiency. Typically, the *North American* hailed consolidation in 1854 as a
measure which removed the "incongruous powers" and "conflicting interests"
of competing jurisdictions. The ultimate metaphor accorded the ideal was
that of a smoothly functioning machine, as the Philadelphia *Commercial
List* put it, "a machine to manufacture order, progress, prosperity and
honor for the whole metropolis."[26]

In light of previous resistance to the centralizing tendency of consolidation, the passage of the act virtually without dissent in 1854 deserves explanation. On the one hand, a provision to tax the rural portions of the
consolidated city at a reduced rate blunted the opposition of less populous
jurisdictions like Germantown.[27] A further provision to absorb all existing
debts clearly appealed to the more built-up suburbs, all of which benefited
except Northern Liberties.[28] A less tangible force seems to have been the
magnetic attraction of becoming an integral part of the expanded metropolis.
In 1849, for instance, Germantown indicated its cosmopolitan orientation
by adopting a new town plan designed to rationalize its street system even
before such plans captured the attention of the mercantile press downtown.[29]
A flurry of expenditures for urban services among suburban jurisdictions
just prior to consolidation stemmed from the desire to take advantage of the
city's promise to absorb local debts. But also at work, at least according to
the *North American,* was the desire to attain the level of amenities hoped
for in the expanded metropolis. Commenting on Moyamensing's reputation
for decay, the paper noted in 1853, "Mud and piles of dirt, stagnant pools,
refuse of every description greet the eye and foot in all directions, and cry
aloud for the besome of the scavenger. No wonder they want consolidation
there. With it they would have clean streets. Without it they are likely to
breed some desolating plague."[30]

Less overt, yet potentially more significant, was another factor which brought working-class natives and middle-class Whigs closer together on consolidation than might otherwise be perceived. As Bruce Laurie has pointed out, the wave of pietism which swept the working-class suburbs where nativism was to thrive after the panic of 1837 emerged not so much from the embrace of church doctrine as from an internalization of the imperatives of industrial capitalism. Convinced that their economic hardship could be attributed to a failure of morality, workers adopted the social norms of piety and expected immigrants to do the same. Newcomers who clung to their old-world drinking habits were thus criticized less for overstepping religious bounds than for being ineffective workers whose productivity was reduced by imbibing on the job or celebrating holidays which carried over into the workweek. Such relaxed attitudes toward work were considered wasteful, frivolous, and even sinful.[31]

Indeed, one of the major trends in the campaign for government reorganization was the rationalization of time as well as space. In 1844 the *North American* denounced the volunteer fire system in pietistic terms for "the gambling, drinking and general depravity" associated with hangers-on at the engine houses. At the same time, however, the paper criticized "the waste of time and habits which the passion for fire alarms and lounging about engine houses are known to produce among a very large class of our youths."[32] By the 1850s the mercantile press was arguing for the professionalization of fire service as part of consolidation to prevent the disruption of routinized work. "Mechanics, clerks, journeymen can no longer come running at the sound of the state house bell," a *City Item* editorial argued. "Time is too valuable now to be spent in that manner."[33] The standardization of city streets was repeatedly proposed as a time-saving device, meeting the approval of the editor of a city shopping guide after adoption of the new law. The *Public Ledger* incorporated time into its arguments for urban development, writing that no public improvement was ever made without ample return: "We gain most precious time by creating opportunity, and this difference between the last century and the present makes the Philadelphia of today as superior to the Philadelphia of 1790 as steam velocity is to mule transportation."[34] Most central to saving time in an expanded city was improved transportation, for as the *Ledger* noted, "It is to the laborer, the mechanic, and the businessman generally that time is valuable; that is a matter of moment whether he is ten minutes going to dinner or half an hour. . . . The revolution that passenger railways would make, in the economy of time alone, would be a mighty one."[35]

Not all supporters of consolidation had the same view of the new act, but in the mid 1850s the emerging consensus behind the bill, which included Democrats as well as natives and Whigs, and suburban as well as downtown jurisdictions, suggests a point of agreement which went beyond the immediate economic or social interests of any one group. The drive for consolidation garnered support from all those who wanted to attain metropolitan status for Philadelphia. In the process, consolidation institutionalized a vision which fits Richard Brown's definition of modernization as a faith not just in greater economic production but also in a "value structure emphasizing rationality, specialization, efficiency, cosmospolitanism, and an interest in the future that can be better than the present in material and social terms."[36] Whether its backers understood this at the time, these values, inherent in consolidation, would most clearly direct the course of the metropolis over the next 100 years.

New Divisions in the Modern Metropolis: Philadelphia in Transition

The prospect of urban unity embraced by the supporters of consolidation did not prevent the crystallization of new social and spatial divisions in Philadelphia. Invoking the centralization of power in the name of developing the outer reaches of the city, consolidation nevertheless encouraged the specialization of urban space that removed home from work and, in addition, set different kinds of residences apart from one another. Although overt ethnic antagonisms of the kind which paralyzed the city in 1844 declined and municipal government took a more active role in mediating between different social groups, if anything the disparate parts of the expanded metropolis became even further divided from one another than they had been before consolidation.

The immediate effect of consolidation was to accelerate the growth of the last relatively undeveloped areas of the city near the central core. As passage of the consolidation bill became assured, newspaper advertisements urged Philadelphians to subscribe to new building associations in anticipation of the extension of urban services to open areas accessible to jobs downtown.[37] Parts of West and South Philadelphia, Spring Garden, and Frankford all boomed in the few years between consolidation and the introduction of street railways. That portion of the original city west of Seventh Street continued to grow while for the first time population declined east of this boundary. Newspaper accounts of the demolition of old residences to make way for stores and warehouses and the introduction of multiple-family dwellings marked this once elite area of the city as an increasingly undesirable place of residence. Setting a pattern which would be shared by the other port cities of the eastern seaboard, Philadelphia's mercantile and business establishment abandoned their residences close to the port for new locations west of Broad Street and north of Vine.

With the completion of an extensive street railway system in the 1860s, the focus of growth shifted from the nearby suburbs along the tracks to the outer reaches of the consolidated city. In 1860 the population of the outer ring of suburbs bypassed that of the original city but still amounted to only half that in the five built-up districts which constituted the inner ring of suburban development. By 1880, however, the outer suburbs had become the largest single sector of Philadelphia's population (see Table 1-2), and as Theodore Hershberg and his associates at the Philadelphia Social History Project have shown, the mean demographic density in the city dropped significantly between 1850 and 1880.[38]

TABLE 1-2   Rate of Population Growth, Philadelphia County, 1820–1880

	Center City	Inner Suburban Ring[b]	Outer Suburbs
1820	63,802 (53.5%)[a]	48,970 (41.0%)	6,553 (5.5%)
1830	80,458 (48.0) + 26.1%	80,892 (48.2) + 65.2%	6,401 (3.8) − 2.3%
1840	93,665 (36.3) + 16.4	122,049 (47.3) + 50.9	42,323 (16.4) + 561.0
1850	121,376 (29.7) + 29.6	204,912 (50.1) + 67.9	82,454 (20.2) + 94.8
1860	137,756 (24.3) + 13.5	284,869 (50.4) + 39.0	142,904 (25.3) + 73.3
1870	124,585 (18.5) − 9.6	318,334 (47.2) + 11.7	231,103 (34.3) + 61.7
1880	112,846 (13.3) − 9.4	361,024 (42.6) + 13.4	373,300 (44.1) + 61.5

SOURCE: John Daly and Allen Weinberg, *Genealogy of Philadelphia County Subdivisions* 2d ed. (Philadelphia: Philadelphia Department of Records, 1966).
[a]Figures in parentheses represent proportion of total county population.
[b]Spring Garden, Northern Liberties, Kensington, Moyamensing, and Southwark.

Given this pattern of decentralized growth, even the most fervent boosters were not disappointed. By the early 1870s the *North American* could boast that the formerly independent villages of the county had been "swallowed up" by urban development.[39] The emergence of these areas as attractive residential locations for city dwellers became the pride of city guidebooks, as the publication *Philadelphia Illustrated* indicated in 1871:

. . . as in every great metropolis, wealth separates the home from the workshop, and the accumulated riches are displayed and spent far from the spot where they are laboriously garnered; so the wealth of our city is not to be seen within the narrow limits of the Philadelphia of William Penn, or of Franklin, or even of a dozen years ago, but in the lovely borders into which her taste and luxury have blossomed into beauty along the shaded walks of West Philadelphia, the sweet lanes that girdle Germantown, the winding waters of the Wissahickon, and the lovely indulations [sic] of Chestnut and Chelton Hills where each wavelet of land is cultivated into luxuriance and crowned with the palaces and towers of our Republican princes and potentates.[40]

Doubt and "croaking" had vanished, the *North American* claimed, "so that in time for the centennial celebration, we shall show the world a reconstituted Philadelphia."[41]

The city provided the most fitting symbol for its pretensions with the erection of a new City Hall at the intersection of the growing commercial district's two most important streets, Broad and Market. Not only were its scale and cost—an estimated $20 million—unprecedented, but the grand eclecticism of its architecture demonstrated the city's ambition to stand out not just locally but around the world. "Intended to be the largest building on the continent," as Alan Gowans has pointed out, "its tower the highest artificial structure in the world, its ornament heaped on from every land and culture, past and present, City Hall dramatized the new ideal of American destiny—no longer so much to be independent from Europe, as to consummate and embody the whole of the historical achievement of Western civilization."[42] Indeed, the same newspapers which had once promoted consolidation to compete with New York turned increasingly to Paris and its monumental baroque planning as the city worthy of emulation. Broad Street, it was hoped, would become the Champs-Elysées of Philadelphia. And with the establishment of Broad and Market as the central point for street railway exchange, it could fairly be said that all lines from the suburbs led to City Hall.

But in the mid-nineteenth century total and uniform urban development did not come to Philadelphia overnight. Land use specializaton as well as zones of high or low status did not become characteristic of every corner of the city immediately after consolidation. In fact, for at least 25 years it could be said that the city remained divided between the old and the new. Even the *North American* had to admit in an 1868 editorial that "the city refuses to obey any laws of growth but its own. It refuses to be concentrated."[43] The very size of Philadelphia, which made it the most extensive city in the United States, prevented the complete urbanization of the outer suburbs. Concentrated populations like those in Germantown or portions of West Philadelphia could exhibit both the physical and social characteristics of mature urban form while remaining within walking distance of self-contained, village-like communities such as Franklinville or Hestonville. Although the outer suburbs attracted increasing numbers of upper- and middle-class residents, they did not begin to approach socioeconomic homogeneity, even among native-born workers. As Penn District grew, it attracted more and more proprietary workers, but even in 1880 the area still contained a higher proportion of skilled workers. Despite its rapid residential development, West Philadelphia's share of manual workers continued to climb until 1880 when for the first time the level of proprietary employment for natives approached that of manual work. Only the western portion of the original city achieved a dominant majority of mercantile and proprietary workers and even there close to a third of its native workers held skilled manual jobs as late as 1880 (see Table 1-3).

TABLE 1-3 Native White American Occupation by Percent, 1850-1880[a]

	CC(E)	CC(W)	M/SW	K	NL	SG	Penn	NW	West P.	South P.
1850										
I	16.4	18.4	2.2	1.9	6.7	6.8	3.0		4.6	
II	27.4	19.5	18.6	10.6	19.4	21.9	17.0		27.6	
III	32.4	41.5	54.8	65.1	56.9	58.1	59.0		44.0	
IV	4.6	6.9	18.7	11.4	10.4	7.0	16.5		12.4	
1860										
I	9.3	14.8	2.0	2.1	6.9	4.5	2.8	5.7	5.4	0.9
II	33.8	20.0	20.4	16.9	28.9	23.1	26.8	25.5	22.0	16.0
III	32.4	33.1	51.9	73.8	41.6	50.4	53.6	37.8	44.1	53.1
IV	18.9	4.1	17.6	12.6	8.7	6.6	9.2	19.8	14.2	16.6
1870										
I	5.3	12.1	2.2	1.7	5.3	5.9	4.7	5.3	7.3	1.4
II	32.2	32.7	20.1	20.9	31.2	37.0	30.2	27.4	24.0	19.7
III	40.4	31.8	48.7	53.4	48.2	39.3	46.9	36.7	40.9	51.0
IV	12.8	11.4	21.5	22.0	12.8	11.7	12.0	22.6	20.5	22.6
1880										
I	4.5	11.3	1.0	1.0	4.8	6.7	4.5	4.2	4.5	1.3
II	38.5	34.6	26.9	20.8	30.7	34.5	37.4	29.7	29.3	20.7
III	28.8	28.4	34.6	54.6	38.4	37.3	40.9	38.8	37.3	47.9
IV	21.5	13.7	22.8	20.6	17.4	14.7	10.6	22.8	21.0	25.5

SOURCE: Multi-Ethnic Files, Philadelphia Social History Project

[a]Not including unlisted or uncertain occupation designations.

Key:
- I   Mercantile and Professional
- II   Proprietary
- III   Skilled Workers (artisans)
- IV   Unskilled Workers
- CC(E)   Center City East of 7th Street (Wards 5, 6 in consolidated city)
- CC(W)   Center City West of 7th Street (Wards 7, 8, 9, 10)
- M/SW   Moyamensing/Southwark (Wards 2, 3, 4)
- K   Kensington (Wards 16, 17, 18, 19, 31)
- NL   Northern Liberties (Wards 11, 12)
- SG   Spring Garden (Wards 13, 14, 15)
- Penn   Penn District (Wards 20, 29)
- NW   Northwest (Wards 21, 22, 23, 25, 28)
- West P.   West Philadelphia (Wards 24, 27)
- South P.   South Philadelphia (Wards 1, 26)

The categories of occupation listed here retain the designations assigned by the Philadelphia Social History Project for Vert 1 (high white collar and professional) and III (skilled artisan), while combining in II PSHP's Vert II (low white collar and proprietary) and Vert VII (possible proprietary) and in IV combining all unskilled laborers (PSHP Vert IV-VI). See *Historical Methods Newsletter* 9 (March-June 1976): 66-8, for a description of the PSHP Vertical File.

The outer suburbs and Spring Garden, which followed a similar development pattern, did attract a disproportionate share of native workers after
consolidation. Penn District, West Philadelphia, and the northwestern
sector of the city all increased their ratios of native to foreign-born workers
after 1860. Kensington, Northern Liberties, Moyamensing, and Southwark,
on the other hand, retained the bulk of the city's immigrant population.
Either unable to pay the relatively high fares charged by the street railways
or to take the time to commute, these immigrants and some of their native
counterparts crowded the existing housing stock near the manufacturing jobs
which were concentrated along the Delaware River[44] (see Tables 1-2 and 1-4).

**TABLE 1-4　Ratio: Native White American to Foreign-Born
　　　　　　 Workers, 1850-1880**

	1850	1860	1870	1880
Center City (E of 7th)	1.44	1.11	1.18	1.64
Center City (W of 7th)	1.33	1.35	1.65	2.48
Moyamensing/Southwark	1.08	1.07	1.35	1.68
Kensington	1.23	.86	1.10	1.61
Northern Liberties	1.49	.94	.85	1.24
Spring Garden	2.50	1.95	1.92	2.71
Penn District	1.38	1.77	2.37	1.94
Northwest		1.94	2.11	2.70
West Philadelphia	.90	1.54	2.10	3.23
South Philadelphia	3.71	1.11	1.59	2.91

SOURCE: Multi-Ethnic Files, Philadelphia Social History Project.

Suburban areas were thus becoming divided between those of necessity,
where residence was dictated by the need of proximity to work, and those of
choice where commuting allowed for such universally acclaimed benefits as
access to work without the necessity of living with its concomitant nuisances.[45]
The new metropolis was thus becoming divided in spite of the concentrated
powers of its government and its vision of bureaucratic unity. To the degree
they could afford it, middle- and upper-class Philadelphians began to follow
the mores of Victorian culture which encouraged a retreat into their homes
in suburban enclaves as a refuge from work. Factory workers, on the other
hand, found government unprepared to improve living conditions near
their work, and as a result their residential areas gradually fell into decline,
establishing the physical as well as the social contours of the classic zone of
emergence. While the actual distinctions among different sectors of the
city remained modest by twentieth-century standards, the expectations for
specialized land use nonetheless remained high. Nowhere was this better
illustrated than in the separation of residence from work.

From the outset of their campaign, the modernist supporters of consolidation proclaimed the benefits of decentralization out of the congested urban core. In a narrow sense this point of view stemmed from the desire of businessmen to take advantage of the better residential opportunities outside the inner city without losing their voice in its politics, an inclination which apparently motivated annexations in other cities.[46] But the mercantile press favored decentralization for more general reasons. Commenting on the prohibitive cost of the omnibus for workers, the *North American* looked forward as early as 1852 to the expansion of railroad commuting, predicting that "the day will soon arrive when the hard-toiling mechanic, whose labors confine him to the heart of the town from dawn till evening, can have his family in the country and give them and himself the advantage of pure air, open grounds, and the quiet comforts of rural retirement."[47]

While even in outlying districts economic realities continued to keep a considerable portion of Philadelphia residences uncomfortably close to the nuisances associated with heavy industrial work, local publications continued to boost the idea of separating work and residence for all income levels. Noting the beneficial effect of building associations in developing new suburban areas, the *Penn Monthly* commented in 1870 that "the working-man finds easy access to his place of business in the city, by the city railroads at a cost of less than $40 a year at the outside, a cost more than made up in the absence of house-rent, and the presence of free pure air in his suburban home."[48] This vision of the benefits of land specialization attained particular power because of the growing concern that the downtown was not only noisy and congested but also unhealthy, all of which were well illustrated in the campaign to establish an urban park system in association with consolidation.

Once again the mercantile press took the lead in developing this issue, harping on the image of a city stifled by development without open space, a "wilderness of brick and mortar." Pointing to the insufficiencies of the parks laid out in Penn's original plan, newspapers drew on the contemporary theory that open space was necessary for the city to breathe. The *North American* extended the metaphor of health to call for an "uncorrupted atmosphere" where "we can sometimes turn the sickened eye from the red glare of man's habitations to the softened hue of bountiful nature."[49] Significantly these advocates favored the idea of an outlying yet concentrated park, and such a facility was built after consolidation to serve workers and their families unable to retreat to suburban homes or summer cottages. Such plans assumed a modern guise in both designating separate space for recreation and offering workers a social outlet on the assumption that they would benefit more from a respite with nature than from exhortations from the pulpit on their day of rest, an assumption which was realized by 1880 in a notably high rate of passenger traffic to the park.[50]

Just as these plans envisioned the outer parts of the consolidated city as places for residence and recreation, they also embraced a modern conception of the downtown as a core for business government, and commerce. The city papers applauded the growth of commercial structures on Walnut, Chestnut, and Arch streets, east of 14th Street. Typically the *Public Ledger* called such enterprise a moral incentive "which demolishes the old shanty of a shop of the last century, and erects on its foundation a palace-like store, ample in dimensions, elegant in form, useful in all its parts."[51] Banks, railroad stations, and department stores all vied for and received attention by putting on display magnificent new buildings in the emerging downtown. Private associations joined the race for attention, as witnessed by the erection in the 1860s of extraordinary new buildings on Broad Street by the Union League and the Masonic Order. In turn, an entirely different style of residential architecture, picturesque and asymmetrical, was promoted for the suburbs, further distinguishing the different sectors of the new metropolis. By 1865 a local judge could affirm the desirability of segregated land use by ruling against the reconstruction of a mill at 20th and Chestnut streets. Located in what had become a residential district, the mill was opposed by home owners who had moved near the site long after its original erection on undeveloped land. But not only did Justice Reed uphold the right of these residents to block the nuisance of business, he also suggested that a private home downtown had no more right to block commercial development around it.[52]

The particular circumstances of Philadelphia's consolidation may have been unique, although other cities including Cleveland, Buffalo, and San Francisco began expanding as well in the 1850s. But the drive to extend both the spatial and social reach of city government over a population flowing out of the urban core could be found in a host of cities in the late nineteenth and early twentieth centuries. More significantly, perhaps, the modern values which coalesced in consolidation would permeate the campaign for urban development over the next 100 years, influencing planners and developers from the City Beautiful movement at the turn of the century to the experts in urban renewal in the 1950s and 1960s. Each generation stressed the development of a monumental urban core tied to suburban residential areas through a vast network of transportation routes, planned in conjunction with land set aside for public recreation.

The first quarter century of Philadelphia's history as a consolidated city can thus best be described as a period of transition. Government had assumed the function of rationalizing urban development in line with the city's aspirations to become a great metropolis. Although the more parochial concerns of ward-based politics tarnished some of these expectations, a substantial measure of orderly growth followed from the elimination of the jurisdictional disputes characteristic of the preconsolidated city. But by choice as much as by necessity Philadelphia was also becoming a divided metropolis, split between work and residence and between the exclusive residential enclaves of the well-to-do around Rittenhouse Square and portions of West and Northwest Philadelphia and the mixed land use areas along the Delaware River. Future generations of planners would draw on the modernist vision of unity through consolidation, but the reality of the divided metropolis would persist.

Notes

1. The research for this chapter was originally undertaken with a grant from the Graduate School of Arts and Sciences of the George Washington University. George Washington's Computer Center provided time for processing the data, which was made available by the Philadelphia Social History Project through support from the Center for Studies of Metropolitan Problems, National Institute of Mental Health (MH 16621); Sociology Program, Division of Social Sciences, National Science Foundation (SOC 76-20069); and Division of Research Grants, National Endowment for the Humanities (RC 25568-76-1156). I wish to extend special thanks to Theodore Hershberg, director of the Philadelphia Social History Project, for his assistance on this and other related projects and to Sandy Moore, Dan Mannix, and David Stokes for their warm hospitality during my many visits to Philadelphia over the past two years.

2. This pattern emerges out of figures printed periodically in the local press listing the number of taxables and the total value of taxable property in each ward.

3. See the Philadelphia *Pennsylvanian,* October 11, 1842, and September 23, 1843, for examples of this Democratic publication's effort to keep the Bank issue alive in the 1840s. On Girard College, see *Pennsylvanian* editorials for October 6, 1842, and October 7, 1843, which included the charge to voters: "Remember that nearly a million and a half have been thrown away upon the useless Grecian Temple. . . ."

4. On October 5, 1843, the *Pennsylvanian* commended the Spring Garden commissioners "for their efforts to break the water works monopoly," adding support on April 11, 1844, for the new facility, "not only in reference to the cheapness and constancy of the supply, but as regards being intensely independent of any and every other corporation for the furnishing of that essential element." The dedication ceremonies were reported in the *Pennsylvanian,* July 2, 1844.

5. Elizabeth N. Geffen, "Violence in Philadelphia in the 1840's and 1850's," *Pennsylvania History* 36 (October 1969): 390.

6. See Michael Feldberg, *The Philadelphia Riots of 1844: A Study of Ethnic Conflict* (Westport, Conn.: Greenwood Press, 1975), especially pp. 41-98; David Montgomery, "The Shuttle and the Cross: Weavers and Artisans in the Kensington Riots of 1844," *Journal of Social History* 5 (Summer 1972): 411-46; and Vincent P. Lannie and Bernard Diethorn, "For the Honor and Glory of God: The Philadelphia Bible Riots of 1844," *History of Education Quarterly* 8 (Spring 1968): 44-106.

7. In a March 14, 1844, editorial, for instance, the *Pennsylvanian* proclaimed, "Our party was the early friend of the naturalization laws," and "every attempt to abridge the present privilege of becoming citizens . . . ought to be resisted with the same spirit which swept the Alien and Sedition laws from our statute-book."

8. These themes can be traced throughout the nativist *Sun,* whose editor, Lewis Levin, was elected to Congress from the southern suburbs of Philadelphia County in 1844. Such issues fit the description of a pietistic strain of Protestant morality described by Paul Kleppner in another context: "The native pietist saw an influx of 'foreigners' who brought with them social customs and mores which were literal expressions of the very sin God commanded him to eradicate. . . . Imbued with a sense of ethical deprivation, these pietists sought to reach out and *change* the world about them; they sought to 'save' themselves by reforming their fellowmen." *The Cross of Culture: A Social Analysis of Midwestern Politics, 1850-1900* (New York: The Free Press, 1968), p. 74.

9. For maps of the new boundaries, see John Daly and Allen Weinberg, *Genealogy of Philadelphia County Subdivisions,* 2d ed. (Philadelphia: Philadelphia Department of Records, 1966), pp. 32, 39. The determination of ethnicity is drawn from the Multi-Ethnic Files of the Philadelphia Social History Project, which comprise a one-in-six sample of males 18 and over in 1850 and 1860 and a one-in-nine sample of males 18 and over in 1870 and 1880.

10. Reported in the *Pennsylvanian,* July 2, 1844.

11. Sam Bass Warner refers to this protest in *The Private City: Philadelphia in Three Periods of Its Growth* (Philadelphia: University of Pennsylvania Press, 1968), p. 152, while Fisher's comments as recorded in February 1845 are found in *A Philadelphia Perspective: The Diary of Sidney George Fisher Covering the Years 1834-1871,* ed. Nicholas B. Wainwright (Philadelphia: The Historical Society of Pennsylvania, 1967), p. 179.

12. Germantown *Telegraph,* September 25, 1850.

13. Ibid., April 18, 1849.

14. Philadelphia *Sun,* April 2, 1845.

15. Warner, *The Private City,* pp. 101, 152.

16. Stephan Thernstrom reports a high incidence of concern about the loss of common "social knowledge" among the established residents of Newburyport, Massachusetts, as the city industrialized at mid-century. *Poverty and Progress: Social Mobility in a Nineteenth Century City* (Cambridge, Mass.: Harvard University Press, 1964), pp. 33, 52. The *Pennsylvanian,* among other Philadelphia papers, sounded a similar note in a December 6, 1845, editorial: "There are thousands of people living in the city of Philadelphia, and in the districts too, who know as little of what is going on in the other parts of the city and districts as the people of Nauvoo or Kamschutka. . . . Why, the very respectable citizens who live in Pine street know nothing of their neighbors half a square from them in *Little* Pine street, much less of those a square off in Lombard."

17. Price's remarks on the partnership he envisioned were reprinted from his 1854 memorial to the Pennsylvania legislature in his study, *The History of the Consolidation of the City of Philadelphia* (Philadelphia: J. B. Lippincott & Co., 1873), pp. 12, 13, 76, 79. A January 11, 1854, editorial in the Philadelphia *North American* struck

a similar theme, complaining that "measures of public improvement, by the city or respective districts, are arrested at each extreme of their narrow limits, and works erected competent to supply the wants of all with but slight additional expense, are curtailed of their usefulness and other works at large expense uselessly erected by other corporations." More recently Kenneth Jackson has suggested a similar motivation for annexation, writing that "one could not deny that many suburbanites did regard the city as their achievement and were willing and even eager to be joined with it. But probably more important than such lofty notions were pragmatic, mundane considerations of sewers, schools, water, and police." "Metropolitan Government Versus Political Autonomy: Politics on the Crabgrass Frontier," in *Cities in American History,* ed. Kenneth T. Jackson and Stanley K. Schultz (New York: Alfred A. Knopf, 1972), p. 450.

18. *North American,* July 18, 1853; Philadelphia *Sunday Dispatch,* March 6, 1853.

19. *North American,* May 11, 1844. The full statement read: "Neither are based upon a true view of the moral and physical character of a great city. Neither are fit for any community of greater extent than a country town."

20. See *Fitzgerald's City Item,* June 19, 1852; *North American,* October 26, 1853, and January 19, 1854; and the Germantown *Telegraph,* November 11, 1853.

21. *Sunday Dispatch,* September 23, 1851; *North American,* October 15, 1853; *Sun,* March 7, 1855.

22. *North American,* December 8, 1853; *Sunday Dispatch,* December 27, 1857.

23. Michael Frisch, *Town into City: Springfield, Massachusetts and the Meaning of Community, 1840-1880* (Cambridge, Mass.: Harvard University Press, 1972), pp. 249-50.

24. See the November 12, 1853, issue of the *Pennsylvanian* for the report of a committee of representatives from the city and suburbs, formed to submit a draft bill to the legislature, which kept previous ward designations intact by proposing the constitution of Ward 2 as Southwark Wards 2 and 5; Ward 3 as Southwark Wards 1, 3, and 4; and Ward 4 as Moyamensing Wards 1, 2, and 3.

25. Conrad Weiler, *Philadelphia: Neighborhood, Authority, and the Urban Crisis* (New York: Praeger, 1974), pp. 39-40.

26. *North American,* January 11, 1854; Philadelphia *Commercial List and Price Current,* February 18, 1854.

27. For commentary on this provision, see the Germantown *Telegraph,* February 1, 1854. By the time consolidation became law the *Telegraph* sounded as enthusiastic as any city booster downtown, commenting in a February 8, 1854, editorial that "Philadelphia, from this point, takes the position among the cities of the earth to which she is entitled by her territory, her population, her wealth, her commerce, and her manufacture."

28. This provision was close to Philadelphia's mercantile interests, dating as a proposal at least as far back as 1844 and reiterated by Price's 1854 memorial to the Pennsylvania Legislature. See the December 18, 1844, issue of the *North American,* and Price, *History of Consolidation,* p. 79.

29. Both a petition to the Pennsylvania legislature "signed by a large number" of Germantown residents and an editorial praising approval of the request for a town plan, stressed its value in providing "regular form and symmetry to the borough." Germantown *Telegraph,* February 14, 1848; March 11, 1849.

30. *North American,* November 22, 1853.

31. Bruce Laurie, "'Nothing on Compulsion': Life Styles of Philadelphia Artisans, 1820-1850," *Labor History* 15 (Summer 1974): 350-51, 366.

32. *North American,* August 6, 1844.

33. *Fitzgerald's City Item,* January 15, 1853. See also *North American,* February 26, 1853.

34. *The Philadelphia Shopper's Guide and Housekeeper's Companion* (Philadelphia: S. E. Cohen, 1859), p. 1166; *Public Ledger,* September 28, 1849.

35. Ibid., September 16, 1853.

36. Richard D. Brown, "Modernization: A Victorian Climax," *American Quarterly* 27 (December 1975): 533.

37. See Philadelphia *Sun,* April 6 and May 18, 1854.

38. Theodore Hershberg, Harold E. Cox, Dale B. Light, Jr., and Richard R. Greenfield, "The 'Journey to Work': An Empirical Investigation of Work, Residence and Transportation, Philadelphia 1850 and 1880," in *Toward an Interdisciplinary History of the City: Work, Space, Family and Group Experience in Nineteenth Century Philadelphia,* ed. Theodore Hershberg (New York: Oxford University Press, 1980).

39. *North American,* January 31, 1871.

40. *Philadelphia Illustrated* (Philadelphia: T. R. Hamersly & Co., 1871), pp. 1-2.

41. *North American,* August 5, 1870.

42. Alan Gowans, *Images of American Living: Four Centuries of American Architecture and Furniture as Cultural Expression* (New York and Philadelphia: J. B. Lippincott, 1964), p. 332.

43. *North American,* June 30, 1868.

44. Theodore Hershberg, Stephanie Greenberg, and their colleagues at the Philadelphia Social History Project make this point forcibly on the basis of quantitative evidence in their contributions to the study, *Toward an Interdisciplinary History of the City.* Another kind of evidence with similar implications is the testimony of an English factory worker as cited by H. J. Dyos and D. A. Reeder: "I always live near the factory where I work, and so do all my mates, no matter how small, dirty, and dear the houses may be. . . . One or two of my uncles have tried the plan of living a few miles out, and walking to business in the morning, like the clerks do in the city. It don't do—I suppose because they have not been used to it from boys; perhaps, because walking exercises at five in the morning don't suit men who are hard at work with their bodies all day. As to railways and omnibuses, they cost money, and we don't understand them, except on holidays, when we have got our best clothes on." "Slums and Suburbs," in *The Victorian City: Images and Realities,* ed. H. J. Dyos and Michael Wolff (London: Routledge & Kegan Paul, Ltd., 1973), 1: 368.

45. Such distinctions between different residential areas reflect what Peter G. Goheen calls the changing social valuation of territory, a process which reflects less an actual change in social differentiation than the way in which the social landscape was perceived. *Victorian Toronto, 1850-1900: Pattern and Process of Growth* (Chicago: University of Chicago Press, 1970), pp. 10, 154-55.

46. *North American,* November 19, 1853; Sam Bass Warner, Jr., *Streetcar Suburbs: The Process of Growth in Boston, 1870-1900* (Cambridge, Mass.: Harvard

University Press, 1962), p. 164; Jackson, "Politics on the Crabgrass Frontier," pp. 354-55.

47. *North American,* April 16, 1852. See also the *Sun* on West Philadelphia, July 16, 1854.

48. "Municipal Characteristics," *Penn Monthly* 1 (February 1870): 71.

49. *North American,* May 1, 1851. See also editorials for May 5 and July 16, 1851.

50. Hershberg, et al., "The 'Journey to Work.'"

51. *Public Ledger,* September 28, 1849.

52. *Sunday Dispatch,* June 24, 1866.

CHAPTER 2 Railroads and
the Downtown:
Philadelphia,
1830-1900

JEFFREY P. ROBERTS

As much as has been written about the railroad's contribution to the transformation of America from an agricultural economy to an urban industrial
one, virtually no attention has been paid to the effect of railroads on the
social and spatial arrangements of American cities themselves. In *The Private
City,* for example, Sam Bass Warner dismisses the railroad's effect on the
emerging industrial city in but a few sentences.[1] Only in England in the
work of H. J. Dyos and John Kellett has this subject been approached in
any systematic fashion. In fact, both Dyos and Kellett have argued that the
railroads were the single most important agent of change in nineteenth-
century cities, affecting their physical and social geography, the distribution
of such activities as housing and industry as well as the urban land market.
Against the benefits offered commuters by suburban development, Dyos
has tried to estimate the social costs resulting from railroad construction,
as measured by housing deterioration and population dislocation in the
central city.[2] Kellett has added that while magnificent railroad terminals
created new symbols for urban pride and unity, at the same time the location
of tracks and adjacent yards proved equally divisive in severing roads and
neighborhoods and created isolated, sometimes disrupted land areas in
their wake.[3]

Such issues form the intellectual foundation upon which to consider the
railroad's contribution to the transformation of Philadelphia from a walking
city in the early nineteenth century to a bustling, industrial metropolis by
1900. How did the railroads with their corporate power, the magnitude of
their terminals, tracks, and steam engines, and the intensity of their competition for passengers, freight, and land contribute to the specialization of
land use and the emergence of the downtown? Moreover, what tensions
were apparent in Philadelphia because of the introduction and expansion of

this new technology? Finally, how was the railroad involved with both the centrifugal and centripetal movement of people and business within the city? What follows will attempt to answer these important questions.

The Pioneer Lines: Railroads and Philadelphia, 1830-1865

The opening of the Pennsylvania System of Public Works in 1832, a state-financed transportation project, gave Philadelphia better access to the trans-Appalachian West than ever before. The system was Pennsylvania's response to New York's Erie Canal, opened in 1825, and Maryland's Baltimore and Ohio Railroad, chartered in 1827. Because of political disputes, the legislature was unable to decide whether the system should be a railroad or a canal. In a stroke of engineering genius or folly, the lawmakers decided to make it both because the steepness of the Allegheny Mountains in Pennsylvania necessitated the use of inclined planes to negotiate their heights. Despite many problems, including bad weather, inefficiency, and the excessive costs prompted by poor design, the system was an improvement over the former network of roads, and it strengthened Philadelphia's competitive position in the West.[4] The eastern third of the system was a railroad—the Philadelphia and Columbia—which connected Philadelphia with Columbia, Pennsylvania, a town on the Susquehanna River about 70 miles to the west. In Philadelphia this line began at Broad and Vine streets, ran north to Noble Street, and then west to 22nd where it turned northwest. It continued through Fairmount Park and crossed the Schuylkill River below the Belmont Plateau on the west bank.

When the state system opened in May 1832, its Philadelphia connection did not penetrate what were then the city limits at Vine Street.[5] A year before, the state legislature had said that a city railroad could be built in Philadelphia on Broad Street between Vine and South streets, but the city councils did not respond until January 1833, and this line on Broad Street did not open until the following December.[6] Although hailed as a major transportation innovation and a boon to commerce, seven long blocks separated it from the city's business center east of Seventh Street. The commercial interests in the eastern part of the city quickly agitated for another section to be built down Market Street to the Delaware River, but enthusiasm for this line was not universally shared. After the City Railroad opened in 1833, Broad Street, which had been undeveloped previously, experienced rapid growth; a number of businessmen, particularly forwarding and commission agents as well as warehousemen, shifted from eastern locations to new sites on this street. These entrepreneurs opposed the extension, for it would eliminate the locational advantages which their Broad Street establishments had over their Delaware River rivals.[7] After considerable debate in the newspapers and in city councils the more powerful eastern interests triumphed, and the Market Street line was authorized in December 1835.[8]

Opened in 1838, the line, extending through the heart of the mercantile district, had three long-term geographic effects. First, by providing equal access to business establishments in the eastern part of town, it reinforced their inclination to remain in that area where, after all, such essential services as banking and insurance could already be found. Second, the Market Street Railroad further congested a thoroughfare which was already crowded by market stalls stretching from the Delaware River to Eighth Street. The crush of traffic, the clogged streets, and the dirt and noise associated with all this activity contributed to the less-than-fashionable appearance of the district. Chestnut Street, capitalizing on Market's misfortunes, soon became known as *the* fashionable avenue in Philadelphia. Even after the City Railroad was removed, this impression persisted, and Market Street was never able to regain its former preeminence. Finally, although a few forwarding agents and warehousemen continued to locate on Broad Street, because of the new extension to the east, Broad Street now acquired many other, less attractive establishments. It "became a very active business center" with "sidings leading out to the numerous coal yards and industries located on both sides."[9] Coal, lumber, and marble yards which supplied customers downtown combined with industrial plants to inhibit the introduction of new activities along the thoroughfare. Not until after the line was removed in the late 1860s did the characteristics of Broad Street change for the better.

In the 1830s other important railroads were constructed in Philadelphia County. Townships and municipalities within the county wanted rail connections to maintain their competitive stance with the city. Businessmen in Germantown, Kensington, and Southwark as well as Philadelphians who owned property in these areas, worked vigorously to establish their own railroads. In April 1831 the Northern Liberties and Penn Township Railroad commenced service on Willow Street, several blocks north of Vine (see Map 2-1). Also called the Willow Street Railroad, it ran from the Delaware River to Broad Street where it joined the state system. One year later the Philadelphia, Germantown and Norristown Railroad, with its southern terminal at Ninth and Green streets, opened for business. It ran to Germantown in the northwest corner of Philadelphia County and carried both passengers and freight.[10] In November 1834 the Southwark Railroad opened, joining with the City Railroad at Broad and South streets. In the same month the Philadelphia and Trenton Railroad began to operate between its depot at Front and Harrison streets in the district of Kensington, and the city of Trenton to the northeast, where passengers could make connections to New York City. The Philadelphia, Wilmington & Baltimore Railroad commenced service in 1838. It crossed the Schuylkill River at Gray's Ferry and gained access to the city via a link with the Southwark Railroad at Broad and Washington streets.

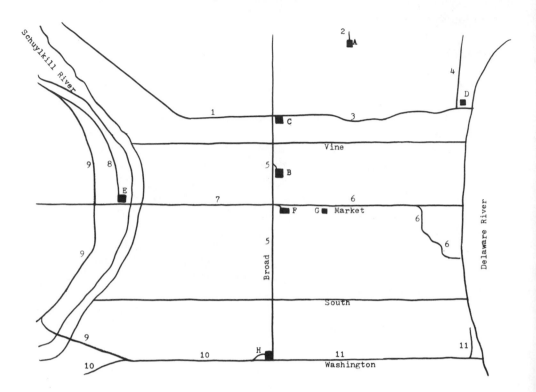

Lines:

1. Philadelphia & Columbia; later Philadelphia & Reading
2. Philadelphia, Germantown & Norristown
3. Northern Liberties & Penn Township (Willow Street Railroad)
4. North Pennsylvania
5. City Railroad: Broad Street line
6. City Railroad: East Market, Third & Dock Streets Line
7. City Railroad: West Market Street line
8. Philadelphia & Columbia; later Pennsylvania
9. Junction
10. Philadelphia, Wilmington & Baltimore
11. Southwark

Terminals:

A. 9th & Green Streets (1832-1893) Philadelphia, Germantown & Norristown
B. Broad & Cherry Streets (1838-1859) Philadelphia & Reading
C. Broad & Callowhill Streets (1859-1893) Philadelphia & Reading
D. Front & Willow Streets (1854-1900) North Pennsylvania (Freight)
E. 30th & Market Streets (1864-1876) Pennsylvania
F. 13th & Market Streets (1852-1875) Pennsylvania (Freight)
G. 11th & Market Streets (1852-1864) Pennsylvania
H. Broad & Washington Streets (1852-1881) Philadelphia, Wilmington & Baltimore

Map 2-1. Railroad Lines and Terminals in Philadelphia, 1830-1865

The discovery of the technology for burning anthracite coal in 1817 stimulated the mining of coal in northeastern Pennsylvania and, ultimately, railroading in Philadelphia.[11] At first, coal was shipped to the city on the Schuylkill Canal, but as demand for anthracite rapidly escalated, the canal was unable to meet it, and together with the questionable reliability of this waterway, its limited capacity prompted a group of businessmen to charter a new railroad in 1833.[12] This line, known as the Philadelphia and Reading, has been closely linked with Philadelphia history ever since. But in the beginning it seemed cursed, for one crisis followed another.

The initial enthusiasm for the railroad was not matched by investments in stock. It was forced to seek foreign financing and was not successful until 1834 when a group of British businessmen purchased $1 million worth of securities. The line's construction was slowed considerably by the panic of 1837 and the ensuing depression which lasted until the mid-1840s. Although a section of the road connecting Reading with Pottstown and Norristown opened in 1838, the portion to Philadelphia was delayed until December of the following year, and even then it handled only passengers, not coal. Finally, during the depths of the depression, one of the railroad's principal investors, the United States Bank of Pennsylvania, the state's successor to Nicholas Biddle's Second Bank of the United States, filed for bankruptcy which nearly forced a sheriff's sale of the Reading in 1841. Not surprisingly, therefore, its coal-carrying line to Mount Carbon was not completed until May 1842, but once opened, this route handled an increasing volume of traffic.[13] In fact, coal production soon outstripped the road's shipping capacity, and the company was forced to secure additional loans to lay a second track and purchase more rolling stock. Born of the demand for coal, the Reading was never able to liberate itself from the vicissitudes of this industry. When times were good in the mines, the line prospered; when times were hard, the road often floundered.

But despite such difficulties, both the railroad and the precious coal it delivered stimulated significant changes in the city. The availability of hard coal encouraged businessmen to switch from water-driven, wood, or soft-coal furnaces to anthracite-fired steam engines. Whereas all railroads had previously provided only the raw materials for production or a link between hinterland markets and the urban entrepôt, the Reading now assumed a major role in supplying energy. For the large-volume coal consumer close access to this line and to its coal yards soon became an important consideration in plant location.

The impact of coal, railroads, and manufacturing on Philadelphia was clearly evident in an area northwest of the central business district.[14] Prior to the advent of the railroads, the only heavy industry in this area was the Bush Hill Iron Works at 16th and Buttonwood streets. The opening of the state system in 1833 made the district attractive to new plants in heavy industry, especially those making products for use by railroads, such as locomotives, cars, rails, and wheels. By 1836 the most notable new manufacturers in the neighborhood were the fledgling locomotive companies of Matthias Baldwin and the Norris Brothers. The Reading, which connected with the state system at Belmont Plateau, used both the Philadelphia and Columbia and the Willow Street railroads to move its coal into Philadelphia. Both of these lines ran through this developing district, and the arrival of coal in the 1840s contributed to its further growth, especially near the tracks shared by these railroad companies. By 1850 iron and machine foundries, railroad car and wheel factories, and other establishments using coal had clustered in the district. These large firms, although small in number, employed nearly two-thirds of all the workers in the area. While the total number of firms grew slowly between 1850 and 1880, the number of large establishments employing 50 or more workers mushroomed, rising by 250 percent. At the same time, the district's overall employment grew rapidly, climbing from 1,005 to 5,009 workers, with the largest increase coming in the big firms.[15] As a result, there was intense competition for land. Most available space soon became densely packed with heavy industrial users. Railroad sidings were laid to firms not adjacent to the main tracks. Worker housing either filled in the gaps between the factories or was located a few blocks away. By 1890 the district was filled with businesses conforming to the modern image of industry in late nineteenth-century America; its plants were huge, smoky, and frenetic places, employing thousands of workers, and connected by rail to vast resources and markets. The specialized use of land, which distinguished the district after 1850, was guided if not fixed by the railroads and the pattern of land use that they established between 1833 and 1850.

During the late 1830s and early 1840s Philadelphia business leaders became increasingly disgruntled with the State System of Public Works, the city's link to the West. Requiring more raw materials and wider markets than ever before, Philadelphia's industrial economy had to rely on this inefficient and expensive arrangement, and given the intense competition from both New York and Baltimore, a sobering if not depressing prospect for the future confronted the city's business community. Newspaper editorials decried the neglect of Philadelphia's "great advantages" while New York "through the superior enterprise of its citizens," had "acquired the ascendency." Unless Philadelphians renewed themselves, one *Public Ledger* editorial commented, "this ascendency [will] continually increase, until our city shall become stationary."[16]

The answer clearly lay in a direct railroad to Pittsburgh and the Ohio and Mississippi River valleys beyond. Although a single, unified canal system was considered, it was rejected because of attempts by the Baltimore and Ohio Railroad to secure authorization for a line to Pittsburgh. In 1846 Philadelphia interests gained approval for a railroad to connect their city

with Pittsburgh. Both the organizers of this line and its first board of directors reflected the commitment of Philadelphia's business community to the
success of this railroad, known as the Pennsylvania. All 13 directors were
from Philadelphia, and they were deeply involved through their business
dealings with the future of the city. They included Samuel V. Merrick, iron
founder and first president of the line; Thomas Cope, transatlantic shipper;
and George W. Carpenter, drug manufacturer. The Pennsylvania was
greeted with great optimism; it would give Philadelphia the chance to regain
"her former pre-eminencey in the contest with her sister cities for the western
markets."[17] In anticipation of the railroad's contribution to the prosperity
of the city and its suburbs, local governments made large investments in
railroad stock. By 1856 the combined Philadelphia city and county stock
subscription was 100,000 shares, valued at $5 million. In fact, the govern-
ment of the newly consolidated city also owned an additional $3,429,000
worth of stock in other railroads which, it was hoped, would also aid the
fortunes of Philadelphia.[18]

Although most Philadelphians welcomed the opportunities presented by
the railroads, many were apprehensive about the new invention. They were
concerned about the dangers posed by trains speeding through the streets,
the fire hazards of wood- and coal-burning locomotives, and the destruction
of the life, commerce, and tranquillity of neighborhoods by the construction and operation of railroads. Such concerns led to legislation governing
the speed, type of motive power, and scheduling of trains. During the 1830s
both the city of Philadelphia and the municipalities in its surrounding county
enacted ordinances restricting speed to four miles per hour.[19] Further, for a
short period of time after the City Railroad was extended down Market
Street, the city banned trains on Wednesdays and Saturdays, so that cars
would not interfere with farmers and shoppers arriving for market.[20] But
most important, the enabling legislation for the City Railroad outlawed the
use of steam locomotives on this line. By law, all cars crossing the city
limits between Vine and South streets on the City Railroad had to "be
drawn by animal power."[21] Since the City Railroad was the only line to be
franchised or to operate within the original city limits between 1834 and
1873, this prohibition eliminated steam from the downtown for nearly 40
years.[22] The ordinance affected only the City Railroad, and other lines
outside these limits continued to use steam, even after the city consolidated
in 1854. However, the necessity of changing from locomotive to horse and
vice versa whenever a train crossed Vine or South Street forced railroad
companies to build major facilities at those points where their main lines
connected with the City Railroad. Thus, while some depots were located on
Market Street for the convenience of travelers, additional terminals were
constructed outside the original city limits to take advantage of the absence
there of any restrictions on steam power.[23]

The ban on steam was an additional thorn in the side of passengers traveling through Philadelphia to other points. All the early lines were independent of each other, and only a few could provide efficient and convenient transfers for passengers. Most people had to disembark at one station and journey by foot, carriage, or omnibus to the next terminal for a connecting train. Those using lines linked by the City Railroad did not fare any better; the time they gained by avoiding transfers was lost switching horses and locomotives or being caught in downtown traffic.

The decentralized pattern of terminals and the necessity of providing passengers with a convenient mode of transit to and from different stations contributed to the growth of Philadelphia's first intraurban transportation system—the omnibus lines. Omnibus companies laid out their initial routes to link the downtown along the Delaware River with the new residential areas that were growing west and northwest of the business center.[24] But while primarily serving a daily commuting public, some omnibus companies created lines to connect the outlying railroad terminals with both the downtown and other railroad stations.[25] Shortly after its inception the Philadelphia, Germantown and Norristown Railroad established omnibus service from the Merchants' Coffee House on South Third Street; its vehicles ran along Chestnut Street and then north to the Ninth and Green Street Depot. As the bus traveled on this route, it stopped at hotels to pick up and discharge railroad passengers.[26] The convenience offered by the omnibus offset to some degree the limited facilities of the City Railroad both by increasing the transportation choices available to passengers and by widening the area to and from which travelers could be conveniently conveyed. Thus, the adjustments made seem to have compensated, at least partially, for the inadequacies of the City Railroad. And viewed from a longer perspective, this line, coupled with the city's ban on steam locomotives and the competition from outlying railroads, may have actually benefited the downtown. The extension of the City Railroad on Market, Third, and Dock streets halted the movement of agents and warehouses to Broad Street. The wholesale district remained along Second and Third streets and stayed centrally located for the rest of the nineteenth century. Meanwhile, the rail lines outside Philadelphia's original limits attracted heavy industries which needed direct access to steam locomotive power. Such a pattern of land use spared most of the central district form the deleterious effects of heavy industry, and although modified after 1850, it would continue to influence the downtown for the next 50 years.

The difficulties created by the City Railroad seem to have been particularly irksome to the Pennsylvania Railroad. The first goods shipped from Pittsburgh on the Pennsylvania arrived in Philadelphia on March 3, 1850.[27] The line entered the area on a new extension of the Philadelphia and Columbia Railroad; it passed through West Philadelphia along Lancaster Avenue, and reaching 30th and Market streets, it crossed the Schuylkill River and continued east on Market on the tracks of the City Railroad. As the volume of freight and passengers rapidly rose, the Pennsylvania's executives became increasingly unhappy about the inefficiency of the City Railroad and their own accommodations for passengers and freight on Market Street. As early as 1852 problems developed with the scheduling of trains. The City Railroad served five different companies, and the Pennsylvania, as well as the other lines, often found itself waiting for the City's tracks to clear. Hermann Haupt, who was the Pennsylvania's superintendent, recommended that instead of a station more centrally located, a passenger depot be constructed at 30th and Market streets which could be served by steam. He further suggested that omnibus companies be hired to convey passengers to this western facility.[28]

The railroad followed his advice and in 1852 purchased a large parcel of land north of 30th and Market streets. However, because westward expansion constituted a greater need for its financial resources, the company continued to occupy its 11th and Market streets passenger depot, purchased from the Philadelphia, Wilmington & Baltimore Railroad in 1852, and its 13th and Market streets freight depot which was erected in 1853. But both the Philadelphia, Wilmington & Baltimore Railroad and the Reading Railroad, which were also increasing their traffic, made changes in their downtown passenger terminals. In 1852 the Reading acquired an entire block of land at the southeast corner of Broad and Callowhill streets where it built a new station, although construction was delayed for seven years because of the line's overextended financial situation and the panic of 1857. The Philadelphia, Wilmington & Baltimore Railroad proceeded with its building program on schedule, and its new passenger depot, located at Broad and Washington streets in South Philadelphia, "the finest . . . in Philadelphia in architectural beauty, size, and internal arrangement," was opened in 1852.[29]

By the 1850s the lack of sufficient facilities to handle incoming and outgoing freight also had become a serious problem for many rail companies. Although the City Railroad was double tracked, its eastern terminus at Dock Street was inadequate to meet the ever growing demand for the movement of goods. The Reading helped itself by building huge coal wharves at Port Richmond during the 1840s and 1850s. But the line had to ship other merchandise over either the Willow Street Railroad or the City Railroad, thereby incurring tolls for their use. In 1857 the Reading acquired the Willow Street line and its dock facilities on the Delaware River, and with this new river outlet avoided both the inconvenience of changing motive power at Broad Street and the City Railroad's tolls. The Pennsylvania Railroad, with its financial success dependent on the volume of merchandise carried, argued at length that improved port facilities were crucial to both its future and that of Philadelphia.[30] While in 1861 the Pennsylvania did solve some of its own difficulties and those of the Philadelphia, Wilmington & Baltimore Railroad by constructing a freight line across Washington Avenue to the Delaware River, the need remained for a better system of local lines to ease the transfer of goods and passengers.

In 1860 a proposal was made by the Reading, the Pennsylvania, and the Philadelphia, Wilmington & Baltimore lines to establish a new railroad that would link the three and bypass both the City Railroad and downtown congestion. The new Junction Railroad was opposed by the city government, since the loss of traffic on the City Railroad would mean a loss of tolls.[31] But the legislature chartered the line in 1860, and three years later a connection was made between the Reading tracks at Belmont Plateau and those of the Pennsylvania at 35th Street. By 1866 a further link had been made at Gray's Ferry between the Pennsylvania and the Philadelphia, Wilmington & Baltimore Railroad. The completion of the Junction Railroad resulted in a loss of business for the City Railroad, and although its traffic declined, maintenance costs did not. At first, city councils passed ordinances that banned the opening of new sidings on Broad Street. But the City Railroad was doomed, and soon the government authorized the removal of the tracks on Broad Street between Vine and Market streets. Finally, in 1869 it directed that the tracks on Broad Street from Market Street to Washington Avenue and on Market Street east to the Delaware River be removed.[32]

The Pennsylvania's board of directors, anticipating the opening of the new Junction Railroad, decided in 1860 to begin construction of their new depot at 30th and Market streets. The decision to build so far from the downtown was influenced significantly by the advent and rapid growth of a horsecar network. The establishment of the first horsecar line in 1858 stimulated an intense battle for lucrative franchises on many city streets. By 1860, 19 lines were in operation, covering all principal avenues in the central district. Faster and more reliable than the omnibus, horsecars meant that either less time was spent traveling over a particular distance or a greater distance was traversed in a specific period of time. For the Pennsylvania Railroad, improved intraurban transit made it possible to plan a larger, though more distant passenger facility.[33] The intervention of the Civil War, however, delayed construction, and the new terminal did not open until 1864.

By 1865 railroads in Philadelphia had achieved considerable maturity in contrast to what they had been 35 years before. Often led by local businessmen and spurred on by the need to establish access to raw materials and new markets, the early rail companies laid out their lines to obtain the maximum possible advantage for themselves as well as for Philadelphia and its surrounding municipalities. The initial geography of railroad construction spared the downtown of much disruption, but this pattern would not prevail for the entire nineteenth century.

Spreading Out: The Philadelphia Central District and the Railroads, 1865-1900

After the Civil War Philadelphians witnessed the expansion and consolidation of their local rail system and a rapid growth in the volume of daily commuting passengers. The Reading and Pennsylvania railroads vigorously competed to acquire previously independent companies and to attract a major share of commuting workers; both developments had a long-term and profound influence on the evolution of the downtown. Moreover, the decision on the site of the new City Hall, perhaps the single most important event in the transformation of the downtown, radically altered the locational patterns of many core activities and had far-reaching effects on railroad development.

In the 1870s and 1880s aggressive and innovative leadership was often what made the difference between success and failure. The management of the Pennsylvania Railroad had always been dynamic and resourceful, and in the chess game of local railroad competition, it usually won. In part, its triumphs were produced by a healthy financial base, particularly in contrast to the Reading. However, its management, under the presidencies of J. Edgar Thomson, Thomas A. Scott, and George B. Roberts, also made the most of every opportunity. The new 30th Street terminal, with its access to steam locomotives and horsecar service, prompted the company to build, in addition to the Junction Railroad, a second intracity link to meet the need for a more direct line to New York City.[34] Chartered in 1863, the Connecting Railroad departed from the "Main Line" track near 35th Street, ran northeast across North Philadelphia for approximately four miles, and turned east to meet the Philadelphia and Trenton Railroad at Frankford. The Connecting Railroad was opened in 1867 and was leased in 1869 to the Philadelphia and Trenton for it to operate. The Pennsylvania, however, leased the Philadelphia and Trenton in 1871 and resumed control of the system.[35]

In addition to their fatal impact on the City Railroad, the Junction and Connecting railroads had important consequences for the downtown. These lines strengthened the tendency for freight shipments to bypass the central district and continued the pattern, established by the ban on steam, of sparing the downtown from the intrusion of extensive rail yards. Moreover, the decentralized location of freight yards and the more reliable service provided by the new intracity lines stimulated growth along the industrial corridors of the Reading in North Philadelphia and the Pennsylvania along Washington Avenue. In addition, they encouraged the development at the city's edge of industries which processed raw materials such as agricultural products, ores, and petroleum.

   The further decentralization of freight traffic and the removal of the City Railroad relieved the downtown of some congestion, but the removal of rail service disrupted the wholesale and manufacturing establishments in the eastern half of the central district. Downtown manufacturing in the middle to late nineteenth century was dominated by such fashion-oriented industries as clothing and accessories, furniture, printing, and publishing, and the number of firms and employees in these fields grew rapidly. Their need for current information and the personal nature of their business relationships made it essential for them to locate downtown where both needs could be satisfied. As these industries grew, so did their suppliers and shippers who operated from nearby warehouses. For both manufacturers and warehousemen, the loss of rail service was an especially difficult problem, for they could not easily relocate nor could they rely on drayage alone to handle their business. Apparently because of either pressure from the affected businesses or the railroad's recognition of the need, a new freight depot was constructed by the Pennsylvania in 1873 at Delaware Avenue and Dock Street. It connected with the company's Washington Avenue Line via a spur that ran up Delaware Avenue and helped to preserve an important part of Philadelphia's downtown economy.[36]

   Meanwhile, the ongoing industrialization of Philadelphia and the concomitant development of its shipping facilities produced increased demand for auxiliary business services, such as import/export banking, insurance, market information, and warehousing. These business needs coupled with rising income levels and increasing population contributed to a post-Civil War expansion of the central district. There was important growth in wholesaling, finance, information services, and the legal profession, activities directly related to the industrial economy of the city. Furthermore, developments in retailing in the downtown reflected changes not only in income and population size but also in the manner in which consumer goods were sold. The days of bartering and personal service were numbered, as new merchandising and marketing techniques, pioneered in Philadelphia by John Wanamaker, revolutionized business practices. Merchants developed sophisticated advertising methods, redesigned their displays, and offered money-back guarantees to attract customers into their shops.

   The expansion of downtown retailing was linked directly to the transportation system. Horsecars funeled thousands of people into the central district to shop and made it possible for that area to become the location for the greatest concentration of commercial employment as well.[37] Beginning in the 1850s and especially after the Civil War, the railroads carried more and more passengers into the core area. At the same time real estate promoters advertised the presence of nearby transportation to sell new housing both in Philadelphia and in its suburbs. Persons responsible for new residential construction in outlying districts like Chestnut Hill were frequently board members of the railroad companies, and this symbiotic relationship worked well as the developers sold their houses, the railroads increased their passenger volume, and new middle-class families found affordable homes in convenient, pleasant neighborhoods. The Pennsylvania Railroad along its Main Line and the Philadelphia, Wilmington & Baltimore Railroad through southeastern Delaware County initiated real estate projects which brought the lines revenue from both land sales and increased commuter ridership.[38] In the 1850s and 1860s the Pennsylvania enjoyed sustained growth in both local and through passenger traffic (see Table 2-1). Except for a few fluctuations, its totals rose through 1875, an indication of the increased importance of passenger revenue to the financial success of the railroad.

Likewise, the Reading Railroad, under the aggressive presidency of Franklin Gowen, recognized the potential for profits in commuting. In 1870 it leased the Philadelphia, Germantown and Norristown Railroad to take advantage of those traveling daily to the downtown from Norristown, Manayunk, Germantown, and Chestnut Hill (see Table 2-2).[39] Moreover, after acquiring these lines, the Reading lowered all its passenger fares, with the greatest reduction being made for those commuting between Philadelphia and the suburbs.[40] As Table 2-1 clearly shows, their policy was quite successful. A similar pattern was evident on the North Pennsylvania Railroad, chartered in 1853 and in operation by 1855. Based in a freight depot at Front and Willow streets and a passenger station at 3rd and Berks streets, it ran trains north to the town of Bethlehem, Pennsylvania, where it connected with the Lehigh Valley Railroad. It was organized to head off a new rail line controlled by interests in New York City, and it provided valuable freight and passenger service to parts of North Philadelphia, the northern suburbs in Montgomery and Bucks counties, and the Lehigh Valley.[41]

The combined efforts of these local railroads to expand and improve commuter service encouraged the movement of population beyond the reach of the horsecar. Whether one lived along the Pennsylvania's Main Line, the Reading's tracks in east Germantown or the Philadelphia, Wilmington & Baltimore Railroad in Delaware County, work in the downtown could now be convenient to a suburban home. The new suburbs did not detract from the downtown; in fact, they contributed to its continued expansion and also strengthened its position as the chief provider of goods and services. The volume of passenger traffic that flowed through it supported hundreds of stores, hotels, boardinghouses, restaurants, and other similar activities catering to a transient population. Small clusters of businesses also sprang up around the rail terminals just outside the central district. In particular, the area surrounding the Reading depot at Broad and Callowhill streets developed a diversified group of eating houses, lodging places, and entertainment attractions, ranging from theater and burlesque to prostitution.

TABLE 2-1   Consecutive Three-Year Passenger Totals, Philadelphia and
Reading Railroad and the Pennsylvania Railroad, 1843-1900

Year	Philadelphia and Reading Railroad	Pennsylvania Railroad[a]
1843	56,554	
1846	88,641	
1849	95,577	
1852	155,164	
1853	211,819	82,750
1855	277,617	92,607
1858	285,651	83,257
1861	368,651	112,119
1864	1,055,529	2,366,213
1867	1,273,644	3,347,486
1870	2,034,039	4,352,769
1873	6,790,088	5,879,683
1876	10,936,157	6,926,016
1879	7,908,648	5,948,645
1882	12,027,420	10,372,894
1885	23,531,057	12,341,459
1888	15,975,839[b]	17,634,467
1891	18,828,090	20,066,268
1894	19,041,293	17,213,157
1897	17,991,326	17,061,656
1900	21,910,349	21,402,972

SOURCE: Pennsylvania Railroad Company, *Sixth to Fifty-Fourth Annual Reports of the Directors* (Philadelphia: various publishers, 1854-1901). Philadelphia and Reading Railroad Company, *Reports of the President and Managers* (Philadelphia: various publishers, 1844-1901).

[a]Statistics between 1853 and 1861 are for Philadelphia only. From 1862 to 1900 data are for Main Line between Philadelphia and Pittsburgh.

[b]Lower figures reflect reorganization of the company and the divestiture of the Central Railroad of New Jersey.

TABLE 2-2 **Philadelphia, Germantown & Norristown Railroad:**
Annual Number of Passengers, 1844–1870[a]

Year	Wissahickon & Manayunk	Spring Mills & Conshohocken	Norristown	Germantown	Chestnut Hill[b]	Total[c]
			Stations			
1844						210,880
1845						249,697
1846						294,194
1847	69,443	34,114	75,221	133,656		324,593
1848	87,582	39,670	83,942	163,821		386,635
1849	90,103	40,190	80,813	172,947		390,945
1850	102,089	38,955	96,366	200,025		446,725
1851	106,610	41,508	106,118	246,971		506,501
1852	95,404	41,232	99,350	277,991		518,402
1853	107,151	51,526	121,239	372,646		672,498
1854	133,187	60,321	160,607	477,252	37,703	869,070
1855[d]	130,932	56,820	151,440	495,444	92,294	826,863
1856	146,986	61,643	184,624	607,521	120,004	1,131,385
1857	154,029	75,015	203,079	710,279	113,300	1,378,228
1858	159,406	69,490	180,196	712,307	113,911	1,243,710
1859	212,268	72,983	178,174	991,780	135,514	1,590,719
1860	211,883	68,025	207,515	972,663	181,386	1,641,472
1861	229,382	50,779	192,376	1,019,811	172,975	1,665,323
1862	228,624	51,053	177,387	992,154	192,243	1,641,461
1863	219,522	58,548	234,842	1,159,562	311,113	1,983,587
1864	285,264	69,243	314,030	1,395,958	334,000	2,398,495
1865	326,351	84,599	357,315	1,417,061	347,976	2,533,302
1866	350,140	83,838	383,280	1,346,840	284,183	2,448,281
1867	366,492	83,769	412,813	1,415,312	282,479	2,560,865
1868	363,535	77,687	405,880	1,425,676	267,789	2,540,567
1869	409,835	95,211	426,505	1,543,909	279,890	2,755,350
1870	455,542	106,928	423,181	1,506,177	283,245	2,775,173

SOURCE: Reports of the President and Managers of the Philadelphia, Germantown and Norristown Railroad, 1844–1870.

[a]Between 1844 and 1854, the reporting year ran from November 1 to October 31. This procedure was changed in 1855 to October 1 to September 30.

[b]The Chestnut Hill Railroad opened in 1854. Statistics between 1854 and 1863 are from its Annual Reports. Thereafter, statistics are from the Philadelphia, Germantown and Norristown Railroad Annual Reports. The totals from the Chestnut Hill RR Reports, with the exception of 1857, 1858, and 1861, were greater than the reported figures from the Philadelphia, Germantown and Norristown.

[c]For a variety of reasons—different reporting techniques, volume from additional stations—the row totals between 1844 and 1863 do not agree with a summation of the row totals. Statistics for the years 1864 to 1870, however, do total across the rows.

[d]11-month total: November 1, 1854, to September 30, 1855. See note (a) above.

But while Philadelphia's railroads significantly contributed to the growth and organization of the downtown during the quarter century between 1850 and 1875, it was the decision to build City Hall at Centre Square that had the most profound effect on spatial patterns in the core in the last third of the nineteenth century. The battle to construct a new City Hall began in the 1830s, and Centre Square always figured prominently in the debate over a site for the building. A decision was finally made in 1870 when Philadelphia voted to erect a new City Hall at Centre Square.[42] Previously the downtown showed a strong affinity for the Delaware River and its long-standing mercantile establishments. Although business development extended farther west along such principal streets as Market, Arch, and Chestnut, the greatest concentration of activities still lay in the area east of Eighth Street between Vine and South. In fact, in the debate about a new City Hall, many thought that it ought to be located at either Independence Hall, the site of the old municipal offices, or Washington Square in the heart of the business community; Centre Square was thought to be too far from the core of activity.[43]

The decision to construct at Centre Square and to consolidate in a single edifice the growing municipal bureaucracy rapidly altered established spatial patterns. The shift westward reorganized the arrangement of workers who relied on such city agencies as the courts or the Department of Vital Records and, in general, meant larger and larger crowds of people concentrated in the vicinity of Broad and Market streets. John Wanamaker was the first to recognize the implications of the new City Hall for downtown business. He saw the new structure as not just an office building but a symbol of Philadelphia's prosperity and urbanity. People would be attracted to it not only for business but also to experience its colossal architectural presence as an expression of the times. Nearby locations, therefore, if used innovatively could benefit from the new building. In 1875 Wanamaker purchased the old Pennsylvania freight depot at 13th and Market streets and commenced a new specialization of the area's land use. In the obsolete depot he opened a clothing emporium which he transformed into a department store in 1878 and which quickly established itself as the premier retail outlet in Philadelphia. The new "Grand Depot" combined with the presence of both City Hall and the Masonic Temple, constructed between 1868 and 1873 on the north side of the square, bestowed a new, more cosmopolitan tone to the district. Representing the downtown's finest qualities of leadership and innovation, the new station quickened the pace of the rivalry between the Pennsylvania and the Reading railroads. Between 1875 and 1895 there was an intense interplay of moves and countermoves as each company sought to obtain an edge over the other in the competition for passengers and terminal locations in the newly emerging heart of the downtown.

But along with Centre Square there was another fresh attraction in the city, and its influence on the railroads would also be profound. Probably more than any other single event, the Centennial Exposition in Fairmount Park convinced railroad management, stockholders, and the general public of the profits to be made from passenger service. The problem of transporting millions of visitors to the fairground in the park prompted a number of railroads to make special plans. The Reading opened a new passenger depot on the west side of the Schuylkill River on the Junction Railroad about three-quarters of a mile upriver from the Girard Avenue Bridge. In 1876 this station handled 247 trains per day and a total of 3,295,120 passengers.[44] The Pennsylvania's plans were even more extensive. In May 1876 it opened a new facility at 32nd and Market streets. Although unveiled during the Centennial, it was intended to be the main station for through and local passengers for years to come. A temporary Centennial station was also constructed at 48th Street on the periphery of the fairgrounds, with an adjoining loop of tracks to facilitate train movement. Both stations handled an incredible number of passengers during the six months the fair was open; the Centennial station handled 22,372 trains and 2,617,213 persons; the 32nd Street station handled 20,231 trains and 2,343,499 persons.[45]

Although the Centennial efforts of both the Pennsylvania and the Reading railroads were important, a construction project by the North Penn Railroad had a more significant effect on the downtown. In 1874 this company announced plans to build a new line from Jenkintown, Pennsylvania, which would run northeast and cross the Delaware River above Trenton. There it would unite with the tracks of the Central Railroad Company of New Jersey which connected with New York City.[46] The new line meant that New York travelers would have an alternative to the Pennsylvania's direct line, and opening for the Centennial, it proved to be an instant success. But its greater contribution was yet to come.

During the 1870s Franklin Gowen vigorously pushed the Reading to expand and become more competitive. Gowen was concerned about the company's reliance on coal revenues, since frequent strikes by miners constantly upset the Reading's financial stability. To gain greater control, the Reading bought many acres of Pennsylvania coal land and mined them itself, but this did not secure the anticipated stability; instead there was increased labor strife, particularly between the Molly Maguires and Gowen's Pinkerton police force.[47] At the same time, Gowen set his mind to breaking the Pennsylvania's dominance of through passenger service to New York City and in May 1879 the Reading leased the North Penn and its New York connection. Unfortunately, the North Penn's passenger depot, located at 3rd and Berks streets in North Philadelphia was nearly three miles from Centre Square. At this distance the Reading and its subsidiary did not threaten the Pennsylvania whose 32nd Street station was but one mile away. The problem was solved in October 1879 when the Reading opened the Tabor Junction line. This route connected the old Philadelphia, Germantown and Norristown Railroad with the North Penn at Tabor, a station on the latter line in North Philadelphia about one and three-quarter miles south of the city limits. The "new three mile road . . . made it possible to run . . . New York trains out of the Reading's downtown station" at Broad and Callowhill streets, a mere half mile from City Hall.[48]

The prospect of a more centrally located terminal for trains to New York was a formidable challenge to the Pennsylvania Railroad. In early August 1879 the managers of the railroad reported to their board of directors that they intended to bridge the Schuylkill River at 30th and Filbert streets, construct an elevated railroad between Filbert and Market, and erect a downtown station on the west side of Centre Square. Apparently, the railroad had been purchasing land in this area for some time, for the *Public Ledger* reported on August 8, 1879, that the Pennsylvania had already acquired "a large proportion of the properties" at "good prices to the sellers" amounting to a total of "over $300,000." By June 1880 some 300 properties had been purchased and demolition was under way.[49] "About 190 dwellings, stores, shops, and stables, of all kinds, were torn down. . . ."[50] In their place the Pennsylvania built a viaduct which bridged every street from the Schuylkill River east to 15th. The number of trains projected for this new downtown terminal was so large that the railroad decided to build elevated tracks rather than cross the north-south streets at grade level. Opened on December 5, 1881, the four-shed Broad Street Station was described by the *Public Ledger* as "magnificent" (see Map 2-2).[51]

The Filbert Street viaduct and the Broad Street Station had an immediate effect on the downtown. First, they attracted more service establishments such as hotels, restaurants, and laundries into the Centre Square locale. Moreover, along Market Street west of City Hall, new freight businesses opened to take advantage of a new freight depot at 15th Street. To the north a district of homes and shops between Filbert Street and the Reading's tracks on Pennsylvania Avenue began to lose its appeal.

The Reading did not respond immediately to the Pennsylvania's downtown challenge because the railroad filed for bankruptcy in May 1880.[52] In receivership for three years, the line again declared bankruptcy in 1884. Part of its difficulties stemmed from its desire to expand westward and rival the Pennsylvania as a national carrier. In the 1880s the railroad became involved in a venture to construct a line across the state, paralleling the Pennsylvania, but the Reading's financial backers, including William Vanderbilt and Chauncey DePew, withdrew from the project in 1885, and the line went even deeper into debt. Fortunately for its creditors, J. P. Morgan and

John Lowber Walsh helped the railroad reorganize itself on a sound financial footing one year later, and as a result the Reading's management was able to consider a new terminal. Nearly 35 years old, the Broad and Callowhill station simply did not have any advantage over the Broad Street Station. In addition, the railroad wanted to bring into one station all its main lines, especially the old Philadelphia, Germantown and Norristown Railroad as well as its original line which ran up the Schuylkill River. In 1888 the railroad proposed to erect a new terminal at 12th and Market streets to be fed by an elevated viaduct between 11th and 12th streets that would extend north to Pennsylvania Avenue.[53] Why the 12th and Market site was chosen is not fully clear, but it was probably a question of land availability and proximity to City Hall. The railroad most likely would have preferred a location one or two blocks farther west, but by the late 1880s the land surrounding Centre Square was very expensive. Moreover, if the Reading had attempted to get closer to City Hall, it would probably have encountered opposition strong enough to stymie the entire project. The 12th and Market site, therefore, appears to have been sensible; it was close enough to the center of activity to benefit but far enough away to prevent any outcry with which the company could not cope.

The public debate over the new Reading terminal lasted for two years. With the exception of property owners adjacent to the line, public opinion favored the new station, and in December 1890 the city councils approved its construction. Opened on January 20, 1893, it was able to handle in excess of 290 trains per day (see Map 2-2).[54] Unfortunately the commitment of a large part of the railroad's financial resources to the structure coincided with a three-year depression which began in 1893, and the line was again forced into bankruptcy. The Reading, despite all its efforts, just never seemed able to escape failure.

The Pennsylvania Railroad, on the other hand, had problems born from success. In the same year that the Broad Street Station opened, the Pennsylvania acquired the Philadelphia, Wilmington & Baltimore Railroad. Transferred to the Broad Street Station, this company's passenger traffic soon accounted for 43 percent of the railroad's total passenger volume.[55] Further, the Reading's success in promoting Germantown and Chestnut Hill as residential areas was not overlooked by the management of the Pennsylvania. Encouraged by Henry Howard Houston, a member of the board of directors and a principal landowner in these two northwest communities, the railroad in 1880 laid out a new commuter line which opened four years later. It ran up the west side of Germantown and Chestnut Hill and was an immediate success. Passenger volume actually exceeded management projections. Traffic from these lines as well as the overall growth of the railroad overtaxed the Broad Street facilities. An enlarged building was opened in 1893;

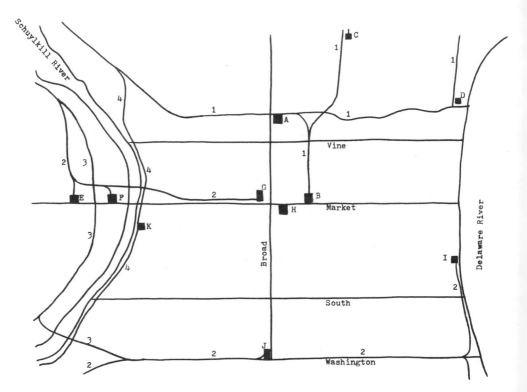

Lines:

1. Philadelphia & Reading
2. Pennsylvania
3. Junction
4. Schuylkill East Side

Terminals:

A. Broad and Callowhill Streets (1859-1893) Philadelphia & Reading
B. 12th and Market Streets (1893-) Philadelphia & Reading
C. 9th and Green Streets (1832-1893) Philadelphia & Reading
D. Front and Willow Streets (1854-1900) Philadelphia & Reading (Freight)
E. 32nd and Market Streets (1876-1881) Pennsylvania
F. 30th and Market Streets (1864-1876) Pennsylvania
G. Broad Street Station (1881-1952) Pennsylvania
H. 13th and Market Streets (1852-1875) Pennsylvania (Freight)
I. Delaware Avenue and Dock Street (1873-) Pennsylvania (Freight)
J. Broad and Washington Streets (1852-1881) Pennsylvania
K. 24th and Chestnut Streets (1886-) Baltimore and Ohio

Map 2-2. Railroad Lines and Terminals in Philadelphia, 1865-1900

its train shed was 306 feet wide, 591 feet long, and 100 feet high, and it arched over 16 tracks. This shelter, the largest single span of its time, was capable of handling 530 scheduled trains and 60,000 people daily. On an average day between 4 and 7 P.M., 50 trains arrived and 80 departed.[56]

In the twentieth century the Broad Street Station would not outlive its major rival, the Reading Terminal. But in 1900 it symbolized much of what had occurred in Philadelphia since the Civil War. The business district had expanded to the west; commuting had become a way of life for many. And the presence of the railroads in the downtown could not be denied. Railroads were playing a central role in the attainment of metropolitan status for Philadelphia, and in the process public attitudes regarding the modern age of steam were changing, too.

Symbol of Unity, Agent of Division

Nineteenth-century Philadelphians were proud of their railroad stations, especially the Pennsylvania's Broad Street facility and the Reading Terminal, both of which were built when the rail industry was at the height of its power and influence. These magnificent new buildings, erected to assert the standing of the railroads, supplied the city with focal points which, as Sam Bass Warner has noted, earlier stations had not done.[57] Along with railroad cars, they brought all types of people together; within them travelers rubbed shoulders, shared pleasures and discomforts, and participated in the leveling of America.

Large city terminals, of course, served very practical goals. The fierce competition among railroads for passengers compelled them "to build their metropolitan terminals on a grand scale, huge in size to handle the volume of traffic, extravagant in facilities and decoration to attract the passenger."[58] But while meeting such business needs, terminals also expressed the progress of civilization, and, more important, a community's degree of urbanity. Banks, hotels, and schools as well as other buildings represented urban sophistication, but they were not uniquely modern. The terminal, on the other hand, symbolized not only the best of America but also its coming of age in the nineteenth century. Railroads were modern and progressive, and railroad terminals, built on a grand scale, declared that a city was up-to-date. Together with city halls and department stores they embodied the energy of the era and gave tangible evidence of Philadelphia's standing near the top of the hierarchy of American cities. In Philadelphia all three building types framed Centre Square by 1881. In contrast, the site of the Reading Terminal at 12th and Market streets, while a symbolic ratification of the westward movement of the downtown, was representative also of the railroad's problems. The Reading's frequent financial difficulties were an embarrassment to

Philadelphia, and it was appropriate that the line's downtown terminal not share the greater limelight of Centre Square.

The benefits of railroads to the nation and the city were not acquired without social costs, a fact which even the most fervent boosters of the cause were willing to acknowledge. Railroads meant ugly scars, thought Daniel Webster, the statesman and promoter of America, but, he said, they represented "a zealous determination to improve and profit by labor."[59] Mocking those who described the locomotive as a "screaming monster" and a "defacer of [the] landscape," Webster made such visions appear "squeamish, effeminate, and trivial. The noise and smoke—the discomfort and visual ugliness, even the loss of peace and repose—these things," Webster proclaimed, were "of little consequence to true Americans."[60] In Philadelphia the early ban on steam locomotives in the downtown kept the monster at bay, at least temporarily, but in the long run the city and Webster seemed to agree. In fact, as early as 1836 the *Public Ledger* heralded the new marvel, its "cars whizzing along like comets," and predicted that it would make Philadelphia into a bustling metropolis. Of course, there would be problems; probably horses would be knocked down, "a cow cut in halves . . . , a score of pigs quartered . . . , a dozen of dogs mangled. . . ." The *Ledger* was even prepared to accept the accidental death of children, "perhaps a dozen or so annually; but this is a trifle. . . ." Men needed machines, even if they occasionally broke arms or legs, "to promote the grand design."[61] Fifty years later the promoters of the Reading Terminal at 12th and Market streets reminded Philadelphians of what they already knew. Railroading, they said, was not "a fine and delicate business," but "a dirty, greasy, [and] smoky" one at best. To build great cities, develop commerce, and maintain a competitive level of manufacturing it was necessary to accept the "disadvantages along with the advantages."[62]

In the nineteenth century the people of Philadelphia were often asked to tolerate the discomforts and dangers introduced by the railroads in the name of progress. But sometimes they demurred. Initially, such conflict occurred in the outer reaches of the developed city. In July 1840 the citizens of Kensington, fearing the disruption of their community and the loss of their principal thoroughfare, rioted to prevent the Philadelphia and Trenton Railroad from building an extension down Front Street.[63] The working class of this neighborhood, no less than those living downtown, found steam railroads to be an intrusion. Later Philadelphians overrun by the railroads turned to litigation for recourse. Between 1879 and 1887 the Pennsylvania Railroad was forced to defend itself in court against the claims of those displaced or disturbed by the Filbert Street viaduct. Called upon for a ruling on two occasions, the Pennsylvania Supreme Court upheld the position of the railroad and the national concerns which it represented. In 1886 the court decided that the Pennsylvania had the authority to buy land in Philadelphia under eminent domain, provided that just compensation was paid.[64] And one year later it said that owners of property near the Filbert Street tracks were not entitled to damages despite the depreciation of their investments due to the noise and smoke of the trains.[65] In Philadelphia local interests would not stand in the way of progress.

Just as their presence caused conflict and division in Philadelphia, the barriers the railroads erected between neighborhoods splintered the metropolis. Property owners on either side of the Reading Terminal were unhappy about its impact on their area. The new facility, they said, would disrupt "free social intercourse and [the] business interchange . . . essential for the proper improvement of their respective neighborhoods."[66] Across Broad Street the Filbert Street elevated reinforced an established pattern in local life. In the nineteenth century Market Street was the accepted boundary between "proper" Philadelphia and the remainder of the city. This understanding began before the Revolution when many Philadelphians abandoned the plain Quaker life for the social graces of the Episcopalians and Presbyterians. Market Street emerged as the dividing line between the traditional Quakers to the north and the highly visible, glamorous social set to the south. When population moved west toward Broad Street after 1835, these settlement patterns persisted, although in new physical spaces. Market Street, in fact, became even more of a psychological and emotional palisade. For high society living to the south it was "one of these 'deadlines,'" said *The Evening Bulletin*, "north of which man or woman may not go and live. Thousands . . . crossed it, only to be lost in the wilderness beyond." Social climbers like the traction magnate P. A. B. Widener, who built stately mansions on North Broad Street, were "heedless until too late, of the clang of the closing doors behind them, shutting them out forever from paradise." Outside the confines of Broad, Pine, and Market streets and the Schuylkill River were those who lived "in *Partibus Infidelium,* beyond the pale of fashionable civilizaton."[67] The Pennsylvania's elevated line gave a physical presence to what once was only an imaginary frontier. Called "a veritable Chinese wall" by Lewis Mumford, the structure dramatically separated the "well-bred district" within which paradise reigned from the world beyond, populated by "ravening beasts."[68]

North of Market Street the "wall" had another effect. In the 1870s this part of Philadelphia was well developed and in places respectable, but it deteriorated rapidly after becoming surrounded by railroads. In addition to the Pennsylvania and the Reading, the Baltimore and Ohio contributed to its decline. For many years the B & O had wanted to build a station in central Philadelphia, but the Pennsylvania had always been able to thwart its efforts to secure the necessary charter. Only the expansion of the Reading Railroad allowed the B & O to arrive in the downtown. Franklin Gowen, president of the Reading, had long been eager to compete with the Pennsylvania between Philadelphia and Washington, D.C. He broke the Pennsylvania's stranglehold on this lucrative run by chartering, together with the B & O, a crucial trunk line called the Schuylkill East Side Railroad. This line connected with the Reading at Fairmount and ran south along the east bank of the Schuylkill River to a point below Grays Ferry. There it crossed the river and joined the Baltimore and Philadelphia Railroad, owned by the B & O, which went south to Baltimore and from there to Washington. This route began operation in 1886, and its terminal, which opened in the same year, was at 24th and Chestnut streets (see Map 2-2).[69] The Schuylkill East Side Railroad added a final link to the chain of railroads surrounding the northwestern end of the central district. Together with the Filbert Street viaduct and the Reading's tracks on Pennsylvania Avenue, the Schuylkill East Side Railroad sealed off this part of town. Between its tracks and the riverbank industrial development eliminated all residential use, while to the east home buyers and developers began to think twice about the desirability of the area. The noise, dirt, smoke, and disruption caused by the constant ebb and flow of trains dampened any enthusiasm for residential and commercial expansion. Housing construction virtually came to a halt, and property values skidded. Buildings were subdivided, overcrowding ensued, and industries formerly excluded from the area began to arrive.

By the late 1870s or early 1880s Philadelphia's rail system was dominated by the Pennsylvania and Reading companies. Only the Baltimore and Ohio avoided being gobbled up by one of these two. Such consolidation may be viewed as a victory for broadly conceived goals over local interests, an outcome which was duplicated in other arenas in the divided metropolis. The railroads linked the inner city and the suburbs, gave focus and definition to the downtown, and raised the prospect of greater prosperity for all Philadelphians. At the same time they proved divisive. Protected by the courts, they made many decisions solely on the basis of corporate self-interest. They contributed greatly to the decentralization of the city, and near the core they helped to separate one neighborhood from another. In many respects, the railroads were a unifying element in nineteenth-century America, but they were also conducive to fragmentation and helped make Philadelphia a divided metropolis.

Notes

1. Sam Bass Warner, Jr., *The Private City: Philadelphia in Three Periods of Its Growth* (Philadelphia: University of Pennsylvania Press, 1968), p. 54*n*. The author would like to express his appreciation to the following agencies whose support of the

Philadelphia Social History Project has made portions of this research possible: Center for Studies of Metropolitan Problems, National Institute of Mental Health (MH 16621); Division of Research Grants, National Endowment for the Humanities (RC-25568-76-1156); and Sociology Program, Division of Social Sciences, National Science Foundation (SOC 76-20069).

2. H. J. Dyos, *Victorian Suburb: A Study of the Growth of Camberwell* (Leicester: University Press, 1961); H. J. Dyos, "Workingmen's Fares in South London, 1860-1914," *Journal of Transport History* 1 (1953-54): 3-19; H. J. Dyos, "Railways and Housing in Victorian London," ibid. 2(1955-56): 11-21 (Part I); 90-100 (Part II); H. J. Dyos, "Some Social Costs of Railway Building in London," ibid. 3(1957-58): 23-30.

3. John R. Kellett, *The Impact of Railways on Victorian Cities* (London: Routledge & Kegan Paul, 1969); J. R. Kellett, "Glasgow's Railways, 1830-1880: A Study in 'Natural Growth,'" *Economic History Review* 17 (1964): 354-68.

4. James W. Livingood, *The Philadelphia-Baltimore Trade Rivalry, 1780-1860* (Harrisburg, Pa.: Pennsylvania Historical and Museum Commission, 1947); Robert G. Albion, *The Rise of New York Port, 1815-1860* (1939; reprint ed., New York: Charles Scribner's Sons, 1970).

5. Prior to the Act of Consolidation of 1854, the City of Philadelphia was one municipality within the County of Philadelphia. The city was bounded by Vine and South streets and by the Delaware and Schuylkill rivers.

6. *A Digest of the Ordinances of the Corporation of the City of Philadelphia, and of the Acts of Assembly Relating Thereto* (Philadelphia: J. Crissy, 1841), p. 268.

7. J. Thomas Scharf and Thompson Westcott, *The History of Philadelphia* (Philadelphia: L. H. Everts & Co., 1884), 3: 2175-76.

8. *A Digest of the Ordinances . . . ,* p. 269.

9. Jay V. Hare, *History of the Reading* (1909-1914; reprint ed., Philadelphia: John Henry Strock, 1966), p. 99.

10. It was the first railroad to operate a steam locomotive made by Matthias Baldwin of Philadelphia, whose firm later gained international fame for its engines.

11. Frederick M. Binder, "Anthracite Enters the American Home," *Pennsylvania Magazine of History and Biography* 82 (January 1958): 82-99.

12. Canal coal tonnage jumped from 6,500 tons in 1825 to 20,271 tons in 1832.

13. Philadelphia and Reading Railroad Company, *Report of the Engineer and General Superintendent of the Philadelphia and Reading Railroad* (Philadelphia: John C. Clark, 1843); Hare, *History of the Reading,* chapter 3.

14. This area, lying within the Spring Garden district and flanking the railroad tracks, was bounded roughly by 13th, 20th, Buttonwood, and Callowhill streets.

15. United States Census Bureau, *Census of Manufacturing for 1850,* manuscript files, processed and addressed by the Philadelphia Social History Project.

16. "Concern Over Lack of Exploration of Philadelphia's Natural Resources," *Public Ledger,* December 10, 1840.

17. Pennsylvania Railroad Company, *Second Annual Report of the Directors* (Philadelphia: Crissy & Markley, 1848), p. 29.

18. City Councils of Philadelphia, *A Digest of the Acts of Assembly Relating to the City of Philadelphia and the (late) Incorporated Districts of the County of*

Philadelphia, and of the Ordinances of the Said City and Districts in Force on the First Day of January, A.D. 1856 (Philadelphia: J. H. Jones & Co., 1856), pp. 193-97.

19. *A Digest of the Ordinances . . . ,* p. 268.

20. The ban lasted only a few months between October 1837 and March 1838. See the *Journal of the Common Council: Beginning October 13, 1837; Ending October 5, 1838* (Philadelphia: Charles Alexander, 1838), pp. 3, 142-43.

21. An ordinance "to regulate the traveling, and providing for the Superintendent of the Broad Street Railroad," was passed on February 27, 1834. It said, in part,. "That every car or other vehicle which shall pass on the said railroad, *shall be drawn by animal power,* [at a rate not exceeding four miles per hour]; and *shall not be drawn or propelled by steam* under a penalty of Ten dollars for each offense. . . ." (italics mine). The ordinance was reaffirmed in Section I of "A Supplement to an ordinance providing for a Superintendent on the railroad along High, Third and Dock Streets, and regulating the travel thereon." It was passed on March 1, 1838. *A Digest of the Ordinances . . . ,* pp. 268, 270-71.

22. No records have been located that suggest the city councils ever repealed the ordinance banning steam. Apparently this section of the ordinance died when the City Railroad ceased to operate. In 1873 the Pennsylvania Railroad built a spur line up Delaware Avenue to Dock Street on which steam locomotives were permitted. Pennsylvania Railroad Company, *28th Annual Report of the Directors* (Philadelphia: E. C. Markley, 1874).

23. Most railroads tolerated the situation for 10 to 15 years before constructing new facilities. The decision to build was influenced by financial considerations which plagued many pioneer railroads. The following is a list of railroads and their terminal dates and locations:

Railroad	Terminal Location	Date
Philadelphia, Germantown & Norristown	9th & Green streets*	1832-1893
Philadelphia & Trenton	Front & Harrison streets*	1834-1867
Philadelphia, Wilmington & Baltimore	11th & Market streets	1842-1852
	Broad & Washington streets	1852-1881
Philadelphia & Reading	Broad & Cherry streets	1838-1859
	Broad & Callowhill streets	1859-1893
	12th & Market streets	1893-
Pennsylvania Railroad	11th & Market streets	1852-1864
	30th & Market streets	1864-1876
	32nd & Market streets	1876-1881
	15th & Market streets	1881-

Limited service continued at these stations after the closing dates indicated.

24. Scharf and Westcott, *History of Philadelphia,* 3: 2199-200; Joseph Jackson, *Encyclopedia of Philadelphia* (Harrisburg, Pa.: National Historical Association, 1933), 4: 940-43.

25. Scharf and Westcott, *History of Philadelphia,* 3: 2200; Jackson, *Encyclopedia,* 4: 943; *Public Ledger,* August 31, 1855.

26. Hare, *History of the Reading,* chapter 46.

27. *Public Ledger,* March 26, 1850.

28. Pennsylvania Railroad Company, *Report of the Superintendent of Transportation* (Philadelphia: Crissy & Markley, 1852), pp. 77-79.

29. Scharf and Westcott, *History of Philadelphia,* 3: 2182.

30. Pennsylvania Railroad Company, *7th, 10th, 12th-14th Annual Reports . . .* (Philadelphia: Crissy & Markley, 1854, 1857, 1859-1861).

31. City of Philadelphia, *Third Annual Message of Alexander Henry* (Philadelphia: n.p., 1861), p. 21.

32. Hare, *History of the Reading,* chapter 15.

33. Pennsylvania Railroad, *14th Annual Report,* pp. 14-15.

34. As of 1863, the only two routes available into New York were via the Philadelphia & Trenton Railroad and the Camden & Amboy Railroad which was reached by ferry boat across the Delaware River.

35. George H. Burgess and Miles C. Kennedy, *Centennial History of the Pennsylvania Railroad Company, 1846-1946* (Philadelphia: privately printed, 1949), chapter 17.

36. See note 20 for documentation.

37. Theodore Hershberg, Harold Cox, and Dale Light, "The 'Journey-to-Work': An Empirical Investigation of Work, Residence, and Transportation, Philadelphia, 1850 and 1880," paper presented at the 89th Annual Meeting of the American Historical Association, Chicago, 1974, pp. 17, 22-23; Stephanie W. Greenberg, "Industrialization in Philadelphia: The Relationship Between Industrial Location and Residential Patterns, 1880-1930," Ph.D. dissertation, Temple University, 1977, pp. 47, 66; Jeffrey P. Roberts, "Continuity and Change in Downtown Land Use: The Evolution of Philadelphia's Central District, 1850-1880," paper presented at the First Annual Meeting of the Social Science History Association, Philadelphia, 1976.

38. Pennsylvania Railroad Company, *22nd and 26th Annual Reports of the Directors* (Philadelphia: E. C. Markley & Co., 1868 and 1872); J. W. Townsend, *The Old "Main Line"* (Philadelphia: privately printed, 1922), pp ^0-85.

39. The Chestnut Hill Railroad opened in 1854. It was leased by the Philadelphia, Germantown & Norristown Railroad in 1868, and the lease was transferred to the Reading in 1870. The line extended north from the Germantown depot of the Philadelphia, Germantown & Norristown Railroad along the east side of Chestnut Hill.

40. Philadelphia and Reading Railroad Company, *Report of the President and Managers* (Philadelphia: H. G. Leisenring, 1871), p. 34.

41. Jay V. Hare, "The Coming of the North Pennsylvania Railroad," *Bulletin of the Old York Road Historical Society* 4 (1940): 18-39.

42. Howard Gillette, Jr., "Philadelphia's City Hall: Monument to a New Political Machine," *Pennsylvania Magazine of History and Biography* 97 (April 1973): 233-49.

43. Ibid., p. 237.

44. Philadelphia and Reading Railroad Company, *Report of the President and Managers* (Philadelphia: Helfenstein, Lewis & Greene, 1877).

45. Pennsylvania Railroad Company, *30th Annual Report of the Directors* (Philadelphia: E. C. Markley, 1877).

46. Hare, "The Coming of the North Pennsylvania Railroad," pp. 38-39.

47. Marvin W. Schlegel, *Ruler of the Reading: The Life of Franklin B. Gowen, 1836-1889* (Harrisburg, Pa.: Archives Publishing Company, 1947), p. 13.

48. Ibid., p. 181.

49. *Public Ledger,* August 7, 1879, and June 10, 1880.

50. Pennsylvania Railroad Company, *35th Annual Report of the Directors* (Philadelphia: n.p., 1881), p. 129.

51. *Public Ledger,* December 3, 1881.

52. *Public Ledger,* May 23, 1880.

53. An additional extension would connect the Philadelphia, Germantown & Norristown depot at 9th and Green streets to the Pennsylvania Avenue tracks.

54. Trades League of Philadelphia, *The City of Philadelphia as it Appears in the Year 1893* (Philadelphia: Geo. S. Harris & Sons, 1893), p. 100.

55. City of Philadelphia, Urban Traffic and Transportation Board, "History of Public Transportation in Philadelphia," Technical Memo No. 1 (Philadelphia: mimeo, 1955), pp. vi-3.

56. Trades League of Philadelphia, *City of Philadelphia . . . 1893,* pp. 98-99.

57. Warner, *Private City,* 54*n*.

58. Carl W. Condit, *American Building* (Chicago: University of Chicago Press, 1968), p. 131.

59. Daniel Webster, *The Writing and Speeches of Daniel Webster* (Boston: 1903), 4: 105-17, quoted in Leo Marx, *The Machine in the Garden* (New York: Oxford University Press, 1964), p. 212.

60. Marx, *Machine in the Garden,* p. 214.

61. *Public Ledger,* October 26, 1836.

62. Philadelphia and Reading Terminal Railroad, *Full Text of the Ordinance* (Philadelphia: Dunlap & Clarke, 1888), p. 19.

63. For additional details of the riots, see *Public Ledger,* July 7-13, 1840, and Scharf and Westcott, *History of Philadelphia,* 3: 2184. For an analysis of the events see, Michael Feldberg, "Urbanization as a Cause of Violence: Philadelphia as a Test Case," in *The Peoples of Philadelphia: A History of Ethnic Groups and Lower Class Life, 1790-1940,* ed. Allen F. Davis and Mark H. Haller (Philadelphia: Temple University Press, 1973), pp. 58-60.

64. Pennsylvania Railroad v. Duncan, 111 Pa 352. *Pennsylvania State Reports,* October-November, 1885, and January, 1886 (New York: Banks Law Publishing Company, 1904), 111: 352-65.

65. Pennsylvania Railroad v. Lippincott, et al. *Weekly Notes of Cases Argued and Determined in the Supreme Court of Pennsylvania,* January-June, 1887 (Philadelphia: Kay & Brother, 1887), 19: 513-17.

66. Joshua L. Baily, *The Reading Elevated Road. Address Delivered Before the Railroad Committee of the City Councils of Philadelphia, May 1st, 1888* (Philadelphia: Sherman & Co., 1888), p. 6.

67. "Philadelphia's Paradise," *The Evening Bulletin,* January 9, 1878.

68. Lewis Mumford, *The City in History* (New York: Harcourt, Brace & World, 1961), p. 461; *North of Market Street Being the Adventures of a New York Woman in Philadelphia* (Philadelphia: Avil Printing Co., 1896), p. 57. Unfortunately, the "Chinese Wall" remained well after the Philadelphia mandarins it protected had moved out of the downtown. The moldering structure sat on the west end of the

downtown for years, while much of the neighborhood north of Market Street and west of Broad Street stagnated. Not until 1952, when the Broad Street Station and the elevated line were demolished to make way for the Penn Center office complex, did private investment and development resume in this area.

69. Hare, *History of the Reading,* chapter 15.

CHAPTER 3 Bank Buildings in Nineteenth-Century Philadelphia

DEBORAH C. ANDREWS

> When Dick went home at night he locked up his bankbook in one of the drawers of the bureau. It was wonderful how much more independent he felt whenever he reflected upon the contents of that drawer, and with what an important air of joint ownership he regarded the bank building in which his small savings were deposited.
>
> Horatio Alger, *Ragged Dick*

A cartoon in a recent *New Yorker* shows a guard chastising two well-dressed but laughing men in line before a teller's window. The caption: "Gentlemen, *please*! This is a bank." The hush in that bank—an air of reverence reinforced by a high ceiling, Corinthian columns, marble, and mahogany—developed in the nineteenth century. It reflects one perception of the image of a bank and the relationship of customers to the bank. Banks also fostered other, rival images to express different functions. The physical appearance of banks comments strongly on their roles. These roles have changed over time, shaping and responding to the development of the communities in which banks grew. Moreover, the modern city runs on money. Understanding the sources of money is essential to understanding the growth of the city. A look at financial institutions in Philadelphia in the nineteenth century—a look at once institutional, architectural, and geographic—suggests much about patterns of development in both banking and the city.

Philadelphia: Financial Center of the New Nation, 1780-1836

In the late eighteenth and early nineteenth centuries, according to Bray Hammond, "Bank credit was to Americans a new source of energy, like steam."[1] Unlike many English and European banks, those in the United States were formed not to consolidate the savings of the wealthy, but to create a circulating medium, to foster expansion. Their origin was not in the abundance of capital but in the lack of it.

The energy for the nation was produced in Philadelphia. The first bank chartered in America was the Bank of Pennyslvania, begun in 1780 to raise subscriptions to finance the Continental Army. It succeeded in its limited goal but fell victim to revolutionary inflation. There was a clear need for a bank with broad powers to issue notes and function as an agent of the government. In 1781 Robert Morris, designated superintendent of finance, submitted a plan for such a bank. A congressional charter was granted, and the Bank of North America began operation in a store on Chestnut Street in January 1782. Thomas Willing was president; he worked with a board of directors and seven employees.

The Bank of North America prospered, although for a time it lost its charter because some citizens thought it opposed paper money. Based in part upon its success, Alexander Hamilton drew up plans for a national bank. The Bank of North America was invited to assume that role but chose to remain small. Subscription books for the new Bank of the United States were opened in July 1791 in Carpenter's Hall. Within two hours more than the set number of shares had been bid in, and the stock commanded speculative prices. It was a central, national bank as well as a commercial one. Thomas Willing resigned the presidency of the Bank of North America to become its president. The bank's location in Philadelphia meant that the local merchants who ran it controlled the finances of the nation (see Figure 3-1).

BANKING RIVALRIES

The new energy of credit attracted many merchants who set up banks to rival the First Bank and the Bank of North America. In what has been called a "mania for banking" several banks were started: the first was the Bank of Pennsylvania, chartered in 1793, and the next was the Philadelphia Bank, which opened 11 years later in 1804. The Bank of Pennsylvania and the Bank of North America were suspicious of this latterday newcomer and refused to accept its notes. In addition to the First Bank, state banks issued bills of credit (bank notes), received deposits, and loaned money at interest or discount. The state of Pennsylvania also participated through its power to incorporate, and thus regulate and make money through these banks.

When the charter of the First Bank came up for renewal in 1811, Congress turned it down. The state of Pennsylvania also refused it a charter, and the bank moved to New York. The renewal was a political tangle, but one early writer on banks assessed the motivation thus: The refusal came "less perhaps from any remains of the old democratic enmity to the system, than from a desire of individuals to get charters for the particular benefit of themselves

Figure 3-1. Bank of the United States, 1795-1797. Samuel Blodgett, Jr., architect. *Courtesy of the Free Library of Philadelphia.*

and their friends.''[2] The First Bank's building was taken over by Stephen Girard's bank, the most prominent of a growing number of new private banks in the city.

In 1814 the state passed its first general banking act, an omnibus bill that set operating limits. Among other things it established the geographic area in which a bank could make loans and the boundaries within which it could build offices. It limited the amount that a Philadelphia bank could spend on its banking house to $50,000 (banks elsewhere in the state were limited to $30,000).[3] For new banks the ceiling on expenditure was unnecessary; like many merchants and shopkeepers, most banks began small, in stores or residences. In addition, architectural technology was still too primitive to allow large, well lighted interior spaces for business or commercial display at anything less than excessive cost.[4] Later, when the limit seemed too low, some prosperous banks simply juggled the books and spent anyway.

The multiplication of state banks and growth of credit-related deposits without a central agency requiring a parallel growth of reserves led to the overextension of credit. This weakened the nation politically and economically as the notes issued by such banks often lost necessary acceptance in circulation. In particular, the federal government had difficulty financing the War of 1812. Stephen Girard's private bank subscribed $5 million to the war loan of 1814, about 95 percent of the total. Thus in 1816 a second Bank of the United States was chartered. Its home, too, was in Philadelphia, although New York City was the government's first choice and the nation's capital had already moved to Washington. Under Nicholas Biddle the Second Bank was generally well run and effective, but it became the focus of controversy, envy, and public agitation over the desirability of any central banking institution with its power for abuse as well as good. Andrew Jackson withdrew federal funds from the Second Bank in 1833 to disperse them to what became known as "pet banks," and engineered the nonrenewal of its charter in 1836. The nonrenewal assured the split of banking powers that continues to this day in our dual system.

PHILADELPHIA'S FINANCIAL DISTRICT

While Philadelphia was the financial center of the nation, the center of finance in Philadelphia was along Third and Fourth streets, between Walnut and Chestnut. Here were the offices of the national banks, merchant bankers, and the Philadelphia Merchants' Exchange, the first stock exchange in America. Such important financial institutions sought impressive physical presences. Banking commissions were coveted, and the outstanding architects of the day vied to supply the designs. The buildings made or enhanced the architects' reputations and set precedents in bank design which belied the relative newness of the occupants.

The contrast between the office of the Bank of North America and that of the First Bank is particularly striking. Small and prosperous, the Bank of

North America remained for 65 years in an unpretentious store owned by its cashier. The First Bank building, however, was monumental in scale, announcing its directors' intention to call up Roman precedents for the new republic (see Figure 3-1). The building was raised above the common level of humanity by impressive steps. Its marble facade was pretentious in a city of brick and frame (although its sides and back were brick). Designed by Samuel Blodgett, Jr., it may have been modeled on the Royal Exchange in Dublin. It included several features that were to be repeated in later bank buildings: an open, domed banking room on the first floor, flanked by offices for the president and cashier, a portico, eagle iconography, and steps leading to a single public entrance. But, while many banks rivaled it, none exactly resembled it. It was impressive. A visitor to the city in 1803 who complained about pigs running in the streets saw only two public buildings of note: the Banks of the United States and Pennsylvania, "which are fronted with polished marble" and porticos "supported by large fluted pillars all of white."[5]

In the early years of the century the Bank of Pennsylvania encouraged more imitation than the First Bank. The first important American building to follow Greek rather than Roman lines, it set a temple precedent in banks (see Figure 3-2). Barely five years after its founding, the bank announced a competition for plans for a banking house. Benjamin H. Latrobe won with a design for a domed marble structure with raised porticos at either end, one for bank officers and one for the public. It was erected between 1798 and 1801 on Second Street between Chestnut and Walnut. Like the First Bank, it introduced a new material—in this case, cut stone—into the city of brick.

The building was based on plates published in Stuart and Revett's *The Antiquities of Athens*. The circular banking room, 45 feet in diameter, was lighted by a cupola and large windows. The interior may have owed something to Sir John Soane's great hall for the Bank of England. The exterior brought the iconography of revolutionary democracy, of Ledoux and others in Napoleonic France, to Philadelphia. Widely admired, the building led Latrobe to settle his practice in Philadelphia, established him as the most important architect of his day, and brought him many other important commissions.

One such commission was for the Bank of Pennsylvania's rival, the Philadelphia Bank. One year after its chartering the bank decided to build. To call attention to itself, and perhaps to avoid confusion with its classical neighbor and rival, the bank erected a building on the southwest corner of Fourth and Chestnut streets conspicuously different from any other in the city. It was perhaps the first specimen of decorated Gothic architecture in the United States (see Figure 3-3). The main banking room on the first floor had a Gothic ceiling including fan vaulting and was flanked by rooms for the bank's officers. The octagonal board room on the second floor was said to be modeled on the chancery of an English chapter house (there was no medieval counterpart to the nineteenth-century bank). In 1810 the cashier

Figure 3-2. The Bank of Pennsylvania, 1798-1801. Designed by Benjamin Henry Latrobe. *Courtesy of the Free Library of Philadelphia.*

Figure 3-3. The Philadelphia Bank, 1807-1808. Benjamin Henry Latrobe, architect. *Courtesy of the Free Library of Philadelphia.*

was given permission to erect his own house on the property, a security measure practiced by several banks.

The Gothic style was not wholly successful. Although in later years "florid financial buildings" would dot the city, this early diversion from classical lines was extreme. The bank itself tore the building down to build a Greek structure on the site in 1836. Extremes of romanticism—Moorish and Egyptian, for example—were only rarely used for banks. But such conspicuousness did anticipate the use of architectural form as a medium of advertising, a practice that in time became widespread.

Aware, perhaps, of the success of the Bank of Pennsylvania's classical building, the directors of the new national bank advertised for a design that would be a "chaste imitation of Grecian architecture, in its simplest and least expensive form."[6] In the competition Latrobe finished second to his student, William Strickland, who was 28 years old at the time. Strickland believed that the friends he made when he helped erect fortifications around Philadelphia during the War of 1812—men later on the board of the Second Bank—influenced the choice of his plan. The building he created was the first public building to be based on the design of the Parthenon (see Figure 3-4). It was the most important Greek revival urban facade in the nation and was widely admired and imitated in both Europe and America. One observer praised the use of a religious form, "for the concept of the nation inevitably takes on a sacred suggestion, which makes even the houses of its merchandise somewhat of a shrine."[7] The building established Strickland's reputation. It led to a commission for the Merchants' Exchange (1834) and to two other banking assignments: the Mechanics Bank on Third Street (1837, now the Norwegian Seaman's Church) and the new Philadelphia Bank. Both were fulfilled with classical structures. A long poem was published about the Philadelphia Bank in the *United States Gazette* in 1837; it begins: "Chaste, classic pile—now tow'ring high above me,/As if in scorne of this vain prizeless earth,/Like a fond parent's first born do I love thee, / And bless the day which ushered thee to birth."[8]

In discussing the use of classical forms for banks, in particular the use of the Parthenon as a model, Strickland observed that "it becomes a difficult task for an architect to preserve *all* the characteristics of a Grecian temple. . . . The flanking columns of a Grecian building produce a decidedly beautiful feature. . . . But they cannot be applied with the proper effect to places of business, without a sacrifice of those principles which have a constant application to internal uses and economy."[9]

Mid-Century Reform in Finance and Commercial Aesthetics

By mid-century, the difficulties Strickland saw in fitting a bank into a Parthenon caused a change in style. Other changes occurred in the institution of banking and the location of banks. The nonrenewal of each of the United States Bank charters coincided with a flurry of state bank births and led to

Figure 3-4. The Second Bank of the United States, 1818-1824. Designed by William Strickland. *Courtesy of the Free Library of Philadelphia.*

changes in banking practices. Commercial banking became more competitive in the nineteenth century. It grew—more slowly in Philadelphia than elsewhere in the country—from a monopolistic privilege to a more widely accessible business. Banks began to appear in developing neighborhoods outside the central business district and rivaled those downtown. Banks often started without real assets. A strong impetus to open banking was the spread of Free Banking Acts, the first of which was enacted by the New York Legislature in 1837. Pennsylvania passed such a law in 1861. It provided that any individual could obtain a charter and start a bank without specific legislative action if certain rules were complied with.

PHILADELPHIA V. NEW YORK CITY

Competition between Philadelphia and New York City prevailed throughout the nineteenth century, but by 1850 Philadelphia had lost its early position as the financial capital of the nation. As early as 1817, New York had begun to take the lead. Because of its better harbor and relative proximity to Europe, its exports exceeded those of Philadelphia. The Erie Canal also gave it cheaper access to the West. The loss of its charter by the Second Bank was a victory for the new entrepreneurs, like those in New York, over the small group of entrenched aristocrats on Third and Chestnut streets. But perhaps as a result of its reduced prestige, Philadelphia banking at mid-century was also marked by hefty speculation and a willingness to suspend specie payments. In 1841 the Pennsylvania Bank of the United States (the rechartered Second Bank) was the first major bank to fail in the United States. New York banks, on the other hand, solidified their lead by taking a more conservative course. They fostered innovations in safe banking. New York banks, for example, established a clearing house in 1853 (Philadelphia followed in 1858), which served to facilitate the exchange of bank notes. It is defined as "a place where all the representatives of the banks in a given city meet, and, under the supervision of a competent officer . . . settle their accounts with each other and make or receive payment of balances and so 'clear' the transactions of the day."[10]

At the beginning of the century, Philadelphia controlled both commercial and government banking. By the 1860s New York was well established as the center of finance, while control over currency and the regulation of banking shifted to Washington. In 1863 Congress passed the National Currency Act, which established one uniform currency for the country, and one year later the National Banking Act. It provided for the chartering of national banks, the first of which was in Philadelphia.[11]

NEW FORMS OF BANKING

To meet changes in city populations and serve new customers, new banking forms grew over the century. In Philadelphia, savings societies, building and loan associations, and trust companies became common.

The first savings bank was organized by a minister in Scotland in 1810. The first in the United States was the Philadelphia Saving Fund Society (PSFS), founded in 1816 and chartered in 1819. In one year, 1835, some 15 new savings institutions went into operation in Philadelphia. These savings institutions were not strictly banks, as such names as "fund," "institution," "association," or "society" indicate. They were without capital and without stockholders. They served mainly "tradesmen, mechanics, laborers, and domestics."[12] In theory such banks encouraged workers to be "industrious and provident." They were often open evening hours to serve customers who were at work all day.

Although some savings funds were located downtown, many appeared in residential neighborhoods. Often they drew on common ethnic or religious wellsprings. The Beneficial Savings Fund Society (1835) was established by "several Catholic gentlemen" at St. Joseph's Church, Willings Alley. The First Penny Savings Bank (1889) was organized by John Wanamaker and others to provide a savings fund for the Bethany Presbyterian Sunday School; its office was at 21st and Bainbridge streets in South Philadelphia. The Kensington Savings Institution (1835) and the Savings Fund Society of Germantown (1854) were organized to be convenient to those growing neighborhoods, while the Western Savings Fund Society (1847) served those residing west of Ninth Street. The distinction in function and customers between commercial banks and savings institutions, as we shall see, bore implications for the kinds of building each would construct.

Workers also formed a special kind of voluntary association that became the main source of money for erecting the city's houses in the 1850s and 1860s: the building and loan association, an important Philadelphia institution. The first of these in the United States was the Oxford Provident Building Association of Philadelphia County, started in Frankford in 1831. Between 1831 and 1849, 50 such institutions were formed in the growing neighborhoods fringing the city. By 1875, there were 600 of them in Philadelphia, and by then they had done more than $50 million worth of business.[13]

These associations were significant in the financing of houses. With their help groups of citizens to whom credit was otherwise inaccessible could borrow money for homes. Typically, a member paid a fee upon joining the group, and then regularly (weekly or monthly) deposited a small sum until he had enough equity to borrow money for a mortgage. Many of these groups were Irish, associated with churches, fraternal organizations, neighborhood or workingmen's groups. Their ties to a club or a church implied a certain honesty and stability as well as a strong emphasis on the family.[14] The associations usually continued until each member had had an opportunity to purchase a home. Then the assets were divided.

Unlike the savings funds and the building and loan associations which had strong immigrant and worker connections, trust companies, like investment banks, grew to serve the needs of the wealthy. Two Philadelphia trust companies were chartered in the 1830s: The Pennsylvania Company for Insurances on Lives and Granting Annuities and the Girard Life Insurance, Annuity and Trust Company. But the real growth of such institutions came after the Civil War to accommodate the large private fortunes being made in manufacturing and railroads. Safe deposit companies also were formed, especially after a rash of robberies in the 1860s. These provided safekeeping for fine jewels and important papers.

NEW COMMERCIAL AESTHETICS

Samuel Sloan was one Philadelphia architect and writer who was concerned at mid-century with the aesthetics of commercial buildings, especially their "fitness" and "convenience." For both Sloan and William Strickland, fitness in a bank building referred to the relationship between its style and its particular economic function and emotional associations. Convenience and utility applied to such technical aspects as the building's operational efficiency, heating, and ventilation. Strickland emphasized the need to adapt classical forms to the exigencies of modern function. In particular, banks required different interior plans from temples: windows for light, fireplaces for heat, and fireproof construction.[15] By Sloan's day, the wholesale copying of models from other times and other functions, which made some early banks exercises in archeology, gave way, at least for a while, to a mingling of historical styles. The results were sometimes equal in their flourishes to the frenzy of finance.

One interesting development in the utility of banks was the technical progress made in protective mechanisms—what one bank advertisement called "contrivances that modern ingenuity can devise to afford security." Robberies, some of them spectacular, and counterfeiters were a real threat to bank operation, equaled only by the threat from the inside—the defalcation of employees, even cashiers and directors. Architects worked on structural systems to prevent robberies, and bankers worked on office procedures to prevent defalcations. The placement of their offices next to the banking room, for example, allowed the president and cashier to keep an eye on the staff and allowed customers to see that the officers were operating above board. Tellers' counters were raised and windows caged. Grills appeared on outside windows. By mid-century there were burglar-proof safes and special fittings for vaults. Time locks, police alarms, and special telephones came by the end of the century.

In addition to technical advances, banks also had to consider the fitness of their aesthetics. Banks had no observable product. They needed to create an image of reliability and productivity to encourage trust. They had to counter popular hostility in an economy punctuated by panics and bank failures. Their buildings would tell customers, especially savers, that the bank would be around, would pay off. In the days before any government insurance programs, before operating statements were made widely available (even stockholders could not see them until the 1950s), bankers looked for an architectural statement to symbolize solvency. Engraved brass plates near the door recited total assets in millions of dollars.

Their buildings also served to differentiate among the many rival banks. By 1873 there were twice as many banks in Philadelphia as in 1859. Early in the nineteenth century, the announcements issued by banks to advertise their services were sober, limited to a brief list of services, and addressed to a small audience. By 1900, with the opening of banking to a wider population, many advertisements became, like the buildings, flamboyant. A description of the building often served as a springboard to claims of excellence in service and diversity of function (see Figure 3-7). This was true even though, as some critics of banking edifices point out, expensive and overbuilt offices represent the least realizable of all bank assets. The directors of the Second Bank of the United States, for example, wanted something gracious "in its least expensive form."

Sloan's concern for fitness led him to advise different styles for savings banks and commercial banks to accommodate differences in function and image. The savings bank was to be "composed on principles of economy, without illiberality, elegance, without display, and attractiveness, without ornament." It should be "simple, yet fine in its very simplicity," giving satisfaction to observers but not calling up in the minds of its patrons "an unpleasant question . . . concerning the use of the capital so outlaid." It should project an air of "modest neatness and well-defined economy." He recommended the Tuscan order and condemned the excessive ornament of some New York savings banks that "cannot be looked on with favor by the thrifty depositor."[16]

Commercial banks, on the other hand, were the "representative temples of the moneyocracy" and should bear "on their front the insignia of their rank."[17] They "bespeak, in their architecture, the profusion of wealth, which is the foundation of their existence." For them as well as for the trust company and investment bank, florid display, ornament, and the Corinthian and Ionic orders were suitable. In addition to these exterior distinctions, the two kinds of banks required different interior spaces. Savings banks served large numbers of customers who needed room to line up. Large, open banking floors thus became common. Commercial banks, and particularly trust companies and investment banks, were likely to serve fewer patrons at any one time. A homier, more clublike atmosphere was thus suitable.

PSFS: SLOAN'S MODEL SAVINGS BANK

In the society's annual report for 1869-70, the president of PSFS attributed a recent increase in business to "the admirable provision made for the safety of the depositors by the construction of the substantial edifice in which the savings from their toil and privation are placed.[18] Sloan praised the second home of the PSFS, designed by his one-time partner, Addison Hutton, as particularly suited to a savings bank (see Figure 3-5).[19] It was, he said, built "for the future as well as for the present, not only with respect to commodiousness and convenience, but also to durability." Until recently "institutions of this kind have been content to occupy buildings of ordinary construction, but various causes have combined to induce some of them to provide better and more substantial facilities for business."[20] The site, at Seventh and Walnut streets, was "convenient to the great business center" but adjacent to Washington Square, whose open spaces provided a vista on the building and fresh air for employees. The open first-floor banking room contained marble-front counters with top screens of walnut and plate glass. The "strongly marked expression of stability" of the facade was "in harmony with the character of the institution."[21]

BANK ROW: MID-CENTURY FINANCIAL DISTRICT

An Italianate style, like that of PSFS, was also adaptable to commercial buildings. Some Italianate banks can still be seen in what came to be called "Bank Row" on the north side of Chestnut Street between Fourth and Fifth streets (see Figure 3-6). Most commercial banks, like those in Bank Row, served common occupational or industrial interests (see Table 3-1). Their names often indicated the group they represented, and their charters restricted their activities to that group. The charter for the Farmers and Mechanics Bank, for example, required that 9 of the 13 directors be "farmers, mechanics, or manufacturers actually employed in their respective professions."[22] These banks usually located near one another to conduct their business with greater ease and efficiency. This concentration of financial activity reflected a larger trend toward more specialized land use in the central business district after the Civil War, although in Philadelphia such spatial differentiation by function was not nearly as marked as in other American cities of the age.[23] But in the 1860s and 1870s, Bank Row in Philadelphia was significant as a center of both finance and architecture. It gave tangible expression to the growing prosperity of the city's financial community and became a showplace for local architects. One observer called the block "well-composed. . . . The total effect is consonant, dignified and strong, altogether in keeping with the trusty and impregnable institutions which inhabit there."[24]

But the air of impregnability surrounding at least one building in the row was false. John M. Gries, a Philadelphia architect, designed the home of the Bank of Pennsylvania at 421 Chestnut Street. Built of Quincy granite, it cost approximately $320,000. Crowds watched its construction. It was to symbolize the "confident and progressive spirit of the times." The books were juggled to show its value (to conform with state regulations) at $50,000. But the bank's finances were not as solid as its house. The bank collapsed before it could occupy its new home, and the building was sold at auction in

Figure 3-5. Main Banking Room of the Philadelphia Saving Fund Society, 1869.
Addison Hutton was the architect of this building at Seventh and Walnut streets.
This interior view shows the bank as it appeared in the 1920s. The bank transacted
business in several languages to appeal to immigrant depositors, and signs outside
each teller's cage indicated what languages he spoke. *Courtesy of the Philadelphia
Saving Fund Society.*

Figure 3-6. Bank Row on the North Side of Chestnut Street between Fourth and Fifth Streets. This photograph shows, from the left: the Pennsylvania Company (partial view), 1873; the Farmers and Mechanics Bank, John M. Gries, architect, 1855; the Bank of Pennsylvania (later owned by the Philadelphia Bank), John M. Gries, architect, 1857-1859; the Philadelphia Trust, Safe Deposit and Insurance Company, James H. Windrim, architect, 1874; and the Provident Life and Trust Company, Frank Furness, architect, 1879. *Courtesy of the Free Library of Philadelphia.*

TABLE 3-1 Commercial Banks in the Central Business District, 1781–1890

Established	Title	First Address
1781	Bank of North America	3rd & Chestnut
1793	Bank of Pennsylvania	2nd between Chestnut and Walnut
1803	The Philadelphia Bank	by 1808, 4th and Chestnut; first site: 3rd near Chestnut
1807	Farmers and Mechanics Bank	first: Chestnut above 4th, then 427 Chestnut
1810	Commercial Bank	314 Chestnut
1810	Mechanics Bank	22 South 3rd
1831	Manufacturers Bank	2nd and Green
1832	Girard Bank	in building of First Bank of the U.S.
1847	Tradesmens Bank	2nd and Spruce; later, 113 South 3rd
1855	City National Bank	1874: 32 South 6th Street
1855	Consolidation Bank	331-33 North 3rd
1857	Commonwealth Bank	4th and Chestnut
1858	Corn Exchange Bank	2nd and Chestnut
1858	Union Bank	1868: 3rd and Arch
1863	First National Bank	315-19 Chestnut (SE corner of 3rd)
1863	Third National Bank	Merrick and Market
1863	Fourth National Bank	Arch near 7th
1864	Sixth National Bank	350 South 2nd
1864	Seventh National Bank	4th and Market
1865	Central National Bank	109 South 4th
1865	National Bank of the Republic	by 1885 at 313 Chestnut
1870	Peoples Bank	435 Chestnut
1880	Merchants National Bank	unavailable
	Keystone National Bank	Chestnut at Juniper
1883	Independence National Bank	Chestnut near 5th
1885	Ninth National Bank	unavailable
1886	Fourth Street National Bank	4th below Chestnut
1887	Market Street National Bank	1107 Market
1887	Chestnut Street National Bank	721 Chestnut
1889	Quaker City National Bank	721 Chestnut
	Franklin National Bank	unavailable
	Textile National Bank	unavailable
	Produce National Bank	unavailable

SOURCE: John Thom Holdsworth, *Financing an Empire: History of Banking in Pennsylvania* (Chicago and Philadelphia: S. J. Clarke, 1928); Belden L. Daniels, *Pennsylvania: Birthplace of Banking in America* (Harrisburg, Pa.: Pennsylvania Bankers Association, 1976).

1857. Francis M. Drexel, who wanted to buy it for his private bank, fell asleep after tea and did not make it to the auction. So the Philadelphia Bank, its old rival, got it for only $163,000 and moved in.

FRANK FURNESS'S BANKS: FINANCIAL
DISTRICT AND NEIGHBORHOOD

Included in Bank Row was the Provident Trust Company, one of five bank buildings on Chestnut Street designed by Frank Furness, who was probably the most widely acclaimed Philadelphia architect of his day. In part through his proper social connections, Furness received commissions to design eight Philadelphia banks, along with additions and alterations to already existing banks (see Table 3-2 and Figure 3-7). Built for the "moneyocracy," they were exercises in richness. They commanded attention—and some criticism—for their extravagance and their nightmarish, out-of-scale ways. They stood out from their neighbors. One reporter said that the facade of the Provident put "a constant strain on the public."[25] The designs

TABLE 3-2   Principal Banking Commissions of Frank Furness in Philadelphia

Date	Bank	Location
1872	Northern Savings Fund, Safe Deposit & Trust Co.	Sixth and Spring Garden
1874	Union Banking Co. (Furness & Hewitt)	310 Chestnut
1875	Guarantee Trust Co. (Furness & Hewitt)	316-20 Chestnut
1876	Centennial Bank	32nd & Market
1877	Kensington Bank	Frankford and Girard
1879	Provident Life and Trust Co.	409 Chestnut
1884	Penn National Bank (Furness and Evans)	Seventh and Market
1884	National Bank of the Republic (Furness and Evans)	313 Chestnut
1898	West End Trust Co. (Furness, Evans and Co.)	Broad and So. Penn Square
1907	Three-Story Building for Girard Trust Co. (Furness, Evans, and Co.)	1413-17 Chestnut

SOURCE: James F. O'Gorman, George E. Thomas, and Hyman Meyers, *The Architecture of Frank Furness* (Philadelphia: Philadelphia Museum of Art, 1973).

Figure 3-7. The National Bank of the Republic, 1884. Frank Furness, architect. This drawing of the bank in an 1894 publication of the Trades League of Philadelphia was accompanied by a text which began, "The attractive building of the National Bank of the Republic, 313 Chestnut Street, commands attention by its unique architecture and prevailing red tone, presenting to the street a striking facade of English redstone, terra-cotta and Philadelphia pressed brick, with [a] steep roof of red slate; the half-arched doorway and round tower, with its conical roof, being prominent features." A detailed description of the building's exterior and interior characteristics followed, including a discussion of its "vaults . . . of massive granite work, with the most approved steel lining"; its interior was "much larger than its exterior indicates, affording ample room in all the apartments, and an unusually large space outside of the counters for customers and the public." The building was, further, "heated by steam and from open stone fireplaces, which form pleasing features" and was "admirably ventilated and lighted, and most conveniently and comfortably arranged." Trades League of Philadelphia, *The City of Philadelphia as It Appears in the Year 1894* (Philadelphia: George S. Harris, 1894), p. 147.

perhaps indicate the taste and preference of the architect more than changing public expectations for a bank building. But the banks boasted of them
and used pictures of their buildings to advertise the grandeur of the bank
(see Figure 3-7).

Furness designed banking houses both for the financial district in town
and for the commercial centers developing in neighborhoods throughout
the city. As Table 3-3 demonstrates, banks began to spring up outside the
central financial district as early as the beginning of the nineteenth century.
In 1810 the Bank of the Northern Liberties appeared, followed by the
Schuylkill Bank and the Bank of Germantown four years later. Several
others appeared in the 1830s, with a new cluster in the 1860s and more
growth in the 1870s and 1880s. These banks began near customers rather
than other bankers and concentrated on making loans to individuals or
small businesses. Many served recent immigrant groups and thus came to
be known in some banking circles as "sauerkraut banks." Located at Franklin
Street and Girard Avenue, the National Security Bank, for example, was
organized by the German residents of the northern area of the consolidated
city. The neighborhood influence was usually preserved directly in the
bank's charter. The Kensington Bank was required to select at least 9 of its
13 directors from residents of that part of Philadelphia.

These banks competed vigorously with those in the financial district. Of
course, financial alliances did not always follow geographic lines. In 1833
Jackson's withdrawal of funds from the Second Bank divided Philadelphia
banks into two camps without geographic significance. The nine banks
which sent a memorial to Jackson supporting restitution came from all over
the city: Bank of North America, Bank of Pennsylvania, Commercial
Bank, Mechanics Bank, Moyamensing Bank, Schuylkill Bank, and Farmers
and Mechanics Bank. Six other widely distributed banks did not join in:
Philadelphia Bank, Western Bank, Southwark Bank, Kensington Bank,
Bank of the Northern Liberties, and Girard Bank.[26] But the rivalry between
neighborhood and city banks surfaced later in response to a bank league
organized by the downtown institutions in 1842. The Kensington Bank and
Bank of Germantown refused at first to participate, although they and
other neighborhood banks were eventually drawn into the clearinghouse.

As they prospered, some neighborhood commercial banks like the Moyamensing Bank (which became the Bank of Commerce) and the Western
Bank moved downtown. On the other hand, new trust and safe deposit
companies grew up in wealthy neighborhoods, saving their patrons the
inconvenience of traveling into the city to retrieve papers and jewels.

Many banks in neighborhoods housed themselves in such modest quarters
as stores or converted residences. The large ones often built in a style similar
to that found on Bank Row, but few anywhere matched the flights of fancy
achieved by Willis G. Hale in his downtown buildings for the Quaker City

TABLE 3-3 Neighborhood Commercial Banks, 1810–1900

Established	Title	First Address
1810	Bank of Northern Liberties	73 Vine
1814	Schuylkill Bank	6th and Market
1814	Bank of Germantown	Germantown Avenue at School House Lane
1825	Southwark Bank	2nd below South
1826	Kensington Bank	Beach below Laurel; later, Girard at Franklin
1827	Bank of Penn Township (Penn National Bank)	by 1829 at 6th and Vine; later, Market at 7th
1831	Western Bank	Market west of 9th
1832	Manufacturers and Mechanics of the Northern Liberties Bank	3rd at Vine
1832	Moyamensing Bank (later became the Bank of Commerce at 207 Chestnut)	5th and South
1864	Eighth National Bank	2nd at Girard
1864	Second National Bank of Philadelphia at Frankford	4348 Frankford Avenue
1869	West Philadelphia National Bank	—
1870	National Security Bank	Franklin and Girard
1871	Manayunk Bank	Main at Levering
1872	First National Bank of Conshohocken	—
1876	Centennial National Bank	32nd and Market
1886	Northwestern National Bank	Girard at Ridge
1886	Tenth National Bank	Broad at Columbia
1886	Southwestern National Bank	Broad and South
1890	Northern National Bank	Germantown Avenue at 6th
1899	Ridge Avenue Bank	Ridge at Spring Garden
—	South Philadelphia National Bank	—

[The Spring Garden National Bank, founded?, failed in 1891; it was located at 12th and Spring Garden.]

SOURCE: John Thom Holdsworth, *Financing an Empire: History of Banking in Pennsylvania* (Chicago and Philadelphia: S. J. Clarke, 1928); Belden L. Daniels, *Pennsylvania: Birthplace of Banking in America* (Harrisburg, Pa.: Pennsylvania Bankers Association, 1976).

National Bank and the Keystone National Bank (see Figure 3-8). Moreover, the move of in-town banks into tall office structures at the end of the century was not imitated in residential areas which maintained a lower skyline.

One suburban bank worthy of special note was the Centennial National Bank at 32nd and Market streets. It built a home which was significant both as an architectural statement and as an indicator of the mobility of the Philadelphia banking community. Designed by Frank Furness, it opened in 1876 to meet the needs of visitors to the Centennial Exhibition. It came to the customer, and the permanence of this structure also revealed its owners' faith in the development of West Philadelphia, a growth which the Centennial spurred and which many Philadelphia banks financed, sometimes at their peril.

Bigger and Broader at the Turn of the Century

At the end of the nineteenth century banking in America became increasingly professional and accessible to the general public. After 1850 the president of a bank gradually moved ahead of the cashier as the chief operating officer of the business. At first he was mostly a figurehead, but the rising significance of his office and of professional bankers in general accompanied an increasing bureaucracy and a more systematic approach to banking in lieu of the countinghouse practices of the cashier. Staff size in the prosperous banks increased, necessitating the redesign of the spaces in which employees would work. At the same time banks became more anxious to broaden their clientele. In the early 1800s the few financial institutions in Philadelphia catered exclusively to a small group of merchants who were usually acquainted personally with the directors, but by 1890 even Horatio Alger's Ragged Dick had a savings account. Banks enlarged their staff to accommodate new customers and introduced new processing techniques to clear out-of-town checks and approve loans.

But the accessibility was not complete. Most commercial banks were still institutions of the moneyed class. Everyone who was anyone had an ownership, directorship, or long-term business relationship with a bank. To have accounts accepted by many banks one had to put up a large opening balance. Even as late as 1954, 25 percent of the customers held 90 percent of the deposits of the First National Bank, whose founder, Jay Cooke, did so much to finance the Civil War.

By 1900 banks also began to consolidate through a series of acquisitions and mergers. The pattern of individual banks, separately owned and operated, growing on street corners in developing neighborhoods, began to give way to another pattern: central banks in the downtown operating branch banks in residential neighborhoods. In Philadelphia the Western Savings Fund Society pioneered this bureaucratic innovation. Downtown banks also bought out one another, a trend which accelerated especially during the 1920s.

Figure 3-8. The Union Trust Company, 1884. Willis G. Hale, architect. Also known as the Singerly Building, this structure was occupied as well by the Quaker City National Bank and the Bank of Commerce. An 1894 Trades League publication called this "one of the most ornate among the many splendid buildings in Philadelphia devoted to the safe keeping of money and valuables." Trades League of Philadelphia, *The City of Philadelphia as it Appears in the Year 1894* (Philadelphia: George S. Harris, 1894).

DOWNTOWN BANKING: TALL OFFICE STRUCTURES

The business and financial district in Philadelphia gradually moved westward during the nineteenth century. From Third Street it advanced along Bank Row to Fourth Street, the center by the 1890s. At this location there were several private banks and the Bullitt Building, home of the Fourth Street National Bank, the leading bank of the decade. Fourth Street was in turn rivaled by Fifth Street, the home of the Philadelphia Bourse and the new site for Drexel and Company, major financiers in the age of finance. By the turn of the century these eastern axes were challenged by the growing center on Broad Street at Market, where the new City Hall had risen.

The pull toward Broad and Market reflected the bankers' need to locate not only near other bankers but also near government offices and nodes of transportation. Girard Trust was a leader of the move when it built in 1889 on the northeast corner of Broad and Chestnut. Another bank drawn to that area was the Market Street National Bank. In 1887 it cast its lot with the main retail section which was passing from a center around Eighth and Chestnut to Market Street. In a Trades League publication, the bank boasted that its new building was "the outgrowth of a conviction of business people in the neighborhood, that a new national bank . . . located on Market Street near the Public Buildings, was a public necessity." This facility, whose vaults were fitted with time locks, an electric police alarm and a guard with direct telephone connections to the police, also purveyed "handsomely fitted rooms, specially arranged for the use of box renters." "This," said the trade publication, "is a great convenience for persons using the Pennsylvania and Reading Railroads, both of which stations are near the bank."²⁷

The moves of the two leading trust companies are indeed instructive of both shifts in the geography of the business district and shifts in building style. The Pennsylvania Company, originally located in the residence of its actuary on South Second Street, moved in 1817 to Chestnut Street near Fifth, and in 1825 to the northwest corner of Walnut Street and Third. Five years later, the increase of business led to another move to Third Street above Walnut. In 1840 it moved to 304 Walnut; in 1873 to 431 Chestnut. In 1883 the bank moved farther west on Chestnut to a site across from the State House. It considered a move then to Broad and Market but assumed that the center of Philadelphia would always be near the State House and built its "permanent home"—now demolished—at 515-21 Chestnut. The five-story Romanesque building was designed by Addison Hutton. It included special rooms with desks and writing materials for the convenience of its safe-renters—with a separate room for "lady patrons" (see Figure 3-9).

But at this location the Pennsylvania Company was bucking the tide. The Girard Trust made a series of moves to keep up with the city. In 1872 it opened its doors at Seventh and Chestnut streets (in a block of business structures, none of which was over 20 years old), and six years later it moved

Figure 3-9. The Pennsylvania Company for Insurances on Lives and Granting Annuities, 1883. Designed by Addison Hutton. *Courtesy of the Free Library of Philadelphia.*

to 2020 Chestnut, which was too residential and too far west to be successful. Finally, in 1889 it settled on the northeast corner of Broad and Chestnut. Designed by Addison Hutton, the firm's eight-story "skyscraper" in the Romanesque tradition was called Morris's Folly (after Girard's president, Effingham B. Morris). But offices for tenants were rented within a few months, and four more stories and two more elevators were added in 1894. By 1900 the company was feeling cramped and moved across the street into a Pantheon that reflected the earlier archeological phase of banking style.

The Girard Trust's addition of four stories in 1894 shows the direction of yet another kind of move: upward. To accommodate larger staffs and respond to rising land values downtown, several banks added floors or erected new, tall office structures. In 1892 the Philadelphia (national) Bank added several stories to its building at 421 Chestnut Street. It also moved its banking room from the back of the building to the front, affording greater convenience to customers and, according to the bank's president, increasing business.[28] Furness uplifted the Provident on Chestnut Street, although the vertical addition which he designed fights hard, stylistically, against being tall. When Drexel and Company needed more room, it hired Wilson Brothers, a Philadelphia firm, to wrap an 11-story office building around its original marble and brick banking temple. The A-frame buttressing system of the design was technically advanced, and the owners considered the structure to compare "favorably with the largest of the new buildings in New York and Chicago."[29]

Other banks built tall structures from scratch, housing themselves on the first few floors and renting out the others. One style, as we have seen, was Romanesque, really a national style for office buildings following the precedent of the major national architect of the period, H. H. Richardson. The influence of Frank Furness, however, kept Philadelphia from being completely overtaken by Romanesque structures as other American cities were during the period.

Philadelphia: Leader in Financial Architecture

During the century, different banking functions and different banking firms sought appropriately different physical presences. Fashions in banks changed. Fashions in the criticism of banks also changed. At the turn of the century a quiet style won praise. Writing in 1904, for example, an "ex-reporter" lamented the loss of geographic and architectural cohesion in the financial community around Third Street and Bank Row. He saw the home of the Second Bank as a model because "it is less pretentious, less suggestive of the architect, more in the unconsciously noble style."[30] Most later banks he thought florid, only "pretty." He liked the "harmonious union of massiveness and elegance" of the 1893-94 building for the Bank of North America designed by James H. Windrim, another leading Philadelphia bank architect. Indeed, in its 1906 self-history the bank called the color scheme of its building "cheerful, yet quiet." True to its heritage as the nation's first bank, it insisted that "while the building gives in every detail the impression of solidity and wealth, no money was uselessly expended in its construction."[31] But recent criticism has praised the merits of the more florid period, of buildings perhaps more suggestive of the architect. In particular, the banks of Frank Furness and, to a lesser extent, Willis G. Hale, are attracting renewed attention.

Any understanding of the development of Philadelphia during the nineteenth century must take its financial institutions into account. They were one mechanism for creating the credit that enabled homes to be built, as well as bridges and factories, offices and railroads, libraries and art museums. If by 1900 national leadership in finance had passed to New York, Philadelphia banks were still strongly contributing to the aesthetic, institutional, and geographic shape of the city and building on a heritage of financial architecture second to none.

Notes

1. Bray Hammond, *Banks and Politics in America from the Revolution to the Civil War* (Princeton, N.J.: Princeton University Press, 1957), p. 195. The author wishes to thank several people who assisted in the preparation of this chapter: William D. Andrews; Robert Dembergh of Boenning & Scattergood Inc.; Anthony N. B. Garvan; Robert F. Looney of the Free Library of Philadelphia; and Peter Parker of the Historical Society of Pennsylvania.

2. Quoted in John Thom Holdsworth, *Financing an Empire: History of Banking in Pennsylvania* (Chicago and Philadelphia: S. J. Clarke, 1928), p. 313.

3. Holdsworth, *Financing an Empire,* p. 320.

4. Antoinette Josephine Lee, "The Rise of the Cast Iron District in Philadelphia," Ph.D. dissertation, The George Washington University, 1975, pp. 1-2, 73-76.

5. Pim Nevin, "Travels in the U.S. 1802-1803," manuscript in the Historical Society of Pennsylvania, pp. 199-201.

6. Independence National Historical Park, *Historic Structures Report on the Second Bank of the United States* (Philadelphia, 1962), p. 2.

7. *Chestnut Street, Philadelphia. Descriptive, Reminiscent, Sentimental,* text by an Ex-Reporter (Philadelphia: Thomson, 1904), p. 8.

8. Quoted in Nicholas B. Wainwright, *History of the Philadelphia National Bank: A Century and a Half of Philadelphia Banking, 1803-1953* (Philadelphia: Philadelphia National Bank, 1953), p. 72.

9. *The Port Folio* 12 (July-December 1821): 204.

10. Elvira and Vladimir Clain-Stefanelli, *Charted for Progress: Two Centuries of American Banking* (Washington, D.C.: Acropolis, 1975), p. 104.

11. The National Banking Act provided for state-chartered banks to be rechartered as national banks with special privileges and responsibilities. In the rechartering,

banks added "National" to their names (as in the "Philadelphia *National* Bank") and new banks often bore numbers (as in the "First National Bank," "Second National Bank," and the like). Only the Bank of North America was allowed to keep its historic name without adding "national" when it received a national charter.

12. Holdsworth, *Financing an Empire,* p. 699. Stephan Thernstrom, in *Poverty and Progress: Social Mobility in a Nineteenth Century City* (Cambridge; Mass.: Harvard University Press, 1964), suggests that in an expanding economy like that of the nineteenth century the savings bank was the least profitable avenue for a worker's money. The banks, he theorizes, became agents of social control, enforcers of the status quo. The worker traded in his mobility for security. *See* pp. 122-31.

13. Dennis Clark, *The Irish in Philadelphia* (Philadelphia: Temple University Press, 1973), p. 56, and Holdsworth, *Financing an Empire,* p. 755.

14. Ibid., pp. 56-58.

15. Agnes Gilchrist, *William Strickland* (New York: Da Capo, 1969), p. 41.

16. Samuel Sloan, ed., *The Architectural Review and American Builders' Journal,* November 1868 (Philadelphia: 1869), p. 298.

17. Ibid., p. 299.

18. Elizabeth Biddle Yarnall, *Addison Hutton* (Philadelphia: Art Alliance Press, 1974), p. 42.

19. PSFS has a notable track record for architectural design. Its first home, a temple at Third and Walnut (1839), was designed by Thomas U. Walter, a leading Philadelphia architect and one of the designers of the national Capitol. Howe and Lescaze's 1931 building on Market Street has become a landmark of modernist international style in skyscrapers.

20. Sloan, *The Architectural Review,* March 1869, p. 550.

21. Ibid., p. 551.

22. Holdsworth, *Financing an Empire,* p. 196.

23. Jeffrey P. Roberts, "Continuity and Change in Downtown Land Use: The Evolution of Philadelphia's Central District, 1850-1880," paper presented at the First Annual Meeting of the Social Science History Association, Philadelphia, 1976, pp. 12-20. See also Martin J. Bowden, "Growth of the Central Districts in Large Cities," in *The New Urban History: Quantitative Explorations by American Historians,* ed. Leo F. Schnore (Princeton, N.J.; Princeton University Press, 1975), pp. 84-88 and 104-7.

24. *Chestnut Street, Philadelphia,* p. 7.

25. Quoted in James F. O'Gorman, *The Architecture of Frank Furness* (Philadelphia: Philadelphia Museum of Art, 1973), pp. 44-45.

26. J. Thomas Scharf and Thompson Westcott, *History of Philadelphia* (Philadelphia: L. H. Everts, 1884), 1: 640. The Girard Bank was already a deposit bank designated by Jackson.

27. Trades League of Philadelphia, *The City of Philadelphia as it Appears in the Year 1894,* 2d ed. (Philadelphia: Geo S. Harris, 1894), p. 148.

28. Wainwright, *History of the PNB,* p. 153.

29. George B. Tatum, *Penn's Great Town* (Philadelphia: University of Pennsylvania Press, 1961), p. 197.

30. *Chestnut Street, Philadelphia,* p. 23.

31. *The Bank of North America: Philadelphia* (New York: Cooke, 1906), p. 23.

CHAPTER 4 Architectural Patronage
and Social
Stratification in
Philadelphia between
1840 and 1920

GEORGE E. THOMAS

The House, the Architect, and the City

Residential location and residential mobility in the nineteenth-century city have long interested social historians. Their investigations have demonstrated that the proximity of housing to work opportunities was a fundamental organizing principle of urban land use, enabling the factory worker to make efficient use of his limited financial and temporal resources by a "commute" of eight to ten blocks' walk.[1] Those requirements led to the common Philadelphia urban form that intertwined factories and new houses in the great mill districts which first bordered the rivers and later spread inland along the railroads. Those mill districts, with their circumscribed opportunities for housing formed the cornerstone of the life experience of the typical urban resident.

For conventional urban planners, sustained by the green images of the city as garden suburb, popularized in 1902 by Ebenezer Howard in his *Garden Cities of Tomorrow,* the factory district and by extension the nineteenth-century city survives as the outmoded vestige of long discarded transportation systems, work patterns, and social conventions, unable to serve contemporary life. Improved public and private transportation augmented by rising income, and shortened work days, have made possible the commuter suburb, widely separated from the workplace. These changes have made the location of housing a matter of personal choice, limited not by the half-hour walk to work but by preferences for schools, social institutions, access to transit and expressways, as well as by the availability of congenial neighbors whose age and values are similar enough to assure community support for child rearing and other family goals.[2] This transformation in life-style, so often discussed by the social historian, has received less attention than it deserves from architectural historians whose interests have been focused more on community form and the stylistic and spatial changes in the house rather than the underlying questions of location and opportunity confronting the expectations and values of the home buyer.

If the connecting tissues of social history are too readily passed over by the architectural historian, the social historian has been equally remiss in concentrating on the urban populace without correlating their activities to the underlying structural skeleton of buildings, streets, and utility systems in the city. Even casual observation of Philadelphia and other nineteenth-century cities shows regional concentrations of buildings that are differentiated by style color, material, and function, corresponding, it can be presumed, to different eras and indicating varying land uses over time. Moreover, because architecture has traditionally served symbolic as well as utilitarian purposes, it has the potential to reflect through style, location, and selection of architect, the values and intentions of the client, offering thereby insight into the decision-making processes affecting the choice of residential location. When these general observations are guided by research into patterns of architectural patronage, the spatial differentiation engendered by social stratification is given visual definition. And viewed over time, the effect of the architectural decisions of various social groups on the stability and success of residential neighborhoods can be evaluated.

These questions are especially relevant in nineteenth-century Philadelphia, for in addition to its working-class districts of factories and row houses, there evolved alternate residential modes that raised many of the discretionary issues of contemporary housing—convenience, fashion, cost, and above all social affiliation. By mid-century two new residential districts had appeared west of Broad Street, one near Rittenhouse Square and another north of Spring Garden Street near the Fairmount Reservoir. Other suburban communities were being developed simultaneously, along the horsecar lines into West Philadelphia, and near the railroads that headed northwest into Germantown and Chestnut Hill. Somewhat more exotic but a part of the same pattern were the residential communities that bordered the Delaware River and depended on river boats to provide a scenic commute to the city.[3] In each of these new districts large single and double villas in the outlying areas and handsome, generous town houses closer to the downtown provided visual evidence of a new level of income and a willingness to expend greater sums on luxury. Size and costliness imply social and economic homogeneity, and as will be shown, the patterns of architectural patronage in Philadelphia suggest that these new residential communities developed in the nineteenth century in response to the forces of social stratification and separation.

Apart from a few comments by social historians in the recent past, the questions of who chose which location and why have been left largely unexamined. Stuart Blumin's essay, "Residential Mobility" in *The Peoples of Philadelphia*, demonstrates how extraordinarily large was the number of individual and family moves both into and out of the city as well as within its borders. But without objective criteria for establishing a prestige rating of each neighborhood, Blumin was unable to proceed beyond description.[4] On the other hand, Nathaniel Burt, whose *Perennial Philadelphia* introduced Philadelphia society to a curious nation in 1963, was able to report that certain zones, particularly Rittenhouse, were more fashionable and hence preferable to those north of Market Street.[5] But how and why this pattern evolved and on what documentation his observations were based were left to the reader's imagination. Burt exited from his discussion of mobility by comparing the pattern of urban residence to "a snail's imitation of America's own continental migration." "Charming cozy neighborhoods," he observed, were created and then abandoned "for newer or more fashionable quarters" just when they began to get "really ripe."[6] That, of course, was not the full story, for numerous old, successful neighborhoods existed as Burt was writing—and for that matter, still exist.

E. Digby Baltzell's cheerfully irreverent *Philadelphia Gentleman* took a more scholarly approach than Burt's anecdotal narrative and looked specifically at the question of location over time, following various identifiable groups across urban space by mapping residential and institutional locations.[7] In several instances Baltzell observed that the various locations paralleled the movements of Theodore Dreiser's fictional hero of *The Financier,* Frank Cowperwood, who rose from a white-collar clerk's home on Front Street above Market, to a house near Girard College, and finally to a great mansion on tree-lined Spring Garden Street, repeating almost exactly the actual course of the Henry Disston family whose tool factory was one of the city's great businesses. If most economically privileged Philadelphians did not finally reside in Moyamensing Prison and then Eastern State Penitentiary, as Cowperwood did before departing for Chicago, nonetheless enough Philadelphians, among them Peter A. B. Widener and Charles Ellis, made similar moves that differed significantly from the gradual westward progress described by Burt to suggest the possibility for a more subtle and telling analysis of mobility.

Dramatic shifts of residence, coupled with spectacular changes in the prestige of certain neighborhoods suggested to Baltzell a significant index to social stratification in Philadelphia. "The rise and fall of the Jenkintown neighborhood," he wrote, "bears out the thesis, stressed by Pitirim S. Sorokin in his *Social Mobility,* that communities distinguished by rapid success and accumulation of great wealth have less staying power than communities with more moderate rates of social mobility."[8] If Sorokin, and thus Baltzell, meant that aristocratic Philadelphia behaved and lived in a different manner and place than the new plutocrats, then they provided a clue to both the meaning and consequences of the various patterns of geographic mobility, one slow and steady, the other rapid and often spanning great distances, that characterized fashionable Philadelphia. Instead of treating all land use by the wealthy as uniform, with uniform implications, this approach not only offers an insight into the variations of upper-class life but also provides an explanation for the stability of some communities and the failure of others.

The residential patterns of the upper classes in Philadelphia between 1840 and 1920 can profitably be studied because at that time the city had both a well-developed, wealthy, and self-consciously exclusive establishment, and a growing, newly prosperous group of professionals, entrepreneurs, and industrialists. Equally important was the vast land area that the city offered for development, in contrast to the relatively limited selection of advantageous sites in island and peninsula cities such as New York and Boston. In Philadelphia, the nation's largest city in terms of land area until Los Angeles took the title in this century, most suburban sites were accessible from the central business district via the vast networks of the Reading and the Pennsylvania railroads, while the inner suburbs could be reached by the equally extensive horsecar lines.

Concentration of wealth, abundance of land, and availability of transit provided the opportunity. But, as we shall see, new values and expectations for the house provided the impetus for the dramatic shifts in residential location and housing type that began by 1840 and continued into this century. The evidence is everywhere—in popular volumes by architects from every region of the country as well as in regular monthly pieces published in journals addressed to the general public but especially in those aimed at women such as *Godey's Ladies Book* and in the various luxury volumes that described the great homes of the United States. The house, the public was informed, was like a "mold" to the "type" of the individual owner, his means of expressing his personality and worth.[9]

Even today, the potential for symbolic expression offered by housing remains great, as Robert Venturi, Denise Scott Brown and Stephen Izenour demonstrated in their Bicentennial exhibition "Signs of Life: Symbols in the American City."[10] Although scholars and critics have often oversimplified their descriptions of the style and embellishment of American homes to the point of stereotyping the owners, the intention of communicating deeply held cultural and social values is apparent even in the development houses of today's bedroom suburbs where American eagles over doors link their owners to the national image and tiny yards with picket fences recall the pastoral ideal of the eighteenth and nineteenth centuries. How much more must such embellishment have communicated when the owner through his own choice could absolutely determine location, architect, style, and ultimately expression as was the case for the moneyed classes in Philadelphia in the nineteenth and twentieth centuries? Moreover, can Baltzell's suggestion of a correlation between social stratification and place of residence be verified by an analysis of the location of the work done for those of wealth, both new and old, by different architects in the city at this time?

The evidence that attests to the social fragmentation of America at mid-century and the architectural representations of that split is plentiful and varied. Particularly informative are the writings of Andrew Jackson Downing (1812-1850) of upstate New York, whose best-known book, *The Architecture of Country Houses,* published in 1850, went through numerous printings until the end of the nineteenth century.[11] There and in his other publications Downing argued for the preservation of the values of the old aristocracy, stressing custom, heredity, and gentility against the encroaching values of show and ostentation of the growing mercantile and materialistic culture which he linked to alien political philosophies. For Downing, the architecture of the nation was a prime vehicle for the expression of its political values; hence he was particularly wary of grandiose architectural display which he viewed as un-American.

Fortunes are rapidly accumulated in the United States and the indulgence of one's taste and pride in the erection of country seats of great size and cost, is becoming a favorite mode of expending wealth. And yet these attempts at great establishments are always and inevitably failures. And why? Plainly because they are contrary to the spirit of republican institutions . . . because they are wholly in contradiction to the spirit of our time and people.[12]

Downing's popularity as a writer was exceeded only by his failure as a seer. The impending shift in values had been evident a decade earlier in New York and especially in Philadelphia. Sidney George Fisher, scion of an old Philadelphia family, whose recently published diaries have provided amusing if acerbic insights into mid-century Philadelphia society described the conflict between old and new money:

At 9 went to Harrison's . . . passed a pleasant evening. This is one of the few houses left in the city where one does not meet the vulgar nouveau riche people who are crowding into society, and are seen at all the parties. The good, respectable old family society for which Philadelphia was once so celebrated is fast disappearing and persons of low origins and vulgar habits, manners, feelings are introduced because they are rich who a few years ago were never heard of.[13]

A decade after Fisher made these observations, Downing himself appeared in the diary's pages, mentioned as the landscape architect for Joshua Francis Fisher's great Germantown residence. His participation in the design of Fisher's "Alverthorpe" suggests the presence of a national network of the upper classes, which had a regional counterpart in Philadelphia.

The Architecture of Country Houses has further significance; it was but one of many books published before the Civil War which held that the housing of gentlemen should be architect-designed and not the result of the collaboration of owner and builder. Concurrently, architecture was undergoing a significant transformation from vernacular craft or the hobby of gentlemen amateurs to a true profession. Office training gave way to schooling, professional organizations replaced local craft societies, and finally professional standards and, more telling, rate structures were formulated. Such changes in occupational practices and status made it increasingly likely that the architects of the city would reflect all levels of society—even the highest— making it possible for a client to select an architect from his own or any other circle in the city.

Finally, the more widespread the interest in architecture, the more likely it became that the press would provide coverage. Shortly after the Civil War, the first architectural journals were published, and soon newspapers were carrying regular columns which discussed construction projects and often mentioned architect and owner.[14] An even more complete source of information on building resulted from the pent up demand for housing among the new industrial middle classes. In the decade after the Civil War, Philadelphia's stock of houses more than doubled, and this tremendous speed was accompanied at times by dangerously shoddy building practices particularly in North and West Philadelphia. Wood shims supported brick party walls; blocks of houses were built above flimsy brick culverts containing underground streams; walls became thinner to the point of collapse. To combat those practices, the building trades were increasingly regulated by the ever enlarging bureaucracy that expanded to fill the newly rising City Hall. Permits were required, and building inspectors were sent to monitor construction practices.[15] Beginning in 1886 the data generated by these activities were published in daily records, newspaper columns, and in a weekly trade journal, the *Philadelphia Real Estate Record and Builders' Guide* (PRER&BG) which listed sales, permits, and work currently in local architectural offices.[16] From 1886 until 1944 the PRER&BG gave a complete picture of building activity in the city, one that confirms and by inference augments much of our information about the pre-Civil War era.

Patterns of Patronage, 1840–1865

For the purposes of this study eight architectural firms have been selected, partly for reasons of architectural merit but also because their commissions are well documented and were sufficiently varied in building type and size to reflect the general range of their era. As will be seen, other architects could have been selected with similar results. The eight firms selected include those of Stephen D. Button (1813-1894) active in Philadelphia from 1850 to 1894;[17] John Notman (1810-1865) active in Philadelphia from 1837 to 1865;[18] Frank Furness (1839-1912) active in Philadelphia from 1866 to 1910;[19] Theophilus P. Chandler (1845-1928) active in Philadelphia between 1872 and 1905;[20] Willis G. Hale (c. 1849-1907) active in Philadelphia between 1870 and 1907;[21] William Decker (1850-c. 1910) active in Philadelphia between 1875 and 1900;[22] Walter Cope (1861-1902) and John Stewardson (1859-1896) active as Cope and Stewardson from 1885 to 1902;[23] and Horace Trumbauer (1868-1938) active in the city between 1890 and 1925.[24] Half of the architects, Furness, Cope, Stewardson, and Trumbauer, were born in Philadelphia; Notman was born in Scotland, Button in Connecticut, and Chandler in the Boston area. Decker was born in Covington, Kentucky, of German parents, while Hale was a native of upstate New York. All had some office training: Button with an English-trained designer in New York; Notman in England; Furness in the office of John Fraser, whose Union League Clubhouse still stands on South Broad Street; Chandler in the Boston office of Peabody and Stearns; Hale with the flamboyant designer of Philadelphia's City Hall, John McArthur, Jr.; and Decker in the office of the machinists Hass and Parsons. Trumbauer spent nearly a decade in the office of G. W. and W. D. Hewitt, former associates of Frank Furness and architects of the old Bellevue-Stratford Hotel, while Cope studied first with the Quaker architect Addison Hutton and later worked in Chandler's office in the company of his future partner John Stewardson, whose earliest training had been with Furness.

Advanced architectural education was rare enough in the nineteenth century that only Furness (atelier of Richard Morris Hunt in New York), Chandler (Harvard University), and Stewardson (Harvard University and a period at the French Ecole des Beaux Arts) had academic training. As could be expected, it was the academically trained architects along with Stewardson's partner Walter Cope who were members of and architects for establishment families.

Affiliation with various professional organizations provides a less reliable index of an architect's social standing or education; instead it indicates the architect's age. The older architects—Button, Furness, Chandler, and Hale—were at one time or another members of the Philadelphia chapter of the American Institute of Architects (A.I.A.). Those who reached professional maturity in the 1880s, such as Cope, Stewardson, and Wilson Eyre, joined the T-Square Club, apparently preferring its guildlike emphasis on teaching and comraderie over the mere regulation of competition afforded by the A.I.A.[25] Of all the architects, only Notman, whose death in 1865 predated the first local professional organization, and William Decker were not members of local professional organizations, although Notman had joined the New York A.I.A.

After his arrival in the 1830s Notman rapidly became the city's leading architect, being pushed to the forefront by that defender of establishment virtues, A. J. Downing.[26] The resulting connections were no doubt instrumental in Notman's receiving commissions for Laurel Hill Cemetery, soon to become the popular place of interment for wealthy Philadelphians, as well as for the city's fashionable Episcopal churches, St. Mark's, St. Clement's, and Holy Trinity on Rittenhouse Square (see Figure 4-1). The same architect

Figure 4-1. Holy Trinity Episcopal Church, 1857, on Rittenhouse Square at Walnut Street. The original design was by John Notman. The tower was added by George W. Hewitt in 1890, and further alterations were made by Cope and Stewardson six years later. The Reverend Philips Brooks served as rector of Holy Trinity before leaving for Boston's equally fashionable Trinity Church. *Photograph by George E. Thomas.*

also designed many of the new buildings for the establishment's most hallowed institutions, beginning in 1839 with the Academy of Natural Sciences on South Broad Street followed by the Athenaeum on Washington Square and, reiterating the Episcopalian connection, the Academy of the Protestant Episcopal Church in 1849.

Notman's career was by no means restricted to public and institutional buildings, although his private commissions were usually dependent on the same circle of men who served on the institutional boards. The Pennsylvania Railroad, foundation of the city's economic renaissance of the 1850s, built an office building from Notman's plans, and he designed city and country houses in the Philadelphia region, including three spectacular Tuscan villas at Princeton, New Jersey. His clients' surnames recall what Sidney George Fisher thought of as "reputable old family society," including in New Jersey, Stockton and in Philadelphia Ingersoll, Harrison, McKean, and Fisher. The location of the new city houses is of particular interest, for without exception they stood within earshot of the chimes of one or more of St. Mark's, St. Clement's, or Holy Trinity. The country houses were more scattered, befitting their English ancestry and their purpose as retreats from the city; only Henry Gibson's West Philadelphia mansion was accessible by horsecar, the rest requiring both train and carriage rides, effectively limiting visits.[27] Notman's circle of clients can thus be described as old Philadelphia Quaker or Episcopalian, and if Fisher is an example, politically conservative.

While Notman's clients restricted their home building to the vicinity of Rittenhouse Square or the deep country, the residential commissions of his near contemporary Stephen Decatur Button were located in totally different sections of Philadelphia (see Map 4-1). Most were built north of Market Street, in the region proscribed by Burt. Several great houses were erected along Broad Street, at Brown, Girard, and Master streets, and more were built in rows along Arch Street and the east-west streets in the newly developing residential districts of Fairmount. When country houses were built, they were generally close enough to train stations to suggest their use as year-round houses rather than summer estates like those for Notman's clientele who preferred the English landed gentry mode of town house and country seat.[28]

Not only do the residential locations and life-styles of the two sets of clients differ, but the private institutions that retained the architects were dissimilar as well. Four of Notman's Philadelphia churches were Protestant Episcopal, one Roman Catholic; Button on the other hand was regularly hired by congregations and institutions associated with the native white working and middle classes, that is, the Methodists and Baptists, but never the Episcopalians (see Figure 4-2). The sole instance of a Button project for a Quaker building occurred when he was hired to make an addition to the old Free Quaker Meeting House when the building was occupied by the Apprentice's Library.

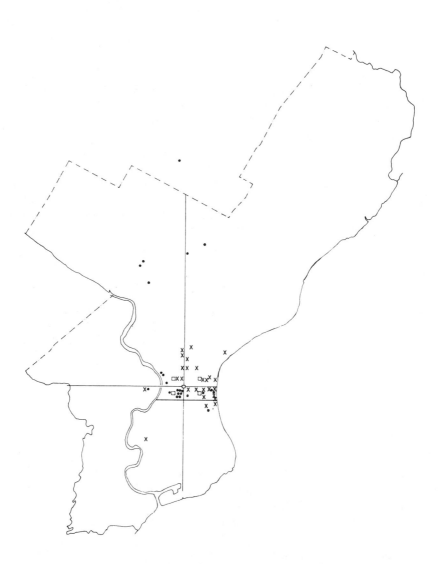

Map 4-1. The Distribution of the Commissions of John Notman, 1840-1865, and Stephen D. Button, 1850-1875. Notman's work appears here as a dot, Button's as an x.

TABERNACLE METHODIST EPISCOPAL CHURCH, PHILADELPHIA.

Figure 4-2. Tabernacle Methodist Church, 1855, at 11th and Jefferson streets, Stephen D. Button, architect. Source: *The National Magazine* 8 (February 1856).

Button's other institutional buildings were of the same general status, among them the Spring Garden Institute, a working-class training school.[29] They were located north and south of the colonial city which was itself becoming increasingly working-class as the upper strata of society moved west to Rittenhouse or northwest to Fairmount. Nothing so directly epitomizes Button's clientele as the firehouses, the Hope Engine Company on South Sixth Street and the Southwark Hose Company on South Third Street. It should be recalled that prior to the organization of the Philadelphia fire department in 1871, firehouses were paid for by local communities whose residents formed the bulk of almost every brigade. As such, fire companies focused neighborhood pride even though at times they also, unfortunately, heightened ethnic and political tensions because of the frequent clashes between rival brigades which often left the fire to be extinguished by the victorious hose crew![30]

The denominations and organizations served by S. D. Button indicate that his residential clientele was probably drawn from the new managerial middle class whose antecedents were often working class. Most probably attended Methodist, Baptist, or Lutheran churches, and many, it can be assumed, were members of one of the fraternal organizations in the city, perhaps the Odd Fellows, whose cemetery Button designed in 1855. In only one area did Button's commissions overlap with Notman's, and that was in the realm of commercial and business architecture. The reasons for this are evident in the structure of Philadelphia. In the middle of the nineteenth century, efficiency of time demanded that most businesses be located near the municipal core around City Hall and the courts at Fifth and Chestnut streets or near the commercial and warehousing facilities that bordered the Delaware River. For the next half century, municipal and private investments reinforced that centralizing tendency, as public transit, communication, and other services all focused first on the old central business district and then on the new district that developed to the west around the new City Hall at Broad and Market streets. Consequently, Button's warehouses and manufacturing lofts stood below Third Street near the port facilities of the Delaware. His office buildings could be found near Independence Hall (including Button's own architectural office which was for years at 430 Walnut Street) while his commercial buildings were built to the west near the new residential and government districts. Since the distribution of Notman's business buildings was identical, it appears that commercial interaction was unimpeded by the social factions which residential location implied.

Does the obvious difference of location between the residential commissions of Notman and Button reveal a social caste system or is this pattern merely the result of a fortuitous selection of architects? Research on the geographic distribution of religious denominations in Philadelphia might confirm this relationship by showing similar sharply delineated zones across the city.[31] If the journey to church, like the journey to work, can be assumed to have been relatively short, and if church affiliation was a reasonable indication of class status, then the location of churches in the communities of choice should provide a strong clue to ethnically and socially distinct districts in the city.

The religious geography of Philadelphia in the middle of the nineteenth century supports these assumptions; of the nearly 30 new Episcopal congregations formed between 1840 and 1860, none were built in the old portion of the city east of Seventh Street, and only three were built to serve its southern reaches, one housing a black congregation. Two of the new churches could be said to have served the Fairmount-Spring Garden districts to the north of what is now the Benjamin Franklin Parkway. But seven new Episcopal churches were constructed within five blocks of Rittenhouse Square, three were built within four blocks of 39th and Walnut streets in West Philadelphia, and five including the wonderfully picturesque St. James the Less were built in rural locations.

Although the combined total of Methodist, Lutheran, and Baptist congregations was more than three times that of the Episcopalians, in 1860 all together accounted for fewer churches in the Rittenhouse Square area than the Episcopalians alone (seven to three). North of Market Street, on the other hand, new Methodist, Lutheran, and Baptist congregations outnumbered the Episcopal congregations nearly six to one. If Quaker meetings, Unitarian, and Swedenborgian congregations are added to the Episcopalian totals, the concentration around Rittenhouse, West Philadelphia, and Chestnut Hill is even more telling, bearing out Nathanial Burt's assumption about the residential location of the establishment. Correlation of the sites of the other denominations with the known residential patterns of ethnic groups and social strata shows that Methodist and Baptist congregations clustered near the growing factory districts along the Delaware River. Lutheran churches appeared in a band stretching across north central Philadelphia, near the homes of those of German origin. Catholic churches, serving larger congregations, were fairly regularly interspersed with Methodist, Baptist, and Lutheran churches, suggesting considerable cultural heterogeneity within working-class districts—contrasting all the more with the elite communities that remained generally homogeneous (see Maps 4-2 and 4-3). The correspondence of the location of the residential commissions of Notman to the elite denominations and of Button to the middle- and working-class denominations suggests that religious orientation is a reasonable indication of the social standing of the architect as well as the neighborhood.

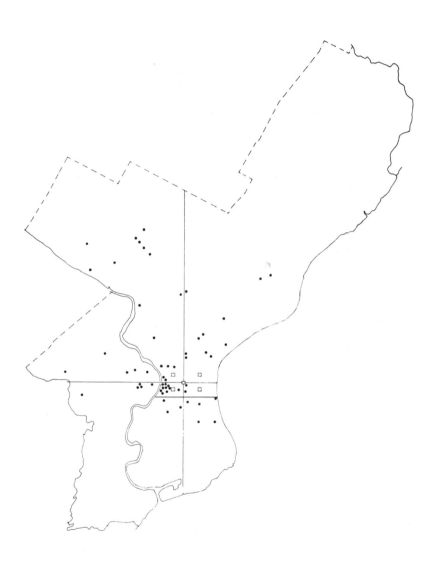

Map 4-2. The Distribution of Philadelphia's Episcopal Churches, 1840-1880. Both new and relocated congregations are shown.

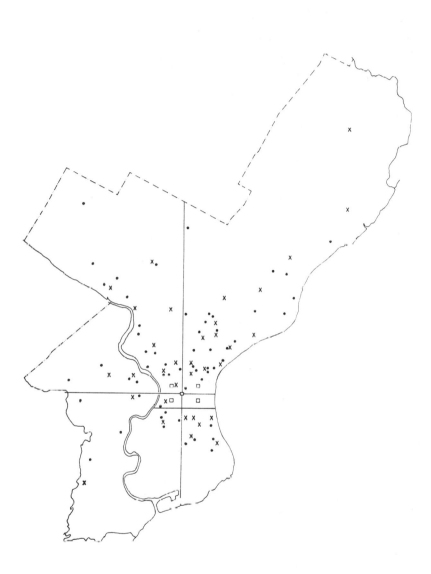

Map 4-3. The Distribution of Philadelphia's Methodist and Roman Catholic Churches, 1840-1880. Methodist churches appear here as a dot, Catholic churches as an x. Both new and relocated congregations are shown.

Patterns of Patronage, 1865–1920

The rapid growth of the city continued after the hiatus of the Civil War, but it was dressed in the often violent clashes of color and form characteristic of high Victorian design which signaled the appearance of a new generation of architects and clients. Of the four architects chosen to represent the post-war generation, only one, Furness, was born in the city and thus may be presumed to have had the social connections on which so many architectural commissions depended. But the prosperity of the others, particularly Chandler, whose clientele overlapped with that of Furness, implies that during the Centennial decade at least, success was as much a matter of talent as social alliance.[32]

Frank Furness was, if not old society, at least respectable, for his Boston-born and Harvard-educated father, William Henry Furness, had been minister of the First Unitarian Church for nearly half a century and a brother and sister married into important Philadelphia families. Furness's ecclesiastical commissions confirm his ascribed status, for in the first generation of his practice, nine Episcopal congregations retained his services for both alterations and new church buildings, and, in addition, he was given the commission for a new Episcopal hospital for consumptives in the salubrious air of Chestnut Hill where by 1886 so many of his clients lived. In part, many of these jobs were received because his partner from 1868 to 1876, George W. Hewitt,[33] had worked with and continued the practice of John Notman. But after the dissolution of their partnership, both architects continued to work for Episcopalians. In addition, Furness and Hewitt, first as partners and later separately, were regularly retained by those institutions whose boards were run by old society Philadelphians, including the Pennsylvania Academy of the Fine Arts, the Pennsylvania Asylum for the Deaf and Dumb, the Zoological Society, the First City Troop, and the University of Pennsylvania. Each of those commissions demonstrated that Furness's originality was no barrier to his successful pursuit of assignments from old Philadelphia families.

As could be anticipated from his institutional clients, most of Furness's residential work was also for old Philadelphia families, including several that had been Notman's clients. For example, Notman had designed the McKean country seat in 1849-50. When the same family required city houses in 1871, Furness and Hewitt provided plans for twin houses at 20th and Walnut streets. Before his career was complete Furness would design two dozen other residences within three blocks of Rittenhouse Square. Other clusters of Furness country houses were erected in Chestnut Hill, and a dozen or more were built on the Main Line in the immediate vicinity of another Furness project, the Merion Cricket Club.

But Furness also served other groups in the city. His father's Unitarian pastorate brought commissions for two Unitarian meetinghouses as well as residences and offices for members of the congregations. Another distinct cluster can be linked to the Rodef Sholom synagogue built at Broad and Mount Vernon streets in 1869-70. It led to other North Philadelphia commissions including the Jewish Hospital complex at Broad and Tabor streets, the Mount Sinai Cemetery chapel in Frankford, and homes for several congregants, mostly in the vicinity of the synagogue.[34] Whether those commissions resulted from the Reverend William Henry Furness's impassioned liberalism or from his son's own contacts in the professional and intellectual community has never been determined.

The last and in many ways the most interesting buildings were those which Furness designed for various commercial enterprises. There the architect's genius for original and eye-catching ornament and composition was put to telling use in the overheated commercial heart of nineteenth-century Philadelphia. But even there Furness's clients were old Philadelphians; Samuel Shipley, the Quaker banker, hired him for three bank buildings and two family homes. Gilles Dallett, whose family had engaged Notman to design a Philadelphia town house, retained Furness for the Penn National Bank, while a grand nephew was sent to learn architecture in Furness's office. These same connections, enhanced by Furness's obvious talents, also resulted in nearly 200 railroad commissions capped by the Baltimore and Ohio Station of 1888 and in 1893 by the massive extension to the Broad Street Station of the Pennsylvania Railroad, a company for which Notman had also worked. Thus, in the final tally, Furness's commissions were distributed in a manner remarkably like those of his predecessor, John Notman: in the business center, the Rittenhouse neighborhood, and the countryside for clients who were mainly Episcopalian and old-money Quaker (see Map 4-4).

Theophilus P. Chandler arrived in Philadelphia from Boston in 1872, hoping to snare some of the Centennial Exhibition projects. Only the bear pits at the zoo were awarded to him, but he was more successful in another venture, for he married a DuPont, assuring financial stability. His first commissions were less spatially coherent, presumably because he had no predetermined connections. Houses on Spring Garden Street in North Philadelphia, churches in North, South, and West Philadelphia as well as commerical buildings in the old city all came his way in the 1870s. By the 1880s, however, that diffuse pattern had more or less given way to the typical establishment pattern, with houses in Rittenhouse, Chestnut Hill, and the Main Line, overlapping almost exactly with the territory, institutions, and clients of Furness (see Map 4-5). It was Chandler who made alterations to the lobby of Furness and Hewitt's Pennsylvania Academy of the Fine Arts and built houses abutting those by Furness on 22nd Street. Chandler, too, built the replacement for Furness's Commercial Union Assurance Company near Independence Hall and, like Furness, stations for the Pennsylvania Railroad. And although Chandler's connections never brought him major

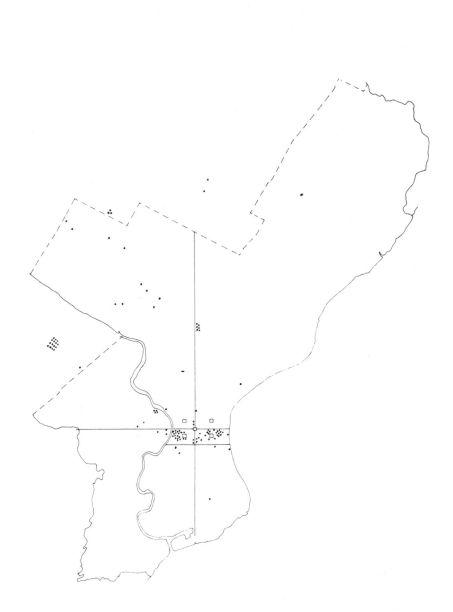

Map 4-4. The Distribution of the Commissions of Frank Furness, 1870-1890.

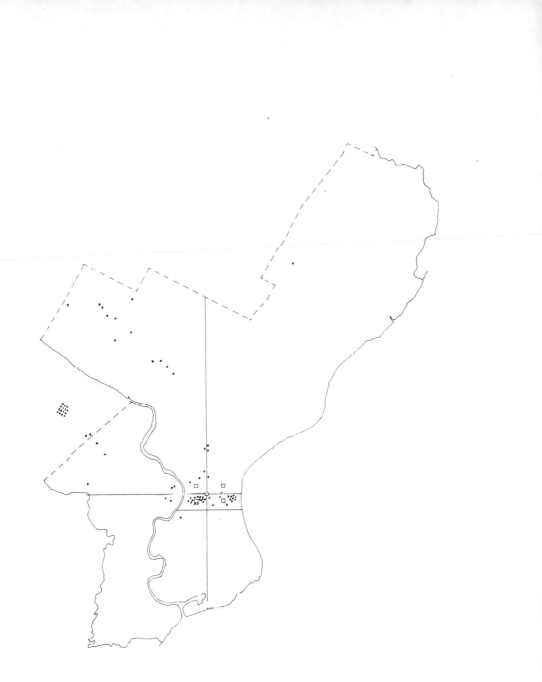

Map 4-5. The Distribution of the Commissions of Theophilus P. Chandler, 1875-1895.

commissions at the University of Pennsylvania where Furness's brother Horace was a leading scholar, nonetheless, it was Chandler who was selected to head the university's School of Architecture when it was reorganized in 1891. Moreover, Chandler's office often provided additional training for young draftsmen who had already worked with Furness. Other architects of the same generation, among them George W. Hewitt (Main Line, Rittenhouse, Pennsylvania Railroad, Episcopal diocese), Addison Hutton (the same spatial pattern but more often Quaker clients),[35] and Henry A. Sims (like Chandler a designer of Presbyterian and Episcopal churches),[36] worked in similar regions and had in common an equally limited group of commissions outside the establishment circle.

Not only were the commissions of Notman and later Furness, Chandler, Hewitt, and others similar, but there was also a striking continuity between the commissions of Stephen Button and the new generation of architects for the nouveau riche after the Civil War. Of that group, the most noteworthy was Willis Hale, a native of upstate New York, whose predilection for exuberant detail was nurtured in the offices of Samuel Sloan and John McArthur, Jr.[37] Like his professional contemporaries, Hale was among the organizers of the A.I.A. and was active in the downtown portion of the city throughout his career, designing banks, office buildings, and stores. But unlike Furness and his elite colleagues, Hale's domestic commissions were located almost exclusively north of Market Street, beginning in the Green Street section of Spring Garden, where Button had worked, and then moving north to Girard Avenue where many of his houses were erected. In addition, his residential clients were of a different sort: Peter A. B. Widener, Civil War profiteer, public transit magnate, and land speculator; Joseph Fleisher, Jewish wool and cloth merchant and devotee of the arts; Benjamin and John Ketcham, building contractors; William Weightman, manufacturing chemist—in short, neither Shipleys nor McKeans, Ingersolls, or Biddles. Hale's commercial buildings were owned by the nouveau riche, and his institutional clients, the Catholic church, the Lutherans, and the Jewish Foster Home, are equally indicative of the different social standing of his patrons.

The distinct pattern of Hale's commissions is also observable in the careers of several of his peers, among them William Decker, the descendant of German immigrants who lived in the North Philadelphia German district. Like Hale, Chandler, and Furness, Decker's commercial buildings were concentrated in the city's original business district east of Seventh Street and after 1885 in the area growing up around the new City Hall at Broad and Market streets. His residential commissions, like Hale's, were situated predominantly north of Girard Avenue and west of Broad Street and showed a considerable range from the great mansions of the traction magnate Charles Ellis to small, three-story shopfront houses (see Map 4-6). Again, like Hale, his clients were drawn not from the establishment but from the new middle

Map 4-6. The Distribution of the Commissions of Willis G. Hale and William Decker, 1880-1900. Decker's work appears here as an x, Hale's as a dot or a dark line, the latter representing a cluster of buildings.

classes. Their names were often German in origin, and they provided types of projects that Furness or Chandler were rarely if ever offered—small enterprises, restaurants, saloons, theaters, breweries and box factories, Baptist churches, and buildings for the Hebrew Sheltering Society. With the exception of one house in West Philadelphia, records show that Decker received no commissions for work in the fashionable suburbs to the west or north of the city. James H. Windrim, architect of the Masonic Temple; Walter Geissinger, factory architect; and Edwin Forrest Durang, theater designer and favorite architect of the Catholic archdiocese, all conformed to this general pattern.[38] Not surprisingly, save for Hale who lived near his place of business in the old commercial district, all lived in the communities that they served.[39]

Two firms from the generation of architects attaining maturity around 1890 confirm the persistence of the residential and architectural schism among moneyed Philadelphians into this century. Walter Cope and John Stewardson, both members of established Quaker families, pupils of T. P. Chandler, and in the case of Stewardson also of Furness, became the principal successors to Furness and Chandler as architects for "Perennial Philadelphians." It was Cope and Stewardson who built the McKeans' new city houses on the site of the family's earlier Furness-designed houses (see Figure 4-3); they added to Notman's St. Mark's Episcopal church and became the principal architects for Quaker Bryn Mawr College as well as the fashionable University of Pennsylvania. Their commissions almost exactly overlapped those of the previous two generations of establishment architects, with Rittenhouse, West Philadelphia, and Chestnut Hill being the sites of their projects (see Map 4-7). Predictably, their clientele was Episcopalian, Quaker, and old Philadelphia, and they designed institutional buildings for organizations whose boards were controlled by the same establishment families. Rarely if ever did public works for the city come their way. But commercial projects, now predominantly around the new rail terminals and City Hall were often theirs, and such structures were built for the Harrisons and other elite friends and relatives.

Horace Trumbauer on the other hand, though a student in the office of George W. Hewitt, took a course that brought him into contact with the Widener and Elkins families and resulted in spectacular commissions for mansions, both in the local suburbs and in the great resorts of Bar Harbor and Newport, as well as grand hotels and office buildings, in short, the grandest projects that such an opulent age might offer.[40] Again, like Hale and Decker, whose clients generally selected sites beyond the built-up regions of the 1860s, Trumbauer's clients broke new ground at the northern edges of the city and beyond, in the suburbs of Jenkintown and Elkins Park. Like Cope and Stewardson and all his predecessors, Trumbauer built extensively in the corporate and commercial center, although usually for the firms controlled by the North Philadelphians (see Map 4-8). But unlike Cope and

Figure 4-3. The McKean Houses, 1897, at 1921-23 Walnut Street, Walter Cope and John Stewardson architects. The use of architectural detail derived from England provided a direct manifestation of the idea of "ethnic continuity" which was further expressed by the sequence of McKean family architects: John Notman, Frank Furness, and finally Walter Cope and John Stewardson. *Photograph by George E. Thomas.*

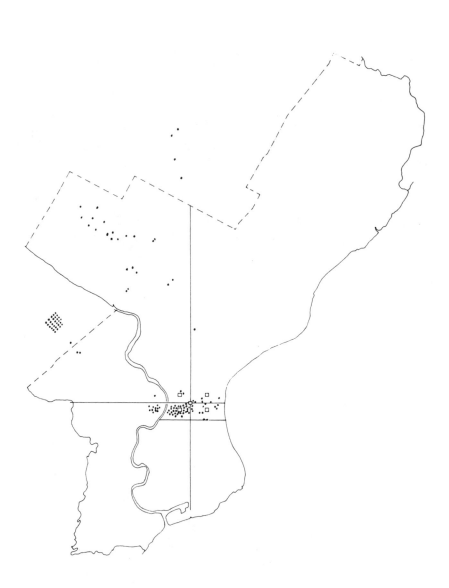

Map 4-7. The Distribution of the Commissions of Walter Cope and John Steward-son, 1887-1902.

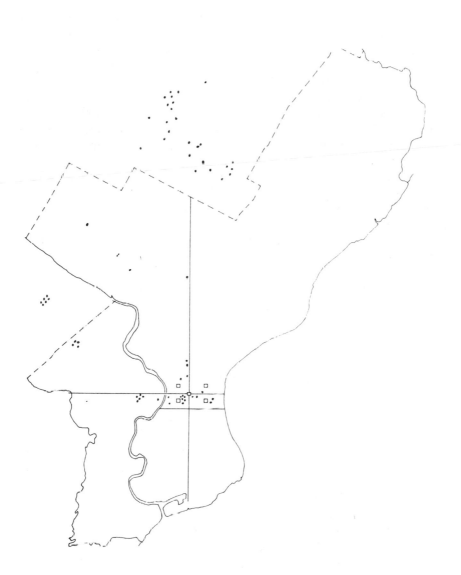

Map 4-8. The Distribution of the Commissions of Horace Trumbauer, 1890-1905.

Stewardson, Trumbauer received important commissions from the city—the Art Museum and the Free Library, for example—indicating perhaps that a continuing interest in city affairs was a characteristic of the newly rich rather than of the old Philadelphians, most of whom had given up political activity when the Whig Party expired.[41]

Trumbauer's career also differed from that of his predecessors and peers in the diverse religious groups for whom he worked—not only Catholics and Methodists, the denominations of the working and middle classes, but the Episcopalians as well.[42] Moreover, Trumbauer's residential commissions were somewhat less spatially distinct, for several of his clients preferred sites in the traditional reserve of the establishment wealthy around Rittenhouse Square rather than in the northern suburbs (see Figure 4-4).[43] Finally, Trumbauer also received several commissions, again with the backing of his usual industrialist patrons, for buildings at old Philadelphia institutions, among them Irvine Auditorium at the University of Pennsylvania, as well as for structures at national institutions such as the Widener Library at Harvard. Those changes in what had been a relatively uniform pattern of affiliation and location mark an important transition in the status of new money (by then becoming, in fact, old money) away from social rejection to tentative tolerance, a process eased by its financial support of some of the establishment's favorite institutions.

Style and Class: Appearances Do Make the Man

For three generations Philadelphia's architectural commissions were distributed across the city's space in relatively fixed patterns. The business and commercial districts were characterized by a richly diverse architecture that represented most, if not all segments of Philadelphia society. With the exception of those few architects whose practices were limited to one or two building types not required in the center of the city, every major architect worked first in old Philadelphia and later in the developing business district around the new City Hall. The legacy of this equality of architectural opportunity is the often harsh visual contrasts of different generations and personal styles which shaped the marketplace of the nineteenth-century city.

That the heterogeneity so evident in the business district did not reappear in Philadelphia's residential quarters affirms the accuracy of J. P. Morgan's assertion, "You can do business with anyone, but you can only sail a boat with a gentleman." And had Morgan continued he might have said join a club, worship, play golf, and reside which would have described the mechanics of social behavior for the era. Still, like the old joke about not being able to afford the cost of the yacht if you have to ask the price, the fact that Morgan was insecure enough to comment about class behavior marks him as a more appropriate resident of the gilded residential communities in

Figure 4-4. E. C. Knight House, 1901, at 1629 Locust Street, Horace Trumbauer, architect. Fashioned of limestone in the *beaux arts* style, the Knight mansion was flanked by the brownstone, gothic parish hall of St. Mark's Episcopal Church and the colonial revival Harrison house by Walter Cope and John Stewardson, 1895. *Photograph by George E. Thomas.*

North Philadelphia than of the old-family zone around Rittenhouse Square.
It is that split between old and new money that is represented in the distribution of architectural commissions and corroborated by the location of
churches in the city's space. But the impact of the split between old and
new money was more than merely geographic, for this social situation
resulted in the useless although psychologically necessary duplication of
many of the city's facilities in the late nineteenth century, including a second
music hall, the Metropolitan Opera House of North Broad Street, and in
the center of the city various clubs to compete with the old Philadelphia
organizations. Even hotels were duplicated when the Widener-commissioned,
Trumbauer-designed Ritz Carlton was completed to house social events in
competition with those at the Bellevue-Stratford, designed by G. W. and
W. D. Hewitt, which hosted old Philadelphia events.

But more important than the duplication of civic facilities, the architectural decisions made in Rittenhouse and North Philadelphia had other consequences for the city and its neighborhoods. At first glance there is little of
a physical nature to differentiate the two areas; land use, access to transit,
availability of city services, house size, and cost are similar enough. The
great differences are aesthetic. Despite the numerous projects of Furness
and his at times equally flamboyant peers, Rittenhouse remained far more
conservative, particularly in the facades of the great town houses on Pine,
Delancey, Spruce, and Locust streets (see Figure 4-5). There the red brick
and marble trim of the eighteenth century remained current into the 1890s,
causing the Reverend William Henry Furness to comment, "Only think
what a long day of it, one particular style of building has had here in Philadelphia." Indeed, more than a few of Furness's commissions on Delancey
Street were simple facade alterations within the existing coloristic and
formal conventions of the street and the region. Flamboyancy in Rittenhouse was, in fact, rare. Instead of responding to the newest fashions,
architecture for the Philadelphia establishment was as daring as its tweedy
conservative garb; as a consequence, neither the buildings nor the region
ever really became dated, and the Rittenhouse area has remained fashionable
for more than a century. The visual evidence of this fact can be seen in the
mixture of architectural periods which still characterize the district in contrast to the relative homogeneity of North Philadelphia. Similar variety
marks the Main Line and Chestnut Hill.

The competitive values of the commercial, newly rich Philadelphians
made for a different architecture. Instead of working within a conservative
tradition, North Philadelphia started with the brownstone, heavy cornices,
and rich carving of the 1840s and proceeded to become even more elaborate,
more expensively and extensively embellished. Whereas the exuberance of
high Victorian design in Rittenhouse was rigorously controlled by proportion and balance, in short by academic discipline, the houses of North

Figure 4-5. Rowhouses in the 1800 Block of Delancey Place, 1856-1857, in the Rittenhouse Neighborhood. The bracketed cornice and paneled window shutters and doors demonstrate the influence of the Italianate style, but the basic composition and colors derive from the eighteenth and early nineteenth centuries. *Photograph by George E. Thomas.*

Philadelphia were endlessly complex but without the necessary ordering motifs and sense of restraint. Thorstein Veblen's analysis of the values of "conspicuous consumption" and the "pecuniary canons of taste" applied to these buildings but not to most old Philadelphia town houses.[44]

Visually the difference can be seen in the contrast between T. P. Chandler's Walnut Street mansion for James P. Scott, the Harvard-educated son of the president of the Pennsylvania Railroad, who "after graduation . . . not being in good health, did not participate in commercial activities,"[45] and the great house Willis Hale designed for the traction magnate and developer of most of North Philadelphia, Peter A. B. Widener. Chandler's work is a beautifully proportioned, carefully balanced and subtle version of a late medieval, French city house (see Figure 4-6). Every detail is carefully studied and the amount of ornament is pared to the essential architectural purpose. Although the Widener house is symmetrical, its effect is the opposite; here, instead of chaste monochromatic, grey stone, brownstone gives way to brick and brick to iron, terra cotta, and finally tile on the structure's roofs (since replaced with copper). No surface, however minute, was left unembellished (see Figure 4-7). It has jokingly been said that Hale could invent a thousand motifs in the development of a design and use most of them, and the evidence here suggests that he could and did. The interior was just as spectacular, the most extraordinary space being the dining room. Its walls were painted away by a German-born decorative artist, George Herzog, whose work simulated views beyond the walls into a sunny seventeenth-century garden peopled with Widener's family in floppy plumed hats and period dress (see Figure 4-8). Although time and space were transcended in the room, date and place—north Broad Street in 1887—were not.

The same dichotomy can be observed in the row buildings of the 1870s and 1880s. On the periphery of fashionable Rittenhouse, where the smaller houses of the up-and-coming were built, simplicity was a virtue, for the children of old elite had the same values as their parents. But in North Philadelphia, which was largely developed by Widener and his partner and neighbor across Broad Street, William Elkins, the row blocks were individualized, and each house was given a separate identity. Their architect, usually Willis G. Hale, used tile, decorative panels, gables, and small mansards to make each as *au courant* as possible (see Figure 4-9). Like the great houses, the rows of North Philadelphia were built at the outer limits of fashion, and like everything a la mode, they went out of fashion just as quickly. Probably that factor was at the root of North Philadelphia's impermanence. In building so fashion-conscious a neighborhood, the residents of North Philadelphia doomed themselves to move on as soon as it became dated. Widener left his home a decade after it was completed for a great Trumbauer mansion, and Elkins moved at the same time. Every decade for half a century after 1850 some new district in North Philadelphia arrived,

Figure 4.6. The James P. Scott House, 1883, at 2032 Walnut Street, Theophilus P. Chandler, architect. The subtle compositional play of balance and refined detail characterized this architect's city houses. *Photograph by George E. Thomas.*

Figure 4-7. The Peter A. B. Widener House, 1886-1888, Broad Street and Girard Avenue, Willis G. Hale, architect. Unlike the restrained Scott house, the Widener mansion is an overwhelming confection which gives an architectural definition to Thorstein Veblen's famous phrase, "conspicuous consumption." *Photograph by George E. Thomas.*

Figure 4-8. The Dining Room in the House of Peter A. B. Widener, 1888-1889, George Herzog, decorative artist. Herzog provided decorations for other important Philadelphia buildings including William Kemble's Green Street mansion, the Masonic Temple, and the William Elkins house. *Photograph by George E. Thomas.*

Figure 4-9. The 2300 Block of West Thompson Street of 1880 in the Fairmount Neighborhood, Willis G. Hale, architect. Individualism, emphasized by separate property breaks, was the hallmark of the late nineteenth-century, North Philadelphia row. The corner storefront is a further indication of the difference between the life-styles of the rich in Rittenhouse and the middle class to the north. *Photograph by George E. Thomas.*

Figure 4-10. Childs, Kemble, and Widener Mausolea, Laurel Hill Cemetery. *Photograph by George E. Thomas.*

and an older neighborhood was stigmatized as being "old-fashioned," confirming the accuracy of Sorokin's views on social mobility and rate of change. Only when new money became old and the traditional values were accepted did the heirs of the great industrial fortunes settle down to one place. For their ancestors, however, permanence was found only in Laurel Hill Cemetery, where they recreated their city residential patterns, recalling in death the social order of the living. But there their pretentious architectural decisions were final, and the nouveau riche street, with George Childs, Widener and his partner William Kemble, and around the corner Hamilton Disston, was stable (see Figure 4-10).

Notes

1. The fundamental issues of this essay were first presented in a seminar for Theodore Hershberg and the Philadelphia Social History Project in the spring of 1977. Their interest made it apparent that the questions that architectural history usually posed were less than vital to an understanding of the nineteenth-century city—but it was equally apparent that architecture and the physical form of the city were ignored by the social historian at his peril. The city's architectural history remains to be written; however, a number of important foundation blocks are already in place: Richard Webster, *Philadelphia Preserved* (Philadelphia: Temple University Press, 1976); Edward Teitelman and Richard W. Longstreth, *Architecture in Philadelphia, A Guide* (Cambridge, Mass.: M.I.T. Press, 1974); George B. Tatum, *Penn's Great Town* (Philadelphia: University of Pennsylvania Press, 1961); Theodore B. White, ed., *Philadelphia Architecture in the Nineteenth Century* (Philadelphia: The Art Alliance Press, 1953). In addition, see The Philadelphia Museum of Art, *Philadelphia: Three Centuries of American Art,* ed. Darrell Sewell (Philadelphia: Philadelphia Museum of Art, 1976). Also, for social commentary on architecture, see Nathaniel Burt, *The Perennial Philadelphians: The Anatomy of an American Aristocracy* (Boston: Little, Brown and Company, 1963) and E. Digby Baltzell, *Philadelphia Gentlemen: The Making of a National Upper Class* (Chicago: Quadrangle Books, 1971).

2. The best study to date of choice in residence is Herbert J. Gans, *The Levittowners: Ways of Life and Politics in a New Suburban Community* (London: Pantheon Books, 1967), pp. 22-43.

3. The Delaware River was one of the major transit systems before the railroad, providing access to Nicholas Biddle's retreat at Andalusia, as well as serving the river suburbs of Burlington, Salem, and so on. Farther south, resorts such as Cape May depended for their success on the Delaware.

4. Stuart M. Blumin, "Residential Mobility within the Nineteenth-Century City," in *The Peoples of Philadelphia: A History of Ethnic Groups and Lower Class Life, 1790-1940,* ed. Allen F. Davis and Mark H. Haller (Philadelphia: Temple University Press, 1973), pp. 37-51.

5. Burt, *Perennial Philadelphians,* pp. 513-35.

6. Ibid., p. 530.

7. Baltzell, *Philadelphia Gentlemen,* pp. 173-222.

8. Ibid., p. 213.

9. Martha Lamb, *The Homes of America* (New York: D. Appleton and Company, 1879), p. 10.

10. Robert Venturi, Denise Scott Brown, Steven Izenour, exhibition at the Renwick Gallery, Washington, D.C., *Signs of Life: Symbols in the American City,* with catalog of the same title.

11. Andrew Jackson Downing, *The Architecture of Country Houses* (New York: D. Appleton and Company, 1850). This was the most popular and influential book on housing of the nineteenth century. The type remained popular until the end of the century with Philadelphians Samuel Sloan, Isaac Hobbs, and William L. Price contributing to the genre. Despite Downing, few later authors argued that republican simplicity was the end of American architecture.

12. Downing, *Architecture of Country Houses,* pp. 266-67.

13. Nicholas B. Wainwright, ed., *A Philadelphia Perspective: The Diary of Sidney George Fisher Covering the Years 1834-1871* (Philadelphia: Historical Society of Pennsylvania, 1967), p. 18.

14. The first American architectural journal was published by the Philadelphia architect Samuel Sloan, *The Architectural Review and American Builders' Journal,* which lasted from 1869 to 1870. Six years later, the Boston-based *American Architect and Building News* was established, lasting nearly three-quarters of a century. The first local building column appeared in *The Philadelphia Inquirer* in 1887.

15. The various codes of the City of Philadelphia depict the evolution of the efforts to regulate building.

16. Apparently other real estate guides were published; see *A History of Real Estate, Building and Architecture in New York City* (New York: Record and Guide, 1898).

17. For biographical materials on Stephen D. Button, see Richard Webster, "Stephen D. Button," M.A. thesis, University of Delaware, 1963; also *American Architect and Building News* 37 (July 16, 1892): 37.

18. John Notman has been discussed by Francis J. Dallett, "John Notman, Architect," *The Princeton University Library Chronicle* 20 (Spring 1953): 127-39. Notman was the subject of an exhibition in the Athenaeum, Philadelphia, with a catalog by Constance Greiff, Autumn 1978.

19. See James F. O'Gorman, George E. Thomas, Hyman Myers, *The Architecture of Frank Furness* (Philadelphia: Philadelphia Museum of Art, 1973); Baltzell, *Philadelphia Gentlemen,* p. 219.

20. A monograph on Theophilus Parsons Chandler is being prepared by Theodore Sande and William Bassett. Sande's unpublished research paper on Chandler (1961) is on file at the library of the University of Pennsylvania.

21. Although Hale has attracted much attention, he has received little research; see Obituary, *The American Architect and Building News* 92 (September 27, 1909): 96; George E. Thomas, "Willis G. Hale," "Peter A. B. Widener Mansion," in *Philadelphia: Three Centuries of American Art,* ed. Sewell, pp. 421-22.

22. Decker regularly advertised in a commercial who's who of the era. See *Philadelphia and Popular Philadelphians* (Philadelphia: The North American, 1891), p. 223.

23. Walter Cope and John Stewardson have been discussed by William Stewardson, "Cope and Stewardson: The Architects of the Philadelphia Renaissance,"

senior thesis Princeton University, 1960; Ralph Adams Cram, "The Work of Mssrs. Cope and Stewardson," *The Architectural Review* 16 (November 1904): 401-38.

24. Trumbauer has attracted the attention of the scholarly organization, Classical America, but he has yet to be the subject of a monograph. See Ralph Adams Cram, "A New Influence in Philadelphia—The Works of Horace Trumbauer," *The Architectural Review* 15 (February 1904): 93-121. See also George E. Thomas, "Horace Trumbauer," in *Philadelphia: Three Centuries of American Art*, ed. Sewell, pp. 480-83.

25. The T-Square Club is discussed in George E. Thomas," William L. Price: Builder of Men and of Buildings," Ph.D. dissertation, University of Pennsylvania, 1975, pp. 63-66.

26. The contacts of Downing and Notman are mentioned in Dallett, "John Notman, Architect," pp. 134-35, and Wainwright, ed., *Philadelphia Perspective.*

27. The Notman-Hewitt connection continued with the Gibson family which hired Hewitt to design a spectacular mansion, "Maybrooke," at Wynnewood in 1881. See the Rev. S. F. Hotchkin, *Rural Pennsylvania* (Philadelphia: George W. Jacobs and Company, 1891), p. 106. Gibson contributed to the Pennsylvania Academy of the Fine Arts (Furness and Hewitt, 1871-1876), and his Gibson collection is one of the cornerstones of the Academy's holdings.

28. Button's parvenu clientele continued in Cape May, where he designed hotels for the railroad magnates and built small cottages and Methodist churches. See George E. Thomas and Carl E. Doebley, *Cape May: Queen of the Seaside Resorts* (Philadelphia: The Art Alliance Press, 1976).

29. Webster, *Philadelphia Preserved*, p. 74.

30. Bruce Laurie, "Fire Companies and Gangs in Southwark: The 1840's," in *The Peoples of Philadelphia*, ed. Davis and Haller, pp. 71-88.

31. The relationship between religion and class affiliation in Philadelphia is discussed in Baltzell, *Philadelphia Gentlemen*, pp. 223-61. Presbyterians have been omitted from this study because they alone consistently bridge the two communities, both in location and in the choice of architect. That would seem to indicate that Presbyterians were the most socially as well as economically mobile Philadelphians.

32. The only similarly fluid period since the post-Civil War era has been the generation after World War II, when many architects from other centers attained success in Philadelphia, in particular Vincent G. Kling and G. Holmes Perkins.

33. George W. Hewitt is mentioned in *Philadelphia and Popular Philadelphians*, pp. 223-24; George E. Thomas, "George W. Hewitt," in *Philadelphia: Three Centuries of American Art*, ed. Sewell, p. 389.

34. The location of the Ashkenazic congregation Rodef Sholom in North Philadelphia corresponds to the known distribution of a significant middle-class German population. The role of the Jewish community in Philadelphia society is discussed in Baltzell, *Philadelphia Gentlemen*, pp. 279-85.

35. Elizabeth B. Yarnall, *Addison Hutton: Quaker Architect* (Philadelphia: The Art Alliance, 1974). Hutton worked for many of the banks of Philadelphia that later hired Furness, notably the Provident Life and Trust Company and the Philadelphia Saving Fund Society. From his office came several important nineteenth-century architects, particularly Walter Cope and William L. Price, both of old Philadelphia Quaker families.

36. Leslie L. Beller, "Henry A. Sims," M. A. thesis, University of Pennsylvania, 1976.

37. Sloan was the author of numerous books on suburban houses and built extensively in the Rittenhouse Square and West Philadelphia regions. His career was wrecked during the Civil War by his obvious pro-Southern sympathies. Harold N. Cooledge, Jr., "Samuel Sloan (1815-1884), Architect," Ph.D. dissertation, University of Pennsylvania, 1963. McArthur was a socially mobile Scots Presbyterian whose connections and talents were rewarded in 1871 with the commission for the Philadelphia City Hall. Lawrence Wodehouse, "John McArthur, Jr. (1823-1890)," *Journal of the Society of Architectural Historians* 28 (December 1969): 271-83.

38. James H. Windrim is mentioned in John C. Poppeliers, "The 1867 Philadelphia Masonic Temple Competition," *Journal of the Society of Architectural Historians* 26 (December 1967): 279-84; *Philadelphia and Popular Philadelphians,* p. 9.

39. In 1880 Button lived in unfashionable Camden, New Jersey; Chandler owned a house near Rittenhouse Square at 318 South 16th Street; Furness resided at the very old but still acceptable 711 Locust Street, near his brother's house on Washington Square; Decker lived in North Philadelphia at 618 Callowhill Street, in the neighborhood of rail yards; Hale lived at 624 Locust Street. Cope and Stewardson still lived with their parents in Germantown and Chestnut Hill; Notman had lived at 1430 Spruce Street from 1842 until his death in 1865.

40. Many of Trumbauer's great houses are mentioned in Vincent J. Scully and Antoinette F. Downing, *The Architectural Heritage of Newport* (Cambridge: Harvard University Press, 1952), and Harry Desmond and Herbert Croly, *Stately Mansions of America* (New York: D. Appleton and Company, 1903).

41. For a discussion of the disengagement of the Philadelphia upper classes from political activity see Sam Bass Warner, Jr., *The Private City: Philadelphia in Three Periods of Its Growth* (Philadelphia: The University of Pennsylvania Press, 1968), pp. 79-98.

42. Several of the Episcopal churches had distinctly North Philadelphia antecedents. For example, Martin Maloney commissioned an Episcopal chapel in a curiously incongruous Roman style at Spring Lake, New Jersey. Trumbauer produced the design; in 1891, nine years earlier, the same Martin Maloney had commissioned Hale to design his Spring Lake resort house.

43. Trumbauer's city houses in the Rittenhouse vicinity are painfully conspicuous, being generally of light limestone with French academic details, while the old families relied on colonial revivals and English styles to express what Ralph Adams Cram called "ethnic community." The most telling contrast occurs on the 1600 block of Locust Street, in the shadow of St. Mark's Episcopal Church where two colonial revival houses by Walter Cope and John Stewardson are overshadowed by Trumbauer's *beaux arts* town house for E. C. Knight.

44. Veblen's views on architecture are notorious—but often accurate. See Thorstein Veblen, *The Theory of the Leisure Class* (New York: New American Library, 1953), pp. 80-118.

45. Scott attended Faires Classical Institute, one of the principal signs of upper-class affiliation. For a listing of its students and their careers, see Charles J. Cohen, *Memoirs of Rev. John Wiley Faires, A.M.D.D.* (Philadelphia: privately printed, 1926), pp. 710-11.

CHAPTER 5 "Ramcat" and
Rittenhouse Square:
Related Communities

DENNIS CLARK

The Historical Context

The precincts of privilege exercise a powerful fascination on people who
have never shared the life-style of the upper class. From Beacon Hill in
Boston to Nob Hill in San Francisco the preserves of wealth and snobbery
have had a magnetic effect upon the imagination of an otherwise democratic
America. This curiosity and interest apply especially to the residential
domains of the elite in the Victorian age when bejeweled matrons in resplendent coaches were trotted up to the graceful doorways of Fifth Avenue
mansions or stately Philadelphia town houses. Indeed, Philadelphia's
Rittenhouse Square in the second half of the last century was something of
a synonym for upper-class status. It came to symbolize architectural elegance, aristocratic demeanor, and elite opulence. But this symbol that we
have known is only a partial reflection of reality.[1]

It is no accident that our vision of upper-class communities in urban
America has been distorted. The dazzling image of their rich and powerful
residents has kept us from placing such neighborhoods in the same context
with the industrial disorder and swelling urbanism which surrounded them.
They have been described more often in romantic than analytic terms. We
have really seen only one level of areas like Rittenhouse Square—the "Upstairs" and not the "Downstairs."[2] Two broad conditions have retarded the
historical study of urban community life and prevented the development of
a complete perspective on wealthy areas. The speed with which many neighborhoods grew and the disorder of the American urban experience in general
have blurred our view of the process of community establishment and
growth. In addition, most American historians in the twentieth century
have emphasized the broad, integrating aspects of life in the United States,

concentrating on the political and military scene at the national level. Only recently have they begun to appreciate the extraordinary range of communities in America which were for too long the exclusive province of the provincial, indeed eccentric writer. Hence, Charles Dickens, James Bryce, and Henry James could all recoil from the apparent chaos and polyglot vitality of American cityscapes while patriotic scholars stood by, unprepared to substitute informed and thoughtful commentaries for the negative observations of such eminent authors.

The growth of sociology and then of social history has done much to eliminate this scholarly oversight. From such pioneering works as Harvey Zorbaugh's *The Gold Coast and the Slum,* published in 1929, we have progressed to computerized studies of community change.[3] But despite its title, Zorbaugh's early book did little to compare the Gold Coast and the slum, and we still lack studies that trace the relationship between one kind of community and another. Analyses of ethnic enclaves, so important for an understanding of our urban past, have tended to fix on one group at a time. The complexity and interrelations of pluralism have not often been shown.[4]

What has been written about Rittenhouse Square and the large Irish area adjacent to it constitutes a clear example of the imbalance in our social history of the nineteenth century and urban studies today. The square itself has been the subject of an impressive literature. There are books on its notable residents, its architecture, and its social structure. E. Digby Baltzell's classic, *Philadelphia Gentlemen: The Making of a National Upper Class,* devotes considerable space to it. Because memoirs, biographies, and guidebooks refer to it repeatedly, we have much material on its wealthy families and their Victorian life-style.[5] But we know all too little about the area behind Rittenhouse Square to the south and west, and yet this neighborhood was as extraordinary in its own way as the square itself. It was the site of an Irish community that formed in the 1830s and persisted for more than a century with remnants still present today. The history of this neighborhood testifies to the endurance of an ethnic identity even in a rapidly changing American city. Only one book deals with the area to any extent, a fine novel of working-class failure called *John Fury* by Jack Dunphy.[6]

The Other Rittenhouse

The Irish neighborhood behind Rittenhouse Square is known as Schuylkill, the name of one of Philadelphia's two rivers. The river borders the central business district on the west and loops around this Irish enclave like an enfolding arm. (see Map 5-1). A nineteenth-century crossing called Gray's Ferry also imparts its name to a portion of the area, but the more colorful appellation of "Ramcat" has been used by local people with casual imprecision to refer to the entire neighborhood.

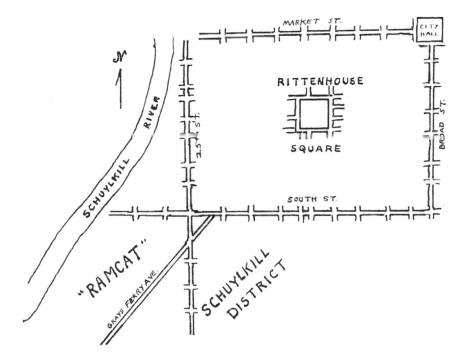

Map 5-1. The "Ramcat" and Rittenhouse Neighborhoods.

Early histories of the city record that the Schuylkill riverfront was a transfer point for trade with the rich hinterlands to the west and south of Philadelphia. Wagon routes led to Gray's Ferry, and the river shore soon became a mooring area for barges and flatboats as well as vessels in the coastwise trade which sailed up the river from Delaware Bay and the Atlantic. Thus, while Philadelphia proper was growing along the Delaware riverbank and moving westward across empty fields, the Schuylkill settlement was expanding and extending eastward to meet it.[7]

In the 1830s the booming city of Philadelphia was caught up in the first full pulse of its industrialization. The docks on the Schuylkill River were busy unloading coal and wood to fuel homes and factories all over the city. Riverfront employers required unskilled hands and strong backs, and since the 1820s the Irish had provided more and more of both. Just as in other areas at the edge of the growing city, the foreign-born were increasing in Schuylkill, and they crowded into jerry-built frame houses and shantytown districts.

The Irish women of the neighborhood took in washing, gathered bones and dung, or worked as ill-paid seamstresses or menial servants while the men performed the heavy dockside labor of coal heavers and longshoremen. In 1835 these men staged one of the first strikes of unskilled labor in American history, but the reaction of the Philadelphia elite was so swift and hostile that all the city's unions felt threatened.[8] In the Irish community children were always expected to work. Some were indentured for 7 or 14 years as tannery boys, hostlers, or carters; others were put out simply to acquire some discipline, especially if they were orphans, runaways, or delinquents. As early as 1837 a soup society was providing nourishment of body as well as soul to the poor of the area. The census of 1841 showed 49 percent of the workers in Schuylkill to be unskilled or semiskilled. Many worked in the numerous brickyards that had sprung up in the district.[9]

During the great influx following the famine of 1845-46 the Irish population of Philadelphia grew swiftly from about 40,000 to 70,000.[10] In the Schuylkill neighborhood the 1850 census listed over 1,700 as Irish born, 43 percent of the total population. Most lived between Lombard Street and Shippen (now Bainbridge), 18th Street and the river bank.[11] Others lived adjacent to the United States Naval Asylum or the Federal Arsenal near the river. In addition to the many who worked as stevedores, some were employed as weavers, wool sorters, stonecutters, carpenters, and shoemakers. There was even a doctor, J. F. Galey, in the area as well as a chemist-pharmacist named John Murry.[12] According to a sample of taxpayers whose ratables were recorded in 1850, some Irish had also begun to accumulate land. "General B. Riley" held 21 acres south of the built-up area. Mary Lafferty owned nine acres and Christianna Lafferty two and one-half along with a dwelling and a barn, while James Lafferty kept an inn. John K. Kane counted 110 acres among his possessions, and John McConnell owned some brick kilns. But they were exceptional. Of the 35 Irish males listed in the surviving tax assessment ledger, 15 were laborers and others were dairymen, basketmakers or small farmers living at the city's edge.[13] Still, these holders of skilled jobs and real property reveal an important feature of the Irish urban condition in 1850. By the middle of the nineteenth century there was a nucleus of example and leadership in the Irish community on the Schuylkill. Originally composed largely of coal heavers, it had diversified and expanded. It was still primarily working-class, but by 1850 it had developed some economic variety and a social structure of its own.

But the growth of the Irish population represented an incremental social threat to the accustomed order of cities like Philadelphia. To the native American the Irish represented disease, especially tuberculosis and cholera, afflictions which were commonly considered to be the scourge of the Great Jehovah upon the superstitious Papists. The Irish were manifestly partial to alcohol, a vice terrible to the mind of the Protestant leadership. They were in need of education, yet would not send their children to the public schools where Protestantism prevailed. They were unskilled in cities where industrial development demanded not only strong bodies but also new skills. As voters, they were enthusiastically democratic, thus imperiling upper-class control of local government. The Irish were also deeply entangled with crime; they were identified not only with gang violence and other disorder but also with the gambling circles of horse racing and illegal boxing. Secret societies and anti-English nationalist groups added a further dimension to the danger which their presence supplied. Finally, they were conceived by educated people to be a separate race, inherently different and inferior. A group alien and intractable, they were seen as fit for servitude but little else. Perhaps most vexatious of all, they refused to accept their public image and contested it with a vanity only exceeded by the vigor of their protest. Their growing numbers were a deeply unsettling intrusion on the social stability of Philadelphia and other American cities.

In the 1840s anti-Irish and anti-Catholic feelings rose dramatically in Philadelphia in part because of the famous riots of 1844. In April of that year Catholic weavers fired on a Protestant political rally in Kensington, and in retaliation Protestant attackers burned two Catholic churches near the Delaware River and later besieged another in South Philadelphia. To the Irish Catholics the disorders were simply the most flagrant example of their alienation from the general community.[14] In Schuylkill one response was the formation of the Rangers, the city's first large-scale criminal gang. More than the poverty and harsh dockside conditions of the area, the Rangers came to signify this Irish community to the rest of the city. Under the leadership of Billy Keating and Jim Haggerty the gang engaged in petty thievery, mugging, burglary, intimidation, and prostitution and controlled the neighborhood. It extorted payments from barge and ship owners along the waterfront and was energetically successful until 1857 when Mayor

Richard Vaux and a tough local police lieutenant named John Flaherty drove Billy Keating from the city and broke the reign of the Schuylkill Rangers.[15]

In the mid-nineteenth century privation and struggle profoundly influ-- enced the Schuylkill area, giving it a tough image and a strong memory of immigrant suffering. Unemployment and low wages took their toll on both family life and individual opportunity, especially when the pace of the city's economy slackened during hard times. To go "over the River" in "Ramcat" meant being sent to the Philadelphia Almshouse at Blockley in nearby West Philadelphia. In 1855 *The Evening Bulletin* observed that an "army of paupers" afflicted the city, requiring a chain of soup kitchens to stave off starvation. "The Irish," the paper said, "generally compose more than two-thirds of the population of the Almshouse."[16] But in "Ramcat" no one had to read the *Bulletin* to know how bad it was.

In Full Flower: "Ramcat" and Rittenhouse in 1880

To view the Schuylkill community in 1880 is to see it greatly enlarged but still with many of the same problems. Its role in the larger fabric of the city had changed. In line with the specialization of social and spatial relation- ships which followed consolidation of the city in 1854, portions of the area closest to the square emerged as an exclusive, upper-class residential enclave amidst the homes and shops of the less well-to-do. This concentration of wealth at the heart of the area created a web of interdependencies between rich and poor, Protestant and Irish Catholic, which marked a new stage in the history of Rittenhouse. The number of blocks occupied by houses and businesses had expanded fivefold. The district now spread between Broad Street and the Schuylkill River for 13 blocks south of Lombard Street in- stead of just six as in 1850. Not four, but 40,000 lived in the area, and more than 22,000 of these were Irish-born or the children of Irish-born. Doubt- less, many others were of Irish background further back in their families. The heaviest concentration of Irish had moved from the eastern edge of the area above Fitzwater Street to the bend in the River above Grays Ferry Avenue. With more than 9,000 Irish-born and their relatives in a neighbor- hood only a mile square, the ethnic identity of the district was patent. It was the most thoroughly Irish section of the city.[17]

Mingled with the row houses in "Ramcat" were many industrial and commercial activities that helped give Philadelphia its manufacturing and business character in the second half of the nineteenth century. There were 18 textile and fabric-processing mills scattered throughout the district. Coal and lumber yards were still very important; there were 38 such fuel and wood businesses, while 98 building and construction enterprises gave work to local men. More than 300 food outlets dotted the streets, and no less than 174 liquor purveyors catered to the thirst of the workers and residents.[18]

But despite all this economic activity "Ramcat" still had many poor people. The Western Soup Society at 1613 South Street was busy in the area, and its register for 1878-79 contained mostly Irish names. Catherine Kane and her four children of 2023 Federal Street received two and a half quarts of soup that winter; Catherine McIlhenny and her five children who lived at 1815 Naudain Street got a similar portion. Barney Clark of 507 South 21st Street brought his eight children to obtain eight quarts, and Annie Conway and her one child took soup home to their ironic address, 202 Prosperous Alley.[19]

To be a "souper" was to risk the contempt of the rest of the Irish community. The charter of the Western Soup Society bound it to give "helpful instructions and guidance" which were usually religious in nature. The pride of these Irish Catholics was doubly offended by having some of their number going as supplicants to a charity that put Protestantism in its soup. According to its subscription book, the society's supporters were Wanamakers and Lippincotts, Yarnalls and Lewises, the same fashionable Philadelphians who lived around Rittenhouse Square.[20] To be forced to take Protestant soup after having resisted all manner of anti-Catholic intimidation in both Ireland and the United States was to accept a potion laced with gall.

As Philadelphia became more prosperous and developed its prime land more intensively, more employment became available, even for the Irish. After the Civil War the downtown greatly expanded its retail and entertainment functions, opening opportunities for the Irish to work in a variety of jobs within walking distance of the Schuylkill neighborhood. The Irish took positions as singing waiters, doormen, bartenders, hotel maids, telegraph runners, cab drivers, firemen, and policemen. Such service jobs supplemented the hard labor in industry with which the Irish were identified and that was swelling the fortunes of the city's most successful entrepreneurs.

The neighborhood was now also linked with the transportation industry in Philadelphia. In addition to working in the factories of Schuylkill, the Irish were fixtures on the railroads by 1880; they were employed in the track gangs and as switchmen, trainmen, freight handlers, and engineers. The Philadelphia, Wilmington and Baltimore Railroad ran across Washington Avenue from Grays Ferry. Later the Baltimore and Ohio would have a terminal beside the Schuylkill at Chestnut Street. The mighty Pennsylvania Railroad owned and operated a huge terminal and switching yard west of the Schuylkill above Market Street. These railroads provided jobs for many of "Ramcat's" males.[21]

At 26th and South streets there were horsecar "turn arounds" and carbarns. Many Irish worked on the horsecar lines as drivers, conductors, and maintenance men. The 1880s were a terrible period for labor unrest on these lines, and many Schuylkill residents suffered accordingly. There were numerous strikes as traction magnates P. A. B. Widener and William L.

Elkins unified the city's 17 transit companies into a transportation empire. Working conditions on the lines were abominable. The daily wage for drivers who worked 15 to 18 hours was a mere $1.50. No time off for meals was allowed. Any labor union activity meant instant dismissal. In 1886 a 12-hour day was achieved as well as some other improvements, but more strikes lay ahead, and they would be both bitter and violent.[22]

Catholic parishes in the Schuylkill area grew with the Irish population. Founded in 1839, St. Patrick's predated the extensive development of either Rittenhouse Square or "Ramcat." It began in a makeshift chapel converted from a warehouse. A lot at 20th and Rittenhouse streets was secured in 1841, but it took 23 years to pay the mortgage. As the new church was being erected, money was so scarce that the struggling parish school had to be closed. St. Charles parish at 20th and Christian streets was begun in 1868 in surroundings described by one writer as having "more brick-clay ponds and frogs" than parishioners. By 1876, however, so great was the post-Civil War housing boom that the area was mostly built up, and the church was the third largest in the city. Farther south a third parish, St. Anthony's, was launched in 1857 at Grays Ferry Road and Carpenter Street. By 1893 a Romanesque structure with sculptures imported from Paris was dedicated in ceremonies illuminated by new devices using electricity.[23]

Through these churches active charitable work helped the hard-pressed in the community. In each parish the St. Vincent dePaul Society distributed food, clothing, and furniture, while the church "poor box" supported additional aid. The parish gave Irish families access to Catholic schools, hospitals, orphanages, and mutual aid societies. The House of the Good Shepherd, located in St. Patrick's parish from 1850 to 1880, was a refuge for those girls who had fallen into a "life of shame," for in Philadelphia prostitution was still a predominantly Irish pursuit at this time.[24]

As early as 1836 there was a little schoolhouse in the Schuylkill area, but public schools did not attract large numbers of area children until the second half of the nineteenth century. By 1880 various public schools in the neighborhood each enrolled between 400 and 600 children. The Pollock School at 24th and Christian streets was the local secondary school, and it drew students from Primary School No. 5 at 20th and Catharine streets and No. 7 at 24th and Christian. St. Patrick's Parish opened a day school under Daniel Devitt in 1839 and later a free school for boys was begun under the same auspices by Richard Patrick McCunney, a graduate of the Irish college in Salamanca. His wife, Bridget Kearney McCunney, instituted a dormitory for girls in her home at 19th and Sansom streets and taught her pupils reading and sewing. The largest parochial school in the city in 1853, St. Patrick's remained one of the most popular for the balance of the nineteenth century. In 1880 only four other parish schools reported more students than the 900 enrolled at St. Patrick's, and together with the nearby schools of St. Charles' and St. Anthony's, it educated the great majority of the Irish Catholic children in the downtown area.

Progress beyond the elementary level was slow for the children of working-class Irish families in Philadelphia. In 1850 only four boys from Schuylkill with Irish names were among the 180 admitted to Central High School, the city's leading post-elementary school. Thirty years later only two boys from this ethnic neighborhood were among the 134 Central entrants. But the desire for advanced education among the Irish grew, and Schuylkill children eventually began to make their way to such Catholic high schools as St. Joseph's and La Salle in the central city.[25]

Thus the Schuylkill community pursued its own well-being at a time when no aid could be expected from government and when the toll upon working people from economic insecurity was harsh. But with the multiplication of employment opportunities and the gradual improvement of their relative job position, the Irish increased their chances for stability. An urban lifestyle developed that included merry christenings at O'Brien's Hall at 20th and Federal streets. There were also political meetings, picnics, and sports at outings of the five local divisions of the Ancient Order of Hibernians. Parish celebrations were frequent. The swift gossip and mocking banter so much a part of Irish life provided daily amusement. Through it all the more serious striving for betterment continued. Education and respectability became the goals of an increasing number of Irish families.

While the drama of working-class community life was being unfolded south of Lombard Street, the land immediately adjacent to Rittenhouse Square was also being developed. Actually, some of the earliest residents of the Square were Irishmen. When its borders were still a jumble of brickyards, stables, and open lots, some shrewd businessmen sensed its promise, for they built good homes on what was then inexpensive land. Thomas Hunter, Irish-born, Protestant, and founder of the Acme Tea Company which would later succeed so handsomely, erected a "mansion" on the square in the 1820s. In the 1840s William Devine, a textile manufacturer of similar background, lived at 1800-1802 Rittenhouse Square. One of the earliest to put up a home on the Square was John O'Fallon, American agent for the Queen of Spain, whose legal fees made him wealthy. He, like the Philadelphia family of Baron John Keating, had ties to the numerous Irishmen who served in the armed forces of France and Spain. Purchasing a brickyard, he built a large home at 216 South 19th Street. These men preceded the wave of fashionable Philadelphians who migrated west of Broad Street after 1850.[26]

The growth of commercial activity east of Broad Street in the mid-nineteenth century made the old city less and less attractive to families who could afford to choose their residential locations. As a result, a movement west along Walnut Street began. Born in Ireland, John A. Brown became a wealthy banker and president of the American Sunday School Union; he lived at 12th and Chestnut streets in 1828 but later moved to Rittenhouse Square. His Episcopalian, Presbyterian, and Methodist peers did the same. E. Digby Baltzell has skillfully described this migration and analyzed upper-class neighborhood concentration in Philadelphia. He has listed Rittenhouse Square property holders between 1850 and 1900, and this catalog is replete with the names of people of enormous wealth—railroad barons, merchant bankers, industrial tycoons, and "old Philadelphia" families with roots in the city's colonial history.

On South Rittenhouse Square Thomas Scott, president of the Pennsylvania Railroad, lived only a few steps from the banker Francis Drexel and Thomas Wanamaker, the son of the founder of the great department store. Diagonally across the Square on 19th Street Tench Coxe, descendent of an eighteenth-century Philadelphia family, shared a block with Samuel Bodine, president of the city's gas monopoly; S. Weir Lewis, China merchant and banker; Joshua Lippincott, publisher; and A. J. Cassatt, another president of the Pennsylvania Railroad. A self-made millionaire in cotton manufacturing, John McFadden resided along the Walnut Street edge of the square, hoping no doubt that his Episcopalianism and his art collection might make his neighbors overlook his Irish name. Nearby were Charles Edward Ingersoll, lawyer; George S. Pepper, philanthropist; Algernon Sidney Roberts, heir to an iron fortune; and Thomas Dolan, owner of the Keystone Knitting Mills. On the 18th Street side of the square Joseph Harrison, railroad entrepreneur, built his huge and ornate mansion. "At no other time in the city's' history, before or since," wrote Baltzell, "have so many wealthy and fashionable families lived so near one another."[27] These were the men who dominated a Philadelphia in which as early as 1860 50 percent of the wealth was owned by 1 percent of the population, while the lower 80 percent owned only 3 percent of the city's real and personal property. This aggregation of money and power was more diverse in its background than might be presumed. Irish Protestants, Germans, and Dutch among others were included, but the standards and manners of Rittenhouse Square were set by the Anglo-American culture that characterized upper-class life in Victorian America.

It is difficult for Americans today to imagine the grandeur of the elite life-style of a Rittenhouse Square at the end of the nineteenth century. Because of geographic dispersal by the "better sort" and the concomitant inner-city poverty, the extraordinary baroque monuments of that age have steadily disappeared from our city streets. The class culture of such neighborhoods created what amounted to a fairyland of elegance and display protected by Victorian codes of civility and discrimination. These enclaves of privilege combined architectural eclecticism with passionate embellishment, lavish furnishings, and an adoration of English upper-class family etiquette. Flamboyant architects like Frank Furness and Theophilus Chandler designed edifices for an almost hysterical display of wealth—here a mansion for the sugar baron James Scott, there a Renaissance palace for Mrs. Sarah Drexel Fell. The structures on the square became wildly adorned shrines to aggressive vanity and the obsessive flaunting of riches.[28]

But an aristocratic way of life requires much more than money and manners if it is to remain in ascendancy. It demands presumptions of superiority, the exercise of assured authority, and the collaboration of a servant class to do the thousands of jobs necessary to guarantee an elaborate system of personal comforts and princely appointments. The *haute monde* of the Victorian elite was perhaps a contradiction in a democratic society, but that society was not yet competent to act on any such judgment. The working people who served were often from such impoverished backgrounds that they had no choice but to serve, and some may even have been beguiled into servility by the mere thought of association with the elegance which they labored to support.

Servants and Masters

In the 1880s Rittenhouse Square was the scene of an interdependent relationship between rich and poor. A wealthy matron going about her morning's business of directing and maintaining her household would have had to deal with Mary Ellen in the nursery, Catharine, the upstairs maid, and Bridget in the kitchen. But, in addition, she would probably have had recourse to the services of a variety of others in the neighborhood. Maria Moran of 2008 Lombard Street might have been summoned to do the heavy laundry. Mary O'Brien of 1938 Locust Street, a dressmaker, might have been engaged to alter a ball gown. Ed McKeown of 521 South 24th Street would have come as arranged to drive madam to the print shop of Stephen Farrelly at 248 South 21st Street to choose designs for an invitation to a musical gala. If madam's nose told her that the privy in the rear used by the servants needed attention, she would send for McAnanny and Brannan of the Quaker City Odorless Excavating Company on South Street. Meanwhile, the household maids would have been pressed to get on with the ironing— some 200,000 square feet of wrinkle-free curtains, linens, clothes, and oddments each year.[29]

The servants required to prepare and serve the meals, shop, clean the household, do the laundry, and care for all the details of the privileged establishments on Rittenhouse Square were drawn for the most part from the South Philadelphia Irish community. After 1850 "Irish" in Philadelphia became virtually synonymous with "servant." According to the United States census of 1870, there were 24,108 domestic servants in the city of whom 10,044 were born in Ireland. Among the remainder a large portion were of Irish parentage.[30] This concentration of Irish in household occupations was believed by most educated people to be inevitable. Sidney George Fisher, a Philadelphia diarist, observed that the Irish had "taken the position of an inferior race in the business of life, because by nature and education [they were] fitted for it."[31] But while the presence of "Bridget" in American homes may have been expedient, it was not necessarily a blessing. From the 1850s forward ladies' magazines and polite journals commonly printed columns and cartoons deprecating the Irish as servants. E. L. Godkin, editor of *The Nation,* saw them as "ignorant, helpless and degraded." Their deportment was often "presumptuous," their culinary skills calamitous, their ideas of cleanliness scandalous. Not one Irish woman in a hundred, wrote Eunice Beecher, "can by any amount of care, patience, or indefatigable teaching, be transformed into a neat, energetic, truth-telling servant."[32] In addition, being Catholics, these servants were seen as threats to the religious integrity of the family and a peril to the Protestant purity of its children.[33]

The great households of Rittenhouse Square were caught in a social dilemma. It was impossible to pursue the extravagant life-style of mannered elegance and luxury without servants, but those most readily available were from a group alien in outlook, habits, and background. Nevertheless, wealth had to make the best of it and be served by such poor as there were. The vast fortunes represented on Rittenhouse Square were created by the labor supply of the city, and the beneficiaries of those fortunes had to enjoy their wealth through the ministrations of that labor supply.

For the Irish a similar ambiguity characterized their connection with Rittenhouse Square. It was demeaning for them to be forced to serve families whose wealth was founded upon notoriously exploitative mills, factories, and railroads. These same families also supported those soup and Bible societies that sought to inveigle the Irish out of their religion by the relief of their hunger. Many a railroad pick-and-shovel man looked with deeply mixed feelings upon his daughters' employment in the great houses of men whose railroads had meant for him a lifetime of miserable toil.

Those who served in the households of the elite sometimes found the extravagance there to be offensive for its great distance from what so many counted as their meager reality. One man, who later worked as a doorman at the Union League Club on South Broad Street, recalled his amazement at the lavish meals served in the house where he was employed while families he knew three blocks away in Donnelly's Court were living mostly on bread and drippings. During a bitter transit strike a woman from county Clare who worked in a fine house on Spruce Street was able to feed her brother's family for weeks by using the scraps from her master's kitchen. Another woman remembered that her employers spoke French so that the servants would not know what was being said. But when she and her friends "below stairs" then spoke Gaelic, her mistress became furious and told her to cease or face dismissal.[34]

Maps prepared in the 1890s make it clear that in the late nineteenth century the Irish still predominated in the neighborhood behind Rittenhouse Square. The properties around the square continued to be solidly upper class, but west of 20th Street and south of Pine Street the blocks were well over 50 percent Irish. On the north side of Lombard Street, west of 23rd, 12 of the 14 row houses were owned by people with Irish names. The 2400 block of Ashburton Street was almost totally Irish. Worsted mills, the Philadelphia Galvanizing Works, and the unlovely Philadelphia Rubber Works were all scattered throughout this area. Tiny "courts" notorious for their crowding and poor sanitation, were still occupied by the Irish poor. Reaney's Court on 26th Street between Pine and Lombard was one such nest of small dwellings. The National Fire Brick Works and the coal yards rimmed the Schuylkill River. Well into the twentieth century this same pattern of ethnic and class concentration remained in the area of Rittenhouse Square.[35]

But the two worlds of "Ramcat" and Rittenhouse gradually changed. Toward the end of the nineteenth century Irish Catholics created their own wealthy class. Born near 26th and South streets, Thomas Cahill struggled as a youth to operate a coal and lumber business along the banks of the Schuylkill. Twice his stocks were washed away by floods, imperiling his efforts to support his widowed mother and her other children. Doggedly, Cahill rebuilt, and eventually he amassed a fortune. Remembering that as a boy he had been rejected by Central High School because he was "too young" even though he had passed the entrance examination, Cahill left his wealth to build Roman Catholic High School, the first such school to be run by a diocese in the nation.[36]

In the early twentieth century some Irish Catholics gravitated into the physical and social orbit of Rittenhouse Square. Constance O'Hara, daughter of a prominent physician, became one of its leading citizens. The Sisters of Notre Dame opened a fashionable finishing school on the west side of the square. Michael Francis Doyle, a brilliant attorney whose work saved the life of Eamon deValera in 1916 when the Irish leader was condemned to death by the British, bought a house on the square. Some say that he vowed to buy the property when he was turned away from the front door as a delivery boy and told to go to the rear. Ultimately, too, John McShain, a wealthy contractor, would purchase the Barclay Hotel, an elite facility best known for debutante parties.[37] But the square was no longer what it once had been.

By the 1930s the great fortunes were under siege. The income tax and the depression had reduced the ability of the rich to disport themselves as had their fathers and grandfathers before them. In 1928 the Republican's party's traditional hegemony in Philadelphia politics had been challenged for the first time, and now a popular Democratic contractor, John B. Kelly, was working furiously for Franklin D. Roosevelt. In "Ramcat" the Republican machine which had provided jobs and contracts for decades was not secure.

In 1928 almost 40 percent of the voters in its two wards, the 30th and the 36th, cast Democratic ballots.[38] A new era was at hand, and the dominance of the "Philadelphia Gentlemen" was passing. Apartment houses were encroaching on Rittenhouse Square, and the elite were leaving the city. Indeed, by 1930 most had already left. The automobile was rapidly eroding many of the old neighborhood identities and altering the geography of class.

As those whose families had reigned resplendent on Rittenhouse Square in the 1880s declined or decamped, the square became drab and unkempt. The great houses were shuttered, demolished, or converted to apartments. The flocks of servants to tend them were no longer affordable or fashionable. The girls from "Ramcat" were becoming secretaries or nurses; some were even going to high school and college. But while old ideas about and among the Irish were being modified, those in the Social Register still could not bring themselves actually to mingle with them in clubs or social activities. The social distance between wealthy Philadelphians and the workers and servants of "Ramcat" had decreased somewhat, but the memory of the earlier gulf and exploitation persisted. Even as late as the second half of the twentieth century it was not all that uncommon to hear Philadelphians of Irish heritage refer to the erstwhile area of social privilege west of Broad Street and south of Market as "Rottenhouse Square."

Notes

1. Charles J. Cohen, *Rittenhouse Square: Past and Present* (Philadelphia: privately printed, 1922), p. vii; Nathaniel Burt, *The Perennial Philadelphians: The Anatomy of an American Aristocracy* (Boston: Little, Brown and Co., 1963).

2. Cleveland Amory, *Who Killed Society* (New York: Harper Brothers, 1960).

3. Harvey Zorbaugh, *The Gold Coast and the Slum* (Chicago: University of Chicago Press, 1929).

4. Two recent exceptions to this unilateral treatment of ethnic communities have been Jay Dolan, *The Immigrant Church* (Notre Dame, Ind.: University of Notre Dame Press, 1975) and Kenneth Kusmer, *A Ghetto Takes Shape: Black Cleveland* (Urbana, Ill.: University of Illinois Press, 1976). Although largely in terms of arithmetic variables, Stephan Thernstrom's *The Other Bostonians* (Cambridge, Mass.: Harvard University Press, 1973) also sets ethnic group development against the broader society.

5. E. Digby Baltzell, *Philadelphia Gentlemen: The Making of a National Upper Class* (Glencoe, Ill.: The Free Press, 1958).

6. Jack Dunphy, *John Fury* (New York: Arno Press, 1976).

7. Joseph Oberman and Stephen Kozakowski, *History of Development in the Delaware Valley Region* (Philadelphia: Delaware Valley Regional Planning Commission, 1976), pp. 31-46.

8. Dennis Clark, *The Irish in Philadelphia* (Philadelphia: Temple University Press, 1974), p. 18; Sam Bass Warner, Jr., *The Private City: Philadelphia in Three Periods of Its Growth* (Philadelphia: University of Pennsylvania Press, 1968), p. 75.

9. Studies of the Irish community in the 1840s were pursued by Philip R. Yannella of Temple University in 1975, and his tabulations of census data were provided to the Center City Residents Association. The percentage cited is from the Yannella statistics.

10. The Irish population of Philadelphia in the late 1840s is a subject of some speculation. These figures are for the Schuylkill area and are the computerized grid tabulations of the Philadelphia Social History Project directed by Theodore Hershberg of the University of Pennsylvania. I must express appreciation to Henry Williams of the project for his very diligent aid in compiling figures from its data bank for the Schuylkill area.

11. U.S. Bureau of the Census, *Seventh Census of the United States, 1850,* manuscript files, Philadelphia Social History Project.

12. Ibid.

13. Passyunk Township: County, State and Personal Tax Assessment Ledger (1850), Archives of the City of Philadelphia.

14. David Montgomery, "The Shuttle and the Cross: Weavers and Artisans in the Kensington Riots of 1844," *Journal of Social History* 5 (Summer 1972): 411-46; Michael Feldberg, *The Philadelphia Riots of 1844: A Study of Ethnic Conflict* (Westport, Conn.: Greenwood Press, 1975).

15. George Foster, "Philadelphia in Slices," *Pennsylvania Magazine of History and Biography* 43 (January 1969): 23-72.

16. *The Evening Bulletin* (Philadelphia), December 29, 1855.

17. Philadelphia Social History Project, Selected Population Statistics (Schuylkill).

18. Philadelphia Social History Project, Selected Commercial and Industrial Statistics (Schuylkill).

19. Register of Recipients (1878-1879), Western Soup Society, Urban Archives, Paley Library, Temple University.

20. Subscription Book, Western Soup Society (1850), Urban Archives, Paley Library, Temple University.

21. These lines are shown on the maps of the Philadelphia Social History Project.

22. Sister M. Consuela, "The Church of Philadelphia (1884-1918)," in *The History of the Archdiocese of Philadelphia,* ed. James F. Connelly (Philadelphia: The Archdiocese of Philadelphia, 1976), p. 295.

23. Daniel H. Mahoney, *Historical Sketches of the Churches and Institutions of Philadelphia* (Philadelphia: Daniel Mahoney, 1895), pp. 63, 122, 149.

24. Ibid., p. 198.

25. School enrollment information for the Schuylkill area is not complete for the mid-nineteenth century, thus making comparisons between 1850 and 1880 difficult. Some information is provided in John Trevor Custis, *The Public Schools of Philadelphia: Historical Biographical, Statistical* (Philadelphia: Burk and McFettridge Co., 1897); *Sixty-Second Annual Report of the Board of Public Education of Philadelphia* (Philadelphia: E. C. Markley, 1881), pp. 79-82; *General Catalogue of the Central High School of Philadelphia* (Philadelphia: Cressey and Markley, 1855); *Semi-Centennial Celebration of the Central High School of Philadelphia* (Proceedings of the Public Meeting, October 29, 1888) Information on Catholic Schools is contained in Thomas J. Donaghy, *Philadelphia's Finest: A History of Education in the Archdiocese of Philadelphia* (Philadelphia: American Catholic Historical

Society, 1972); John E. O'Breza, "Philadelphia Parochial School System from 1830 to 1920: Growth and Bureaucratization," Ed. D. dissertation, Temple University, 1979, pp. 87-150.

26. Hunter, Divine, and John A. Brown are mentioned in Cohen, *Rittenhouse Square: Past and Present,* pp. 14, 81, 200. For O'Fallon see Clark, *Irish in Philadelphia,* p. 14.

27. Baltzell, *Philadelphia Gentlemen,* 181-86.

28. Richard J. Webster, *Philadelphia Preserved* (Philadelphia: Temple University Press, 1976), p. 108-9.

29. These names and addresses are from the Philadelphia city directories of the 1880s.

30. Blaine Edward McKinley, "The Stranger in the Gates: Employer Reactions Toward Servants in America, 1825-1875," Ph.D. dissertation, Michigan State University, 1969, p. 155.

31. Ibid., p. 161.

32. Cited in ibid., p. 162-70.

33. The "Nun of Kenmare" counselled Irish servants to be very careful of the religious issue. Mary Frances Cusack, *Advice to Irish Girls in America* (New York: F. Pastet, 1886).

34. Interviews with James Patterson, June 8, 1975; Margaret Dougherty, January 12, 1974; and Honora Conn, April 12, 1975.

35. The residential characteristics are clearly seen in the *Atlas of Philadelphia,* Vols. 2 and 7 (Philadelphia: G. M. Bromley and Co., 1889 and 1896).

36. Dennis Clark, *Proud Past: Catholic Laypeople of Philadelphia* (Philadelphia: Catholic Philopatrian Literary Society, 1976), p. 24.

37. Reflections on the decline of the square's residents and their socioeconomic class are provided by E. Digby Baltzell in his "The Protestant Establishment Revisited," *The American Scholar* 45 (Autumn 1976): 499-518. Recollections about Rittenhouse Square at the turn of the twentieth century are given by Constance O'Hara in "The Square with a Past," Golden Anniversary Lecture, The Philadelphia Art Alliance, October 1965.

38. John L. Shover, "The Emergence of a Two-Party System in Republican Philadelphia, 1924-1936," *Journal of American History* 60 (March 1974): 985-1002.

CHAPTER 6 The Relationship
between Work and
Residence in an
Industrializing City:
Philadelphia, 1880[1]

STEPHANIE W. GREENBERG

A number of studies of urban life have concluded that the social and spatial characteristics of neighborhoods have a profound impact on a variety of social processes. Geographic propinquity has been tied to friendship formation, spouse selection, and voluntary association membership.[2] All these are strongly linked to social mobility and assimilation; one's associates are critical in determining success or failure in American society.[3] While urban residential structure has been examined in great detail in twentieth-century cities, it has received relatively little attention for the nineteenth century. But it is upon the cities of this era that modern cities were built. This study examines the relationship between the location of job opportunities and the organization of residence in Philadelphia in 1880.

Review of the Literature

The urban model developed by the sociologist Ernest W. Burgess has exercised perhaps the most pervasive influence of any on the study of urban form and development. Even those who have challenged or qualified prevalent notions of urban ecology use this model as one of their main points of reference. Because of its importance we must begin with it in order to study the organization of residence in the nineteenth-century city.

Burgess and other human ecologists of the same period posited that urban spatial patterns were the result of competition among diverse groups for scarce land. The area referred to as the central business district was usually the most accessible spot in the city. Often centrally located and adjacent to a lake or river, it was the most desirable location for a wide variety of activities. Finance, retailing, wholesaling, and some types of manufacture made the most intensive use of central land and as a result were able to edge out other land uses, such as residence. In turn, the area directly surrounding the core deteriorated as landowners neglected their property in anticipation of profitable sales to businesses in an expanding central district. As the affluent and, later, middle-income groups moved away from the center to escape its noise and congestion, this adjacent area became a haven for newly arrived immigrants and other lower-class groups. This process, according to the Burgess model, accounts for the development of concentric zones of residence and increasing economic status with increasing distance from the center that have been widely observed.[4]

Others have argued that urban land use is not determined by pure competition. According to this position, the organization of urban space depends upon the needs of different economic interests. Dissimilar forms of private enterprise require different types of locations within the city. Commerce needs accessibility; some manufacturing depends upon proximity to nonlocal transportation routes and a large amount of space, and so on. These land needs are served first. Residence, particularly of working-class people, takes shape around job opportunities, wherever they may be located. The social composition of many urban neighborhoods is thereby determined by the needs of industry for specific types of labor. Thus, immigrant and working-class ghettos are not the product of the abstract ecological processes of competition, dominance, and succession but rather develop as a response to the demand for large numbers of laborers.[5]

Several studies of large cities have argued that Burgess' failure to consider carefully the work-residence relationship produced distortions in his model. For example, Maurice Davie found in a study of New Haven and Chicago in the 1930s that many of the qualities attributed to centralized immigrant ghettos, such as high population density and high rates of crime and delinquency, could be found in any area of the city that contained a large number of manufacturing jobs.[6] Hence, the deterioriation found near the center was not so much the result of an expanding business district as it was the consequence of many workers living in aging, inexpensive housing close to factories. Similarly, Eugene Ericksen and William Yancey found that in Philadelphia in 1930 it was not centrality per se which attracted workers but rather the availability of jobs and inexpensive housing.[7] To the extent that these are centralized, the city will resemble the Burgess model; in situations where this is not the case, the spatial structure of the city will deviate from the model. Studies of New York[8] and of Chicago[9] also stress the importance of the location of work opportunities in determining urban residential patterns.

But the presence of job opportunities and the location of work also influenced urban structure before the 1930s. In the preindustrial and industrializing city of the nineteenth century, mass transit was in its infancy. Slow, relatively expensive, and often inconveniently routed, it was not likely to have carried many people to work. The result was a severe limitation on where people could choose to live.[10] In Philadelphia, for example, workers in a number of industries settled in concentrations near their place of employment.[11] Sam Bass Warner's study, *The Private City,* gives careful attention to the work-residence relationship in Philadelphia over three centuries.[12] He traces the decline over time of the residential segregation of workers in some industries and the increased segregation of workers in other industries. What Warner fails to do is to evaluate systematically the effects of specific factors on this relationship.

This previous research raises a number of questions. Did industries differ in the extent to which they attracted nearby settlements of workers, and what were the characteristics of these industries that might explain such differences? Did workers in the most centralized (downtown) industries travel into the center from adjacent areas because business and manufacturing displaced housing; or was it still possible in 1880 for housing to remain in areas of intense economic activity? It is also worth asking whether or not industries that clustered at the outskirts of the city employed workers who lived apart from the rest of the population, creating, in effect, mill towns. In addition, did people avoid living close to nuisance industries whose production process involved especially high levels of noise, noxious odors, or air pollution?

The answers to these questions can be found in part by analyzing the geographic, social, and economic structure of Philadelphia in 1880. While manufacturing increasingly dominated urban economies throughout the nineteenth century, the preindustrial, walking city had not entirely disappeared. In 1880 the Industrial Revolution had yet to reach its peak in the United States. Owing to the paucity of inexpensive, fast, overland transportation routes, the markets for finished products in most industries were still small, usually no greater than regional. Even though the transcontinental railroad was completed in 1867, railroads did not become a practical means of shipping goods long distances until an efficient method of steel production was developed and put into widespread use in the 1870s.[13] Hence, most production was limited by a narrowly circumscribed market and was characterized by low mechanization and an emphasis on skilled hand trades.[14] While some of the changes in the organization of production usually associated with industrialization began to develop early in the nineteenth century, such as the "putting out" system, the assembly line, and skill debasement, manufacturing could not dominate the urban economy until the technology of steam and steel was more developed.

Owing to the relatively small scale of production, it was possible for many factories to operate near private homes. Situated in a few rooms or single small buildings, such businesses did not have to displace the local population, and their employees could live next door to or even on top of the places of production.

Data and Methods

This analysis is carried out in three steps: an examination of (1) the degree to which workers formed settlements around jobs in specific industries; (2) the effect of accessibility to jobs versus access to the center in the location of industrial workers; and (3) the relationship between the spatial pattern of industries and the residential context of workers.

The two major data sources are the original manuscripts from the United States Census of Population and the United States Census of Manufactures for Philadelphia in 1880. Beginning in 1870 the government collected detailed information on the occupation of gainfully employed persons from which that person's economic sector and industrial affiliation were inferred. The most detailed population information is currently available for adult males only. In this study statements about the industrial affiliation of the population are based on the work experience of adult males employed only in manufacturing. The Census of Manufactures provides the location of manufacturing jobs. But there are too few data on non-manufacturing workplaces in 1880, and the city's business directories can provide only a location, not the number of persons employed at a given site.[15] The industries were grouped into 44 categories in order to examine the relationship between work and residence.[16]

The individual data on population and jobs were aggregated into areal units. The roughly 7,300 one-by-one-and-a-quarter block grid units adopted by the Philadelphia Social History Project were grouped into the 404 census tracts into which the city was divided in 1930. Each individual and each job was assigned to the tract he (it) would have occupied had the city been tracted in 1880. It is assumed that jobs and population were located at the centroid of each tract. The purpose of using census tracts rather than grid units is to trace change and to permit direct comparisons of spatial measures in one city over a period of time spanning 1850 to 1970.[17]

Workplace accessibility is expressed by measuring the total number of manufacturing jobs within one mile of the center of a census tract.[18] The distance of one mile is used because it is a good approximation of the likeliest maximum distance for a one-way daily trip on foot, as described in a study of the journey to work in Philadelphia at the end of the nineteenth century.[19]

The spatial distribution of population and jobs is expressed through several measures. The two most widely used measures to express locational dissimilarities have been the indices of dissimilarity and segregation. The former indicates the proportion of one group that would have to change its location in order to be distributed identically with another group, and the latter shows the proportion of a group that would have to move in order to have the same distribution as the rest of the population. There are two other dimensions of spatial distribution which are as important as segregation in the description of the spatial distribution of population. The index of relative clustering shows the degree to which a group is clustered, on average, compared to the average amount of clustering in the entire population. The index of density shows the population per acre in the areal unit inhabited by the group's mean individual.[20]

Findings

As a first step in the analysis, a spatial typology of industries was constructed. It organizes the 44 industries under scrutiny according to those characteristics that are hypothesized to affect the work-residence relationship. The two spatial variables that are included in the classification scheme are distance from the central business district and the degree of spatial clustering of an industry's jobs. A third variable included in the scheme is the nuisance factor. A nuisance industry is defined as one whose production process creates noxious odors, noise, or filth. These characteristics are expected to repel the population, making the work-residence relationship weaker for these industries.[21]

The typology appears in Table 6-1. Four industrial spatial types are delineated. Centralized industries were typically small in scale and low in mechanization; they produced nonstandardized products and depended on frequent personal interaction between the producer and consumer during the production process.[22] Such industries were therefore dependent on the supplies and services that tended to concentrate in the central district. Next were those industries which located primarily in the second ring out from the center and were spatially dispersed. They fell into two categories—consumer-oriented and building-related. Consumer-oriented industries, such as baking, brewing, and butchering, were found in many neighborhoods just outside the core.[23] Building-related industries like lumber and stone, clay, and glass were located close to natural resources such as clay deposits, while the construction business was especially attracted to undeveloped land. Nuisance industries were located in this second ring but were concentrated into a few areas. Many of these industries embodied the coming age of steam and steel. Their location, outside the center in specialized areas, anticipated the pattern found in twentieth-century cities. Finally, highly mechanized, large-scale industries dominated the outer ring. These industries tended to be spatially concentrated, often near a swiftly running stream upon which some of them depended for power.

Having organized the 44 industries according to the variables that are hypothesized to affect the work-residence relationship, let us now examine this relationship.

WORK AND RESIDENCE AMONG 44 INDUSTRIES

It is hypothesized that workers in centrally located industries had a weaker work-residence relationship than workers in other industries because private

TABLE 6-1 Typology of Industries by Spatial Characteristics
and Nuisance Factor, Philadelphia, 1880

	Non-Nuisance		Nuisance	
	Index of relative clustering:		*Index of relative clustering:[f]*	
	1.5+	*≤1.5*	*1.5+*	*≤1.5*
Mean Distance from center:				
≤1.00 mile	Apparel	Leather[b]		
	Boots	Precious metals, jewelry		
	Brass[a]	Paper boxes		
	Confection	Printing, publishing		
	Furniture	Shirts		
	Harnesses	Tailoring		
	Instruments			
1.01 – 2.00 miles	Brewing	Baking		Food (not elsewhere classified)
	Hardware, fabricating metals	Blacksmithing		Chemicals
	Rope, twine	Construction		Iron, steel
	Silk	Meat[c]		Locomotives
	Sugar refining	Lumber, wood products		Machinery
	Tobacco			Petroleum refining
	Tools			Railroad cars
				Stoves, boilers
				Tin[d]

146

Non-Nuisance		Nuisance
		Copper, other metals[e]

2.01 + *miles*

Carpets	Cotton	
Dying, textiles	Stone, etc.	
Hosiery, knits		
Miscellaneous textiles		
Paper		
Ships		
Woolen goods		

SOURCE: Original manuscript, U.S. Census of Manufactures, Philadelphia, 1880.

[a] Primarily brass casting rather than smelting and refining.

[b] Primarily the working of tanned leather and therefore not predominantly a nuisance industry. According to the published reports of the Census of Manufactures, 1880, 98.1 percent of jobs in the Philadelphia leather industry were in curried leather and dressed skins and only 1.9 percent in leather tanning.

[c] In the data used in this study, the meat industry consists primarily of small butchering firms, rather than slaughtering and meat packing. While the former were not included in the Census of Manufactures aggregate statistics, they comprised the vast bulk of the jobs found in the original manuscripts.

[d] Primarily tin sheets or tin sheets combined with copper and iron sheet rolling.

[e] Primarily sheet work.

[f] Index of Relative Clustering: $C_i = \frac{1}{G_i} \sum_{j=1}^{404} (g_{ij} \cdot \frac{g_{ij}}{G_j})$; $C_t = \frac{1}{G_t} \sum_{j=1}^{404} (g_{ij} \cdot \frac{g_{ij}}{G_t})$; $I_{rc} = C_i / C_t$; where G_t = total manufacturing jobs; G_i = total jobs in industry i; g_{ij} = total jobs in industry i located in tract j; g_{ij} = jobs in industry i located in tract j.

housing was displaced by the high concentration of economic activity in the center; that workers in clustered, decentralized industries formed tight residential concentrations around their workplaces, creating, in effect, mill towns; and that workers avoided living near nuisance industries.

One way of measuring the work-residence relationship is to compare the average number of jobs in an industry within a mile of workers in that industry to the average number of jobs in the same industry within a mile of the entire population. The resulting ratio shows the relative degree of residential concentration among workers around potential workplaces compared to the population as a whole. A ratio greater than one indicates that there are more jobs, on average, in an industry within a mile of workers in that industry than there are for the general population. A ratio of one or less shows that workers in a given industry are no more or possibly even less oriented to specific job locations than the entire population.

It can be seen (Table 6-2) that for 32 out of the 44 Philadelphia industries, there were more jobs on the average in a given industry within a mile of workers in that industry than there were for the total population. For example, there were over three times as many shipbuilding jobs within a mile of the homes of shipbuilders, on the average, as there were within a mile of the entire population. In the remaining cases, there was either an approximately equal number or a slightly lower number of jobs within local access to workers in those industries compared to the rest of the population. This suggests that with few exceptions, workers were drawn to areas with high accessibility to their particular type of workplace. This is not to say, for example, that all woolen workers living within a mile of a woolen mill worked in that mill. Without employee lists, such a statement is not possible.[24] But given the difficulties involved in commuting long distances and the fact that workers had local accessibility to more jobs in their industry than other workers, it is not unreasonable to suggest that workers usually clustered near job opportunities.[25]

Do the three variables of centralization, concentration, and the nuisance factor affect this relationship? Looking first at distance from the center controlling for the other two variables, highly clustered, non-nuisance industries located in the city's outer ring such as ship building, carpet making, and paper production had a substantially stronger work-residence relationship, on the average, than those in the first two rings. The density of economic activity in the first two rings apparently did not permit the concentration of workers around potential workplaces to the same extent as in the more isolated outer regions. But this is not to say that residence was not oriented to jobs close to the center of the city. Of the 13 industries located in the core, all but one had residential ratios greater than one, and the ratio was exceptionally high in the case of the paper box and leather industries. Residence was similarly oriented to job opportunities in the second ring.[26]

It appears that spatial concentration among industries also has an effect. Comparing non-nuisance industries between one and two miles from the center, concentrated industries such as rope making or sugar refining show a much closer orientation of workers to jobs than do dispersed industries like construction or butchering. Jobs in the latter category were scattered throughout the second zone, and similarly, their workers were dispersed with no clear-cut orientation to workplaces. Of course, many bakers, butchers, or blacksmiths may have lived close to their shops or even in them.[27] But in these industries large numbers of workers did not live in clusters near their workplace as did those employed in rope making or sugar refining. With regard to industries at the city's edge, it seems clear that workers in concentrated non-nuisance industries had a greater orientation to their workplaces than those in dispersed industries; the ratios for both industries in the latter category are lower than those for all but one industry in the former.

Finally, let us look at the effect of the nuisance factor. Virtually all nuisance industries were spatially concentrated and located in the ring between one and two miles from the city center at Seventh and Market streets. Residence for the workers in these industries was markedly less oriented to jobs than was the case for those employed in clustered but non-nuisance industries in the same location. Six out of seven industries in the latter group had residential ratios well above one. But among nuisance industries, only three out of nine had such high ratios, which suggests that even when jobs were highly concentrated, a manufacturing process which produced noxious odors or loud noises may have discouraged workers from living nearby.[28] However, there were two notable exceptions: locomotives and railroad cars. Both these industries were in the near northwestern section of the city. The Baldwin Locomotive Works, located at Broad and Spring Garden, was the only firm of its kind in Philadelphia, and its products were sold nationwide. The number of males in the population stating that they worked in either of the two industries represents only a small fraction of the total jobs. But those who did mention them clearly lived within local access to a far greater number of jobs of these types than did the rest of the population.[29] In other nuisance industries, high concentrations of jobs were not accompanied by noticeable concentrations of workers. In iron and steel and heavy machinery, a high concentration of workplaces was not associated with any particular proximity of workers, a pattern which anticipated the trend in contemporary cities.[30]

The evidence suggests that both the spatial distribution of jobs and the nuisance factor accounted for variations in the formation of residential clusters close to workplaces. With almost no exceptions, workers in spatially concentrated industries had greater access to these jobs than the rest of the population, as long as the industry was not unpleasant to live near. This was especially the case for industries located far from the city center.

TABLE 6-2 Relative Access of Workers to Jobs in 44 Industries, Philadelphia, 1880

Industry[a]	A_i	A_t	R[b]	Male Workers
≤ 1 mile from center, highly clustered, non-nuisance				
Apparel	1,730	1,250	1.44	1,622
Boots and shoes	1,396	936	1.49	6,877
Brass	106	85	1.25	547
Confection	202	127	1.60	773
Furniture	830	666	1.24	3,636
Harnesses, saddles	70	65	1.08	619
Instruments	388	238	1.63	867
Leather	1,479	508	2.91	2,052
Paper boxes	104	29	3.60	118
Precious metals, jewelry	190	133	1.43	1,412
Printing, publishing	1,197	757	1.58	5,003
Shirts	239	131	1.83	198
Tailoring	148	98	1.52	3,291
Weighted Mean	—	—	1.58	27,015
1-2 miles from center, highly clustered, non-nuisance				
Beverages	70	55	1.26	842
Hardware, other fabricated metal	556	479	1.16	2,082
Rope, twine	84	42	2.02	233
Silk	216	161	1.34	216
Sugar refining	390	124	3.15	235
Tobacco products	548	421	1.30	2,141
Tools	591	468	1.26	800
Weighted Mean	—	—	1.34	6,557
1-2 miles from center, dispersed, non-nuisance				
Baking	302	280	1.08	2,953
Blacksmith	61	66	0.92	3,013
Construction	1,114	1,156	0.92	17,715
Lumber, wood products	677	689	0.98	4,257
Meat	84	111	0.75	3,346
Weighted Mean	—	—	0.95	31,284
1-2 miles from center, highly clustered, nuisance				
Chemicals	594	504	1.18	1,045
Food (not elsewhere classified)	222	230	0.97	931
Iron, steel	562	556	1.01	3,635

Industry[a]	A_i	A_t	R[b]	Male Workers
Locomotives	714	165	4.34	42
Machinery	543	585	0.93	6,514
Petroleum refining	202	136	1.49	216
Railroad cars, parts	418	95	4.38	190
Stoves, boilers	187	171	1.10	907
Tin	161	175	0.92	1,263
Weighted Mean	—	—	1.04	14,743
2 + miles from center, highly clustered, non-nuisance				
Carpets	2,480	956	2.59	2,947
Dying of textiles	239	174	1.38	1,167
Hosiery, knit goods	699	385	1.82	637
Miscellaneous textiles	520	436	1.19	3,080
Paper	193	57	3.38	591
Ships	916	300	3.05	1,089
Woolen goods	279	170	1.65	1,506
Weighted Mean	—	—	1.99	11,006
2 + miles from center, dispersed, non-nuisance				
Cotton goods	377	374	1.01	1,673
Stone, clay, glass	599	455	1.32	4,446
Weighted Mean	—	—	1.24	6,119
2 + miles from center, highly clustered, nuisance				
Copper, other metal goods	97	64	1.51	237
Total[c]	15,391	15,391	1.00	100,503

SOURCE: Original manuscripts, U.S. Census of Population, U.S. Census of Manufactures, Philadelphia, 1880.

[a]See Table 6-1 for explanation of industrial categories.

[b]A_i = number of male jobs in industry i within one mile of the mean male worker in industry i

A_t = number of male jobs in industry i within one mile of the mean individual in the total male population.

$R = A_i/A_t$

[c]Total male workers and male jobs includes miscellaneous manufacturing.

Conversely, dispersed industries did not attract large residential concentrations of workers. Finally, although there were a few notable exceptions, industries that polluted the surrounding areas tended to discourage worker concentrations.

THE BURGESS MODEL AND THE WORK-RESIDENCE RELATIONSHIP

Most of the traditional models of urban form and development, the Burgess model foremost among them, assert that the central district is the magnet to which population is attracted.[31] Whether the city is believed to develop along zonal, sectoral, or axial lines, the center is posited to be the focal point of urban spatial organization.

But there is a growing body of evidence that suggests a different view about the twentieth-century city. The classic models of urban form were developed in the 1920s when workplaces of all kinds and inexpensive housing were centralized. At that time, the dominance of the center in organizing residence was unquestioned.[32] However, it has been argued that residential areas develop around economic opportunities, wherever they may be, rather than around the city center.[33] But if this was the pattern in the 1930s, should it not have been even more pronounced 50 years before when mass transit was still in its infancy and wages were low relative to expenses?[34] Especially at that time the location of jobs should have been more important than proximity to the center in accounting for the residence of workers. When job accessibility is controlled, centrality should have no effect.

The two independent variables, job accessibility and centrality are defined as the number of jobs in a given industry within a mile of the centroid of each tract and distance of each tract from the center point of the city, respectively. The residential location of workers, the dependent variable, is defined as the proportion of the total population in a tract employed in a given industry. A dummy variable was added to account for whether or not a tract was located within a mile of the center, since population may have been displaced by the high concentration of economic activities in the center. Within the core there may actually be a negative relationship between access to jobs and proportion of workers. In tracts located outside the core, it is predicted that there will be a positive relationship.[35]

The set of regression equations for the 44 industries by spatial characteristics and nuisance factor appears in Table 6-3. For many of the centralized industries like apparel, boots and shoes, and jewelry, distance from the center was the most important variable in predicting the proportion of workers. This is demonstrated by the size of the standardized beta coefficients, or beta weights, which show the relative contribution of each independent variable in predicting the dependent variable. In over half the cases, workers decreased with distance from the center, although in a few instances, the effect was weak. In contrast, the beta weights for job accessibility were low in most industries, but in the positive direction. It is also the case that the dummy variable for central tracts usually had a weak negative effect. Centralized industries like apparel and printing and publishing needed to be close to a wide range of services, and, as the beta weights suggest, they outbid their workers for downtown space. But given the expense and slowness of mass transit, the employees had to live nearby, in other words just outside the central district. This would account for both the importance of centrality in predicting the location of workers and the fact that they were clustered closer to corresponding workplaces than the rest of the population. For such industries, it appears that the Burgess model is appropriate.[36] To the extent that an industry was centralized, workers concentrated in the ring surrounding the core. However, the low explanatory power of the independent variables for most industries suggests that within areas of accessibility to the center, the specific location of residence may have been determined by housing availability or proximity to streetcar lines.[37]

The dynamics of the relationship between work and residence for decentralized industries like textiles, paper, and ships were very different. For the ten industries with an average distance of two or more miles from the center, the location of workplaces was the single most important variable in the prediction of residence. The effect of centrality worked in the opposite direction to that predicted by the Burgess model. The proportion of workers in these industries *increased* with distance from the center. This was especially true for cotton and woolen goods and textile dying, some of the most decentralized industries. The proportion of variance explained by the combination of job accessibility and decentralization was usually much greater for concentrated non-nuisance industries than for either concentrated nuisance or dispersed industries. For non-nuisance industries which were far from the center of town and whose jobs were concentrated into a few small areas, a "mill town" effect was created. In an era when the technology of transportation and communication was in its infancy, such areas may have developed almost independently, as self-contained entities.[38]

There was some evidence of this pattern among concentrated non-nuisance industries in the second ring from the center, although not to the same degree. Of the seven industries in this group, the effect of the location of workplaces reached statistical significance in three. Because of the density of business and residential land uses in this narrow ring (over a quarter of all the jobs and almost half the population were located here) the concentrations of workers around jobs could not form to the extent that was possible in sparser, peripheral areas. The greater the distance from the center, the greater the opportunity for the emergence of industrially based residential areas.

There were two industrial categories for which neither distance from the center nor access to jobs was important in determining where workers lived:

TABLE 6-3 Regression of Location of Residence of Workers in 44 Industries on Accessibility to Jobs, Distance from the Center, and Central Tracts,[a] Philadelphia, 1880

Industry[b]	Beta Weights			R^2	$\bar{R}^2$
	X_1	X_2	X_3[c]		
≤ 1 mile from center, highly clustered, non-nuisance					
Apparel	.13	−.33**	−.13	.1198	.1022
Boots, shoes	.16	−.33**	.01	.1967	.1806
Brass	.05	−.25*	−.15	.0537	.0320
Confection	.31*	.13	−.06	.0494	.0276
Furniture	.48**	.04	−.30*	.0742	.0530
Harnesses, saddles	.05	.25*	.04	.0461	.0243
Instruments	.00	−.11	.10	.0339	.0118
Leather	.74**	−.01	−.20**	.4788	.4684
Paper boxes	.57	−.00	−.14	.2166	.1987
Precious metals, jewelry	−.07	−.26*	−.02	.0503	.0286
Printing, publishing	.13	−.22*	−.03	.0834	.0651
Shirts	.08	−.19	−.14	.0399	.0179
Tailoring	.15	−.32**	.09	.2340	.2165
1-2 miles from center, highly clustered, non-nuisance					
Beverages	.03	−.03	−.06	.0028	.0000
Hardware, other fabricated metal	.28	.08	−.23	.0295	.0073
Rope, twine	.34**	−.02	−.16	.1261	.1061
Silk	.02	−.01	.03	.0021	.0000
Sugar refining	.37**	−.22**	.01	.2425	.2252
Tobacco products	.18	−.16	−.06	.0731	.0519
Tools	.25*	.27**	−.09	.0836	.0626
1-2 miles from center, dispersed, non-nuisance					
Baking	.03	−.03	.00	.0035	.0000
Blacksmithing	−.11	.11	−.06	.0586	.0370
Construction	−.09	.02	−.22	.0971	.0770
Lumber, wood products	−.12	−.31**	−.17	.0694	.0405
Meat	−.17	.03	−.04	.0501	.0284

	Beta Weights				
Industry[b]	X_1	X_2	X_3[c]	R^2	$\bar{R}^2$
1-2 miles from center, highly clustered, nuisance					
Chemicals	.26	.02	− .23	.0201	.0000
Food (not elsewhere classified)	− .12	− .08	− .05	.0148	.0000
Iron, steel	.20	.20	− .25*	.0824	.0614
Locomotives	.09	.03	− .03	.0074	.0000
Machinery	.12	− .02	− .28*	.0444	.0253
Petroleum refining	− .07	− .18	− .09	.0265	.0000
Railroad cars, parts	.31**	− .02	− .08	.1069	.0865
Stoves, boilers	− .22	− .07	− .26*	.0426	.0207
Tin	− .11	− .03	.01	.0081	.0000
2 + miles from center, highly clustered, non-nuisance					
Carpets	.56**	.21**	.05	.3075	.2936
Dying of textiles	.25**	.36**	.01	.1560	.1367
Hosiery, knit goods	.42**	.21*	.07	.1961	.1777
Miscellaneous textiles	.30**	.21	.10	.0904	.0696
Paper	.65**	.19*	− .38**	.3531	.3383
Ships	.56*	− .02	− .12	.3241	.3106
Woolen goods	.36**	.49**	.07	:3548	.3419
2 + miles from center, dispersed, non-nuisance					
Cotton goods	.37**	.58**	.00	.3378	.3246
Stone, clay, glass	.45**	.08	− .40**	.1629	.1462
2 + miles from center, highly clustered, nuisance					
Copper, other metal goods	.30*	.01	− .14	.0453	.0234

SOURCE: Original manuscripts, U.S. Census of Population, U.S. Census of Manufactures, Philadelphia, 1880.

[a]Tracts with a population of less than 200 were eliminated.

[b]Table is based on male jobs and male population.

[c]Y = percent of the population in tract j comprised of workers in industry i

X_1 = number of jobs in industry i within one mile of tract j

X_2 = distance of tract j from center

X_3 = tract j is or is not within one mile of center

*Beta weight is significant at 5% level.

**Beta weight is significant at 1% level.

nuisance industries and dispersed industries. The latter did not attract large numbers of workers to a particular place of residence. In fact, in the building trades, in which jobs were located in relatively underdeveloped areas, the major problem for workers was to find housing at all, let alone near the worksite. In order to have a ready market, consumer industries had to locate in neighborhoods that were already developed. Their workers had no more access to workplaces than the rest of the population who purchased the products on a daily basis.

In nuisance industries, too, neither job accessibility nor distance from the center counted heavily in the decision about where to live. Given the unpleasant atmosphere created by these industries, workers apparently avoided residing near such firms. But these Philadelphians were not attracted by access to the center either. In fact, for several industries, such as iron, steel, and machinery, the only important predictor variable was distance from the center. These workers avoided central tracts; they lived everywhere in the developed city except downtown.

In sum, there were four types of relationships between work and residence in Philadelphia at the end of the nineteenth century. Outside the core, those industries that were highly clustered but not unpleasant to be near developed a very strong relationship between work and residence—the farther from the center, the stronger the relationship. Proximity to the center was of little importance in the locational decisions of workers in these industries.[39] Furthermore, if the industry was extremely distant from the center, it may have formed the backbone of a separate labor market. To the extent that a city of this period specialized in industries with these spatial characteristics, the Burgess model of residential structure is inappropriate. By contrast, the Burgess model is well suited to describing the spatial distribution of workers in highly centralized industries. Philadelphia in this period displayed characteristics of both the centrally dominated city of the Burgess model and a loose confederation of mill towns. Half of all manufacturing jobs and the bulk of jobs in finance and commerce were located within a mile of Seventh and Market streets. Workers were displaced by this intense economic activity. But there were also relatively autonomous communities, such as Manayunk, Germantown, and Frankford. Third, objectionable production processes seemed to repel workers, and they looked elsewhere for housing. Since many of the nuisance industries constituted the growth sector of manufacturing, this pattern of segregated residential and industrial areas foreshadowed the city of a later era. Finally, those industries which were scattered around the city outside the center exerted no special pull on workers, and as was the case with nuisance industries, other factors came into play in residential locational decisions.

A study of Philadelphia in 1930 reports results that are quite similar to the findings for 1880.[40] The major difference is that the attractive force of industry was typically much stronger in the earlier year, as would be expected. This suggests that while the basic form of the work-residence relationship did not change between the walking and the streetcar city, the expense and slowness of commuter transportation strengthened the relationship in the earlier period.

THE SPATIAL CONTEXT OF RESIDENCE

The spatial characteristics of neighborhoods, that is, degree of centrality, density, and the like, have been found to have considerable impact on a wide variety of social processes. Therefore, it is important to find the degree to which the spatial distribution of industries predicted the residential characteristics of workers in those industries.

Four spatial measures are used to define the spatial context of jobs and residence—mean distance from the center and the indexes of segregation, relative clustering, and density. For each of the 44 industries, the locational characteristics of the workers' residences are regressed on the corresponding characteristics of jobs.

The relationship between the spatial distribution of jobs and workers is a close one (see Table 6-4). Over half of the variance in the centrality of workers is accounted for by the single variable of job centrality. This strong positive relationship held true regardless of the other industrial characteristics, in other words, whether the industry was a nuisance or not.

The correlation between the segregation of jobs and workers is similarly close; about three-quarters of the variance in the latter is explained by the former. Industries with jobs that were the most segregated from other jobs—highly clustered industries more than two miles form the center—had workers who were the most segregated from the rest of the population. In contrast, workers in jobs that were the most integrated with other work-places—consumer- and building-related—were distributed like the rest of the population.

With respect to clustering, the spatial concentration of jobs explained over half of the variance in the concentration of workers' residences. In decentralized industries, where the work-residence relationship was particularly close, both jobs and workers were highly clustered relative to the entire population. These concentrated workplaces probably had workers tightly clustered around them. This relationship was also true, although to a lesser extent, for highly concentrated industries located in the second ring from the center. But for the most centralized industries, this relationship was different. Although they were among the most highly clustered, their respective work forces, with a few exceptions, had only moderate levels of clustering. As noted earlier in a separate analysis, workers in those industries were forced to live just outside the core. Similar to centralized industries, workers in nuisance industries tended not to be as spatially concentrated as

TABLE 6-4 Spatial Distribution of Jobs and Workers in 44 Industries, Philadelphia, 1880

Industry	Mean Distance from Center—Miles[a]		Index of Segregation[b]		Index of Relative Clustering[c]		Index of Density[d]	
	Jobs	Workers	Jobs	Workers	Jobs	Workers	Jobs	Workers
≤ 1 mile from center, highly clustered, non-nuisance								
Apparel	0.61	1.57	59.25	34.60	6.75	1.92	56	25
Boots, shoes	0.70	1.68	51.35	25.00	3.97	1.64	45	25
Brass	0.76	1.61	61.65	50.35	4.41	2.47	50	25
Confection	0.80	1.53	52.20	41.35	2.39	2.12	27	25
Furniture	1.00	1.86	41.15	26.90	1.70	1.54	28	24
Harnesses, saddles	0.99	2.07	51.45	44.45	2.66	2.23	37	23
Instruments	0.81	1.64	63.15	49.20	2.45	2.31	28	25
Leather	0.98	1.56	81.35	61.50	3.52	7.00	18	28
Paper boxes	0.54	1.04	74.80	76.65	11.40	10.43	65	37
Precious metals, jewelry	0.62	1.54	60.90	41.05	4.18	1.91	42	25
Printing, publishing	0.58	1.69	61.05	27.20	5.16	1.49	44	25
Shirts	0.86	1.45	75.55	67.95	11.87	4.73	27	26
Tailor	1.00	1.59	55.15	31.90	3.32	2.01	38	26
Weighted Mean	0.74	1.67	57.93	33.44	4.67	2.21	42	25
1-2 miles from center, highly clustered, non-nuisance								
Beverages	1.04	2.02	79.55	58.20	2.73	5.28	17	20
Hardware, other fabricated metal	1.47	1.88	62.55	33.90	2.08	1.60	22	23
Rope, twine	1.46	2.40	78.60	73.80	11.31	4.20	22	14
Silk	1.28	1.80	64.55	63.80	5.14	3.57	46	21
Sugar refining	1.84	1.21	86.95	56.20	9.14	4.00	21	27
Tobacco products	1.11	1.66	45.95	33.95	1.87	1.88	24	26
Tools	1.31	3.43	81.35	67.85	5.97	3.97	22	18
Weighted Mean	1.35	2.01	66.48	44.42	4.21	2.70	25	23

1-2 miles from center, dispersed, non-nuisance

Baking	1.43	1.85	49.80	21.85	0.58	1.38	15	23
Blacksmith	1.86	2.37	53.90	29.15	0.77	1.15	12	19
Construction	1.51	2.23	42.10	18.40	0.79	1.03	21	20
Lumber, wood products	1.43	2.08	41.65	25.15	0.68	1.24	18	21
Meat	1.43	2.46	45.25	40.70	1.34	1.54	24	18
Weighted Mean	1.48	2.21	43.35	23.06	0.76	1.16	19	20

1-2 miles from center, highly clustered, nuisance

Chemicals	1.38	1.97	49.20	42.05	2.10	1.75	28	22
Food (not elsewhere classified)	1.24	2.08	63.05	44.45	6.05	1.65	19	22
Iron, steel	1.39	2.18	54.30	30.85	1.64	1.71	23	21
Locomotives	1.12	1.65	97.60	89.75	20.16	15.49	24	20
Machinery	1.62	2.15	43.65	22.80	1.61	1.15	26	21
Petroleum refining	1.04	1.71	76.60	72.50	9.89	4.37	23	19
Railroad cars, parts	2.00	2.02	90.55	72.10	9.92	4.95	9	19
Stoves, boilers	1.01	1.96	57.20	47.40	2.72	2.46	33	23
Tin	1.04	2.09	45.80	41.15	2.74	1.66	37	20
Weighted Mean	1.38	2.11	60.72	32.16	5.55	1.63	25	21

2+ miles from center, highly clustered, non-nuisance

Carpets	2.69	2.65	85.85	66.30	2.64	5.20	12	19
Dying of textiles	2.97	3.12	72.90	62.45	1.73	2.88	13	16
Hosiery, knit goods	3.01	2.77	73.80	70.45	1.55	4.76	12	19
Miscellaneous textiles	2.21	2.53	71.80	56.00	1.71	5.02	12	17
Paper	2.51	4.68	70.80	74.35	3.91	6.79	25	12
Ships	2.10	1.78	90.65	64.45	6.78	8.01	10	22
Woolen goods	3.92	4.52	81.00	69.80	2.08	3.82	9	9
Weighted Mean	2.74	2.95	80.00	64.04	2.75	5.06	12	17

(cont.)

Industry	Mean Distance from Center—Miles[a]		Index of Segregation[b]		Index of Relative Clustering[c]		Index of Density[d]	
	Jobs	Workers	Jobs	Workers	Jobs	Workers	Jobs	Workers
2 + miles from center, dispersed, non-nuisance								
Cotton goods	3.53	3.87	63.10	59.15	1.32	3.15	18	13
Stone, glass, clay	2.06	2.15	61.70	33.40	0.57	1.31	13	19
Weighted Mean	2.72	2.62	62.33	40.44	0.91	1.81	15	17
2 + miles from center, highly clustered, nuisance								
Copper, other metal goods	2.48	1.60	62.40	58.55	2.69	3.62	26	26
Total	1.62	2.07	—	—	—	—	26	21
	$R^2 = .5598$		$R^2 = .7298$		$R^2 = .5268$		$R^2 = .3575$	

SOURCE: Original manuscripts, U.S. Census of Population, U.S. Census of Manfactures, Philadelphia, 1880.

[a]Spatial measures are based on male jobs and male workers.

[b]Index of Segregation $= \dfrac{1}{2} \displaystyle\sum_{j=1}^{404} \left| \dfrac{g_j - g_{ij}}{G_t - G_i} - \dfrac{g_{ij}}{G_i} \right|$, where G_t = total jobs or population; G_i = total jobs or workers in industry i;

g_{ij} = total jobs or population in tract j; g_{ij} = jobs or population in industry i located in tract j.

[c]Index of Relative Clustering—See Table 6-1.

[d]Index of Density $- \dfrac{1}{G_i} \displaystyle\sum_{j=1}^{404} \left(g_{ij} \cdot \dfrac{g_{ij}}{acres} \right)$.

their jobs. They tended to disperse rather than clustering around job opportunities.

There is a close association between job density and residential density. Workers in industries located in dense manufacturing areas lived in dense residential areas. As distance from the center increased, the density of both jobs and population decreased, as would be expected. It should be noted that the relationship between density of jobs and workers is not as strong as the other spatial measures. In several cases, workers lived where there were many people but few other manufacturing jobs per acre. In these areas, manufacturers may have had to compete for space with a great many other employers who attracted population.[41] Water-oriented industries like sugar refining and ship building may have typified this pattern, inasmuch as ports drew many types of employers.

Industries were good predictors of the corresponding residential characteristics of workers. The industry in which one was employed in 1880 in Philadelphia defined the context in which one was likely to live. Thus, there was no one set of living conditions that characterized manufacturing workers as a whole. Rather, the residential characteristics of workers depended on the spatial distribution of their jobs.

Summary and Conclusions

The following is a summary of the major findings of this study:

1. In three-quarters of the manufacturing industries in Philadelphia in 1880, workers in a given industry lived in areas that had local access to a greater number of manufacturing jobs in this industry than the population as a whole.
2. There were four types of relationships between work and residence. Among industries that were concentrated into one area but not extremely centralized, the location of potential jobs was the best predictor of the location of workers, as long as the industries were not unpleasant to live near. For centralized industries, the best predictor was distance from the center, as outlined in the Burgess model. Neither the location of jobs nor distance from the center was a good predictor of the location of workers in highly dispersed industries or nuisance industries.
3. There was a strong relationship between the spatial characteristics of manufacturing industries and the residential context in which the workers in these industries were likely to live.

There are three major implications of this research. First, the Burgess model is incomplete and should be revised. Second, employment opportunities may be at least as important as ethnicity and social class in explaining where people lived in nineteenth-century cities. Finally, the availability of jobs is important to neighborhood stability and social composition.

Because it was ahistorical, the Burgess model incorrectly identified the center as the focus of urban spatial structure. This model was developed in an era when the core dominated urban economic activities and mass transit was developed only to the extent that the middle and upper class could afford to use it for a daily commute. The model, therefore, confused centrality with the location of jobs in determining residential patterns.

It is inappropriate to apply any one model of residential structure to the late-nineteenth-century city. The spatial distribution of industries defined the residential context in which workers lived. Workers in industries with different spatial characteristics were themselves differentially distributed. For this reason, the residential structure of cities would be likely to vary according to their industrial structure. Cities which specialized in such centralized industries as apparel and publishing would probably approximate the Burgess model. Cities specializing in textiles and paper might have resembled a cluster of small mill towns. Philadelphia at the end of the nineteenth century was actually a combination of both. The area surrounding Seventh and Market streets was the largest of a number of industrial concentrations. In addition, it was the seat of the city government and the prime location for a wide variety of commercial activities. But there were several other industrial concentrations, each constituting a well-defined community—Spring Garden with its railroad and machinery works, Kensington with iron, tools, and textiles, Manayunk, the historic center of paper and textile production, and Germantown, the center of Philadelphia's woolen industry, to name just a few. Thus, no single model is adequate to describe Philadelphia's residential structure in this period.

A second implication concerns the effect of industrially based residence on class and ethnic communities. To what degree did job location constrain the formation of residential neighborhoods based on common cultural heritage or economic status? The dominant theme in the literature on urban communities, beginning with the studies by the Chicago sociologists in the 1920s, has been that residence is a reflection of shared life-styles. Members of a particular class or ethnic group are believed to carve out their own neighborhoods as a means of maintaining their culture. In turn, these areas of common residence are thought to reinforce group consciousness and shared social networks. An analysis of this question, using the same data presented in this paper, suggests that the location of job opportunities and common industrial affiliation were more important than shared ethnicity or occupation in determining the location and patterns of residence.[42] But this is not to say that culture was of no importance in residential organization. It may have been that class and ethnic communities developed within a larger industrial context. An analysis of the residential patterns of leather workers in nineteenth-century Philadelphia shows that the large concentration of workers close to leather factories was divided into small Irish and

German segments.[43] There were probably a number of areas like this in Philadelphia, each existing within easy access to a particular industry.

Finally, the evidence presented in this study has implications for our understanding of change and stability in urban neighborhoods. Given the finding that industry was one of the major organizing factors in urban residence in the late nineteenth century, one might expect that a change in the location of jobs over time would affect the residential stability and social composition of surrounding areas. In other words, were areas of the city that maintained a large and constant supply of jobs residentially stable compared to those undergoing rapid economic growth or decline? Were immigrants attracted to areas with expanding job opportunities? Did areas that lost jobs deteriorate? In an analysis of residential patterns in Philadelphia between 1880 and 1930 it was found that change in the location of employment opportunities had an important impact on the residential stability, economic status, and ethnic composition of districts in the city.[44] The characteristics of urban neighborhoods cannot be fully understood without reference to their economic development over time. Unfortunately, social scientists, urban planners, and policy makers who are concerned with the viability of modern cities have too often ignored this factor.

Notes

1. For their help in the preparation of this paper special thanks are due to David Elesh, Eugene Ericksen, Theodore Hershberg, William Whitney, and William Yancey. Most of the data for this study were drawn from the files of the Philadelphia Social History Project at the University of Pennsylvania, and the author would like to express her appreciation to the following agencies whose support of the project has made this research possible: the Center for Studies of Metropolitan Problems, National Institute of Mental Health (MH 16621); Sociology Program, Division of Social Sciences, National Science Foundation (SOC 76-20069); and Division of Research Grants, National Endowment for the Humanities (RC 25568-76-1156).

2. Wendell Bell and Maryanne Force, "Urban Neighborhood Types and Participation in Formal Associations," *American Sociological Review* 21 (February 1956): 25-34; J. H. S. Bossard, "Residential Propinquity as a Factor in Marriage Selection," *American Journal of Sociology* 38 (September 1932): 219-24; Elizabeth Bott, *Family and Social Network* (London: Tavistock, 1957); Theodore Caplow and Robert Forman, "Neighborhood Interaction in a Homogeneous Community," *American Sociological Review* 15 (June 1950): 357-66; William H. Michelson, *Man and His Urban Environment: A Sociological Approach* (Reading, Mass.: Addison-Wesley Publishing Co., 1976); Michael Young and Peter Willmott, *Family and Kinship in East London* (London: Routledge & Kegan Paul, 1957).

3. Eugene R. Ericksen and William L. Yancey, "Using Connections: Antecedents and Consequences of Personal Networks in the City," paper presented at the annual meeting of the American Sociological Association, New York, 1976; Mark S. Granovetter, "The Strength of Weak Ties," *American Journal of Sociology* 78 (May 1973): 1360-80.

4. Ernest W. Burgess, "The Growth of the City—An Introduction to a Research Project," in *The City* by Robert E. Park, Ernest W. Burgess, Roderick D. McKenzie (Chicago: University of Chicago Press, 1925), pp. 47-62.

5. David Harvey, *Social Justice and the City* (London: Edward Arnold, 1973); John R. Logan, "Industrialization and the Stratification of Cities in Suburban Regions," *American Journal of Sociology* 83 (September 1976): 333-48; Harvey Molotch, "The City as a Growth Machine: Toward a Political Economy of Place," *American Journal of Sociology* 82 (September 1976): 309-32; Seymour Spilerman and Jack Habib, "Development Towns in Israel: The Role of Community in Creating Ethnic Disparities in Labor Force Characteristics," *American Journal of Sociology* 81 (January 1976): 781-821.

6. Maurice Davie, "The Pattern of Urban Growth," in *Reader in Urban Sociology,* ed. Paul K. Hatt and Albert J. Reiss, Jr. (Glencoe, Ill.: Free Press, 1951), pp. 244-59.

7. Eugene P. Ericksen and William L. Yancey. "The Organization of Residence in an Industrial City," unpublished manuscript, Department of Sociology, Temple University, 1976.

8. Edgar M. Hoover and Raymond Vernon, *Anatomy of a Metropolis* (Garden City, N.Y.: Doubleday, 1962); Edward E. Pratt, *Industrial Causes of Congestion of Population in New York City* (New York: Columbia Univesity Press, 1911).

9. Beverly Duncan and Otis D. Duncan, "The Measurement of Intra-City Locational and Residential Patterns," *Journal of Regional Science* 2 (Fall 1960): 37-54; Otis D. Duncan and Beverly Duncan, "Residential Distribution and Occupational Stratification," *American Journal of Sociology* 60 (March 1955): 493-503.

10. Stuart Blumin, "Mobility and Change in Ante-Bellum Philadelphia," in *Nineteenth Century Cities*, ed. Stephan Thernstrom and Richard Sennett (New Haven: Yale University Press, 1969), pp. 165-208; Ian Davey and Michael Doucet, "The Social Geography of a Commercial City, ca. 1853," Appendix 1 in *The People of Hamilton, Canada West* by Michael B. Katz (Cambridge, Mass.: Harvard University Press, 1975), pp. 319-42; Clyde Griffen, "Workers Divided: The Effect of Craft and Ethnic Differences in Poughkeepsie, New York, 1850-1880," in *Nineteenth Century Cities,* ed. Thernstrom and Sennett, pp. 49-97; Theodore Hershberg, Harold E. Cox, Richard R. Greenfield, and Dale B. Light, Jr., "The 'Journey-to-Work': An Empirical Investigation of Work, Residence, and Transportation, Philadelphia, 1850 and 1880," in *Toward an Interdisciplinary History of the City: Work, Space, Family and Group Experience in Nineteenth Century Philadelphia,* ed. Theodore Hershberg (New York: Oxford University Press, 1980); Robert Lynd and Helen Lynd, *Middletown* (New York: Harcourt, Brace & World, 1929); Stephan Thernstrom, *Poverty and Progress: Social Mobility in a Nineteenth Century City* (Cambridge, Mass.: Harvard University Press, 1964); David Ward, *Cities and Immigrants* (New York: Oxford University Press, 1971).

11. Hershberg, et al., "The 'Journey-to-Work' "; Sam Bass Warner, Jr., *The Private City: Philadelphia in Three Periods of Its Growth* (Philadelphia: University of Pennsylvania Press, 1968), p. 169.

12. Warner, *The Private City,* pp. 169-71.

13. Harlan W. Gilmore, *Transportation and the Growth of Cities* (Glencoe, Ill.: Free Press, 1953).

14. W. Lloyd Warner, J. O. Low, Paul S. Lunt, Leo Srole, *Yankee City* (New Haven: Yale University Press, 1963).

15. For a more detailed discussion of the data sources, see Stephanie W. Greenberg, "Industrialization in Philadelphia: The Relationship Between Industrial Location and Residential Patterns, 1880-1930," Ph.D. dissertation, Temple University, 1977; and Theodore Hershberg, "The Philadelphia Social History Project: An Introduction," *Historical Methods Newsletter* 9 (March-June 1976): 43-58.

16. These categories were derived from a more detailed coding scheme primarily on the basis of comparability both with the scheme used in a recent study of manufacturing location in Philadelphia in 1930 and with the Standard Industrial Classification used today by the Census of Manufactures. For the 1930 study, see Eugene P. Ericksen, "The Location of Manufacturing Jobs in a City: Changes in the Pattern, 1927-1972," unpublished manuscript, Department of Sociology, Temple University, 1976.

17. Greenberg, "Industrialization in Philadelphia."

18. Ericksen and Yancey, "The Organization of Residence."

19. Hershberg, et al., "The 'Journey-To-Work.' "

20. Alan N. Burstein, "Residential Distribution and Mobility of Irish and German Immigrants in Philadelphia, 1850-1880," Ph.D. dissertation, University of Pennsylvania, 1975.

21. The classification of industries according to the nuisance factor in the present study was accomplished by combining the Hoover and Vernon listing with the one constructed by Whitney. Hoover and Vernon, in their study of the New York Metropolitan Region in the mid-twentieth century, found that nuisance industries tended to locate away from population centers in peripheral areas of the region. In a study of industrial location in mid-nineteenth-century Philadelphia, Whitney also found that nuisance industries were located away from the population, even prior to the advent of zoning laws. See Hoover and Vernon, *Anatomy of a Metropolis* and William G. Whitney, "The Uses of Urban Space in Nineteenth Century Philadelphia: Manufacturing Location at Mid-Century," paper presented at the First Annual Meeting of the Social Science History Association, Philadelphia, 1976.

22. The center is defined here as the intersection of Seventh and Market streets, a point along the major east-west axis midway between the Delaware River, the eastern boundary of the city, and the present nucleus of the core, City Hall.

23. At this time, almost half the population lived in the ring between one and two miles from the center. See Greenberg, "Industrialization in Philadelphia."

24. A study of the journey to work in nineteenth-century Philadelphia, which utilizes the employee lists of several firms and indirect measures of the work trip, also suggests that workers clustered around the places in which they worked or were likely to work, although there were some differences by occupation and industry. See Hershberg, et al., "The 'Journey-to-Work.' "

25. That the accessibility of jobs to workers seems to be more important in 1880 than in the early twentieth century can be inferred from the fact that the ratios observed in the former year are generally higher than those in a comparable study of Philadelphia in 1930. See Ericksen and Yancey, "The Organization of Residence." Ericksen and Yancey used the same measure of job accessibility and the same areal units as are used in the present study, basing their analysis on data from the 1930

population census and the 1928 Pennsylvania Industrial Directory. They calculated the job access ratio for 11 industries. The highest ratio they found was 2.80, for auto workers, and all but four industries had ratios below 1.50.

26. It is difficult to make the same comparison for the effect of distance on dispersed non-nuisance industries and clustered nuisance industries since there are no industries of either of these types in the core and almost none more than two miles from the center.

27. A scan of the census manuscripts of population and manufacturing shows, for example, that George Ludy, a first-generation German baker lived at 2024 Lombard Street and had his shop on the premises. The same was true of Neil McCarrick, a first-generation Irish blacksmith of 619 South 19th Street and Frank Schweizer, a first-generation German butcher of 928 Poplar Street. These are just a few instances of what was probably a common occurrence.

28. For example, Baeder Adamson and Company, one of the largest chemical firms in Philadelphia at the time, was located in Port Richmond, a sparsely developed section of the city. The I. P. Morris Company, a large iron works, was located in a fairly undeveloped part of Kensington.

29. One explanation for the close orientation of residence to work among railroad car and locomotive workers is that the large companies that characterized these industries may have built employee housing near the factories. However, an examination of the Baist Atlas maps of 1880, which showed buildings, and a review of several contemporary histories of Philadelphia's industries and industrialists yielded no evidence of this. See Ellis P. Oberholtzer, *Philadelphia: A History of the City and Its People, A Record of 225 Years* (Philadelphia: S. J. Clarke, 1912), 2: 420-39; J. Thomas Scharf and Thompson Westcott, *History of Philadelphia* (Philadelphia: L. H. Everts, 1884), 3: 2226-340. Owner intervention in the housing market does appear to have taken place in the J. B. Stetson Company, the largest hat manufacturer in the world until well into the twentieth century. Located in Kensington, the company owned the Stetson Savings and Loan, which provided low-interest loans to workers. However, this type of intervention was very indirect; company housing in the usual sense apparently did not exist in Philadelphia. See Bill Lynskey, "How Tom Mix's Hat Built a Philadelphia Neighborhood," *Today Magazine, The Philadelphia Inquirer,* June 19, 1977, p. 25.

30. Laurie, et al., found that these capital-intensive, nonfinal market industries so characteristic of the nuisance category had the highest wages. See Bruce Laurie, Theodore Hershberg, and George Alter, "Immigrants and Industry: The Philadelphia Experience, 1850-1880," *Journal of Social History* 9 (December 1975): 219-48. Therefore, it might be that this higher wage level permitted a greater separation of work and residence than was the case for low-wage industries. This hypothesis was examined in a more detailed analysis of these data, and in general there was no strong relationship between average per capita wages and the work-residence relationship. Some very low-wage industries, such as food processing and cotton goods, had a weak tie between work and residence. High-wage industries, such as locomotives, petroleum refining, instruments, and printing and publishing, to name a few, had sizable residential concentrations of workers. See Greenberg, "Industrialization in Philadelphia."

31. Burgess, "The Growth of the City"; Homer Hoyt, *The Structure and Growth of Residential Neighborhoods in American Cities* (Washington, D.C.: U.S. Govern-

ment Printing Office, 1939); Richard Hurd, *Principles of City Land Values* (New York: The Record and Guide, 1903).

32. Ward, *Cities and Immigrants;* Sam Bass Warner, Jr., and Colin B. Burke, "Cultural Change and the Ghetto," *Journal of Contemporary History* 4 (October 1969): 173-87.

33. Davie, "The Pattern of Urban Growth"; Duncan and Duncan, "The Measurement of Intra-City Locational and Residential Patterns"; Ericksen and Yancey, "The Organization of Residence"; Chauncy D. Harris and Edward L. Ullman, "The Nature of Cities," in *Reader in Urban Sociology,* ed. Paul K. Hatt and Albert J. Reiss, Jr. (Glencoe, Ill.: Free Press, 1951), pp. 222-32; Amos Hawley, *Urban Society: An Ecological Approach* (New York: Ronald Press, 1971); Hoover and Vernon, *Anatomy of a Metropolis.*

34. Eudice Glassberg, "Work, Wages, and the Cost of Living, Ethnic Differences and the Poverty Line, Philadelphia, 1880," *Pennsylvania History* 46 (January 1979): 17-58.

35. In a study of the location work and residence in Chicago during the same period, it was found that there was, in fact, a negative relationship between central location and population owing to the displacement of homes by firms. See Raymond L. Fales and Leon N. Moses, "Land-Use Theory and the Spatial Structure of the Nineteenth Century City," *Papers and Proceedings of the Regional Science Association* 28 (November 1972): 49-80.

36. It should be noted that there were several exceptions to the rule for centralized industries. Particularly in the case of leather and paper boxes, accessibility to job opportunities was the the most important variable and centrality had no effect. It was shown earlier that workers in these industries had an extremely large number of jobs within local access relative to the rest of the population. It is not clear why these industries followed a pattern so different from the other centralized industries, since the leather and paper box industries are not alike in ethnic or occupational composition or wage level. See Greenberg, "Industrialization in Philadelphia."

37. Ericksen and Yancey, "The Organization of Residence"; Fales and Moses, "Land-Use Theory."

38. Margaret Marsh described this phenomenon in her study of northern West Philadelphia prior to 1880. Autonomous industrial neighborhoods developed around meat packing and textile firms. See Margaret S. Marsh, "The Transformation of a Community: Suburbanization and Urbanization in Northern West Philadelphia, 1880-1930," Ph.D. dissertation, Rutgers University, 1974, and "Suburbanization and the Search for Community: Residential Decentralization in Philadelphia," *Pennsylvania History* 44 (April 1977): 104-5. Sam Bass Warner described a similar pattern in the lower northeast section of Philadelphia, where workers were attracted by a great diversity of industries. See Warner, *The Private City,* pp. 178-83. Also see the essay by Meredith Savery in this volume.

39. A study of Chicago in the same period found that the location of jobs had a negative effect on population. However, this study does not differentiate among types of employment. See Fales and Moses, "Land-Use Theory."

40. See note 25. Ericksen and Yancey used distance from the center, number of jobs in an industry within one mile, and average value of housing to predict the location of workers in 11 industries. They found that centrally located industries, concentrated noncentral industries, and dispersed industries had the same effects on

the residence of workers as those reported in the present study. They also found that workers in 10 out of 11 industries were attracted to tracts with inexpensive housing. Unfortunately, housing values were not collected by the census in 1880 and are not easily obtainable in Philadelphia through other sources.

41. It is impossible to measure total job density, since there are no data on the location of wholesale, retail or service jobs.

42. Greenberg, "Industrialization in Philadelphia"; Stephanie W. Greenberg, "Industrial Location and Ethnic Residential Patterns in an Industrializing City: Philadelphia, 1880," in *Toward an Interdisciplinary History of the City,* ed. Hershberg.

43. Timothy Cook and Andrew Pollott, "A Fronting Block Analysis of the Residential Patterns of Late Nineteenth Century Philadelphians: Morocco Workers, 1880," Philadelphia Social History Project Working Paper, Spring 1975; Hershberg, et al., "The 'Journey-to-Work.'"

44. Greenberg, "Industrialization in Philadelphia."

CHAPTER 7 The Impact of the
Market Street "El"
on Northern West Philadelphia:
Environmental Change
and Social Transformation,
1900-1930

MARGARET S. MARSH

What happens to a community when its physical environment is suddenly
and drastically altered? This essay considers that question, concentrating on
the interplay between an abrupt physical change—the rapid construction of
the Market Street Elevated Line—and social transformation.[1] Promoters of
rapid transit viewed the Market Street Line as the first of a number of
subways and "Els" that would bind the outlying residential areas to the
central business district. Although the grand designs were never fully realized,
the Market Street El was a success. Functioning as a tangible link between
central Philadelphia and the communities of the outer city, the El facilitated
a shift of residents' attention from their neighborhoods to downtown, not
only for work but also for shopping and entertainment. Yet if the El succeeded as a symbol of physical unification, it served to promote fragmentation and divisiveness as well. In the late nineteenth century neighborhood-based institutions such as churches, clubs, and civic associations had
helped to unify the residents. The El altered the functions of such groups as
people began to focus on the downtown for both work and recreation.
Unwilling to forgo either the advantages of the larger urban community or
the comforts of a homogeneous neighborhood, residents now started to
insist on external signs of coherence, such as shared socioeconomic, ethnic,
and racial backgrounds, trusting in them to ensure similarities in values
and behavior patterns.

The process of transformation can be traced in northern West Philadelphia, which contained the six communities of Mill Creek, Haddington,
Hestonville, Morris Park, Overbrook, and Wynnefield (see Map 7-1). The
Market Street El, built in the first decade of the twentieth century along the
southern boundary of this area, was the city's first and only rapid transit

line until 1922. Construction of the line brought sudden and extensive residential development in several of the six communities and significantly affected the future course of growth in the others.

Northern West Philadelphia Before the El, 1880–1900

Prior to the building of the El, Northern West Philadelphia emerged as a group of middle-class, suburban communities. In 1880 the area was less densely settled and more homogeneous than the communities which immediately joined the downtown section. Mill Creek, the closest of the six communities to urban Philadelphia, housed the nuisance industries needed by the nineteenth-century city but which the more densely settled neighborhoods could not tolerate—tanneries, slaughterhouses, stockyards. Hestonville and Haddington had been independent villages before consolidation in 1854. In addition to the old inns and taverns which had once welcomed visitors traveling into the city on the unpaved turnpikes, each of these two districts maintained a small-scale textile industry which relied on the locally available water power. Haddington's clay soil also supported several brickyards. The people who lived in these three communities were for the most part working-class family members who labored in the nearby industries. Haddington's population also contained a squatter settlement, a shantytown built by Irish immigrants but by 1880 inhabited mostly by black families, the men working usually as unskilled laborers in the brickyards and the women frequently as laundresses.

If Mill Creek, Hestonville, and Haddington were only partially developed, socially and industrially, Overbrook, Morris Park, and Wynnefield might be described as pastoral. They contained farms, country estates, a few boardinghouses for summer tourists escaping the heat of the city, and little else. Parts of northern West Philadelphia were beautiful, with rolling hills, magnificent foliage, and clear flowing streams. Such natural beauty can still be found in Fairmount Park, but in the half century after 1880 much of the loveliness was obliterated by seemingly endless lines of red brick rowhouses, with the streams paved over to serve as sewers.

During the last two decades of the nineteenth century, northern West Philadelphia became a suburban residential area. Its jumble of industrial-residential enclaves, stockyards, estates, squatter shacks, and the villages of Hestonville and Haddington, was replaced by a group of well-defined communities. Prompted by the introduction of electric trolley lines along the principal thoroughfares—Lancaster Pike, Haverford Road, and Lansdowne Road—suburban development resulted in the tripling of population, from 14,250 in 1880 to 43,708 twenty years later. In the northern part of Haddington, through which ran both Lansdowne and Haverford roads, the number of houses increased from 250 to 908. In the western portion of Mill Creek, the increase was proportionately greater, from 91 to 550 dwellings.[2]

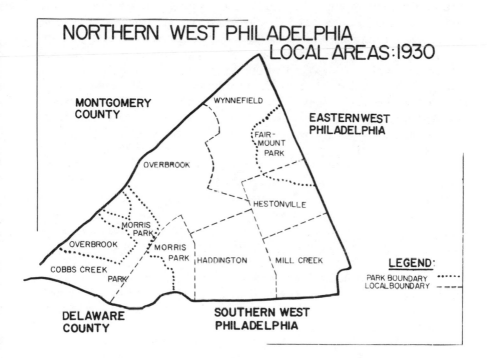

Map 7-1. Neighborhoods and Parks of Northern West Philadelphia, 1930. *Map by Robert H. Marsh.*

In part because of the differential patterns developed during the preurban period, in part because of the type of transit introduced during the last two decades of the nineteenth century, the communities which developed during this initial phase of growth were distinct from one another, both physically and socially. The planned suburb of Overbrook Farms, located on the western edge of the city and isolated from the rest of the area, attracted corporate executives and independent professionals. In Haddington and Mill Creek, on the other hand, bookkeepers, clerks, teachers, and some skilled workers purchased or rented the new red brick row houses modeled on the traditional urban pattern but larger, with more light and air and often with small front lawns. In both communities most industries were driven out before the turn of the century by the residential expansion; in Haddington the black shantytown, the last vestige of an earlier stage of development, was completely destroyed by fire in 1900. Hestonville alone retained a pattern which combined industrial and residential land use, a pattern encouraged by the site advantages afforded by the rail line and numerous track extensions for industrial transport. It would have been both impractical and prohibitively expensive to demolish them (see Map 7-2).[3]

Alterations in the fabric of community life accompanied the physical changes brought on by the first wave of suburbanization. For the first time, formal community institutions became important. The majority of the residents of Overbrook Farms participated in the creation of a country club and two social-civic organizations. In the middle-class communities of Haddington and Mill Creek neighborhood churches, fraternal clubs, and other social organizations proliferated. Between 1880 and 1900 the number of churches—most of them neighborhood-based—grew sevenfold, and fraternal organizations more than quadrupled, with several of the clubs initiating women's branches. The principal significance of the growth of such institutions was that they provided a measure of "instant" communality for the thousands of newcomers. The rigid racial and ethnic exclusivity practiced by most of them assured potential members of association with people of similar background, while it harshly anticipated the segregated neighborhoods of the twentieth century.[4]

This initial phase of residential growth was thus characterized by an informal order, regulated to some extent by nascent community institutions which brought a measure of cohesiveness to the neighborhoods of the outer city. Physical developments also contributed to that informal order in several ways. Because the residential construction industry rested in the hands of a multitude of independent, small-scale builders, land tended to be brought into residential use in small tracts. (Overbrook Farms was the one exception to this pattern.) This building process encouraged steady but not overly rapid growth, a stable pattern which was also promoted by a second factor, a trolley system which extended along two of the major

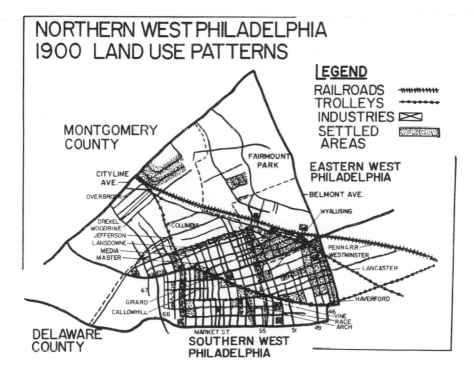

Map 7-2. Land Use in Northern West Philadelphia, 1900. The blocks immediately north of Market Street were still relatively undeveloped in 1900. *Map by Robert H. Marsh.*

arteries from the central business district, Lancaster Pike and Haverford Road. These lines were complemented by others along Vine Street and Lansdowne Road, and together they eliminated any spatial need to concentrate construction excessively in a single area. Finally, northern West Philadelphia as a whole represented only one of a number of residential choices for the suburban-bound city dweller. The concurrent development of other areas of the outer city, particularly to the northeast and north of the central business district, helped to maintain a steady and manageable rate of growth.[5]

Initial Impact of the El, 1900–1910

The introduction of rapid transit altered the entire fabric of community life, both spatially and socially, in northern West Philadelphia. Opened six years after completion of the plans for it, the Market Street subway-elevated Line lured tens of thousands of new residents to northern West Philadelphia. The promise of a 15-minute ride from the western edge of the city into the center of town caused commuters to make West Philadelphia the fastest-growing section of the city during the first decade of the twentieth century. Although some urban analysts such as Andrew Wright Crawford of the *Public Ledger* deplored the chaotic and excessively rapid growth of the areas in the vicinity of the El, the city administration was pleased, publishing a transportation study which showed substantial public acceptance of the El as indicated by a very high level of use. The city subsequently planned, on a grander scale, the construction of new subway and elevated lines, goals which were delayed by World War I and never implemented completely.[6]

Although northern West Philadelphia was only one of four areas within West Philadelphia, in some respects it experienced the most severe effects of the El's construction. Of the other three, Southwest Philadelphia was the farthest away, too far to be affected. Eastern West Philadelphia, on the other hand, had become almost fully urbanized by the early twentieth century. A business and residential area, it was an extension of the Rittenhouse neighborhood to the east. Southern West Philadelphia was virtually undeveloped until the El opened it to mass settlement in 1907. In northern West Philadelphia substantial growth had already occurred; however, there was still room for new construction, and the El's impact there was most profound, for it disrupted established communities in the process of further development. In addition, the decision to locate the rapid transit line along Market Street was of particular significance. West of 44th Street it had been a comparatively unimportant thoroughfare, and now the entire traffic pattern of the area was shifted southward from Lancaster and Haverford avenues. Perhaps more important was the determination that in West Philadelphia the Market Street Line would be an elevated railway. Once completed, this unsightly structure overshadowed its surroundings and became the dominant feature of the environment (see Figure 7-1).[7]

Figure 7-1. The Market Street Elevated, October 1919. Looking east on Market Street from the corner of 62nd, who could deny that the El dominated its surroundings? *Courtesy of the Philadelphia City Archives.*

The construction boom which began in anticipation of the completion of the El continued for a decade. More than 5,000 new structures were erected in Southern Haddington between 1905 and 1915, more than 2,600 in western Mill Creek, and 1,000 in Morris Park, the communities closest to the El. Northern Haddington and lower Overbrook, which were somewhat farther from the El but accessible to it by trolley, together acquired 3,000 new residential structures. By 1910 northern West Philadelphia's population had grown to 89,024, while the proportion of Philadelphians who lived there had increased to 5.7 percent, up from 3.4 percent in 1900.[8]

Most of the newcomers lived in newly built single-family, red brick row houses. A measure of the importance of such dwellings may be found in the scarcity of apartment houses. Only eleven were constructed, almost all in lower Overbrook, designed for middle-class single adults or childless couples. Although the single-family row house predominated, the introduction of two-story, two-family houses in Mill Creek and Southern Haddington served as a harbinger of the future development of the area, had people taken notice. These houses, built practically in the shadow of the elevated tracks along Market Street and adjacent streets, were comparatively inexpensive to build, since the stringent laws concerning "tenement" or apartment house construction only applied to structures with three or more units. Shoddily constructed, these two-family houses were usually put up as rental properties and were rarely owner-occupied. Because they were thought to be less desirable than single-family homes, high rents could not be charged. Most tenants did not expect to remain in them permanently but only until they could buy their own homes.[9]

Between 1905 and 1915 from 20 to 30 percent of the residents of Southern Haddington and Mill Creek lived in housing of this type. After 1920 these two communities would become the center of black expansion in northern West Philadelphia. But initially their new residents as well as those in the entire area were in the same socioeconomic and ethnic categories as those who had moved to northern West Philadelphia during the 1880s and 1890s. The majority were whites of native parentage, while those ethnic groups represented were primarily of the "old" immigration: Germans, English, and Irish (see Table 7-1). Italians, Russian Jews, and blacks combined to total only 5.3 percent of the population. In fact, during the decade when the El was planned and completed there was a proportional decline in the black population. Consequently, despite the El northern West Philadelphia in the early twentieth century must have seemed little changed to many observers. With the exception of the rental flats in the immediate vicinity of the El itself, the houses remained more expensive than those in the working-class, ethnic neighborhoods to the east. The absence of industry in most of the area, the comparative spaciousness of the homes, and the convenience of rapid transit combined to form an almost irresistible attraction for the city's middle class in the pre automobile era. Bookkeepers, clerks, lower-

TABLE 7-1 Population Composition of Northern West Philadelphia, 1900–1920

	1900		1910		1920	
	Number	*Percent*	*Number*	*Percent*	*Number*	*Percent*
Total City Population	1,293,697		1,549,008		1,823,799	
Population of Northern West Philadelphia	43,708		89,024		117,783	
Native white—native parents	21,950	50.3	46,403	52.1	57,109	48.5
Native white-foreign or mixed parents	12,819	29.3	25,399	28.5	34,506	29.3
Foreign-born white	7,122	16.3	14,716	16.5	18,962	16.1
Irish-born	—		5,713	6.4	5,741	4.9
English-born	—		1,994	2.2	1,621	1.4
German-born	—		1,994	2.2	1,548	1.3
Italian-born	—		1,527	1.7	4,340	3.7
Russian (usually Jewish)			618	0.7	2,538	2.2
Nonwhite	1,805	4.1	2,460	2.9	7,152	6.1

SOURCE: U.S. Department of Commerce, Bureau of the Census, *Twelfth Census of the United States, 1900: Population,* 1: 639; *Thirteenth Census of the United States, 1910: Population,* 3:607-8; *Fourteenth Census of the United States, 1920: Population,* 3: 898-99.

level managers, and other white-collar workers whose jobs were in the central business district and whose salaries were improving flocked to northern West Philadelphia which could still promise both a quasi-suburban environment and rapid transportation to the downtown. The trolley lines that served as feeders to the El meant that many commuters could enjoy its advantages without having to endure its accompanying visual and aural discomforts.[10]

Between 1900 and 1910 the communities of northern West Philadelphia which received the most new residents were Mill Creek, Haddington, Morris Park, and lower Overbrook. Upper Overbrook and Wynnefield experienced fewer immediate changes. Their populations did not grow rapidly, and on the surface these neighborhoods appeared to have been untouched by the frenzy of development to the southeast (see Map 7-3). Nevertheless the isolation was more apparent than real. For example, Overbrook Farms had been able to maintain itself as a closed upper-class community in part because of its remote physical location. When the El was built, the country estate which had served as a buffer between it and the rest of northern West Philadelphia was sold to developers. The houses later built on that estate were row and semidetached styles, priced for upper middle- and middle-income buyers. The long-term effect was to lessen the attraction of Overbrook Farms for wealthy Philadelphians.[11]

An analysis of commutation patterns in northern West Philadelphia underscores the direct and indirect impact of the introduction of rapid transit. Data collected for a city-wide study of urban transportation in 1912 showed that the population of northern West Philadelphia had risen to approximately 99,300. Haddington and Mill Creek as a result of spectacular growth had reached their population peaks, while Overbrook and Wynnefield continued the slow and steady pace of development begun in the late nineteenth century (see Table 7-2). Of these nearly 100,000 residents, about half used mass transit every day. Researchers who canvassed commuters leaving the city's central business district for northern West Philadelphia in the evening learned that about 80 percent of them traveled downtown each day. The remaining 20 percent journeyed between their homes and intermediate destinations such as Hestonville (on the trolley) or the industrial sections of eastern West Philadelphia. Not surprisingly, the downtown commuters lived for the most part in Mill Creek, Haddington, and lower Overbrook. Only about 500 Wynnefield residents used either the trolley or the Market Street Elevated, and they lived for the most part in the southern portion of the area. Few, if any, upper Overbrook residents used rapid transit.[12]

By 1912 rapid transit had profoundly affected residential patterns. The Market Street subway-elevated facilitated commuting and shifted the emphasis of urban transit to the goal of moving people into and out of the center of the city. As a result, it became more difficult for a resident to travel within

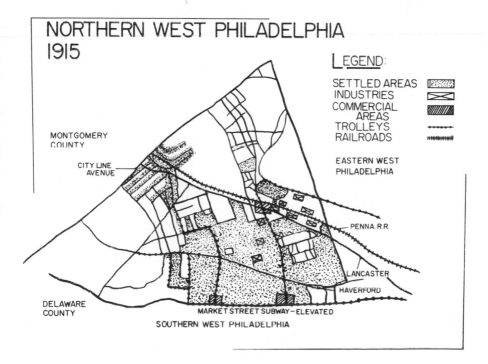

Map 7-3. Land Use in Northern West Philadelphia, 1915. In contrast to 1900, note the extensive settlement, encouraged by the construction of the Market Street subway-elevated, in Mill Creek, Haddington, Morris Park, and lower Overbrook. *Map by Robert H. Marsh.*

TABLE 7-2   Population of Northern Western Philadelphia, 1912

	Number	Percent
Total Population	99,300	
Overbrook		
Overbrook Farms and vicinity	2,500	2.5
Other Upper Overbrook	1,900	1.9
Lower Overbrook	2,800	2.8
Wynnefield	1,700	1.7
Morris Park	6,400	6.5
Haddington	41,800	42.1
Mill Creek	30,300	30.5
Hestonville	11,900	12.0

SOURCE: Department of City Transit, *Report of the Transit Commissioner,* "Electric Railway Traffic and Earnings by Traffic Sector," map, unpaged. Population figures were computed using this map.

northern West Philadelphia for work or recreation. Trolley lines, which had once seemed nearly ubiquitous, were by 1912 relegated principally to the role of feeder lines to the El. It had become easier and quicker to travel from southern Wynnefield to the central business district, a distance of five miles, than to travel from Morris Park to Hestonville, a distance of only a mile and half.[13]

Changing Neighborhoods, 1910–1930

This discussion of residential and transportation patterns suggests that although the initial thrust of development brought greater numbers of the same types of people to northern West Philadelphia, there were several indications that the future might be fundamentally different. In the first place, the decision to build an elevated line, rather than a subway, affected the choices of developers who owned property in the immediate vicinity. Commercial development was one obvious possibility, but only at selected locations. Many types of residential construction would be unfeasible near the hulking, unsightly tracks. Most housing contractors chose to construct the cheap and profitable two-story, two-family rental dwellings along the El. It is not clear whether these builders realized that the creation of a housing market with rents comparable to those in several of the combined industrial-residential sections of the city would ultimately transform the socioeconomic and ethnic character of much of northern West Philadelphia. Nevertheless, that was the result.

Second, the rapidity with which the Market Street Line was planned and constructed, combined with its position as the only system of its kind within the city, encouraged builders to erect dwellings as cheaply and quickly as possible in order to take advantage of the potential market along the El. Even where the construction itself was not shoddy, there was a carelessness about siting and design which resulted all too often in architectural repetitiveness and visual boredom. Because these instant residential areas were aesthetically unappealing, when automobiles allowed the middle classes to abandon them for the relatively more open spaces of suburban Montgomery and Delaware counties, these groups were lured from Philadelphia. A sense of community, which might have held them in northern West Philadelphia, was no longer strong. The restructuring of the transportation system, which after 1912 emphasized almost exclusively movement to and from downtown, combined with the elimination of those lines which had primarily served the local areas, spurred the decline in community identification. The weakening of local ties was most pronounced among the middle class and the upwardly mobile, those groups which had been most active in the social and civic groups of an earlier era. The growth of such organizations had not kept pace, after 1905, with the population increase. Most of the fraternal societies still in existence in the second decade of the century were located in Mill Creek and Hestonville, the least affluent of the residential areas. In her book, *The Urban Neighborhood,* Suzanne Keller has pointed out that in the mid-twentieth-century American city the principal "users" of neighborhoods are those aged or poor residents most socially isolated from the city as a whole. That development appears to have already begun to emerge in northern West Philadelphia during the first and second decades of the century.[14]

The advance guard of the new population began to arrive during the 1910s as blacks moved into Haddington and Mill Creek and Italians into Morris Park. Given the racial bigotry evident in northern West Philadelphia as recently as 1900 when the homes and belongings of the blacks of Haddington's shantytown were destroyed with the approbation of the rest of the community, one might have expected that the increase in the black population, occurring after a decade of racial stability, would have caused consternation. Initially, however, that did not happen. Just before World War I blacks moving into northern West Philadelphia encountered little overt opposition. As Clement Price observed in his study of Newark, before the great migration during World War I blacks were perceived more as a group to be ignored or patronized rather than feared. Then, too, blacks generally moved to northern West Philadelphia in family units; they were quietly respectable, Philadelphia-born, and modestly prosperous. To be sure, there were some migrant black families in the city as a whole before World War I, but they tended to move into the established black community in South Philadelphia or to the more recently formed black settlement in North Philadelphia, not to northern West Philadelphia. A study completed by the Philadelphia Housing Association in 1930 reported "a general tendency for migrant families to settle first in the southern sections of the city and then, with an improved economic status, to move to better rental dwellings and homes which they can purchase."[15]

The comparative freedom which blacks had enjoyed in northern West Philadelphia ended in 1917 as the migration from the South reached major proportions and the city was gripped by a severe housing shortage. Intolerance and hostility became the norm. Landlords in Hestonville and Mill Creek attempted to halt the influx of black residents by refusing to sell or rent to them. An investigator for the Philadelphia Housing Association canvassed an extensive area in Mill Creek (and part of eastern West Philadelphia as well) that had already become "occupied by colored people (more or less)" and could find only one house that the agent was willing to rent to them. But the attempt to call a halt to black population increase was unsuccessful; by 1920 blacks were a substantial minority in several areas. They comprised 18 percent of the total population of southern Haddington in that year; in Mill Creek they were 37.8 percent, and in Hestonville 10 percent.[16] The pattern of black residential distribution—newcomers to the city moving first into the established racial communities, then into other areas as their financial situation improved—seems to have also applied to the Russian Jewish immigrants and perhaps to the Italians as well, although the evidence in the latter case is not conclusive. The majority of both immigrant groups lived in the older sections of the city, the Jews in South and North Philadelphia, the Italians mostly in South Philadelphia. From these areas they fanned out to other sections of the city.

A sociological study of West Philadelphia completed during the 1920s suggested that the Jewish population of northern West Philadelphia came from the older Jewish settlements of North Philadelphia. "There has been a steady westward movement" of Jews, it said, "along the line of Girard Avenue." This influx into northern West Philadelphia began just before 1920; by that year many Jewish families had settled in Hestonville, where they comprised 14 percent of the population, and adjoining southern Wynnefield. Evidence regarding the original residential patterns of the Italian population is considerably less clear. About all that can be said with certainty is that they moved to Morris Park and Hestonville, where they formed about 6 percent of the population. Since most Italians in the city lived in South Philadelphia, which was the locus of immigrant associations and community institutions, it seems logical that these two communities in northern West Philadelphia were areas of second settlement, not an initial place of residence upon arrival from Italy. Because Italians had been employed extensively in the construction of the El, it is likely that many of them simply moved to the area from South Philadelphia.[17]

Whatever their racial or ethnic background, new residents of northern West Philadelphia had to be able to pay somewhat more for housing than they would have in North or South Philadelphia. Most of the dwellings in this area cost more than the typical working-class Philadelphian could afford, and consequently the majority of those who moved into this growing section of the city were undoubtedly either middle-class or relatively well-paid blue-collar workers. Before World War I the mean selling price of a new house in northern West Philadelphia ranged between $3,500 and $4,200. But according to housing experts, the average worker could afford to pay only approximately $1,400 to $2,000 for a home. Rents, too, were somewhat higher here on the average than in the older sections of the city.[18] Nevertheless, northern West Philadelphia by 1920 had changed. Blacks now formed 6.1 percent of the population, while in 1910 their proportion had been only 2.9 percent. The proportion of Russian Jewish immigrants had grown from 0.7 to 2.2 percent, while the Italians had increased from 1.7 to 3.7 percent. Of course, these percentages represented small populations in terms of absolute numbers, but they marked the beginning of a trend which would become quite pronounced by 1920 (see Table 7-1).

During the 1920s, the incipient pattern of the previous decade became firmly established. Following the classic sociological model of residential dispersion, that of invasion and succession, substantial numbers of blacks, Italian Americans, and Jews continued to be attracted to northern West Philadelphia. The most dramatic development of the decade was the spectacular and selective increase of the black population in the area. While it is true that black migration to the city as a whole was high during the 1920s, the total proportion of blacks in Philadelphia only grew form 7.4 to 11.4 percent. Within northern West Philadelphia, however, blacks increased to 19 percent of the total, with Mill Creek and southern Haddington attracting the greatest numbers. By 1930 blacks made up more than 40 percent of each area's total population. Wynnefield, upper Overbrook, and Morris Park, on the other hand, still had extremely small black populations, ranging from 0.2 to 2.6 percent. But while the emergence of southern Haddington and Mill Creek as predominantly black neighborhoods was the most significant residential transformation of the 1920s, changes also occurred in the settlement patterns of other groups. Italian Americans continued to settle in Hestonville and Morris Park, and to a somewhat lesser extent in Haddington. Jewish families concentrated for the most part in Wynnefield, with smaller settlements in upper Overbrook and Hestonville (see Table 7-3).

Because manuscript census data are unavailable for 1920 and 1930, it is impossible to determine with precision either the economic status or the geographical mobility patterns of newcomers to northern West Philadelphia. Nevertheless, through the use of census tract data, city directories, and voter registration lists, it is possible to offer some tentative observations. After 1920 the trend in the area towards second settlement for upwardly

TABLE 7-3 Population of Local Areas in Northern West Philadelphia, 1930

	Wynnefield	Upper Overbrook	Hestonville	Lower Overbrook/ Northern Haddington	Southern Haddington	Morris Park	Mill Creek
Total number	14,996	6,478	13,400	35,523	27,054	12,509	29,271
Native white-native parents	23.6%	53.2%	20.3%	50.8%	22.1%	33.6%	34.5%
Native white-foreign or mixed parents	45.0%	28.1%	38.0%	27.7%	20.1%	42.2%	20.6%
Foreign-born white	29.0%	16.1%	23.0%	13.0%	12.3%	24.5%	10.6%
Nonwhite	2.1%	2.6%	8.6%	7.5%	45.2%	0.2%	34.2%
Foreign-born:							
born in England	0.9%	1.1%	0.6%	1.2%	0.6%	0.8%	0.6%
Germany	0.8%	0.9%	0.4%	1.0%	0.5%	0.5%	0.8%
Ireland	1.5%	4.4%	3.6%	5.4%	2.0%	3.0%	5.1%
Italy	0.2%	0.7%	12.0%	2.5%	5.1%	17.3%	0.5%
Russia	20.6%	5.2%	3.3%	1.1%	1.8%	1.0%	1.2%

SOURCE: Computed from unpublished census tract data for Wards 34 and 44, 1930.

mobile immigrants and blacks became more pronounced. By 1929 a sub-stantial minority of the residents in the six communities under consideration had moved there from poorer neighborhoods east of the Schuylkill River. Of those who could be traced, 57.2 percent of those who came from outside northern West Philadelphia had been living in Jewish, Italian, or black sections of South or North Philadelphia in 1921. But most geographical mobility was modest; for example, 32.7 percent of the total number of movers came from other sections of West Philadelphia (see Table 7-4).

TABLE 7-4   Residents of Northern West Philadelphia Who Changed Addresses, 1921–1929

Total in Table: 204

Address 1921	Number	Percent
North Philadelphia	38	18.6
South Philadelphia	25	12.3
Northwest Philadelphia	8	13.9
Central Business District	3	1.5
West Philadelphia (outside northern West Philadelphia)	36	17.7
Within northern West Philadelphia, from one section to another	41	20.1
Changed address within section	53	25.9

SOURCE: Table based on sample data.

The existence of a pattern of short-distance moves may also help explain the gradual and measured pace of the process of invasion and succession in northern West Philadelphia. Changes occurred at a rather moderate rate in the area perhaps because between 1910 and 1920 native whites of native parentage began to move out of the area in stages—from southern Haddington and Mill Creek to northern Haddington and lower Overbrook, then to upper Overbrook and out of the city entirely.[19]

Contemporary observers remarked on the dispersal of long-term, estab-lished black Philadelphians from the seventh Ward in the heart of the black community. They appeared to be fleeing the migrants from the southern states whom they fiercely resented. One young scholar who investigated the situation noted that "Negro preachers invited new arrivals into the church but many of the congregations made [the newcomer] know he was not wanted." Some black Philadelphians showed their distaste for the migrants not only by refusing to welcome them into their churches but also by moving out of the neighborhood. Many of them moved to West Philadelphia, initially expanding the black settlement in Mantua (in eastern West Philadelphia). They also settled in Mill Creek and fanned outward from the inexpensive rental housing along the El in Haddington. Jewish and Italian residents seem to have followed a similar pattern of migration accompanying economic mobility, although the evidence is somewhat less clear. In any of these cases, the role played by "blockbusting" realtors is difficult to assess. Blockbusting occurred, but it appears likely that it was substantially less prevalent during the 1920s than it would later become. The existing evidence suggests that it was not the major factor in altering the ethnic or racial composition of the communities of northern West Philadelphia.[20]

Occupational analysis also supports the argument that it was the upwardly mobile who settled there. In 1929 only 21.1 percent of northern West Philadelphia's residents worked in unskilled, semiskilled, or service occupations (see Table 7-5). More than half the working population, 54 percent according to sample data, either owned their own businesses or were engaged in white-collar or professional work. Even in Mill Creek and Haddington, the center of black population, only a little more than one-fourth of the workers were employed in lower-level manual labor. Although with the data available it is impossible to link specific occupations with individual members of ethnic or racial groups, the overall pattern seems clear. Northern West Philadelphia was perhaps a cut below what it once had been, but its socioeconomic status had not drastically declined. With one exception, the area had emerged as a residential district for skilled working and middle-class blacks and ethnics.

The one exception was upper Overbrook, which continued to attract native whites of native parentage. Like the other communities during the 1920s, Overbrook's physical structure was largely determined by land use decisions made in the late nineteenth and early twentieth centuries. Overbrook's first development had been Overbrook Farms. By the 1920s this community had long since lost its splendid isolation, and some of its larger lots had been divided to make room for more houses—smaller detached and semidetached models. Affluent families still occupied many of the homes, particularly the largest and most expensive ones, even though it was no longer true as it had been in 1900 that all of the household heads of Overbrook Farms were corporate executives or independent professionals. By 1925 teachers, other white-collar workers, and at least one skilled worker lived in Overbrook Farms. But despite its slight decline in status overall, Overbrook, particularly upper Overbrook, retained more of the suburban qualities that had been present in 1900 than any of the other areas. There appear to be two reasons. First, upper Overbrook was virtually untouched by the land use changes accompanying the rapid transit line; those who needed the cheap and quick transportation of the El never moved here. This explains the absence of the lower middle class, but does not reveal why

TABLE 7-5　Occupational Classification by Area of Residence in Northern West Philadelphia, 1929

Total in sample: 1,305; total in table: 1,138, total unemployed: 167

	Total		Unskilled, Semiskilled, Service		Skilled		Clerical, Sales, and Protective Service		Managerial, Professional, Business	
	Number	Percent	Number	Percent	Number	Percent	Number	Percent	Number	Percent
Wynnefield	86	100.0	4	4.7	4	4.7	17	19.8	61	70.8
Overbrook	246	100.0	18	7.3	52	21.1	90	36.6	86	35.0
Hestonville	79	100.0	24	30.4	23	29.1	24	30.4	8	10.1
Haddington	392	100.0	100	25.5	120	30.6	96	24.5	76	19.4
Morris Park	40	100.0	11	27.5	8	20.0	10	25.0	11	27.5
Mill Creek	295	100.0	83	28.1	77	26.1	70	23.7	65	22.1
Total	1,138		240		284		307		307	
Total Percent	100.00		21.1		24.9		27.0		27.0	

SOURCE: Based on sample data. Because the voting lists did not provide occupational information, each name was checked in the city directory for occupation.

affluent Jews did not move here but did move to Wynnefield. Apparently, Jewish migrants moved in a line from the Spring Garden section to Strawberry Mansion, then to Hestonville, and beyond to Wynnefield. Residents may have pushed out only a small distance each time because they wanted to be close to a familiar congregation, old friends, and services. They may not have wished to be exposed to anti-Semitism, a likelihood if they ventured too far from familiar territory.[21]

Although the overall population figures for northern West Philadelphia in 1930 seem to suggest that the area was quite heterogeneous, such an interpretation would be inaccurate. The increase in the proportion of minorities in the area was accompanied by higher levels of racial and ethnic segregation, as indicated in the index of dissimilarity for northern West Philadelphia in Table 7-6. The index shows the proportion of each ethnic and racial group which would have had to move to another area in order to have a population distribution like that of whites of native parentage. An index figure higher than 40 is usually considered an indicator of a significant level of segregation.

Analysis of a different type, based on the census tracts, not only strengthens the conclusion regarding racial segregation but also sheds new light on the importance of ethnic segregation. The results of racial and ethnic correlation analysis suggest that in 1920 ethnic segregation was more important in determining residential patterns than was racial segregation, but that by 1930 the reverse was the case. Table 7-7 shows the correlation coefficients for this analysis. Briefly, the correlation analysis shows that a much stronger negative association existed between the black population and the white population in 1930 than had been present in 1920. Conversely, the negative relationship had grown weaker during that decade. Regression analysis of ethnic and racial variables also suggests that ethnicity was relatively less important than race in determining the population composition in northern West Philadelphia by 1930.[22]

There are several reasons for this reversal. The proportion of black residents in the city as a whole had remained relatively stable during the last decades of the nineteenth century and into the first decade of the twentieth. After 1910 that pattern changed, as the migration of blacks from the South grew heavy. However, the first substantial increase in the number of blacks in the city did not precipitate immediate intensification of racial clustering, in part because of the acute housing shortage that gripped the city between 1917 and 1921. Whites found it extremely difficult to move during those years, but by 1921 the situation had altered, and they were no longer compelled to remain in their old neighborhoods. The growth of the suburbs in Delaware and Montgomery counties and of new quasi-suburban communities in the northeastern and northwestern sections of Philadelphia provided alternatives. These new communities owed much of their growth to the mass production of the automobile. Thus, three factors—the end of the housing shortage, the development of new suburbs, and the popularization

TABLE 7-6 **Comparative Index of Dissimilarity, 1880–1930** (Index is for segregation of various groups from native whites of native parentage)

	1920	1930
Native whites of native parents from all foreign-born whites	8	25
Irish	13	10
English	6	8
German	4	8
Italians	37	55
Russian Jews	36	52
Blacks	45	52

SOURCE: Index based on unpublished census tract data for 1920 and 1930, computed for the six communities. There are slight differences in the tract boundaries for 1920 and 1930, but these differences do not appear to affect the analysis appreciably.

TABLE 7-7 **Racial and Ethnic Segregation in Northern West Philadelphia: Correlation Analysis, 1920–1930**

	Correlation Coefficient (r)	Variance Explained r^2	Significance
1920			
White population with black population	−.7280	.5300	.001
Native whites of native parents with foreign-born population	−.8107	.6572	.001
Native whites of native parents with first-generation native-born	−.5950	.3540	.006
1930			
White population with black population	−.9550	.9120	.001
Native whites of native parents with foreign-born population	−.5569	.3101	.005
Native whites of native parents with first-generation native-born	−.6233	.3885	.002

SOURCE: The correlation analysis is based on census tract data for 1920 and 1930. The correlation coefficient squared (r^2) indicates the proportion of variance in variable x which is explained by variable y. Partial correlations failed to reveal the existence of spurious relationships.

of the automobile—contributed to the final triumph of racial segregation in northern West Philadelphia. At the same time, as immigration came to a halt, fear of and hostility toward the immigrant began to level off, although it did not abate completely. By 1930 the nature of twentieth-century development in northern West Philadelphia had become clearly defined. In the next three decades much of the area would become predominantly black, while retaining its residential, home-owning characteristics.

In shaping the physical and social structure of northern West Philadelphia in the twentieth century, the Market Street El was unquestionably of major significance. It contributed to the eventual emergence of the six communities as skilled working- and middle-class, black, and ethnic residential areas. The decisions which accompanied the El's construction—the introduction of rental housing, the siting of commercial areas, even the choice not to build another rapid transit line simultaneously—created the conditions for the transformation of northern West Philadelphia from a group of middle-class, native-white suburbs into more urban but still residential communities for somewhat less affluent but nevertheless upwardly mobile black and white, ethnic Americans. Clearly, without the impact of other social and economic forces, such as the black migration from the South, the immigration from southern and eastern Europe, or even the widespread use of the automobile during the 1920s, that transformation would have occurred differently. Nevertheless, those other forces do not explain why it was particularly the areas which the Market Street El affected, rather than the northeastern or northwestern sections of the city, which first experienced such changes. The development of rapid transit, while not the sole determinant of later development, was of substantial importance in reshaping the residential fate of northern West Philadelphia.

Notes

1. Roy Lubove has observed that cities are "physical container[s]" whose "social organizations and relationships are greatly influenced by land-use and housing patterns." See *The Urban Community: Housing and Planning in The Progressive Era* (Englewood Cliffs, N.J.: Prentice Hall, 1967), pp. 1-2.

2. Pennsylvania State Emergency Relief Administration, *Report of the Philadelphia Real Estate Survey: Residential Structures,* 2 vols. (Philadelphia: City of Philadelphia, 1934) 1: 339-72, and 2: 361-66; Office files of the Philadelphia Housing Association, "Demolitions" (Philadelphia, 1923-1927), n.p. (typewritten).

3. On the black shantytown, see W. W. Weaver, *West Philadelphia: A Study of Natural Social Areas* (Philadelphia: by the author, 1930), p. 83. On the emergent suburbs in northern West Philadelphia, see Margaret Marsh, "Suburbanization and the Search for Community: Residential Decentralization in Philadelphia, 1880-1900," *Pennsylvania History,* 44 (April 1977): 99-116.

4. Gospill's Philadelphia Business Directory (Philadelphia: Gospill, 1895 and 1912); Arthur A. Preuss, *A Dictionary of Secret and Other Societies* (New York:

Herder Book Company, 1924). Robert Cross, ed. *The Church and the City* (New York: Bobbs-Merrill, 1967), introduction.

5. Cf. Sam Bass Warner, Jr., *Streetcar Suburbs: The Process of Growth in Boston, 1870-1900* (Cambridge, Mass.: Harvard University Press, 1962), p. 124; Roy Lubove, *The Progressives and the Slums: Tenement House Reform in New York City, 1890-1917* (Pittsburgh: University of Pittsburgh Press, 1962), pp. 36-39. Both confirm that such diffuse construction practices were the norm for late-nineteenth- and early-twentieth-century urban and suburban areas.

6. Andrew Wright Crawford, "The Interrelation of Housing and City Planning," *Annals of the American Academy of Political Science* 51 (January 1914): 162-71; Department of City Transit, *Report of the Transit Commissioner* (Philadelphia: City of Philadelphia, 1913), passim.

7. William S. Twining, *A Study and Review of the Problem of Passenger Transportation in Philadelphia by a United System of Lines* (Philadelphia: City of Philadelphia, 1916), pp. 52-53; Department of City Transit, "History of Rapid Transit in Philadelphia," Philadelphia, 1930 (typescript); Philadelphia City Planning Commission, *The West Philadelphia District Plan* (Philadelphia: City of Philadelphia, 1964), p. 14; Weaver, *West Philadelphia,* p. 114; Market Street Elevated Passenger RR Co., "Chronology of Construction," January 11, 1927, Philadelphia City Archives.

8. Philadelphia Real Estate Survey, 1: 339-72, and 2: 363-66.

9. Ibid.; Crawford, "Interrelation of Housing and City Planning," *Property Atlas, City of Philadelphia* (Philadelphia, 1911), Wards 34 and 44.

10. Oliver Zunz, "Technology and Society in an Urban Environment: The Case of the Third Avenue Elevated Railway," *Journal of Interdisciplinary History,* 3 (Summer 1972): 89-102, discusses a similar case of delayed transformation; housing costs were computed from the office files of the Philadelphia Housing Association for 1910 in conjunction with figures given in Helen L. Parrish, "The Housing Awakening," *Survey* 27 (January 1911): 232.

11. Tello J. D'Apery, *Overbrook Farms* (Philadelphia: Magee Press, 1936): 17-20.

12. *Report of the Transit Commissioner* (Philadelphia: City of Philadelphia, 1913), "Diagram Showing Volume and Distribution of Traffic out of the Central Delivery District, October-November, 1912," map, unpaged.

13. Department of City Transit, *Report of the Transit Commissioner,* "Official Rapid Transit Map, 1904," unpaged, illustrating transit lines as they existed in 1904 and as they would exist in 1912.

14. Regional Planning Federation of the Tri-State District, *The Regional Plan of the Philadelphia Tri-State District* (Philadelphia: Regional Planning Federation, 1932), pp. 114-15, 128; Leo F. Schnore, "Metropolitan Growth and Decentralization," *American Journal of Sociology* 63 (September 1957): 175-76; *Gospill's Philadelphia Business Directory* (Philadelphia: by the author, 1912); Suzanne Keller, *The Urban Neighborhood: A Sociological Perspective* (New York: Random House, 1968), pp. 105-6.

15. Clement Price, "The Beleagured City as Promised Land: Blacks in Newark, 1917-1947," in *Urban New Jersey Since 1870,* ed. William C. Wright (Trenton: New Jersey Historical Commission, 1975), p. 18; Bernard Newman, "Philadelphia's Negro Population" (Philadelphia, 1930), n.p., (typescript) from the office files of the Philadelphia Housing Association.

16. Philadelphia Housing Association, "Negro Migration Study" (Philadelphia, 1920[?]), n.p., (typescript); Weaver, *West Philadelphia,* p. 87.

17. Caroline Golab, "The Polish Communities of Philadelphia, 1870-1920: Immigrant Distribution and Adaptation in Urban America," Ph.D. dissertation, University of Pennsylvania, 1971, 164n.

18. Office Files of the Philadelphia Housing Association, 1910; Parrish, "The Housing Awakening," p. 232.

19. My analysis of migration patterns within the city is based on systematic samples taken from two sources: the 1929 City Directory (one of the few in which residents were listed geographically) and voting lists for 1928. Both are flawed, biased towards citizens and household heads; nevertheless, there is little else available for individual sampling. Further, the overall distribution was compatible with the observations of other scholars, for example, Weaver, *West Philadelphia,* and Mary Herman, et al., *Introductory Survey of Social Areas in West Philadelphia* (Philadelphia: Health and Welfare Council, 1963), mimeographed. The sample totaled 1,305 persons, whose addresses were traced back to the 1921 City Directory.

20. Sadie Tanner Mossell, "The Standard of Living Among One Hundred Negro Migrant Families in Philadelphia," *Annals of the American Academy of Political and Social Science* 98 (November 1921): 171-218.

21. D'Apery, *Overbrook Farms,* p. 90, lists the charter members of a women's club formed in Overbrook Farms in 1926. None of the women was employed; the occupations of their husbands were checked in the City Directory. The land use changes were evident from analysis of the city's *Property Atlases* for 1911 and 1927.

22. The dependent variable in the regression analysis was the total population composition. The independent variables that were found to be the best "predictors" of the dependent variable in 1920 were, in order, the proportion of Russian-born immigrants (usually Jews), Italian immigrants, whites of native parentage, and blacks. The F-statistic in each case was significant at 0.05. The same equation was computed for the 1930 sample, using the identical racial and ethnic variables. This time, however, the only independent variable that could be used to "predict" the dependent variable was the proportion of black population. The F-statistic again was significant at 0.05. None of the other variables had a sufficient level of significance.

CHAPTER 8 Instability and Uniformity:
Residential Patterns in
Two Philadelphia
Neighborhoods,
1880-1970

MEREDITH SAVERY

The Neighborhood Movement Today

The 1970s may, at some later date, be remembered as the decade of the neighborhood. The virtues and charms of the neighborhood are everywhere trumpeted as the answer to urban decay and the solution to urban anomie. When she announced in 1978 that she planned to focus her attention on American cities, Rosalynn Carter said, "I think the neighborhood is the answer to the problem of the cities," while Henry Reuss, speaking as chairman of the congressional subcommittee on the city, said, "We must focus on a human-scale neighborhood as the basic unit in urban revival."[1] In 1977 Congress created a National Commission on Neighborhoods, charging it with recommending public policy to conserve and revitalize existing neighborhoods.[2] Organizations like the National Association of Neighborhoods and the Alliance for Neighborhood Government have formed to make the neighborhood a viable political force and to influence public policy decisions. The popular press brims with reports of neighborhood revivals—Brooklyn Heights in New York, Mount Auburn in Cincinnati, Bunker Hill in Los Angeles, the Vieux Carré in New Orleans. In short, neighborhoods are fashionable.

Philadelphia, which has for many years called itself "a city of neighborhoods," has been in the vanguard of the neighborhood movement. The reconstruction of Society Hill in the 1960s, planned and financed largely with federal money, was one of the earliest and most successful instances of neighborhood renewal in the country,[3] and other inner Philadelphia neighborhoods, drawing primarily on private funds and the energy of individual urban pioneers, have followed suit with astonishing rapidity—South Street, Queen Village, Olde Town, Spring Garden, Powelton, and University City among others. Philadelphians believe in the neighborhood as a positive force, and both politicians and the media pay homage to it. This faith was given substance when, during the Bicentennial, an immense stainless steel map was constructed in City Hall courtyard, the city's geographic and symbolic center; the map's distinguishing feature was its partitioning of the city into neighborhoods. Many of Philadelphia's neighborhoods have strong historic associations with specific ethnic groups, and these identities persist in the popular imagination despite significant demographic shifts.

Nationally, the resurgence of neighborhood dates from the early 1960s and can be traced to public policy decisions and trends in the national economy. During the presidency of Lyndon Johnson the government began to direct large sums of money toward the nation's cities for urban renewal, education, poverty relief, health care, and other social programs. Unlike earlier efforts which had been highly centralized, many of these new federal programs mandated citizen involvement, and the resulting citizens' advisory councils, action coalitions, coordinating committees, and task forces trained thousands of people in the rituals of the political process.[4] Also, by the early 1960s patterns of urban land use, in transition for more than a century, had been redefined. The central city's position as a government, banking, retailing, recreational, and cultural area was solidified while industry and wholesale trade were removed to outer city and suburban locations adjacent to nodes in the national transportation network. Thus, central cities, and Philadelphia's downtown in particular, became areas of employment for white-collar and professional workers, and the sturdy, if somewhat seedy, nineteenth-century housing stock found there became convenient, relatively inexpensive, and potentially attractive shelter for them. During the 1970s, as inflation and energy problems have intensified and the number of households has proliferated with the coming of age of the postwar babies, the rationale for the reinhabitation of older parts of the city by the upper middle class has gained force and has even spilled into less centrally located neighborhoods.[5]

Although the genesis of the neighborhood movement can be traced back to the 1920s,[6] the current movement owes a considerable debt to one book, *The Death and Life of Great American Cities,* published in 1961, and to its author, Jane Jacobs. A believer in the richness and vitality of urban life, she was dismayed at the results of urban renewal programs, and during the 1950s she set out to analyze "neighborhood" and to identify the factors that successful neighborhoods had in common. "Neighborhood," she said, existed at three levels: the street, the district, and the city itself. While the street and the city were established and viable, the district desperately needed shoring up to act as a political intermediary between the cohesive but powerless street neighborhood and the disjointed but powerful city. Looking for viable district neighborhoods, she pointed to the ethnic, working-class communities of Boston and New York as areas that delighted the senses and cosseted the soul, and she concluded that diversity and stability were the two common components of these neighborhoods. Diversity in the Jacobs' lexicon has both social and physical dimensions; "exuberant diversity" exists where both people and their life-styles as well as buildings and their functions are varied yet interdependent, concentrated yet dynamic. Stability, while less carefully defined, refers to the continuous habitation of an area by significant numbers of residents—or in her words, "they [heterogeneous and cohesive neighborhoods] contain many individuals who stay put."[7]

During the 1960s Mrs. Jacobs' arguments attracted an enormous popular following, but historians have pointed out that, despite the small amount of research that has been done on individual neighborhoods, the available evidence indicates the existence of massive and chronic transiency in urban populations. Jacobs' enthusiasm for diversity has also been challenged, most notably by Lewis Mumford, who, using Harlem as his example, argued that diversity in itself does not create a successful neighborhood.[8] But these challenges notwithstanding, the essentials of the Jacobs' thesis are still widely accepted and in certain quarters have taken on a mythic character that transcends both *The Death and Life of Great American Cities* and historical reality.

The current neighborhood movement has accepted Jacobs' dictum about the necessity for local political power; "there is," according to one observer, "a widely shared perception that many of our most serious urban problems can be solved best . . . at the local level."[9] Implicit in this argument for the decentralization of political power has been the assumption that neighborhoods not only have a stable power base but are also more representative of diverse interests than elected politicians and the central bureaucracies they direct. While City Hall and its allies in business and finance are said to destroy neighborhoods, tearing down buildings and uprooting families, the neighborhood movement seeks to preserve them, thus encouraging stability and protecting diversity. In 1977 Congress made this viewpoint explicit in its National Neighborhood Policy Act. Based on the assumption that the nation's neighborhoods are a national resource, this act was intended to promote community continuity and heterogeneity.[10]

Stability and diversity are legitimate goals in a pluralistic, postindustrial society, but are they realistic? What does the historical record reveal about neighborhoods? In general, have they been stable and diverse? To answer these questions, let us examine two Philadelphia neighborhoods, Strawberry Mansion and East Mount Airy. They are neither unique nor archetypal. Although they developed at different rates, both have been recognizable entities for almost a century. Neither has undergone any significant redevelopment, and Strawberry Mansion, a modest streetcar suburb, and East Mount Airy, a middle-class railroad suburb, are representative of two kinds of residential development in post-Civil War Philadelphia. Each neighborhood was subdivided and its housing designed along distinct lines that were almost identical to other Philadelphia neighborhoods of the same type, and these development patterns have profoundly affected the socio-economic, racial, and ethnic composition of the two neighborhoods throughout the twentieth century.

Built almost entirely during the great construction boom of the 1890s, Strawberry Mansion was perhaps Philadelphia's first true suburb in that it was entirely residential and therefore wholly dependent on the mass transportation system. Located about two and a half miles from City Hall, it is and always has been basically a working-class area; some middle-class Philadelphians lived there in the early twentieth century, but in recent years the neighborhood has lost most of them and become so badly deteriorated and racially segregated as to restrict sharply its chances for improvement. The other neighborhood, East Mount Airy, is approximately seven miles from City Hall and is now a racially mixed, middle-class residential community. While it has within it a small industrial village of eighteenth-century origins, referred to here as Franklinville, most of the neighborhood began as a railroad commuter suburb in the early 1860s[11] Its growth continued into the mid-twentieth century as the automobile and bus provided access to areas which lay at a distance from the railroad tracks.

From 1880 to the present neither East Mount Airy nor Strawberry Mansion has been particularly stable or diverse. In both neighborhoods there has been constant and unremitting residential mobility, and with the exception of some racial and ethnic integration for short intervals in both areas, the turnover in population has not been accompanied by significant socio-economic diversification. In Philadelphia's post-Civil War neighborhoods, the physical environment, that is, the quality and character of the land division and housing stock, not only determined the social class, family characteristics, and ethnicity of the first residents but also imposed powerful constraints on the nature of the population changes which occurred in succeeding years. Intended for homogeneous populations, whether of working, middle, or upper class, these neighborhoods have remained homogeneous, their short periods of pluralistic disequilibrium being followed rapidly by the familiar pattern of social and economic uniformity. Thus, for a large fraction of the city individual neighborhoods have been not only unstable but also socially and economically homogeneous for a long time.

Strawberry Mansion and East Mount Airy: How They Began

Strawberry Mansion takes its name from a large eighteenth-century country house on the western boundary of the neighborhood in what is now Fairmount Park. This rather elegant federal mansion is an anomaly in the community. With one exception, it is the only single house, the only house surrounded by grass and trees, the only house overlooking the Schuylkill River, and the only house faced with white stucco. Strawberry Mansion, the neighborhood, is almost entirely a settlement of red brick row houses, some large and semidetached, but most of modest dimensions, crowded onto blocks that have neither grass nor trees.

By 1880, although largely undeveloped, the neighborhood had a discernible outline (see Map 8-1). Its boundaries were defined by Fairmount Park[12] and the Pennsylvania Railroad on the west and south and by two large streets, Lehigh Avenue and 29th Street, on the north and east. The area's chief attraction was its cemeteries, in particular Laurel Hill, which, when it was laid out in 1834, was nationally recognized for its beautiful site and superb landscaping. More important for its destiny as a residential suburb, the Ridge Avenue streetcar ran diagonally through the neighborhood. In regular operation from 1859, it terminated at the Park, where a depot was built to house the horses and later the trolley cars used on the line. In 1880 the streetcar was not yet suitable for most commuters. It was still relatively expensive and, being drawn by horses, not very fast, but with electrification, which came in the 1890s, it became more popular. It is apparent from atlases drawn at the time[13] that developers and the city engineers had already envisioned the basic configuration of Strawberry Mansion. In dotted lines the strict orthogonal grid system laid out by William Penn in the seventeenth century was extended through the working-class neighborhoods of North Philadelphia to the undeveloped countryside along the Schuylkill. With the imposition of those tidy rectangles over the rolling land, the neighborhood was clearly intended to be an extension of North Philadelphia. In fact, by 1875 the first tiny subdivision had already appeared at a point where two streetcar lines intersected.

East Mount Airy is a part of the larger community called Mount Airy; it is defined by its modern neighborhood association as the area between Cresheim Drive on the north, Stenton Avenue on the east, Washington Lane on the south, and Germantown Avenue on the west (see Map 8-2). Although this is not a large area,[14] there are within it two very distinct neighborhoods, each with its own history and its own distinct demography. The two neighborhoods now have only one name and are interrelated to some extent, but they are separate and unequal.

Settlement in the Mount Airy region began in the eighteenth century as the wilderness gave way to farms and the Cresheim and Wissahickon creeks were harnessed to provide power for mills. The Germantown Turnpike, from downtown Philadelphia to Bethlehem, Pennsylvania, became an important artery early in the century, and there are still a number of eighteenth-century buildings—inns, farmhouses, and large summer estates—along Germantown Avenue. Two churches were associated with early East Mount

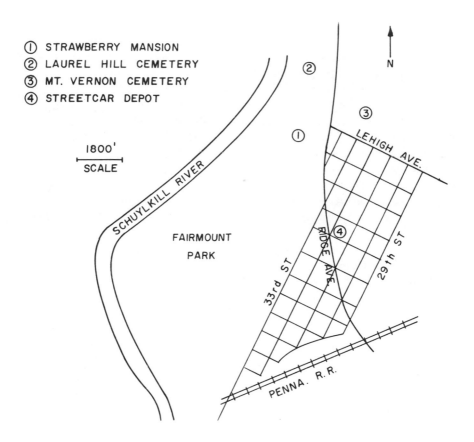

Map 8-1. Strawberry Mansion, Philadelphia, showing the neighborhood's major streets and landmarks.

Airy, St. Michael's Lutheran and the Church of the Brethren (Dunkards), both of which served the poor and around which a community known as Beggarstown developed. The vestiges of this community are still visible on the streets immediately adjacent to these churches where the traditions of poverty and hardship established in the eighteenth century have persevered into the twentieth.

By the 1860s Beggarstown had expanded to become a mill village known as Franklinville which included Franklin Mills as well as other, smaller wool, hosiery, and yarn mills.[15] Throughout the nineteenth century this community provided a pool of cheap labor not only for the mills but also for the construction and maintenance of the country estates in the area and for the improvement of Germantown Pike. This road was successively macadamized, provided with sidewalks (1835-1860), equipped with tracks for the streetcar (1850s), and paved with Belgian block (1880s and 1920s). After 1859, when a depot for the streetcar was built in Franklinville, conductors, brakemen, drivers, and hostlers settled in the neighborhood.

The development of the rest of East Mount Airy followed the more classic pattern of the upper middle-class railroad suburb. The Reading Railroad was extended from Germantown to Chestnut Hill in 1854; by 1886, there were three stations in East Mount Airy.[16] The first church to operate in the railroad suburb was Grace Episcopal which began in 1858 as a mission of Christ Church, Germantown, and established itself as an independent parish in 1868. The fact that the Presbyterians and Methodists did not build churches in East Mount Airy for another 15 to 20 years is an indication not only of the newness of the neighborhood but also of its exclusivity.[17] The respectable character of the neighborhood was enhanced in the 1880s when the Pennsylvania School for the Deaf moved from its downtown location to a 32-acre site on Germantown Avenue and the Lutheran Seminary took over the spacious grounds of Mount Airy College (formerly the Gowen estate). In 1900 the Leamy Home, a model retirement facility, was commissioned by the Leamy sisters to provide a gracious setting for Episcopalian gentlewomen in their declining years.

The street atlas issued by G. M. Hopkins in 1876 clearly reveals the two communities of East Mount Airy.[18] The Germantown Avenue "strip" was uniformly, if sparsely, developed, taken up by the great houses and summer estates of the rich, including the Chews, Johnsons, Bostwicks, Carpenters, and Gowens. The nucleus of an upper middle-class suburb had also appeared near the neighborhood's first railroad station on Mount Pleasant Avenue. A few blocks away Franklinville was an established, self-contained community with three churches, a public school, at least two good-sized mills, the streetcar depot, and whole blocks of small single and semidetached houses. The rest of East Mount Airy was farm land, particularly east of the railroad tracks.

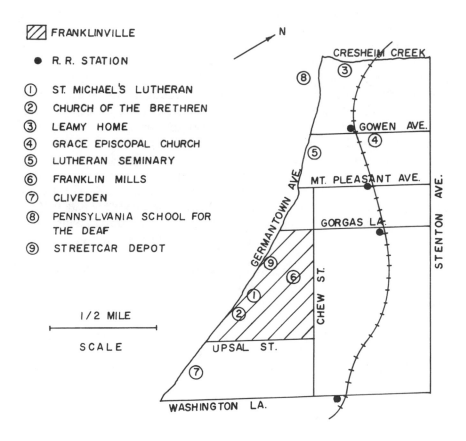

FRANKLINVILLE

● R.R. STATION

① ST. MICHAEL'S LUTHERAN
② CHURCH OF THE BRETHREN
③ LEAMY HOME
④ GRACE EPISCOPAL CHURCH
⑤ LUTHERAN SEMINARY
⑥ FRANKLIN MILLS
⑦ CLIVEDEN
⑧ PENNSYLVANIA SCHOOL FOR
   THE DEAF
⑨ STREETCAR DEPOT

1/2 MILE

SCALE

N

CRESHEIM CREEK
③
⑧

GOWEN AVE.
④
⑤

MT. PLEASANT AVE.

GORGAS LA.

GERMANTOWN AVE.

STENTON AVE.

CHEW ST.

⑨
⑥
①
②

UPSAL ST.

⑦

WASHINGTON LA.

Map 8-2. East Mount Airy, Philadelphia, showing the neighborhood's major streets and landmarks, including the Reading Railroad. Franklin Mills has been torn down; the Leamy Home closed in 1979. Cliveden, the home of the Chews for more than 200 years, is now owned by the National Trust for Historic Preservation. The rest of the neighborhood's landmarks, however, are still serving their original purposes.

Stability and Diversity, 1880–1900

According to the manuscript census, the population of Strawberry Mansion was about 1,800 in 1880.[19] Most of the residents lived either along the route of the Ridge Avenue streetcar or on Lehigh Avenue across from the cemeteries. Households were large, averaging six persons apiece; almost 40 percent of the heads of household were foreign-born with Germans predominating, and more than half of the male heads of household worked as craftsmen. Many of these men were in the building trades—brickmasons, brickmakers, carpenters, and painters—but there were also stonecutters turning out headstones for the ordinary dead and crypts, sarcophagi, obelisks, and statuary for the fashionable who were interred at Laurel Hill. Street railway employees were also well represented in Strawberry Mansion in 1880. It is likely that most men walked to work, either to construction jobs in nearby areas of North Philadelphia or to the street railway depot and the cemeteries in the immediate neighborhood.

By 1900 significant changes had occurred in the neighborhood's demographic profile (see Table 8-1). The population had more than quadrupled, increasing to 9,000 people, and households were much smaller, averaging 4.2 people. Heads of household were more likely to be native-born than in 1880, and there were more white-collar workers than there had been 20 years before. The number of craftsmen and operatives had declined correspondingly, from 54 percent of the total in 1880 to 43 percent in 1900. Unlike the 1880 population, with its building tradesmen and stonecutters, there do not appear to have been any occupational clusters in 1900, with the possible exception of street railway workers.

Between 1880 and 1900 Strawberry Mansion had changed from an urban outpost to a residential suburb. Single-family row houses, stamped endlessly from the same mold, accounted for 90 percent of the land use in 1903. While this pattern was typical for Philadelphia, the speed—20 years—with which this neighborhood developed was unusual.[20] The spacious blocks measuring approximately 400 by 500 feet had been trisected to form three narrow rectangles; on each street there were 40 to 60 row houses, with the original blocks now containing as many as 300 or 400 homes (see Map 8-3). The row houses on the perimeter of the original blocks were usually larger and slightly more ornate than those on the interior streets, but the distinctions were slight. The similarities—the red brick facades, the two bays per floor, the miniscule front porches, the front doors raised above street level, the interior floor plans, the lack of open space—were far more noticeable (see Figure 8-1). Nonetheless, as the advancing population totals suggest, Strawberry Mansion was a desirable address in the early 1900s, and it is not hard to imagine why. Unlike most other neighborhoods in the city, and North Philadelphia in particular, it had no industrial or large commercial

TABLE 8-1   **Strawberry Mansion: Population Profile, 1880 and 1900**

	1880		1900	
Total population	1,850		9,000	
Number households (estimated)	300		2,143	
Average household size	6.1	(n = 90)	4.2	(n = 152)
Average size nuclear family	4.8		3.4	
Heads of household-race & ethnicity				
Percent foreign-born	38[a]		25[a]	
Percent black	0		0	
Heads of household—occupation				
Percent professional	6		6	
Percent managerial	9		13	
Percent sales & clerical	6		23	
Percent craftsmen & operatives	54		43	
Percent laborers & domestics	25		15	

SOURCE: U.S. Bureau of the Census, *Tenth Census of the United States, 1880* (Federal Archives and Record Center, Philadelphia), manuscript files, Reel T9/1187; *Twelfth Census of the United States, 1900* (Federal Archives and Record Center, Philadelphia), manuscript files, Reels T 623/1470, 1472 and 1469.

[a] 1880: 20% from Germany; 1900: 8% from Germany.

sites whatsoever. With the exception of the street railway, the only jobs available in Strawberry Mansion were those in small retailing establishments. Men and women rode to work on the newly electrified trolleys, which now provided not only linear service to the central business district but also crosstown service to Kensington and other parts of North Philadelphia. Adjacent to the neighborhood was Fairmount Park and beyond that the Schuylkill River; thus, the flavor of country living was permanently preserved within walking distance at city expense.

In 1880 East Mount Airy was similar to Strawberry Mansion (see Table 8-2). Its population was less than 2,000, its households were large, and more than a third of its heads of household were foreign-born. But in 1880 East Mount Airy, as a whole, had considerably more socioeconomic diversity than Strawberry Mansion; laborers, craftsmen, salesmen, and professionals were all well represented in the neighborhood. By 1900, households had grown smaller, as in Strawberry Mansion, and the number of foreign-born heads of household had declined. The socioeconomic heterogeneity of the entire area remained about the same, although, not surprisingly, the proportion of agricultural workers had declined by the same percentage as that by which sales and clerical occupations had increased. Population density was low throughout the neighborhood, and ward atlases for this 20-year period reveal slow but steady growth.[21]

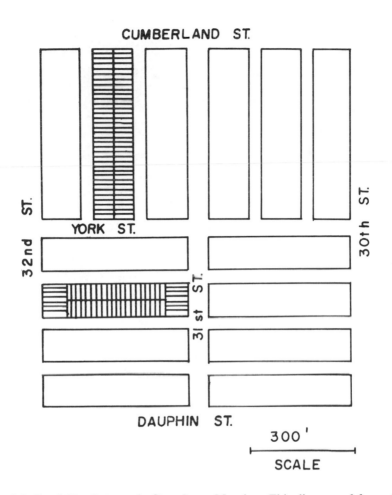

Map 8-3. Land Use Patterns in Strawberry Mansion. This diagram of four of the original blocks in Strawberry Mansion shows how they were subdivided to create fourteen separate blocks. Individual building lots are indicated on two of these blocks.

Figure 8-1. The 2400 Block of North 31st Street, Strawberry Mansion. These brick rowhouses were erected in approximately 1899. *Photograph by Meredith Savery.*

But if East Mount Airy appeared to be somewhat diverse at the end of the nineteenth century, that appearance is deceptive, for Franklinville and the rest of East Mount Airy were still two separate communities, and when examined independently, the differences between them, both in 1880 and 1900, are not only obvious but dramatic (see Table 8-3). In Franklinville the remaining open land was being subdivided in much the same manner as in Strawberry Mansion; that is, row houses and small semidetached houses were being built on small lots. In the rest of East Mount Airy, large single and semidetached houses were under construction on large lots (see Figures 8-2 and 8-3).

TABLE 8-2 **East Mount Airy: Population Profile, 1880 and 1900**

	1880	1900
Total population	1,500	3,000
Number of households (estimated)	270	600
Average household size	5.6 (n = 80)	5.0 (n = 165)
Average size nuclear family	4.6	3.8
Heads of household—race & ethnicity		
Percent foreign-born	36[a]	25[a]
Percent black	<1	5
Heads of household—occupation		
Percent professional	16	13
Percent managerial	5	7
Percent sales & clerical	13	21
Percent craftsmen & operatives	30	35
Percent laborers & domestics	23	19
Percent other (agricultural workers)	13	5

SOURCE: Tenth and Twelfth Census of the U.S., manuscript files.
[a]1880: 17% from Ireland; 1900: 7% from Ireland.

The male heads of household in Franklinville were employed as craftsmen, factory operatives, laborers, or agricultural workers. On the average, they were younger (under 40), had smaller households, and, if foreign-born, were more likely to have been born in Ireland. In the rest of East Mount Airy the male heads of household were older; if foreign-born, they were more likely to have been born in England, and they were employed as professionals, merchants, salesmen, or agents. In Franklinville household members beyond the nuclear family were likely to be boarders; elsewhere in East Mount Airy servants and relatives filled out the extended family. Black families lived only in Franklinville and within that community only on the smallest and oldest streets. In short, East Mount Airy in 1880 and 1900 was clearly divided along socioeconomic, racial, and ethnic lines.

TABLE 8-3   East Mount Airy and Franklinville:
Population Profile, 1880 and 1900

	1880 Frankl. (n = 47)	E.M.A. (n = 24)	1900 Frankl. (n = 87)	E.M.A. (n = 32)
Average household size	5.2	6.4	4.2	6.2
Average size nuclear family	4.4	5.0	3.5	4.0
Heads of household—race & ethnicity				
Percent foreign-born	37	37	29	6
Percent black	∠1	0	7	0
Heads of household— occupation				
Percent professional	3	42	1	43
Percent managerial	0	16	1	21
Percent sales & clerical	14	11	17	32
Percent craftsmen & operatives	38	16	47	4
Percent laborers & domestics	30	11	27	0
Percent other (agricultural)	15	4	7	0

SOURCE: Tenth and Twelfth Census of the U.S., manuscript files.

In the 20 years between 1880 and 1900 were Strawberry Mansion and East Mount Airy either stable or diverse? They were certainly not stable; the population of Strawberry Mansion quintupled, that of Mount Airy doubled, and the demographic profiles of the two neighborhoods reveal distinct changes in their composition. The question of their socioeconomic and ethnic diversity is somewhat more complex. In Strawberry Mansion in 1880 one in three heads of household was foreign-born, three of four worked with their hands either in skilled trades such as stonecutting and building or in unskilled jobs such as hostling and laboring. In 1900 only one in four heads of household was foreign-born, and there had been a fourfold increase in the number of heads working in sales and clerical jobs. However, this apparent occupational diversification masked segregation by income. Almost all the housing was new, and variations in size and style were slight or nonexistent. Since there were no jobs within walking distance and no local stop for the railroad, the entire neighborhood was dependent on one mode of transportation. Consequently, it was settled by a fairly narrow group: families, primarily native Americans, of modest prosperity having sufficient income and job security to take on the cost of new but inexpensive housing. While some ethnic and socioeconomic diversity existed on given blocks, the neighborhood as a whole, that collection of almost identical brick row houses, was extraordinarily homogeneous.[22]

Figure 8-2. The 200 Block of East Hortter Street, Franklinville. The semidetached brick twin houses shown here were built about 1890. *Photograph by Meredith Savery.*

Figure 8-3. Twin House in the 200 Block of East Cliveden Street, East Mount Airy.
This semidetached, brick and fieldstone twin house was put up in approximately
1890. *Photograph by Meredith Savery.*

In East Mount Airy, although there appears to have been socioeconomic diversity, the reality was two relatively homogeneous communities, East Mount Airy and Franklinville, existing side by side. Blacks and the foreign-born were concentrated in Franklinville, and even as late as 1900 its residents were in occupations suitable for the immediate neighborhood, that is, within walking distance. In the rest of East Mount Airy, workers were generally in the professions or in jobs with companies located in the central business district; these people were railroad commuters. The socioeconomic difference between the two communities was clearly reflected in lot size and available housing. As in Strawberry Mansion, subdivision patterns and housing stock dictated segregation by income.

Thus, these two neighborhoods illustrate well the turn-of-the-century suburban development patterns described by Sam Bass Warner in *Streetcar Suburbs*.[23] Strawberry Mansion, with hundreds of small houses and multiple streetcar lines, was predominantly an upper working-class neighborhood. East Mount Airy, despite the anomalous pocket of settlement in Franklinville, was an upper middle-class railroad suburb. By 1900 each neighborhood had attained a distinct socioeconomic identity which found its most visible expression in lot size and housing style.

Stability and Diversity, 1901–1940

The patterns of residential mobility and socioeconomic homogeneity, which had been established in both neighborhoods by 1900, continued and were reinforced in the twentieth century. While the two neighborhoods differed in their population growth rates and land use patterns, they were remarkably similar in the pace of their residential mobility and the consistency of their socioeconomic status over time.[24] Between 1900 and 1920 the population of both Strawberry Mansion and East Mount Airy continued to grow, but thereafter Strawberry Mansion began to lose population while East Mount Airy gained in size into the 1960s. Throughout the twentieth century there has also been an accelerating increase in the black population of both neighborhoods. The population figures for the period 1900 to 1930 appear in Table 8-4.

Population growth did not alter the land use patterns established by the early subdividers and building contractors.[25] Strawberry Mansion, which was almost totally developed by 1910, became more densely inhabited, while in East Mount Airy development continued along the lines previously established. As late as 1940 large portions of the area east of the Reading Railroad tracks remained unimproved, although much of it was coming under the ownership of one developer, Ashton Tourison. During the 1920s Mount Airy, East and West, became a center for colonial revival architecture. Large and imposing homes replete with fanlights, pediments, dormers,

TABLE 8-4 **Strawberry Mansion and East Mount Airy:**
            Population Growth, 1900-1930

	Total Population[a]		Black Population	
	Str. Man.	*E.M.A.*	*Str. Man.(%)*	*E.M.A. (%)*
1900	9,000	3,100	0	5
1910	22,338 (+ 148%)	6,303 (+ 103%)	no data available	
1920	28,623 (+ 28%)	9,329 (+ 48%)	1	7
1930	27,335 (− 4%)	11,972 (+ 28%)	5	11

SOURCE: Twelfth Census of the U.S., 1900, manuscript files; U.S. Bureau of the Census, *Thirteenth Census of the United States, 1910,* enumeration district manuscripts (Urban Archives, Temple University); U.S. Bureau of the Census, *Fourteenth Census of the United States, 1920,* enumeration district manuscripts (Urban Archives, Temple University); U.S. Bureau of the Census, *Fifteenth Census of the United States, 1930,* census tract manuscripts (Urban Archives, Temple University).

[a]The compilation of demographic data by neighborhood was complicated by shifting tract boundaries. See note 24 for further explanation.

and columned entranceways replaced the mansard-roofed, gabled, and bracketed styles of the late nineteenth century (see Figure 8-4). Like the commuter suburb, Franklinville, too, underwent rapid development during the first 30 years of the twentieth century, but there row houses with more modest colonial motifs were the rule. By 1930 Franklinville was fully developed. With very little open space and high population density, it had a very different ambiance from the commuter suburb.

Despite the increasing maturity of both neighborhoods, the residential stability which might have been anticipated by 1930 did not materialize. The Philadelphia city directories of 1921, 1929, and 1935-36 have been used to analyze residential stability and the persistence of neighborhood residents. The results appear in Tables 8-5, 8-6, and 8-7.

Clearly, between 1929 and 1936 both Strawberry Mansion and East Mount Airy experienced significant turnover in population. At the end of this seven-year period in both neighborhoods only four of every ten heads of household had been at the same address since 1929 (see Table 8-5). These data are not unique; in fact, because they are taken from the 1930s, a period when residential mobility was at a city-wide low, they are probably conservative.[26] Other research on residential mobility, whether among ethnic or socioeconomic groups, or among urban populations as a whole, points to the same conclusion—widespread and persistent transiency.[27] Most recently, the findings of Caroline Golab, writing about the Polish in Philadelphia before World War I, typify work in this field. The tightly knit, stable ethnic

Figure 8-4. Colonial Revival Single in the 100 Block of East Sedgwick Street, East Mount Airy. This fieldstone house was built about 1920. *Photograph by Meredith Savery.*

TABLE 8–5   Strawberry Mansion and East Mount Airy:
Residential Stability, 1929–1936

	Str. Man.	E.M.A.
Sample: heads of household, 1929	462	229
Population, 1930	27,335	11,972
Population, 1940	25,969	14,752
Percent change	−5%	+23%
Number in 1929 sample at same address in 1935-36	185	116
Percent of 1929 sample at same address in 1935-36	40%	51%
Percent of 1935-36 population which had lived at same address since 1929	42%	42%

SOURCE: In 1929 and 1930 one section of the directory listed the names of all heads of household in order of street address. The 1929 directory was used noting every fifteenth name (a 6 percent sample of heads of household) from the streets of Strawberry Mansion and East Mount Airy. The 1921 and 1935-36 alphabetical directories were then searched for the same names. City directories were not published after 1935-36. *Boyd's Philadelphia Combined City and Business Directory* (Philadelphia: C. E. Howe Co., 1921); *Polk's (Boyd's) Philadelphia City Directory V. 1929* (Philadelphia: R. L. Polk Co., 1929), p. cv; *Polk's (Boyd's) Philadelphia City Directory V. 1935-36* (Philadelphia City Directory, Inc., 1935), p. cvii.

ghetto was, she has said, an imaginary phenomenon: "If the Polish experience in Philadelphia is at all typical, fluidity and transiency, not stagnancy and immobility, were the chief characteristics of large, urban immigrant neighborhoods."[28]

While the 1929 and 1936 city directory data for Strawberry Mansion and East Mount Airy reveal clearly the magnitude of residential mobility, the introduction of the data from the 1921 directory permits a closer analysis of the persistent resident (see Table 8-6). In the 1920s and 1930s Strawberry Mansion and East Mount Airy each had a core of households which was significantly more stable than a random sample of the neighborhoods' populations. Between 10 and 20 percent stayed for 15 years or longer (see Table 8-7). But was this group large enough or effective enough to provide continuity for a neighborhood and its institutions? Did its existence give the neighborhood an "identity"? If so, how was that identity transmitted, and what distinguished the family that stayed from the one that moved?

In an effort to answer those questions, occupational data were taken from the city directories for each persisting head of household in 1936 and compared with 1940 census distributions. As Table 8-8 indicates, residents of higher socioeconomic status were more likely to persist than those from

**TABLE 8-6 Strawberry Mansion and East Mount Airy:
Residential Persistence, 1921–1936**

	Str. Man.	E.M.A.
1929 total sample	462	229
Number in 1929 sample at same address in 1921	113	45
Number in 1929 sample at same address in 1936	185	116
Number in 1929 sample at same address in 1921 and 1936	73	34
Percent of sample persisting from 1929 to 1936	40%	51%
Percent of those persisting from 1921 to 1929 who also persisted to 1936	65%	76%

SOURCE: Philadelphia city directories, 1921, 1929, 1936.

**TABLE 8-7 Strawberry Mansion and East Mount Airy: Residential
Persistence Equalized for Population Change, 1921–1936**

Population	Strawberry Mansion	East Mount Airy
1920	28,623	9,329
1930-percent change	27,335 (−4%)	11,972 (+28%)
1940-percent change	25,969 (−5%)	14,752 (+23%)

Samples of heads of household equalized for population change by decade

1920	481	179
1929	462	229
1936	439	281

Stable core by number and as a percentage of the total population

	Number	Percent	Number	Percent
1921	113	—	45	—
1929	113	24	45	20
1936	73	17	34	12

SOURCE: Philadelphia city directories 1921, 1929, 1936; *Fourteenth Census of the
U.S., 1920,* enumeration district manuscripts; *Fifteenth Census, 1930,* census tract
manuscripts; U.S. Bureau of the Census, *United States Census of Population and
Housing: 1940, Statistics for Census Tracts, Philadelphia, Pa.* (Washington: Government Printing Office, 1942).

other groups.[29] The presence of widows among the persisters is also worthy of note; perhaps, as women alone, they could not be as mobile as those still living with their husbands. Finally, significant persistence is also evident among a large group of craftsmen and operatives in Strawberry Mansion.[30] To the extent that these persisters staffed neighborhood institutions, such as churches and saloons, or provided goods and services, as doctors and merchants would have done, they undoubtedly provided a *sense* of continuity. In addition, they may have created a physical presence—churches and synagogues, stores and shops, signs and symbols—which remained long after their founders had died or moved away. But there is no evidence to suggest that such people and institutions exerted a significant influence upon the residential stability of their neighbors or on the neighborhood as a whole.[31]

Turning to an investigation of social diversity in these two neighborhoods between 1900 and 1940, it is apparent that the nineteenth-century pattern of segregation by income remained in force despite ethnic turnover.[32] In both Strawberry Mansion and East Mount Airy significant ethnic changes occurred, although the transformation in Strawberry Mansion was larger and more dramatic. In 1900, 25 percent of its heads of household were foreign-born with people from Germany and Ireland in the majority. Only one head of household had been born in eastern Europe, and surnames for neighborhood residents were overwhelmingly Western European. But by 1929 at least 80 percent of the names listed for Strawberry Mansion in the city directory were Jewish. According to the census of the following year, 34 percent of the population in the area was foreign-born; another 38 percent had foreign or mixed parentage, and the vast majority of these people were from eastern Europe and thus were, most likely, Jewish.[33] Such ethnic data alone suggest remarkable population turnover in Strawberry Mansion in the 30 years between 1900 and 1930.

For east Mount Airy ethnic change was less profound but significant nonetheless. Like Strawberry Mansion 25 percent of its heads of household in 1900 were foreign-born with people from Ireland, Germany, and England predominating. In 1930 only 11 percent of the population was foreign-born. Almost half of them had been born in Ireland, and most now lived in Franklinville. In the same year 23 percent of those in East Mount Airy had parents of foreign or mixed birth, more than one-third of whom were from Ireland. Not surprisingly, most of these second-generation immigrants (65 percent) also lived in Franklinville.[34] Thus, although population mobility and persistence (see Tables 8-5 and 8-7) were approximately the same in both Strawberry Mansion and East Mount Airy, the ethnic composition of the latter was somewhat more stable, the result perhaps of the higher social status of the neighborhood as well as its substantial distance from the older sections of the city.

TABLE 8-8   Strawberry Mansion and East Mount Airy: Socioeconomic
Profile of General Population and Persisters, 1940

Occupations	Strawberry Mansion		East Mount Airy	
	1940 *Census (%)*	*1936* *Persisters (%)* *n = 73*	*1940* *Census (%)*	*1936* *Persisters (%)* *n = 34*
Professional	4	13	14	30
Managerial	11	7	16	17
Sales & clerical	28	15	30	10
Craftsmen & operatives	43	31	19	10
Domestics & laborers	14	13	21	17
Widows	—	14	—	10
No occupation	—	7	—	6

SOURCE: Philadelphia city directory, 1936; *U.S. Population Census, 1940.*

Clearly, there was a high degree of residential turnover in both neighborhoods and extreme discontinuity in the ethnic composition of Strawberry Mansion. But when one examines the socioeconomic profile of these two neighborhoods over the same period, one finds remarkably little change. In Strawberry Mansion residential instability and ethnic discontinuity were accompanied by high degrees of socioeconomic continuity and homogeneity (see Table 8-9). Different ethnic groups arrived and departed, but the neighborhood remained predominantly working-class.

In East Mount Airy there was some occupational diversification in 40 years, but Franklinville and the rest of East Mount Airy did not merge (see Table 8-10). The commuter suburb remained primarily white-collar, while Franklinville continued to be largely blue-collar, although it experienced a significant increase in the number of its professional and managerial jobholders.[35] Thus, although the evidence is not as compelling as that for Strawberry Mansion, it appears that East Mount Airy, particularly when considered in its two sections, was also both unstable residentially and relatively homogeneous socioeconomically.

Between 1900 and 1940 socioeconomic status was the most stable feature of Strawberry Mansion and East Mount Airy, and it was, in turn, both reflected in and influenced by the spatial arrangements of these neighborhoods and the quality of their housing stock. The essential identity of a neighborhood is transmitted largely through its physical structures. Residents come and go, ethnic groups leave their signatures behind, but the essence of a mature neighborhood, especially a post-Civil War one, derives from something more. What matters perhaps more than anything else is remarkably simple: housing and land use. In the developed neighborhood they determine socioeconomic status as much as, if not more than, they are determined by it.

TABLE 8–9 Strawberry Mansion: Occupational Distribution, 1900 and 1940

Occupations	1900 (%)	1940 (%)
Professional & managerial	19	15
Sales & clerical	24	28
Craftsmen & operatives	42	43
Laborers & domestics	15	14

SOURCE: *Twelfth Census of the U.S., 1900,* manuscript files; *U.S. Population Census,* 1940.

TABLE 8–10 East Mount Airy and Franklinville: Occupational Distribution, 1900 and 1940

Occupations	East Mount Airy 1900 (%)	1940 (%)	Franklinville 1900 (%)	1940 (%)
Professional & managerial	64	42	2	13
Sales & clerical	32	35	17	23
Craftsmen & operatives	4	11	47	31
Laborers & domestics	—	12	27	32
Other (agricultural)	—	—	7	1

SOURCE: *Twelfth Census of the U.S., 1900,* manuscript files; *U.S. Population Census,* 1940.

Stability and Diversity After 1940: A Postscript

After 1940 the patterns previously established in both Strawberry Mansion and East Mount Airy persisted, but external factors introduced modifications. In the 1950s the automobile and the truck continued to open vast areas to industrial and residential development. Mount Airy, which was at the edge of the city and which still had much undeveloped land, was the beneficiary of this sudden boom, but Strawberry Mansion, a classic streetcar suburb, was isolated from many jobs which were now accessible only by car or train. Between 1949 and 1959, 306,379 housing units were built in the Philadelphia metropolitan area, a 100 percent increase over the preceding decade.[36] This abundance of housing construction, greater than in any previous decade and available with attractive financing and GI loans, was an irresistible inducement to middle-class whites. The neighborhoods they left behind were then available to blacks, who with lower incomes and fewer skills as well as insufficient access to credit, were unable to maintain the 50-year-old, deteriorating housing they inherited (see Figure 8-5).

For Strawberry Mansion the story is told in Table 8-11. Here is homogeneity with a vengeance. By 1960 in this neighborhood as well as in the rest of North Philadelphia, all vestiges of racial diversity had disappeared, and whatever socioeconomic diversity may have existed within the limits imposed by the housing stock was greatly reduced. A relative change in the housing stock, which by 1960 was no longer in a desirable location and was neither new nor well maintained, was reflected in an absolute, if not drastic change in the socioeconomic composition of the neighborhood. Between 1940 and 1960 Strawberry Mansion lost its standing as an upper working-class community and became instead one in which many more of its workers than ever before were at the bottom of the occupational ladder. Residential turnover, moreover, continued. According to the 1970 census, 41 percent of the residents of Strawberry Mansion had lived there for less than five years, 59 percent for less than ten years. Of course, these turnover rates were *not* unique; they were approximately the same as the rates for the period from 1921 to 1936. Therefore, while the 1950s is commonly thought of as the period of white flight, it might more accurately be thought of as part of a historical continuum, a national habit of moving on, which, if Strawberry Mansion is typical, was as prevalent among urban blacks in the 1960s as it was earlier among whites.

In East Mount Airy after 1940 the population continued to grow as the remaining undeveloped areas, mostly east of the Reading Railroad, filled with semidetached houses, quadriplexes, and apartment buildings (see Table 8-12). Such growth and the concomitant proliferation of multifamily housing did not affect significantly the preexisting socioeconomic identity of the neighborhood. As always, there were still two separate communities

TABLE 8-11   Strawberry Mansion: Population Characteristics, 1940-1970

	1940 (%)	1950 (%)	1960 (%)	1970 (%)
Total population				
Percent white	88	74	9	2
Percent black	12	26	91	98
Occupations				
Professional & managerial	15	14	4	6
Sales & clerical	28	26	12	21
Craftsmen & operatives	43	43	48	38
Domestics & laborers	14	17	36	35

SOURCE: *U.S. Population Census, 1940;* U.S. Bureau of the Census, *United States Census of Population: 1950, Census Tract Statistics, Philadelphia, Pa.* (Washington: Government Printing Office, 1952); U.S. Bureau of the Census, *United States Census of Population and Housing: 1960, Census Tracts Philadelphia, PA-NJ.* (Washington: Government Printing Office, 1952); U.S. Bureau of the Census, *United States Census of Population and Housing: 1970, Census Tracts Philadelphia, PA-NJ* (Washington: U.S. Government Printing Office, 1972).

in East Mount Airy (see Table 8-13), but their racial compositions, while different from one another, had changed. Franklinville remained a working-class neighborhood, and by 1970 it was predominantly black. The remainder of East Mount Airy was overwhelmingly white collar, and while whites were in the majority in 1970, that situation will not last through the decade. Despite their proximity, Franklinville and white-collar East Mount Airy do not mix much; their children go to different schools, they ride to work by different conveyances, they attend different churches, they have different recreational facilities. And these patterns have existed in East Mount Airy for at least a century, if not longer.

Like Strawberry Mansion the turnover rates in East Mount Airy, as reported in the 1970 census,[37] were not significantly different from what they had been throughout the century. In 1970, 42 percent of the population had lived in the neighborhood for less than five years, 60 percent for less than ten years. Not only are the 1970 figures similar to those for 1921 and 1936, but they are also similar to the figures for Strawberry Mansion for the same period. Residential turnover in East Mount Airy and the gradual aging of its housing stock over the next two or three decades are likely to result in increasing racial homogeneity and socioeconomic decline. However, the range of housing types, from the large villas of the 1890s and 1920s to the apartment houses of the 1940s, as well as the neighborhood's well-established reputation as a middle-class area make it unlikely that these changes will be as rapid or as precipitous as in Strawberry Mansion.

TABLE 8-12 East Mount Airy: Population Characteristics, 1940–1970

	1940 (%)	1950 (%)	1960 (%)	1970 (%)
Total population				
Percent white	88	86	66	44
Percent black	12	14	34	56
Occupations				
Professional & managerial	29	32	31	32
Sales & clerical	31	31	32	35
Craftsmen & operatives	19	22	21	17
Domestics & laborers	21	15	16	16

SOURCE: U.S. Census 1940-1970. The seeming consistency in the percentage of residents who are professional and managerial obscures the decrease in self-employed professionals and managers and the increase in the number of professionals working in the public sector. In 1970 East Mount Airy, while thoroughly middle-class, was no longer upper middle-class.

TABLE 8-13 East Mount Airy and Franklinville: Population Characteristics, 1970

	Franklinville (Tract 253)	East Mount Airy (Tracts 254, 255, 256)
Population	5,890	12,452
Percent white	13%	59%
Percent black	87%	41%
Occupations		
Professional & managerial	16%	39%
Sales & clerical	32%	37%
Craftsmen & operatives	25%	13%
Domestics & laborers	27%	11%

SOURCE: U.S. Census, 1940-1970.

Figure 8-5. The Corner of 30th and Cumberland streets, Strawberry Mansion. The corner building in this picture was torn down in 1978. *Photograph by Meredith Savery.*

Conclusion

Although they are in the same sector of the city, Strawberry Mansion and East Mount Airy are significantly different in origin and in pace and pattern of development as well as in physical appearance and socioeconomic identity. Nonetheless, data from the two neighborhoods suggest some similar conclusions.

For both neighborhoods residential change was constant and substantial. Whether a result of new construction or the resale or rental of existing housing, it appears that, at the end of each decade in the twentieth century, about six out of every ten faces in the two neighborhoods were new. This constant turnover, which has been discovered by other researchers for other times and other places, amounts to a national obsession.[38] It has been variously attributed to the throwaway mentality of a consumer society, to the eternal quest of Americans for a rural utopia, and to a national character that thrives on challenges. But whatever the cause, the fact remains that Americans do not "stay put." For Rosalynn Carter, Henry Reuss, and Jane Jacobs, for the National Commission on Neighborhoods and a host of neighborhood-related federal and state programs which assume that the neighborhood can become the basis for political action and power, this pattern of mobility does not augur well. Lacking wealth and patronage, the strength of neighborhoods must arise from the determination of individuals or small groups acting in their own interest. Is this possible if six out of every ten people in the area move away in the course of a decade?

Assuming that residential stability is desirable, what can be done to encourage it? According to the 1970 census, 11 percent of the residents in Strawberry Mansion and 16 percent in East Mount Airy had moved into their dwellings at least 20 years earlier. Persistence appears to be related to job stability, home ownership, income, and high socioeconomic status. But there is nothing to indicate that persisters are influential in determining neighborhood policy. Nor is it clear that a core of them makes any neighborhood either more stable or a better place to live. With or without them, the modern neighborhood is a fragmented place. Urban neighborhoods have a long history of instability, and left to the forces of history, they will probably continue to be so transient as to make concerted political action all but impossible.[39]

As to diversity, the evidence indicates that for these two neighborhoods, homogeneity was the rule rather than the exception. Both areas, Strawberry Mansion in its entirety and East Mount Airy in two parts, possess a housing stock which is remarkably similar in size, style, and in the case of Strawberry Mansion, date of construction. Considerable socioeconomic homogeneity has been the result. At the same time there have been, for both neighborhoods, radical changes in ethnic and racial composition and for Strawberry

Mansion a significant decline in socioeconomic status. The direction of these changes, however, has been toward homogeneity. Thus, while there have been intervals of disequilibrium (for example, the 1920s in Strawberry Mansion when the neighborhood changed from Irish and German to Jewish and the 1960s in East Mount Airy as the population has become increasingly black), the trend has been toward uniformity. Curiously, the same phenomenon also appears to be occurring in the city's older (pre1850), traditionally heterogeneous neighborhoods. Known as "gentrification" because the direction of change is generally up, this process is nowhere more clearly evident than in Society Hill, the city's oldest and, by many accounts, most comprehensively redeveloped neighborhood. Evidence from most quarters suggests that Americans specifically reject racial diversity and view land use diversity with suspicion.

With some minor exceptions, then, these two neighborhoods were neither stable nor diverse. Mobility and homogeneity have been two of their chief characteristics from the beginning, and in the absence of any major changes in the economy or public policy, they are likely to continue to be dominant.

Notes

1. *The Philadelphia Inquirer,* January 16, 1978; United States Congress, House Committee on Banking, Finance, and Urban Affairs, Subcommittee on the City, *Toward a National Urban Policy,* committee print, 95th Congress, April 1977, p. 139.

2. United States Congress, *National Neighborhood Policy Act,* Title II of Public Law 95-24, 95th Congress, 1977.

3. Valerie S. H. Pace, "Society Hill Philadelphia: Historic Preservation and Urban Renewal in Washington Square East," Ph.D. dissertation, University of Minnesota, 1976.

4. Housing legislation in the 1950s had included provision for citizen participation, but it did not have a widespread effect.

5. For a description of the demographic and economic roots of the return to the cities and the social implications, see Peter Nye and Clint Page, "America's Cities: The Country's New Frontier?" *Nation's Cities* (March 1978): 29-35.

6. The concept of the neighborhood unit is not a new one; in the 1920s reformers and social theorists, reacting to turn-of-the-century living conditions in the large, industrial cities, proposed planned communities in which social and aesthetic considerations received full attention. Unlike the current neighborhood movement which is basically conservative, the earlier movement was essentially progressive, implying relatively major social change. For a discussion of the achievements of these planners, see Lewis Mumford, *The Urban Prospect* (New York: Harcourt Brace, 1968), pp. 56-78.

7. Jane Jacobs, *The Death and Life of Great American Cities* (New York: Vintage Books, 1961), p. 139.

8. Lewis Mumford in his review of the book contended that "some of [Jacobs'] boldest planning proposals, indeed, rest on faulty data, inadquate evidence, and startling miscomprehensions of views contrary to hers." Mumford, *The Urban*

Prospect, p. 187. Mumford, who believes strongly in planning, took exception to Jacobs' celebration of urban life which he characterized as pathological, congested, and disordered, and to her attack on planning and planners as the cause of urban ills. Mumford and Jacobs agree, however, that the neighborhood, because it is stable and continuous, is a vital entity in the revitalization of urban life: "the stabilities of the family and the neighborhood are the basic sources of all higher forms of morality, and when they are lacking, the whole edifice of civilization is threatened." Mumford, *The Urban Prospect,* p, 200. See also Richard Sennett, "An Urban Anarchist," *NY Review of Books* (Jan. 1, 1970), pp. 22-24, and Charles Abrams, "The Economy of Cities," *The New York Times Book Review* (June 1, 1969), p. 3.

9. Paul R. Levy, *Queen Village: The Eclipse of a Community.* Public Papers in the Humanities No. 2 (Philadelphia: Institute for the Study of Civic Values, 1978), p. 7. For a fuller elaboration of this position, see Milton Kotler, *Neighborhood Government: The Foundations of Political Life* (New York: The Bobbs-Merrill Co., 1969), and David Morris and Karl Hess, *Neighborhood Power* (Boston: The Beacon Press, 1975).

10. Section 204 of the National Neighborhood Policy Act, Public Law 95-24, 1977, empowers the National Commission on Neighborhoods to make recommendations for the following, among others: more effective means of community participation; policies to encourage the survival of economically and socially diverse neighborhoods; policies to prevent such destructive practices as blockbusting, redlining, resegregation, and speculation in reviving neighborhoods; policies to promote home ownership in urban communities; policies to encourage better maintenance and management of existing rental housing; policies to make maintenance and rehabilitation of existing structures at least as attractive from a tax viewpoint as the demolition and development of new structures; and policies to modify local zoning and tax laws to facilitate the preservation and revitalization of existing neighborhoods.

11. The Chestnut Hill branch of the Reading Railroad opened in 1854. Mount Pleasant (now Sedgwick) Station is shown on the *Map of the Vicinity of Philadelphia, 1609-1884* (Philadelphia: J. E. Gillette and Co., 1861).

12. The section of Fairmount Park adjacent to the neighborhood was added to the park in 1868. J. Thomas Scharf and Thompson Westcott, *History of Philadelphia, 1809-1884* (Philadelphia: L. H. Everts, 1884), 3: 1856.

13. *City Atlas of Philadelphia By Wards, 21st and 28th Wards* (Philadelphia: G. M. Hopkins, 1875), vol. 2.

14. The neighborhood's area is approximately two square miles.

15. Franklin Mills may well have been a subsidiary of a much larger firm of the same name, with mills downtown and in Conshohocken, which manufactured wool blankets for Union troops during the Civil War. In any event, Germantown was a major nineteenth-century milling center specializing in hosiery and knit goods. Small mills, operating independently or as a part of a mill complex, proliferated throughout Germantown/Mount Airy. The name Franklinville is no longer applied to this section of Mount Airy; we shall continue to use it in order to distinguish it from the rest of Mount Airy.

16. The Pennsylvania Railroad serving West Mount Airy and West Chestnut Hill was not in service until 1884; thus, the east side of Germantown Avenue was suburban-

ized first, beginning in 1832 when the Philadelphia, Germantown and Norristown Railroad initiated service from the central business district to Germantown.

17. For a discussion of the relationship between social class and church locations, see Norman Johnston, "The Caste and Class of the Urban Form of Historic Philadelphia," *Journal of the American Institute of Planners* 32 (November 1966): 247-49.

18. *City Atlas of Philadelphia By Wards, 22nd Ward* (Philadelphia: G. M. Hopkins, 1876), vol. 1.

19. U.S. Bureau of the Census, *Tenth Census of the United States, 1880* (Federal Archives and Record Center, Philadelphia), Reel No. T 9/1187.

20. Henry Muller, *Urban Home Ownership: A Socio-Economic Analysis with Emphasis on Philadelphia* (Philadelphia: College Offset Press, 1947), pp. 73-79. Muller suggests that the proliferation of single-family row houses, many of them owner-occupied, in Philadelphia can be traced to (1) the tradition of home ownership encouraged by the ground rental system established by William Penn, (2) plentiful and cheap building materials, (3) the surplus capital generated by the post-Civil War industrial boom which was available to entrepreneurs both from individuals and from the savings and loan associations established by numerous groups, and (4) the Philadelphia plan of home financing (voided in 1933) in which most lending institutions accepted second mortgage security for loans. These factors were responsible for Philadelphia's reputation as a city of homes.

21. *Atlas of the City of Philadelphia, 22nd Ward* (Philadelphia: G. M. Hopkins, 1885); George W. and Walter S. Bromley, *Atlas of the City of Philadelphia* (Philadelphia: G. W. Bromley, 1895); George W. and Walter S. Bromley, *Atlas of the City of Philadelphia, 22nd Ward* (Philadelphia: G. W. Bromley, 1899). East Mount Airy's slow growth can probably be attributed to the opening of West Mount Airy and Chestnut Hill in the mid-1880s. Henry Houston, through whose efforts the Chestnut Hill commuter line of the Pennsylvania Railroad was constructed, was an energetic entrepreneur and real estate speculator and was successful in attracting upper-class Philadelphians, who had formerly lived downtown, to the new area. E. Digby Baltzell, *Philadelphia Gentlemen: The Making of a National Upper Class* (Glencoe, Ill.: Free Press, 1958), pp. 205-9.

22. There are some, Lewis Mumford among them, who would claim that Strawberry Mansion as described was not a neighborhood at all but a "caste quarter." While it is true that income segregation, nineteenth-century transportation technology, and the grid system were in many ways destructive, there can be no doubt that "neighboring" as a basic social activity existed as it has wherever people have lived in groups.

23. Sam Bass Warner, Jr., *Streetcar Suburbs: The Process of Growth in Boston, 1870-1900* (Cambridge, Mass.: Harvard University Press, 1962).

24. For the period 1901-1929 neighborhood-specific data are scarce. Aggregate population figures are available for the 1910 census enumeration districts; similar information, with racial designations, is available for 1920, but other population characteristics are reported only by wards, which are too large to be useful. In 1930, for the first time, demographic information was reported by census tract. Although the new tract boundaries were not identical to the old enumeration district borders, it is possible to extrapolate from one to the other for a reasonably accurate population continuum.

25. George W. and Walter S. Bromley, *Atlas of the City of Philadelphia* (Philadelphia: G. W. Bromley, 1901); George W. and Walter S. Bromley, *Atlas of the City of Philadelphia* (Philadelphia: G. W. Bromley, 1910); George W. and Walter S. Bromley, *Atlas of the City of Philadelphia, 22nd Ward* (Philadelphia; G. W. Bromley, 1923).

26. Muller, *Urban Home Ownership,* p. 88.

27. Muller found that in 1939, at the end of ten years of depression, 45 percent of the family accommodations in the city had been occupied for less than five years and 63 percent for less than ten years. Muller, *Urban Home Ownership,* p. 88. See also Alan Burstein, "Immigrants and Residential Mobility: The Irish and Germans in Philadelphia, 1850-1880," unpublished manuscript, Philadelphia, 1976, who found that in each decade between 1850 and 1880 approximately 60 percent of the German- or Irish-born adult males were mobile. Burstein's findings echo those of Stephan Thernstrom, *The Other Bostonians* (Cambridge, Mass.: Harvard University Press, 1973) who analyzed the persistence of adult males in Boston over a 90-year period. He found that in some decades, like the 1910s and 1960s, less than 50 percent of the adult males stayed in the city for the ten-year period; even in the decade of greatest stability, the 1880s, only 64 percent of the adult males persisted. Thernstrom's study, of course, does not consider intercity mobility. Howard Chudacoff, "A New Look at Ethnic Neighborhoods: Residential Dispersion and the Concept of Visibility in a Medium-Sized City," *Journal of American History* 60 (June 1973): 76-93, who researched Omaha at the turn of the century, drew similar conclusions. On the average, less than 20 percent of Chudacoff's sample stayed at the same address for eight years.

28. Carolyn Golab, *Immigrant Destinations* (Philadelphia: Temple University Press, 1977), p. 134.

29. The records of Grace Episcopal Church, East Mount Airy's first and until recently major church, provide additional evidence of the persistence of upper-class residents. Vestrymen of the church, who were all in professional or managerial occupations, served lengthy terms averaging in excess of ten years, with the median term being approximately 15 years. In several cases, a man was succeeded on the vestry by his son, suggesting the existence of a mini-aristocracy.

30. These findings must be viewed within the larger context of city-wide residential patterns in the twentieth century. Sociologists William Yancey and Eugene Ericksen have demonstrated that the most stable neighborhoods are those with a high proportion of manufacturing workers—that is, neighborhoods which have access on foot or by transport to many industrial jobs. Most of East Mount Airy was never intended for industrial workers, and thus the occupational group most likely to be stable was largely absent. Strawberry Mansion did afford relatively easy access to industrial jobs, and indeed 31 percent of the 73 people in the sample who persisted for 15 years were craftsmen or operatives. It is clear that in both Strawberry Mansion and East Mount Airy higher-status residents persisted out of proportion to their numbers in the local population; the effect of their persistence is unclear. Eugene P. Ericksen and William L. Yancey, "The Industrial Antecedents of Ethnic Segregation, 1910-1970," unpublished manuscript, Philadelphia, 1977.

31. Yancey and Ericksen have determined that in addition to access to industrial jobs, three other variables relate significantly to stability. They are the age of the neighborhood, the distance from the center of the city, and family income. The

presence of local institutions, that is, those facilities popularly associated with "community," are not significantly related to stability. W. L. Yancey and E. P. Ericksen, "The Antecedents of Community: The Economic and Institutional Structure of Urban Neighborhoods," unpublished manuscript, Philadelphia, 1977.

32. The relationship between ethnicity and residential stability has been investigated elsewhere. See the work of Burstein, Yancey and Ericksen, and Stephanie Greenberg, "Industrialization in Philadelphia: The Relationship Between Industrial Location and Residential Patterns," Ph.D. dissertation, Temple University, 1977.

33. *Twelfth Census of the United States, 1900* (Federal Archives and Records Center, Philadelphia), manuscript files; U.S. Bureau of the Census, *Fifteenth Census of the United States, 1930,* census tract manuscripts (Urban Archives, Paley Library, Temple University); *Polk's City Directory, 1929.*

34. *Twelfth Census of the United States, 1900,* manuscript files; *Fifteenth Census of the United States, 1930,* census tract manuscripts.

35. Franklinville, with its eighteenth-century origins, may conform more to a pre-industrial than a streetcar suburb model; in the preindustrial village, although residential turnover was high, there was more socioeconomic, ethnic, and racial heterogeneity.

36. U.S. Bureau of the Census, *Census of Population and Housing: 1960, Census Tracts Philadelphia, Pa.-N.J.* (Washington, D.C.: U.S. Government Printing Office, 1962.

37. U.S. Bureau of the Census, *United States Census of Population and Housing: 1970, Census Tracts Philadelphia, Pa.-N.J.* (Washington, D.C.: U.S. Government Printing Office, 1972).

38. Stuart Blumin, "Residential Mobility within the Nineteenth Century City," *The Peoples of Philadelphia: A History of Ethnic Groups and Lower Class Life, 1790-1940,* ed. Allen F. Davis and Mark H. Haller (Philadelphia: Temple University Press, 1973), p. 49, suggests that high transiency rates were the norm in the early-nineteenth-century city: "The migration of Philadelphians, consisting of their movements both beyond *and within* the city, was truly immense in its proportions." See also Stephan Thernstrom, *Poverty and Progress: Social Mobility in a Nineteenth Century City* (Cambridge, Mass.: Harvard University Press, 1964).

39. According to Suzanne Keller in *The Urban Neighborhood,* both neighboring and neighborhood are essentially obsolete. "Neighboring" she says, "is no longer part of a tight network of interdependent activities and obligations concentrated within a small physical and social space; it is simply one more segmentalized activity." As for the physical reality of neighborhood, "Local areas or neighborhoods are but stepping stones—not necessarily devoid of sentimental value—in the pursuit of happiness." Suzanne Keller, *The Urban Neighborhood* (New York: Random House, 1968), pp. 119, 123.

CHAPTER 9 **Public Housing in the Depression: Slum Reform in Philadelphia Neighborhoods in the 1930s**

JOHN F. BAUMAN

Prospects for Comprehensive Reform

Nineteenth-century industrialism bequeathed to depression Philadelphia a grim heritage of moldering back-alley courts and blocks of decrepit row housing. In 1930 thousands of families in the city's 2nd, 3rd, 4th, 7th, and 30th wards along the Delaware River front and in South Philadelphia still crammed these scabrous, tottering structures. Moreover, epidemic evictions and sheriff sales in the early 1930s compounded the problem of a deteriorating housing stock, forcing many of the 91,500 Philadelphians whose homes fell under the sheriff's hammer between 1929 and 1933 to double up with relatives or move into already overcrowded and inadequate housing.[1]

The depression decade brought major urban policy changes to Philadelphia, not the least in the area of housing. Clinging to Philadelphia's much-touted reputation as "a city of homes," city officials and reformers alike had spurned arguments in the 1920s from reformers like Edith Elmer Wood who believed that despite the development of housing codes, zoning ordinances, and philanthropic housing experiments, only state-aided housing projects could revitalize the city and decently rehouse its mushrooming low-income population. From 1924 to 1929, this deep-seated tradition of home ownership together with the establishment of hundreds of new building and loan associations, prevented more active government intervention in housing. But the depression, with its massive sheriff sales, evictions, and plummeting urban land values and tax revenues, jarred even the most stalwart city booster and stirred interest in the housing nostrums of the reformers. They, in turn, drew upon two distinct traditions—communitarian and professional reform—to devise a mongrel housing policy which ultimately satisfied none of the participants. Rather than relieving inner-city congestion and affording decent shelter to Philadelphia's low-income working class, public housing invidiously hardened patterns of racial segregation and exacerbated such problems as crime and poverty which were already eroding the vitality of the city's central neighborhoods. Thus in its evolution this policy contributed to many of the unfortunate social and physical patterns which continue to plague Philadelphia today.[2]

Communitarians and professionals propounded distinctive solutions for the city's housing crisis, one stressing the design of modern cooperative communities, and the other, in the progressive tradition, emphasizing the building of good, low-cost housing as one part of a broad program of restrictive legislation aimed at ridding the city of the slum. Both schools of housing reform arose in the late nineteenth and early twentieth centuries. Communitarians found their moorings in the Garden City plans of the English civil servant, Ebenezer Howard, and in the ideas propounded in the 1920s by the Regional Planning Association of America. The professionals looked for inspiration to Lawrence Veiller, author of the 1901 New York Tenement Law and the arch spokesmen for the passage and enforcement of strict city housing codes and ordinances.[3]

In Philadelphia Bernard Newman championed the professional housing position. As executive director of the Philadelphia Housing Association (PHA), Newman undertook numerous housing studies which produced diagrams, charts, and other statistical ammunition to fight for tough city housing codes and to combat slums, which according to the Association bred diseases, crime, and immorality. While favoring restrictive legislation to restrain the venality of private builders and realtors, professionals like Newman remained staunch defenders of private housing. Like Veiller, Newman vigorously opposed government intervention in the free housing market, referring skeptics to the rows of attractive, new working-class homes in the $5,000 range lining blocks in North Philadelphia. "It is only through the education of the builder and their financial backers to the greater profits in lower sales costs," argued Newman, "that lower construction costs" will be stimulated.[4]

But Newman's solicitude for the accomplishments of the private builder never compromised his battle against the slum. In the wake of the depression he and his PHA cohorts tirelessly informed city officials about the enormity of the city's deteriorating housing conditions, stressing especially the rising costs of fighting slum crime, fire, immorality, and disease. With the municipality financially distressed in 1931, Newman hedged his position enough on public intervention to urge the state to support limited-dividend companies which would buy and clear city slum sites and rebuild them with safe and sanitary low-income housing. Two years later Newman openly supported federal funding for limited-dividend projects to house "the forty percent of [Philadelphia] families with small incomes who have been unable to rent hygienic and attractive houses."[5]

Significantly, professionals like Newman considered themselves technicians and housing efficiency experts dedicated to marshaling hard data and awakening concern for both the slum and the need for decent, low-income housing. Housing design and sound construction impressed them, but housing starts, demolitions, vacancy rates, and housing code violations stirred even greater interest. They essentially ignored theoretical excursions into either neighborhood form or the composition of modern environments. Newman accepted the maxim that good housing was safe and sanitary housing, and *ipso facto*, good housing made good people.[6]

No doubt, communitarians like Henry Wright, Lewis Mumford, Clarence Perry, Clarence Stein, and Catherine Bauer agreed with the professionals that sound housing had behavioral consequences. However, their conception of good housing embodied far more than Newman's simple admonition that it be safe and sanitary. Following the ideas of Patrick Geddes, Thorstein Veblen, and Simon Patten, they believed that the era of unbridled competition, characteristic of the nineteenth century, was passing and would give way to a new cooperative order. Captivated by the communitarian vision, Mumford envisioned slums replaced by "cellular cities" wherein "no act, no routine, no gesture" would be "devoid of human value," or would "fail to contribute to the reciprocal support of citizen and community," and where life would have "despite its broken moments, the poise and unity of a collective work of art.'"[7]

Accordingly, communitarian housers like Mumford and Bauer abjured what they considered to be anachronistic single-family housing in favor of tastefully planned communities "for the machine age" like Stein's Radburn, New Jersey, or Stein and Wright's, Sunnyside, Long Island. Bauer's conception of modern housing incorporated the new functionalism of her mentor Walter Gropius, the German housing theorist and founder of the Bauhaus school of architecture. Simple, "direct, moderately presupposing architecture," invoking both light and the efficient use of space, characterized Bauer's concept of acceptable shelter. In addition, she favored enough bedrooms to enable parents and children to sleep separately, running water, flush toilets, ample closet space, modern kitchens, and well-landscaped lawns and gardens visible from all windows. Significantly, the communitarian vision encompassed society at large, not merely the currently ill-housed. Moreover, it extolled a concept of social reconstruction which would restore the elements of community presumably abraded in the whir of nineteenth-century industrialism. Therefore, in communitarian language, modern housing was not only safe and sanitary but also the sine qua non of a truly modern society.[8]

While the depression deepened the housing crisis in Philadelphia, it simultaneously raised hopes for massive relief. Loula Lasker, a social worker gravely concerned about housing, likened its impact on housing to the Tokyo earthquake and declared that it was "a chance to rebuild the U.S.A."

President Herbert Hoover quickened those hopes in December 1931 by calling a White House Conference on Homebuilding and Housing, which, while affirming the nation's traditional commitment to the private home, also recommended government subventions in housing. Prodded by the newly formed National Public Housing Conference, in 1932 Hoover's Reconstruction Finance Corporation (RFC) authorized federal loans for the building of limited-dividend housing projects.[9]

As part of his New Deal, Franklin D. Roosevelt took even firmer action on the housing front. In 1933 he established under the Public Works Administration a Housing Division headed by Robert D. Kohn, an architect-planner with imposing communitarian credentials earned as a member of the Regional Planning Association of America. Kohn promptly went to work, organizing a $125 million program for urban slum clearance and low-cost, limited-dividend housing. Washington's heralded assault on urban blight and slums excited the prospect of modern housing which in the more individualistic 1920s had produced numerous theoretical expositions but few experiments. Philadelphia architects and planners hastily dusted off their drawing boards and tuned up their imaginations. Kohn's generous offer of low-income housing funds equally inspired Newman who, as the city's dean of housing experts, acted as chief adviser to a host of anxious architects. In the fall of 1933 a torrent of housing proposals streamed from Philadelphia to Washington.[10] But only one Philadelphia proposal for a limited-dividend project escaped Kohn's rejection bin. The Carl Mackley project not only epitomized the essence of "modern housing" but also prompted the enlistment of organized labor into the crusade.

Named for a member of the Philadelphia hosiery workers' union slain in 1931 by a strikebreaker, the Mackley project owed its existence to the force and dedication of three men: John Edelman, secretary of the American Federation of Full-Fashioned Hosiery Workers (AFFFHW), Oscar Stonorov, a Russian-born but German-educated architect and housing activist who moved from New York to Philadelphia in 1931 to form the architectural firm of Stonorov and Kastner, and William Jeanes, a wealthy Quaker whose 1930 grand tour of European housing converted him into a disciple of functional, low-cost, modern housing.[11]

Early in the depression Edelman became aware of the tragedy of unemployment among hosiery workers and their families who lost their homes and found their belongings dumped haphazardly at the curbside. Naturally, he was excited by Oscar Stonorov's idea for a workers' cooperative housing project. Once a student of Le Corbusier, Stonorov helped Edelman and Jeanes construct a detailed model for such a project based on an extensive sociological survey of the housing needs of Philadelphia hosiery workers. The plan was rejected as preposterous by both Philadelphia philanthropists and Hoover's RFC, but in 1933 it received financial backing from Kohn and the Housing Division as the Juniata Park Housing Corporation. When ready for occupancy in March 1934, the Carl Mackley Houses graced the Juniata section of Northeast Philadelphia, not far from the factories, mills, and two-story brick homes of industrial Frankford and Kensington. But in the mid-1930s Juniata was still a relatively undeveloped area in Philadelphia, and the project's open setting suited the holistic and environmentalistic philosophy of the communitarians (see Figure 9-1). Containing 284 units of two rooms apiece, its four-story block buildings basked in sunlight and fresh air on a four-and-one-half-acre site overlooking Juniata Park.[12] Its tenants shared a community pool, a wading pond for children, an auditorium, and a laundry facility. Edelman and Stonorov strove to infuse a cooperative spirit into the project. In addition to the shared community facilities, the Mackley social universe included a cooperative store, a federal credit union, a mother's club, nursery school, drama school, and hobby workshop.[13] Clearly, housers like Edelman, Stonorov, and Jeanes regarded the project as a landmark in the effort to lure working-class families away from their anachronistic attachment to home ownership and toward the new world of community living. In Jeanes' words, the "unexpected dividends which our residents receive are not of course in cash, because the tenants do not participate in ownership. They consist largely in the enjoyment of community activities. . . . This community life is every bit as valued by our tenants as the exceptionally comfortable homes Carl Mackley House affords at reasonable costs within the means of low-income workers."[14]

The national interest aroused by the announcement of the new housing project encouraged Stonorov to enlist the support of the youthful housing idealist, Catherine Bauer, in the Philadelphia effort. In her recently published work, *Modern Housing,* Bauer had argued that the European experience had demonstrated that to be successful, a housing movement must spring from the anger, militancy, and organized determination of the working class.[15] Together with Edelman she formed the Labor Housing Conference (LHC) in Philadelphia in 1934 to organize blue-collar support for low-cost public housing. She hoped to transform the Mackley initiative into a ground swell for modern housing, and she soon succeeded in establishing local labor housing committees outside Philadelphia in New Jersey, New York, and North Carolina. Spurred on by Kohn and the Housing Division's allocation of $4 million to Philadelphia for slum clearance and low-cost housing, Bauer and the LHC printed countless statements and flyers and hosted numerous mass meetings and conferences to advance the cause of modern housing.[16]

According to Bauer and the Philadelphia LHC, "good housing in the right place for everyone must be the major objective of all resource planning . . . and only the national government in collaboration with local planning and housing authorities and with groups of workers and consumers can . . . finance large-scale planned housing developments on a non-profit, public utility basis." Bauer traced the slum problem to "the criminal waste

Figure 9-1. The Carl Mackley Houses, M and Bristol streets. Opened in 1934, this project was built in an unfinished neighborhood where, surrounded by open land, its communitarian philosophy could express itself. Note the golf course in Juniata Park across the street. *Courtesy Urban Archives, Paley Library, Temple University.*

of land speculation, . . . jerry-building, . . . and chaotic and exploitative proprietorship," and denied that either ordinary private enterprise or "disinterested private citizens (philanthropists)" could solve the problem. Only large-scale methods, pleaded Bauer, "planning for use and not for quick profits, the construction of complete community developments designed to fit the needs of real groups of people, will prevent the erection of new slums."[17]

But the need for good modern dwellings obsessed Bauer and her LHC compatriots more than the problem of the slum. According to the LHC, "the housing problem in Philadelphia can never be completely solved as long as the program is limited to central slum clearance." High priced inner-city land at $1.00 to $4.00 a foot could never accommodate good, standard low-cost housing. Bauer urged the city to find "so-called 'blighted' areas" where land could be bought "with comparative ease and where the requirements of good city planning" could be satisfied "more thoroughly perhaps than in the worst 'most ancient sore spots.'"[18]

Understandably, then, Bauer shared the disillusionment of many, including Newman, when in mid-1934 Secretary of the Interior Harold Ickes accepted the resignation of the communitarian Kohn and scuttled all but the few limited-dividend projects already under way. Ickes appointed Horatio Hackett to be the new director of the PWA's Housing Division. A military man with experience mostly in skyscraper construction, Hackett confined the agency to a few "demonstration" housing projects and to the clearance of some of the nation's worst city slums.[19]

Precedents for Slum Clearance

In June 1934 the Housing Division launched a new $144 million program primarily aimed at slum clearance and model housing. In Philadelphia the LHC joined with the Housing Study Guild, which included Wright, Mumford, and Carol Arnovici, to accuse Ickes of paying lip service to the cause of housing and yielding to the "pressures of organized real estate and financial interests." Bauer and her colleagues charged that the Housing Division had allowed the obstruction of its original goal of building "thousands of modern, low-rental dwellings in planned communities," and spurned "the cooperation or participation of workers and consumers."[20] Professional housers like Bernard Newman also contributed to the criticism. In the early 1930s Newman had vigorously supported the Housing Division's limited-dividend venture, and although not a communitarian, he endorsed the Mackley project. But in 1934 he fiercely attacked the division for its inefficiency and shortsightedness. In a stinging rebuke aimed at Ickes, entitled "How to Stall," Newman accused the Division of miscalculating the fiscal merits of limited-dividend projects. Ignoring hard data on residential vacancies, demolitions, and new construction, the agency, he said, had deferred to bankers, mortgage lenders, and jerry-builders, and neglected such vital objectives as increased employment in the building trades and housing for the ill-housed.[21]

Newman struck hardest at the Division's failure to consult known "housing experts," like himself, and to formulate a comprehensive housing program embracing not only the construction of low-income housing but slum clearance, housing renovation, code enforcement, and zoning as well. Later, in a 1935 communication to Ickes, Newman observed that the Public Works Administration had "not over-emphasized the importance of slum clearance." Although "it should not be . . . the sole contribution to better housing," the amount budgeted for it, he thought "should be greatly increased."[22] Of course, the relative merits of housing and slum clearance would continue to inform the debate over the future of urban shelter through the 1940s. However, in Philadelphia it was the demolition of moldering slums and not the construction of modern, low-cost housing for the poor which attracted business and civic support. In addition, slum clearance comported with the popular attitude that bad housing bred criminality and disease and imposed a costly tax burden upon the hard-working middle class. Professionals like Newman acknowledged the need for low-cost housing, but they remained staunchly convinced that the target of any comprehensive housing program must be the eradication of the slum. Meanwhile, by 1935 Roosevelt and the New Deal had begun to back away from experiments with cooperative, collectivistic democracy, including communitarian housing. Despite the ongoing agitation of Bauer, Wright, Mumford, and the LHC, the federal government was moving toward a policy more in keeping with the progressive, professional tradition in housing reform.

In 1934 the Housing Division of the PWA urged those in Philadelphia to create an advisory committee on housing composed of "leaders of public opinion in the community who can advise us regarding what kind of a start should be made and where, in slum clearance. . . ." The 12-member Philadelphia Advisory Committee on Housing (PACH) included a panoply of housing experts as well as representatives from business, labor, education, and philanthropy. With Newman as secretary, the PACH met for the first time in October 1934. It promptly declared slum clearance as its mission and aimed its attack on the skid row haunts near the Vine Street approach to the Delaware River Bridge and on the excrescent bandbox slums surrounding Old Swedes' Church in the Queen Village area. Obviously, decades of antislum literature, reinforced by a heavy barrage of PHA statistics and lurid case studies had etched a deep impression on Philadelphia consciences. Advisory Committee members never questioned the view that slums bred violent, immoral, and diseased people. In fully developed areas whose housing had outlived its usefulness slum clearance would excise a festering sore, while simultaneously relieving city taxpayers of costly police, fire, health, and welfare services.[23]

Unfortunately, many of the Advisory Committee's neat housing axioms floundered on the issue of race. In 1934 blacks lived in the city's worst slums. During the "Great Migration" to Philadelphia between 1916 and 1930 the city's black population rose over 13 percent to 219,599, and most of these newcomers crammed the ancient bandbox rookeries of the Second, Third, Fourth, Fifth, and Seventh wards in the Society Hill, Washington Square, and Queen Village sections of the city. Concerned by the increasing wretchedness of such housing, black leaders such as Raymond Pace Alexander, Leslie Pinckney Hill, and Wayne Hopkins unsuccessfully lobbied for a limited-dividend project. As housing conditions worsened in 1935, organizations like the Armstrong Association enlisted the black press and settlement house workers behind a black housing movement. In 1934 black Philadelphians had supported the New Deal at the polls, and this benefited their housing cause. In addition, Harold Ickes had long been concerned about the treatment of blacks in America, and in 1935 he placed two prominent blacks, Crystal Bird Faucett and Major R. R. Wright, on the Philadelphia Advisory Committee. He also ordered the PACH to concentrate on a black housing project. But despite its good intentions the committee failed either to destroy slums or to rehouse the city's blacks. Proposed sites for black housing were either too costly or racially too sensitive. Land values at one likely location near the historic Pennsylvania Hospital in West Philadelphia proved exorbitant; a vacant site near the city's baseball stadium on Lehigh Avenue in North Philadelphia could not be used because a nearby white, middle-class neighborhood wanted the land for recreation.[24]

Ironically, the Hill Creek houses, the only PWA demonstation project built, represented neither slum clearance nor black housing. Located near the Mackley Houses in a fringe area, they went up at Adams and Rising Sun avenues overlooking Tacony Creek Park. Significantly they included such communitarian features as cul-de-sac parking, integral shopping facilities, excellent landscaping, and a two-story, two-room-deep design which satisfied the communitarian prescription for light and air. However, Hill Creek's affinity for communitarian appurtenances mired it in the same dilemma as Mackley. The high cost per room at Mackley made it impossible for truly low-income families to live in the units. In fact, hosiery workers comprised fewer than 60 percent of this project's first residents. Like Mackley, most of Hill Creek's early residents were stable, middle-class teachers, lower-echelon management personnel, and skilled or semiskilled workers. Such a socioeconomic composition might have been predicted, given their suburban locations. But the failure of both the Mackley and Hill Creek homes either to solve the problems of slum clearance or house the ill-housed convinced skeptical Philadelphians like Arthur Binns of the Philadelphia Real Estate Board that modern housing for low-income families was indeed a folly.[25]

Actually, the Hill Creek Homes, which opened for occupancy in 1936, proved the last glimmer of the communitarian vision in Philadelphia. Events between 1934 and 1937 suggested that, while the issue of slum clearance excited considerable social and political interest in Philadelphia, little commitment existed for modern, communal low-cost housing. Because public housing became the handmaiden of slum clearance, as Catherine Bauer feared it would, it did not develop in a cooperative, biotechnic form but merely in reaction to the slum, perhaps even mirroring the tenement itself.

The merger of housing reform and slum clearance began in late fall 1934 when professionals like Newman joined the Bauer communitarians of the Labor Housing Conference and organizations like the National Association of Housing Officials to sponsor a drive to replace the erstwhile Housing Divsion with a permanent federal housing agency. To spearhead the campaign for a real housing program in the communitarian mode, Bauer and her allies at the National Association of Housing Officials hosted a multicity tour by distinguished European housers including the architect and town planner Raymond Unwin and Ernest Kahn, economist, banker, and the former manager of public housing projects at Frankfurt am Main. The tour, which included a stroll through Philadelphia's maze of horrendous courts and alleys, produced numerous memoranda on American housing conditions and a final report read before an enormous assemblage of housing officialdom at the landmark Baltimore Housing Conference. At this meeting the Europeans helped to make influential recommendations for a permanent housing program, although Bauer and her supporters must have been disappointed at the visitors' apparent lack of enthusiasm for the American communitarian position. Public housing, they declared, "should be large-scaled in which every effort . . . was made to reduce [the] cost of dwelling construction through care in [the] design and purchase of materials." But, stated the experts, public housing must be closely related to slum clearance, and only heavy subsidies could recoup the great expense of demolishing acres of tottering slums.[26]

In the early 1930s the Philadelphia political climate had foreclosed any possibility of combining housing and slum clearance on the scale outlined by Unwin. Between 1933 and 1935 all New Deal programs in the city had faced the stubborn opposition of Philadelphia's Old Guard Republican mayor, J. Hampton Moore. He flatly refused to cooperate with the Housing Division, proclaiming that as a "City of Homes . . . [Philadelphia] was too proud to have slums." "Of course," he said "there are cases of two or more families living in one house. . . . There may be some dilapidated houses . . . [but] that does not constitute slums. People are merely living within their means."[27]

But by 1935 the political climate in Philadelphia had warmed somewhat to the idea of federal action on housing and slum clearance. With street lights unrepaired, storm sewers failing, and blight spreading, many once-loyal Moore supporters rejected the mayor's blind devotion to economy and retrenchment. Convinced with Newman that slums cost the city in crime, dirt, and poverty, and faced with the reality of a declining tax base, the Chamber of Commerce, for one, spurned Moore's intransigence and implored the city to allow PWA slum clearance.[28]

The resurgence of the Democratic party in the early 1930s furnished a political foundation for slum clearance and low-cost housing. In 1934 a fledgling but clearly dynamic Philadelphia Democratic party captained by John B. (Jack) Kelly helped George Earle win the state's governorship. One year later Kelly entered the mayoral race, parading slum clearance as a main issue. During one publicized tour of the slums he paused to lash out at Moore's blunder that Philadelphia was "too proud to have slums." Viewing the dingy housing around Fourth and Bainbridge streets, Kelly inquired "how children raised without sunlight, running water, or toilet facilities could remain patriotic citizens." He departed pledging to "Wipe out all [the] City Slums."[29]

Although Kelly lost the mayor's race, the victor, S. Davis Wilson, a political "chameleon" masquerading in 1935 as a Republican, coveted federal funds as eagerly as any Democrat. However, his willingness to feed at the New Deal trough meant little for new housing. Until late 1936 Philadelphia's business and civic elite clamored for subway completion and an airport more than housing or slum clearance.[30] But suddenly in December of that year the city's housing crisis gripped its attention. At midnight on December 19, 1936, seven black residents died in the fiery collapse of several moldering bandbox tenements. The tragedy horrified the public and gruesomely reminded proper Philadelphians that bad housing could involve scandalous human tragedy.[31]

Philadelphia's widely publicized bandbox disaster aroused a city-wide outcry against the slums. Only days before the collapse, the Real Property Inventory conducted by the Works Progress Administration had carried a statistical exposé of the city's South Central district where the holocaust had occurred. According to the survey, 60 percent of the area's ramshackle tenements were over 100 years old; a quarter of the dwellings lacked indoor plumbing, forcing residents to bucket water from yard pumps and share ancient feces-encrusted water closets. For a while, at least, Philadelphians felt branded by the stigma. An axe-wielding Mayor Wilson unleashed an all-out war against the slum, personally helping demolish one of the city's notorious bandboxes.[32]

As the victims of the tragedy, Philadelphia blacks were especially outraged by the disaster. The NAACP and the Armstrong Association summoned black slum tenants to a series of meetings protesting the actions of slumlords, the squalid living conditions, and the city's inaction on housing. Out of these meetings emerged the Philadelphia Tenants League, an organization pledged to defending tenants' rights, enforcing city housing codes, fighting unfair evictions, and looking after the housing rights and needs of the unemployed.[33]

Plainly, the bandbox tragedy served to isolate further the slum as the target for ameliorative action. Since 1933 professionals like Newman had tirelessly stressed that slum eradication involved building low-cost public housing. Moreover, communitarian reformers in the federal government's Housing Division significantly advanced the welding together of the two housing positions by portraying massive, well-designed housing projects as likely to help rehabilitate the defective poor. Such homes, said Arthur DuBois, the Philadelphia district manager of the Housing Division, would create "a nucleus in the slum and blighted district" which would act "as a spreading point for the regeneration of valuable and intensely developed districts in the heart of the cities."[34] But by 1937 the communitarian crusade for modern housing found itself more enmeshed than ever before in the campaign to rid the city of the slum.

In the spring and fall of 1936 housing reformers testified at congressional hearings on the Wagner-Steagall Housing Bill, and gradually the lineaments of the permanent housing program began to appear. Modern housing was grafted to slum clearance, and the hybrid housing which resulted would bear the markings of the communitarian design but lack any of the socially normative attributes of the neighborhood plan. The housing units would reflect rigid architectural simplicity as well as the sunlight-drenched lines of the superblock. But as housing communities in the spirit of the Carl Mackley Houses, that is, buildings skillfully articulated on spacious sites, replete with amenities and responsive to their residents' social and cultural needs, projects in Philadelphia such as the Richard Allen Homes at Tenth and Poplar streets or the Tasker Homes at Third and Morris streets, failed. Of course, these projects went up in two of the city's most built-up neighborhoods where greenery and open space were at a premium (see Figure 9-2). And yet, conceived as slum clearance rather than ideal communities, they also neglected the fundamentals of good neighborhood design. Instead of shared values, work experience, or child rearing as the basis for social cohesion, they came to rest on the weak foundation of mutual poverty. For contrary to the wishes of the communitarians, the 1937 National Housing Act did not assert that Americans have the right to decent housing but only that society must provide minimum shelter to those low-income families outside the reach of the private real estate market.[35]

The Wagner-Steagall Act, signed into law September 1, 1937, created the United States Housing Administration (USHA) under which a decentralized system of local policymaking replaced the centralized bureaucracy of the PWA Housing Division. Community housing authorities would now decide upon project clientele, sites, and layouts. Designating federal housing for

Figure 9-2. The Richard Allen Homes, Tenth and Poplar streets, in 1950. These buildings never had much breathing room, being pinched in on all sides by working-class row homes and the Reading Railroad tracks. *Courtesy Urban Archives, Paley Library, Temple University.*

only the lowest-income families, Washington guaranteed loans to municipal authorities for up to 90 percent of the cost of slum clearance and project construction, and it directly funded local governments to assure that rents would be truly low. In effect, the USHA's decentralized administrative apparatus assured local authorities the autonomy to erect public housing in accord, not in conflict, with existing housing values and land use configurations.[36] But any possibility that such housing would ever escape slum neighborhoods or be truly communitarian was now effectively foreclosed.

Philadelphia's Mongrel Housing Policy

Between 1937 and 1940 the program of the Philadelphia Housing Authority took clear form, and it only vaguely resembled the communitarian vision. The Authority found the basic design principles of the communitarians appealing. As the key to low-cost housing, planners eagerly accepted the efficiency and economy of the superblock. Accordingly, multifamily neighborhood units were arranged artistically on vacant as well as slum-cleared land. Among the three projects completed in Philadelphia in the early 1940s only the Allen Homes replaced slums. Both the Johnson Homes at 25th Street and Ridge Avenue and the Tasker Homes in South Philadelphia were built on vacant sites, although in the midst of crowded and poor surroundings. Such superblock communities featured the basic elements of sun and air, as well as schools, recreation and shopping facilities, auditoriums, and meeting rooms. But the functionalism and efficiency of the superblock design comported too easily with the money-saving priorities of the bureaucrats who ran the Housing Authority. In the name of strict economy project directors instructed architects and landscapers to substitute curtains for closet doors, shave square footage from bedrooms and living rooms, strip exterior decor or architectural frills, and replace decorative plantings with hearty, childproof shrubbery and ground cover.[37] In a short time such denuded structures acquired a sterile, uninviting appearance which reflected their didactic mission. Although the Philadelphia Authority fused low-income housing with slum clearance, it defined the housing project client as an upwardly mobile member of the lower class, a "working adult known to have regularly lived as an inherent part of a family group whose earnings are an integral part of the family income. . . ."[38] As way stations, projects would serve clients until they gained a firm economic foothold and entered the private housing market. The authority's goal was not to build stable communities, and accordingly its projects sought to instill in their residents those values and habits which would enable them to move into the housing mainstream. Aware of the moral problems once created by lodgers, project managers did not allow relatives to stay overnight as guests in the units. Other rules forbade gambling, outlawed dogs and cats, and attempted to teach good citizenship by urging participation in project government. Yards were included in the basic layout for the occupants to tend, an arrangement which, according to an Authority manual "maintained low rents as well as . . . cultivated self reliance." Casting aside communitarian principles, the Authority affirmed that "arranging open space for the private use of individual families who will be expected to maintain it and care for it and use it as their own . . . accords with American Custom."[39]

As the designers of twentieth-century asylums, project planners closed the book on "frills" or "delux service." An active member of the Authority's Committee on Sites, Bernard Newman argued that such "delux services . . . added to the operating costs [of projects], raised rent levels, [and were] a doubtful expenditure of public funds for projects designed to house poor slum families in safety and sanitation. . . . The object of authority housing," expounded Philadelphia's professional expert, "is not to save tenants from ordinary household duties, a saving which is always a luxury, but to provide more safe and sanitary houses for more slum families. Luxuries are a questionable innovation for low income families."[40] Given its commitment to slum clearance and housing for the poor, the Philadelphia Housing Authority found it difficult to locate suitable sites and construct low-income housing. The cost of slum land was high. Philadelphia continued to value its reputation as a city of homes, and racial antipathy confined black housing to black neighborhoods.[41] Between 1937 and 1940 several neighborhoods rebelled against the intrusion of project housing. Despite a public relations campaign by the Housing Authority which pointed out that low-cost housing replaced dangerous slums with safe and sanitary dwellings, Philadelphians in the predominantly white Germantown, Kirkbride, and Queen Village areas rallied behind the Philadelphia Real Estate Board's slogan that housing projects were "un-American."[42]

Even an obvious site for public housing in the bandbox-infested neighborhood around Old Swedes' Church in South Philadelphia proved politically volatile in the prewar years. As early as 1935 the Octavia Hill Society joined area settlement houses and John Roak, the rector of historic Old Swedes', in a campaign to demolish 668 "decadent" buildings and erect 950 two- and three-story low-income units on a 26.3-acre site at Front Street and Washington Avenue. However, project boosters overlooked the social dynamics of the area. Its Italian population was remarkably stable but on the defensive in a changing neighborhood.

Between 1920 and 1930 the size of this group in the Second Ward, where the project was to be located, fell by 20 percent, but in 1940 half of the ward's residents were still Italian or of Italian parentage. Russian Jews, on the other hand, declined from 3,500 in 1920 to less than 500 20 years later while blacks rose from only a handful in 1920 to comprise 20 percent of the ward's 6,000 families by the beginning of the depression. As late as 1940

well over 4,000 Italians lived in the Second Ward and many of these Philadelphians (38 percent in 1930) owned modest but well-kept homes valued
at between $2,000 and $7,000. While these homes frequently lacked modern
sanitary facilities and needed structural repairs, in 1934, 48 percent were
mortgage-free. These Italian home owners made up much of the opposition
to the Old Swedes' project. When proponents of "Old Swedes'" pleaded
that the "White Only" project would guarantee neighborhood stability,
Italian home owners appealed plaintively for their homes with their vine-
yards and vegetable gardens nestled in the rear. Supplications aimed at the
symbol of home ownership carried political weight in Philadelphia.[43]

Although the Housing Authority considered a "white" project like Old
Swedes' important, in 1938 a black project stood on record as the lingering
business of the city's now dissolved Advisory Committee on Housing.
Furthermore, because of the bandbox collapse in December 1936 black
housing loomed as the inescapable priority. For some like Bernard Newman
it was humanitarian; for others, those white realtors, planners, and architects who were alarmed by the increase in the city's black population, housing projects for blacks could contain or "Harlemize" the expanding black
population if they were strategically located. In fact, in its official policies
the Authority reinforced segregation by insisting that the racial composition
of a project "conform to the prevailing racial composition of the surrounding neighborhood."[44]

Located on the fringe of a large black neighborhood, the Glenwood
Cemetery site at 25th Street and Ridge Avenue fit the Housing Authority's
bill for black housing. Built at a cost of $3 million the complex opened on
October 1, 1940. It was named the James Weldon Johnson Homes in honor
of the black playwright and author, and it became the first of only three
prewar low-cost housing units built in Philadelphia. Like its mates, the
black Richard Allen and the white Tasker homes, the Johnson units bore
the marks of a housing policy premised upon sheltering families outside the
private housing market or the communitarian dream. Bounded on one side
by a railroad right-of-way, the 535-unit Johnson project afforded well-
built, "clean, sunny homes for [black] families with net incomes below $15
weekly" without endangering white real estate values.[45]

Because of their low incomes and substandard housing, hairdressers,
schoolteachers, public health workers and other middle-class blacks moved
into the new Johnson homes. The Armstrong Association, the NAACP,
and black newspapers like *The Philadelphia Tribune,* fought for this public
housing, but the units were inferior in style and amenities to the new private
housing being built for middle-class whites in Northeast Philadelphia and
beyond.[46] Moreover, in sharp contrast to the communitarian vision, the
planners of the James Weldon Johnson, Tasker, and Richard Allen homes
never designed the projects to be stable neighborhoods. Ideally, mobile low-
income families would be rehabilitated, leave the projects, and achieve the

nirvana of private housing; meanwhile, project residents would neatly tend their grounds making superblock neighborhoods model environments which would contribute to the eradication of the slum and the renewal of the city.

In 1939 and 1940 this ideal seemed attainable. The presence of an enormous pool of poor families anxious for any decent housing allowed managers to select "worthy" tenants as the first project residents. However, by the 1950s project clients were increasingly either "multiproblem" families or blacks kept in the inner city by limited housing and job opportunities. Under these circumstances frill-less housing projects designed as way stations for the upwardly mobile quickly became custodial accommodations stigmatized by outsiders as "islands of poverty" and despised by the residents as the apotheosis of a social system which imprisoned them in a cycle of despair.

The Philadelphia case illustrates the obstacles which obliterated the modern housing vision and produced a mongrelized housing program bent ultimately only on the destruction of the slum. Although they built public housing only at the fringe, the communitarians sought to reconstruct the city as a whole. Professionals like Newman also hoped to achieve widespread reform, but by aiming their panaceas directly at the slum, close to the core, they often encountered local opposition. The city's symbolic dedication to the single-family house, its racial prejudices, and its imbedded tradition of privatism doomed public housing. But Catherine Bauer detected the major fallacy in 1950. Physical rehabilitation, she observed, did not decree the amelioration of urban social decay. Yet, it was this assumption which informed the 1937 legislation as well as the Wagner-Ellender Housing Act of 1949 and the urban renewal philosophy of the 1960s. Sadly, out of the hopes of Bernard Newman, John Edelman, and Catherine Bauer, professionals and communitarians alike, emerged a modern slum, often far more pernicious than the alleys and bandboxes demolished in its wake.[47]

Notes

1. Bernard Newman, *Housing in Philadelphia, 1931* (Philadelphia: Philadelphia Housing Association, 1932); Edith Elmer Wood, *Recent Trends in American Housing* (New York: Russell Sage, 1931), pp. 39-44; John F. Bauman, "The City, the Depression, and Relief: The Philadelphia Experience, 1929-1939." Ph.D. dissertation, Rutgers University, 1969, pp. 126, 186, 225.

2. Mel Scott, *American City Planning Since 1890* (Berkeley: University of California Press, 1969), p. 133; Sam Bass Warner, Jr., *The Private City: Philadelphia in Three Periods of Its Growth* (Philadelphia: University of Pennsylvania Press, 1968), pp. 211-12; Edith Elmer Wood, "Is Government Aid Necessary in House Financing," *Housing Problems in America, Proceedings of the 10th National Conference on Housing* (Philadelphia: Philadelphia Housing Association, 1930), pp. 55-61.

3. On "professional housers" see Roy Lubove, *The Progressives and the Slums: Tenement House Reform in New York City, 1890-1917* (Pittsburgh: University of Pittsburgh Press, 1962); on "communitarian housers" see Roy Lubove "New Cities for Old: The Urban Reconstruction Program of the 1930s," *Social Studies* 53 (November 1962): 203-6.

4. For Newman's Perspective see Bernard Newman, "Low-Cost Housing—What the Rest of the Country Can Learn from Philadelphia," *The American City* 40 (April 1929): 101-3; Newman, *Housing in Philadelphia, 1931*, p. 7; on Newman see John F. Bauman, "Disinfecting the Industrial City: The Philadelphia Housing Commission and Scientific Efficiency, 1909-1916," in *The Age of Urban Reform: New Perspectives on the Progressive Era,* ed. Michael H. Ebner and Eugene M. Tobin (Port Washington, N.Y.: Kennikat Press, 1977), pp. 124-25.

5. Bernard Newman, "Can We Afford Not to Build," *Housing in Philadelphia, 1933* (Philadelphia: Philadelphia Housing Association, 1934), pp. 10-11; Bernard Newman, "The Problem of Shifting Population," *Housing in Philadelphia, 1931,* pp. 16-17.

6. Lubove, *Progressives and the Slums,* pp. 151-84; see Newman correspondence in the papers of the Housing Association of the Delaware Valley, Temple Urban Archives, Paley Library, Temple University, Philadelphia (hereinafter, HADV).

7. Lewis Mumford, *The Culture of Cities* (New York: Harcourt Brace and Company, 1938), p. 484; on Clarence Perry's "cellular city," see Scott, *American City Planning*, pp. 258-60; also see Henry Wright, *Rehousing Urban America* (New York: Columbia University, 1935), pp. 9-35.

8. Catherine Bauer, *Modern Housing* (Boston: Houghton Mifflin, 1934), pp. xv-xvii, 218-19, 254-55; Lubove, "New Cities for Old," pp. 210-11.

9. Loula D. Lasker, "The Chance to Rebuild the U.S.A.," *Survey Graphic* 22 (August 1933): 420-21; on Hoover's housing conference, see Arthur Evans Wood, "Home and the Housing Experts," *The Nation* 133 (December 23, 1931): 693; Lawrence M. Friedman, *Government and Slum Housing: A Century of Frustration* (Chicago: Rand McNally, 1968), pp. 98-101.

10. Lasker, "Chance to Rebuild," pp. 420-42; on Philadelphia limited-dividend projects, see J. A. MacCallum, president of Philadelphia Housing Association to Victor Abel, architect of Earlington project, and numerous other correspondence and blueprints relating to the limited-dividend proposals sent to Washington, D.C., all in Record Group (RG) 196, File H-3000, Housing Division Records (HDR), National Archives (NA); see also, Bernard Newman, *Housing in Philadelphia, 1935* (Philadelphia: Philadelphia Housing Association, 1936), pp. 18-23.

11. Mary Susan Cole, "Catherine Bauer and the Public Housing Movement," Ph.D. dissertation, The George Washington University, 1975, pp. 214-15; PWA Press Release No. 3052, December 7, 1936, in RG 196, "Miscellaneous Materials—Carl Mackley Housing," File H-1, HDR, NA.

12. Cole, "Catherine Bauer," pp. 215-20, 225, 227.

13. PWA Press Release No. 3052, "Carl Mackley Housing," File H-1, HDR, NA; *The New York Times,* January 6, 1935; Washington *Evening Star,* September 9, 1936.

14. PWA Press Release No. 3052, "Carl Mackley Housing," File H-1, HDR, NA.

15. Cole, "Catherine Bauer," pp. 225-27; "Housing in Philadelphia: Union-Sponsored Project Hailed as Model for U.S.," *Christian Science Monitor,* November

2, 1937; on the Juniata Park setting see Simon Breines, "The Philadelphia Experiment in Low-Cost Housing," *Real Estate Record* 135 (April 20, 1935), p. 21; Social Base Map, 1939, WPA Project 20879, Plate 6B.

16. "Statement on the Housing Situation in Philadelphia: Excerpts from a Petition Submitted to the Pennsylvania State Planning Board by the Philadelphia Labor Committee," August 31, 1934, mimeographed, HADV; Mark Gelfand, *A Nation of Cities: The Federal Government and Urban America, 1933-1965* (New York: Oxford University Press, 1975), p. 135.

17. "Statement on the Housing Situation in Philadelphia," August 31, 1934, HADV; "Resolution on a Labor Housing Program," a copy of which was forwarded to Newman in a letter, James McDevitt, Chairman of Philadelphia Labor Housing Committee, to Newman, September 12, 1934, HADV; for Newman's dim view of the LHC, see Newman to Carol Arnovici (a communitarian with whom Newman regularly corresponded), July 10, 1934, HADV.

18. "Statement of the Housing Situation," August 31, 1934, HADV.

19. "Public Statement on the Abolishment of the Housing Division and the Passage of the National Housing Act," submitted by the Labor Housing Conference, the Housing Study Guild, and the Federation of Architects, Engineers and Chemists, June 25, 1934, HADV; National Association of Housing Officials, *Housing Yearbook, 1935* (Chicago: National Association of Housing Officials, 1935), pp. 4-5; Charles Ascher, "The Puzzle of Public Housing," *Survey* 70 (August 1934): 242.

20. "Public Statement on the Abolishment of the Housing Division and the Passage of the National Housing Act," June 25, 1923, HADV.

21. "Recommendation on How to Stall on a Federal Housing Program," n.d., circa June 26, 1934, RG 196, File H-3000.09, HDR, NA.

22. Ibid.; Transcript of Conference with Col. Horatio Hackett, Washington, D.C., June 26, 1934, URB 3/111/408, HADV; Arnovici to Newman, July 7, 1934; Newman to Harold Ickes, March 1, 1935, HADV.

23. See Minutes of Philadelphia Advisory Committee on Housing (hereinafter PACH Minutes), October 31, 1934, RG 196, File H-3000.703, HDR, NA; in the PACH Minutes of October 31, 1934, it was observed that "all parties expressed greater interest in slum clearance (than another Mackley type project). Moreover, the change in the policy of the federal government from limited-dividend housing to slum clearance created widespread expectations that a PWEC [Public Works Emergency Housing Corporation] project would be undertaken in Philadelphia. Therefore, if the committee recommended housing on vacant land in preference to wiping out a city slum, there would undoubtedly be a great deal of local opposition. . . ."; note also PACH Minutes, October 24, 1935, that "When we approached this problem [of housing] as we did it in Philadelphia, we approached it with the idea of cleaning up slums."

24. On black housing see John F. Bauman, "Black Slums/Black Projects: The New Deal and Negro Housing in Philadelphia," *Pennsylvania History* 41 (July 1974): 311-33.

25. On Hill Creek Homes, see Memorandum from M. D. Carrel to A. R. Clas, Regional Project Manager PWAHD, July 16, 1934, RG 196, File D-106, HDR, NA; transcript of meeting of Technical Advisory Committee of PHA, September 11, 1935, HADV and Frank Smith to Newman, October 30, 1937; on Mackley see, Leon Keyserling to William Jeanes, January 19, 1938, RG 196, File Pa-H-1, Miscel-

laneous Material, NA; and Memorandum from Norman Miller, Counsel to United States Housing Authority to Leon Keyserling, January 11, 1938, RG 196, File Pa-H-1, Miscellaneous Material, NA; on Hill Creek's location see Social Base Map, 1939, WPA Project 20879, Plate 7B.

26. On Unwin's tour see Scott, *American City Planning,* pp. 324-25; Newman to Col. Horatio Hackett, September 25, 1934, RG 196, HDR, requesting Hackett visit Philadelphia and tour the city slums with the Unwin party; "Summary of Report on the American Housing Program Drafted by the European Authorities," October 24, 1934, in Official File (OF), 63, Box 2, Franklin D. Roosevelt Library, Hyde Park (FDRL).

27. Statement of J. Hampton Moore, July 4, 1933, in the Collection of J. Hampton Moore, Historical Society of Pennsylvania, Philadelphia; Newman explained Moore's intransigence to A. R. Clas, July 8, 1935, HADV.

28. "Is the Northeast Part of the City?" Frankford *Dispatch,* February 2, 1934; Minutes of the Philadelphia Chamber of Commerce, April 11, 1935, in Historical Society of Pennsylvania, Philadelphia.

29. Irvin F. Greenberg, "The Philadelphia Democratic Party, 1911-1934," Ph.D. dissertation, Temple University, 1973, pp. 434-533; Philadelphia *Record,* June 12, 1934, and other clippings found in the Scrapbooks of John B. Kelly, Free Library of Philadelphia, Philadelphia (hereinafter Kelly Papers); Philadelphia *Public Ledger,* August 13, 1935, Kelly Papers.

30. *The Philadelphia Inquirer,* October 25, 1935, Kelly Papers; *Journal of City Council,* March 8, 1934; *The Evening Bulletin* (Philadelphia) January 18, 1936, Kelly Papers.

31. Bauman, "Black Slums/Black Projects," 328-29; *The Evening Bulletin,* December 22, 1936, Kelly Papers; *The Philadelphia Inquirer,* December 22, 1936, Kelly Papers.

32. Works Progress Administration, Philadelphia Real Property Survey, Philadelphia Survey, Colored Housing, Bulletins 26 and 27, West and East Central Philadelphia Districts A-1 and A-2, April 10, 1936, RG 196, File H-3000, HDR, NA; the South Central inventory covered the area between Spruce and Wharton streets from river to river in the city's 2nd, 3rd, 4th, 5th, 7th, and 13th wards; S. Davis Wilson to Arthur DuBois, February 14, 1936, RG 196, File H-3000, HDR, NA; *The Philadelphia Inquirer,* December 30 and 31, 1936.

33. Tenant's League Flyer, "Join-To-Help Our Own Third of a Nation!" in HADV; "Mass Action Sought on Local Housing," *The Philadelphia Tribune,* December 9, 1937.

34. Arthur DuBois, report to FEA of PW, Housing Division, n.d., RG 44, Box 77, NA; in a letter to Ann Jarvis, founder of Mother's Day Incorporated, dated November 15, 1935; Harold Ickes noted that small-scale projects hardly sufficed to combat deteriorating neighborhoods, RG 196, File I-276, HDR, NA; see also M. A. Carrel, Associate Project Manager, Housing Division, "Social and Economic Reasons for Slum Clearance and Low-Cost Housing and the Progress of the Housing Division," address at Minnesota State Conference, September 20, 1935, RG 196, File H-3000, HDR, NA.

35. Timothy McDonnell, *The Wagner Housing Act* (Chicago: Loyola University Press, 1957), pp. 106-7; Testimony of Helen Alfred, J. David Stern, S. Davis Wilson,

and Catherine Bauer, U.S. Senate, Committee on Education and Labor, *Hearings on S. 4424*, "Bill to Provide Financial Assistance to the States and Political Subdivisions for the Elimination of Unsafe and Unsanitary Housing Conditions . . . and the Stimulation of Business Activity to Create a U.S. Housing Authority and for Other Purposes," 74th Congress, 2nd Sess., April 20-29, 1936, 132-51; NAHO, Bulletin No. 119, August 24, 1937, contained a meticulous analysis of the Wagner housing legislation, in John Ihlder Papers, FDRL.

36. John Ihlder to Leon Keyserling, February 24, 1937, Ihlder Papers, FDRL.

37. A sketch of the various Authority policies is found in a press release, Philadelphia Housing Authority, "Public Housing Under the Philadelphia Housing Authority," April 28, 1938, in HADV; USHA, Bulletin No. 4, "Development Costs of a Low Rent Housing Project," RG 196, Bulletins on Policy and Procedure, HDR, NA; Housing Authority *Minutes*, September 6, 1939.

38. USHA, Bulletin, No. 22, "Initial Steps in Tenant Selection," RG 196, Bulletins on Policy and Procedure, HDR, NA; also, Bulletin, No. 31, "Suggested Procedures for Initial Tenant Selection and Renting," RG 196, HDR, NA.

39. USHA, *Design of Low-Rent Housing Projects* (Washington, D.C.: Government Printing Offices, 1939), p. 10; note the National Association of Housing Officials, *Report of the Committee on Physical Standards and Construction* (Chicago: NAHO, 1939), p. 6, which emphasized tenant care of facilities; see Philadelphia Housing Authority, "Recommendation on Tenant Selection Policy of the Board of Review Committee on the Philadelphia Housing Authority—1938-1939," July 7, 1939, mimeograph, HADV.

40. Draft by Bernard Newman, "Outstanding Progress in Local Housing," n.d., mimeographed, HADV; Nathan Straus, "Architects and the U.S.H.A.," USHA, Division of Research and Information, Release, n.d., HADV.

41. On the Authority's neighborhood formula for race, see Philadelphia Housing Authority *Minutes*, December 29, 1937, found in the Philadelphia Housing Authority Offices, Philadelphia (hereinafter HA *Minutes*).

42. On the Philadelphia Housing Authority's search for suitable sites, see HA *Minutes*, February 12, 1938; HA *Minutes*, September 27 and December 29, 1937; March 11 and June 12, 1939.

43. Report on Old Swedes' Site, found in RG 48, Emergency Housing Corporation Records, Central Classified Files, NA; see also Philadelphia Housing Association, comp., maps showing "Location of Foreign Born . . . 1920, 1930, 1940," Urban Archives, Paley Library, Temple University; "Outline Map Showing Ratio of Negro Population, 1930," comp. by Research Department of the Armstrong Association, and Philadelphia Housing Association, HADV; U.S., Bureau of the Census, *Fifteenth Census of the United States: 1930*, data taken by "Work Sheets," for Census Tracts, 2 A, B, C, 3 A, B, and 4 A, B, in Free Library of Philadelphia; "Excerpts from Southwark Public Hearings," April 15, 1940, HADV.

44. J. D. Goodman to Newman, October 1, 1935, HADV; Frank Smith, chairman of the Philadelphia Housing Authority, to Newman, July 20, 1937, HADV; *The Philadelphia Tribune*, May 18, 1939; PHA, in "Housing for Negroes in Philadelphia," December 29, 1944, HADV.

45. Philadelphia Housing Authority, Release, No. 12, May 12, 1939, announcing ground breaking for James Weldon Johnson Homes, HADV; Philadelphia Housing

Authority Release, June 10, 1940, announcing the opening of the Johnson Homes for occupancy, HADV. The Glenwood Cemetery tract had been originally selected as a housing site by the PACH. The fact that it was an abandoned cemetery and bounded on one side by a railroad right-of-way and on the other by black neighborhoods minimized objections. In 1937 the new United States Housing Authority demanded immediate action in Philadelphia on housing and insisted that the first sites be on relatively inexpensive vacant land. Therefore, in several ways the Glenwood location was ideal. See Philadelphia Committee on Public Affairs, "The Public Housing Program in Philadelphia," March 15, 1940, mimeograph, Housing Authority Papers, NA.

46. On the absence of frills see Housing Authority, *Minutes,* September 6, 25, 1939, and March 4, 1939, and June 24, 1940; on the first residents see *The Philadelphia Tribune,* July 18, 1940.

47. On project tedium see Dorothy Canfield, "I Visit a Housing Project," *Survey Graphic* 29 (February 1940): 89-90; on the devolution of the communitarian ideal, see Catherine Bauer Wurster, "The Dreary Deadlock of Public Housing," and John P. Dean, "The Myths of Housing Reform," in *Urban Housing,* ed. William L. C. Wheaton, Grace Milgram, and Mary Elgin Meyerson (New York: Free Press, 1966), pp. 246-47, 255-58.

CHAPTER 10 The Persistent Dualism: Centralization and Decentralization in Philadelphia, 1854-1975

WILLIAM W. CUTLER, III

Since the beginning of the nineteenth century American cities have been moving in two opposite directions at once. On the one hand, there has been centralization, meaning a commitment to a strong central business district, a dense and concentrated population, and decision making by a comprehensive governmental body. Meanwhile, decentralization has taken effect, bringing among other things demographic dispersal and business relocation as well as neighborhood loyalty and local control. Such centrifugal developments have tested the cohesive and magnetic powers of the urban core and prompted many efforts to achieve a balance. In 1937, for example, a special study of American cities commissioned by the National Resources Committee called for "a moderately decentralized and yet integrated urban structure.[1]

But tension rather than balance better characterizes the relationship between the constituent parts of the modern metropolis. Zones of residence and work, commerce and industry, wealth and poverty give form to the city but strain against one another as well. Competition between the downtown and the suburbs accents the differences among the city's many different neighborhoods. In the twentieth century the centripetal elements in urban life have struggled against those forces which would tear the city apart.

Philadelphia: A Developmental Overview

No less than other American cities, Philadelphia has experienced the conflict of concentration with dispersal. For nearly 200 years it has been divided and yet kept together by competing political, economic, and technological developments. On the whole, the forces of decentralization have triumphed, but since 1850 the city government at times has labored vigorously to counteract the decline of the old city in the face of unplanned growth and suburban dispersal.

Perhaps more than any other event in the city's history, the political consolidation of Philadelphia in 1854 concentrated power and decision making. To the delight of reformers interested in order and efficiency, not to mention land speculators with purely private motives, the city added 127 square miles to its area, making its boundaries coterminus with those of Philadelphia County. The prior existence of county-wide special service districts in such fields as education, health, and public utilities facilitated consolidation, but since 1854 even the promise of city services has not opened the way for further growth. With the exception of 0.121 square miles acquired from Montgomery County in 1916, Philadelphia is the same size today as it was in 1854.[2]

Political centralization did not end with consolidation. In the half century after 1854 politicians and elite reformers gradually diminished the powers granted to the city's wards by the act of consolidation. In 1873 centralized appointment replaced the ward election of tax assessors, while in 1905 the ward boards of education lost virtually all their power in a bureaucratic shake-up which advanced the importance of city-wide school leadership.[3] When Philadelphia's bicameral council was abolished just after World War I, enlarged councilmanic districts were put into effect, and later after World War II police district lines were redrawn to minimize partisan politics and local influence in the administration of justice. At the same time a new home rule charter, adopted in 1951, gave City Hall added leverage in its quest to manage and control all Philadelphia.[4]

In general, technology, business, and industry have done far more to disperse the city since 1800 than to hold it together. Of course, as long as Philadelphia has existed, there has been a concentration of economic activity along the Delaware River north and south of Market Street. But in the twentieth century the geographic patterns of employment have changed, and at work, only white-collar professionals now cluster to any great degree in the old city. Introduced in the United States in the 1880s, the electric elevator and the skyscraper opened the way for more intensive land use in the downtown than ever before; however, not everyone would benefit equally from these innovations. Without them there would be no department stores or high-rise apartments, and law firms, banks, and insurance companies among others have profited because multistory office buildings have enabled those in these interdependent occupations to maintain propinquity in a centralized location. But benefits to the working class from these technological developments have been more indirect, and white-collar businesses probably paid the salaries of most of the 600,000 people who commuted to work every day in downtown Philadelphia in 1955.[5]

Economic growth in the United States for the past 150 years has been not only gigantic but also largely unplanned by any public authority, and the distended metropolis is one tangible result. In the nineteenth century turnpikes, canals, and eventually railroads tied cities like Philadelphia to an expanding market for manufactured goods, while in the city itself more factories meant more jobs in general. The appearance of related industries such as cotton processing and clothing production kept the demand for labor on the increase in Philadelphia. In turn, a rising pool of factory workers created more and more employment opportunities in local industries like housing, education, and food retailing. Between 1860 and 1900 factories making such goods as textiles, carpets, and paper often moved to the outskirts of the developed city, but their workers settled nearby, and the differentiation of land use, commonly associated with suburbanization, was not advanced very far. At the same time cities other than Philadelphia in the Delaware Valley became important manufacturing centers. In Camden, Trenton, Norristown, and Chester many factories sprang up, but Philadelphia's economy was always the most diversified, and its expansion animated not only Philadelphia's physical and demographic growth but that of its region as well.[6]

Suburbanization in Philadelphia is by no means a recent phenomenon. Even within William Penn's original boundaries there were large areas where few people lived before 1840, and prior to consolidation the development of residential neighborhoods from which people commuted to work occurred both within as well as outside the political limits of the city. Near the Schuylkill River south of Market Street the Rittenhouse neighborhood became a suburb by the middle of the nineteenth century. Population increased to a moderate level, elite town houses appeared, and many residents walked or rode to their jobs east of Broad Street every day. Along the Delaware between Vine and South streets demographic density peaked in 1830, and for the rest of the century Philadelphians spread out into the vastness of the city's vacant territory to the north, west, and south. Carried by old radial roads like Germantown and Ridge avenues, they settled in such northern districts as Spring Garden, Kensington, and Germantown, while to the south Moyamensing and Southwark became well-developed neighborhoods. (see Map 10-1).[7]

Innovations in public transportation profoundly affected urban population distribution in the nineteenth century, but at first the city was unaware that any revolution was under way. Little more than a stagecoach, the omnibus made its debut in Philadelphia in 1831, offering bone-jarring service on Chestnut Street at a cost few could afford. Horse-drawn streetcars began to move the middle class on rails between the old city and North Philadelphia in 1858 and soon linked the downtown with outlying communities like Germantown. Widely adopted in the 1890s, the electric street-

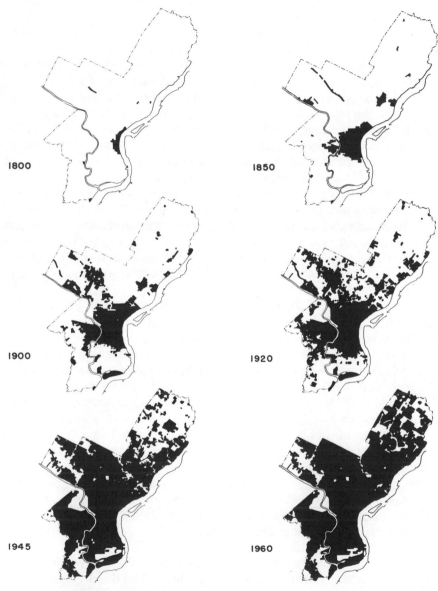

URBAN GROWTH IN PHILADELPHIA   1800-1960

1800

1850

1900

1920

1945

1960

Map 10-1. The Built-up Areas of Philadelphia, 1800-1960. These maps reveal how the county and city's land area gradually became covered over by houses, stores, factories, and so on. Note in particular what the automobile did to extend development between 1900 and 1945. *Courtesy of the Philadelphia City Planning Commission.*

car meant increased speed and the great extension of commuting limits. The first trolley line in Philadelphia opened in 1892, and in a mere five years this electric marvel had driven the horse from the mass transportation business in the city. Impressive additions to the city's transit network came soon after. In 1907 the Market Street subway-elevated commenced service; the Frankford elevated followed in 1922, and the Broad Street subway in North Philadelphia six years later.[8]

The commuter railroad proved to be especially important to the Philadelphia elite. Fast and expensive, it gave the wealthy access to distant suburbs where they could find or build housing to suit their status. In the 1860s the Pennsylvania Railroad first provided service to what soon became the fashionable Main Line, while within the consolidated city rail connections reached Chestnut Hill in 1854. Railroad companies actively promoted development along their routes. The directors of the Chestnut Hill Railroad speculated in local real estate, hoping to profit from their area's " 'elevated situation' " and " 'beauty of prospect.' "[9] The Pennsylvania Railroad laid out a community in Bryn Mawr after the Civil War and set regulations for housing quality and value, while the financier Henry Howard Houston convinced the railroad to build its own line to Chestnut Hill in 1884. Within five years Houston had erected a country inn, an Episcopal church, and, according to one report, between 80 and 100 houses in the vicinity of this line.[10]

But Chestnut Hill was not to remain the exclusive preserve of the elite. In 1894 the People's Traction Company brought trolley service as far as Rex Avenue in the center of Chestnut Hill, and when the route was extended to the front gates of an amusement park in eastern Montgomery County four years later, the Hill was no longer as private as before. By then some traction money was also being invested in suburban development. In the early 1880s William L. Elkins and Peter A. B. Widener consolidated under their control all the streetcar lines in Philadelphia, and over the next 25 years they bought property and built houses for the upwardly mobile middle class both in North Philadelphia and in the Montgomery County suburbs of Jenkintown and Elkins Park. At the same time the ambitious realtor William T. B. Roberts saw the potential brought to Montgomery County by the arrival of the Reading Railroad, and his "Easy Roberts Plan" of ten dollars down and ten dollars a month contributed to the settlement of such outlying communities as Glenside Farms and Latham Park.[11]

Because these early transportation innovations were intended to move people more than goods, they did not release most industries from their dependence on freight railroads or, more often, the Delaware and Schuylkill rivers. Whether for reasons of cost or convenience most workers also continued to congregate near their place of employment, and the differentiation of land use commonly associated with suburbanization advanced unevenly. But after 1900 the availability of motorized transportation extensively influenced both the residential and industrial structure of the city. The motorbus, automobile, and truck brought unparalleled flexibility to transportation and opened the way for the complete, if not always coordinated, development of the urban hinterland. In Philadelphia the first local bus line commenced operations in 1923, and over the next 40 years such vehicles not only replaced trolleys on many routes but also allowed passengers to travel across town more directly than could be done by rail.

Even the motorbus could not compete with the automobile. It released Philadelphians from any dependence on mass transit and enabled developers to build clusters of single-family dwellings in every corner of the suburbs.[12] Beginning in the 1920s and accelerating after World War II, the widespread ownership of automobiles allowed the middle class to become independent of even the city itself and helped to create the intra-suburban commute to work. At the same time motorized trucks allowed industry to move farther away from the inner city than ever before and along with the development of electrical power and the telephone, gave the businessman unprecedented freedom in his search for the best place to build his headquarters. The extension of the Philadelphia metropolitan area by six to nine times since 1930 is due in large part to the truck and the car.[13] Without government aid, of course, such vehicles would never have become as important as they have. Federal support for road construction began as early as 1916, and the interstate highway system, first funded in 1944, has encouraged metropolitan sprawl. In Philadelphia two major bridges were constructed over the Delaware River in the 1920s, and while a rapid transit line to Camden was opened on one in 1936, it was the motorists and the New Jersey land speculators who benefited most from these spans. Between 1950 and 1973 the city acquired more than 160 miles of interstate highway, including six expressways; consequently, the suburbs grew faster and faster while the downtown struggled with more and more traffic.[14]

According to some geographers, the more people there are in urban areas, the more extensive settlement must be.[15] But as great as it has been, the suburban boom is hardly new and need not still be out of control. As long ago as 1920 population in the outlying districts of Atlanta, St. Louis, Cleveland, Buffalo, Pittsburgh, and Philadelphia was growing twice as fast as that in the central city. Since then in Philadelphia, the number of people living in the city has remained relatively stable, but the metropolitan population has nearly doubled in size.[16] Between 1944 and 1954 while Philadelphia developed nine square miles of open land within its borders for residential use, the four adjacent counties in Pennsylvania opened 61 square miles for the same purpose. Simultaneously, those counties added 16 square miles to their industrial tax base compared to only two for Philadelphia.[17] Perhaps the wonder is that there was any unimproved land at all in the city as late as 1944. But industry moved to the suburbs not just because vacant land was no longer as plentiful or suitable housing as available near the downtown as they once had been (see Map 10-1). Suburban locations also offered lower taxes and, in time, immediate access to interstate highways like the Pennsylvania Turnpike which connected business easily with other metropolitan markets. By the 1950s the textile industry was well established outside Philadelphia, and the construction of United States Steel's Fairless Hills Plant in southeastern Bucks County helped create enough demand for worker housing to justify the development of Fairless Hills and Levittown in Pennsylvania and Willingboro township in New Jersey, which the firm of Levitt and Sons also built. Overall, Philadelphia's share of the jobs in its region dropped from 61 percent to 45 percent between 1960 and 1975.[18]

As more and more people decided to live and even work in the suburbs, the demand for consumer services escalated. Critics have sometimes complained about suburban formlessness—the "*nebulous* structure" of such areas—but shopping centers have always brought at least some focus to the city's outlying districts.[19] At the beginning of the twentieth century commercial nodes appeared at major intersections and mass transit stops. In Philadelphia an important shopping center grew up around the 69th Street Terminal of the Market Street subway-elevated line. More recently, shopping malls have become an organizing force in suburbia, offering not only retail outlets but also entertainment and professional services. Together with community colleges and industrial parks, they not only reflect urban decentralization but also act as a recentralizer within the suburbs themselves[20]

Geared to the automobile rather than the train or trolley, the Suburban Square Shopping Center, which opened in Ardmore in 1929, was the first of its kind in the region. But it was not until after 1950 that the shopping mall became commonplace. A location next to a main road meant customers could come from the city as well as the suburbs, and increasingly mall developers recognized the importance of buying up sufficient peripheral land to accommodate automobiles and control related development. The Ashton Shopping Center, opened in northeast Philadelphia in 1961, is still handicapped because it has off-street parking for only 50 cars. The nearby Roosevelt Mall, erected three years later, has room for 3,000, while the Deptford Mall in Gloucester County, New Jersey, which began operations in 1975, owns a gigantic lot with space for 6,500 vehicles.[21] The J. W. Rouse Company, a major developer of malls nationwide, discovered just how unattractive the neighborhood around a shopping center could become after it put up the Cherry Hill Mall across the Delaware River from Philadelphia in southern New Jersey. One of the first of its breed to spawn commercial and residential growth rather than merely pursue it, the Cherry Hill Mall soon became surrounded by a disorderly array of fast food shops, gasoline stations, and other small businesses. In planning the Echelon Mall which opened in 1970, nine years after Cherry Hill, the Rouse Company bought enough land to keep unwanted neighbors at a distance.[22]

Suburban shopping areas have more than held their own in the competition for business with the downtown. Whereas in 1950 there were only five major retail centers outside the Philadelphia business district, by 1975 there were dozens, including 28 enclosed malls in eastern Pennsylvania and southern New Jersey. Over-the-counter sales were increasing much faster in the suburbs than in the downtown, and planners, politicians, and businessmen expressed their concern about the future of the entire region should Philadelphia's business district suffer too many losses (see Table 10-1).[23]

The problems besetting Philadelphia have been political in origin as well as economic. Actions taken in Washington, Harrisburg, and Trenton throughout the twentieth century have subsidized decentralization. In distributing tax revenues, the state governments in Pennsylvania and New Jersey have favored the suburbs over the city even though Philadelphians pay much more per capita in taxes than do their counterparts in the outlying districts. The Federal Housing Authority, created in 1934, has made it possible for many Americans to purchase new homes outside the city. Meanwhile, local governments have not supported the integration of the suburbs with the city. In 1950 there were no less than 703 separate governmental units in the eight-county area, and their suspicions of one another, not to mention Philadelphia, have made metropolitan government little more than a topic for debate.[24]

Given the obvious popularity of living outside the city, it is hardly surprising that government at all levels has backed decentralization. Yet Philadelphia has not died. The city retains an important hold on the Delaware Valley as a whole. Its offices and stores still attract millions to the downtown. But like a solar system the region works because its elements are in tension, a relationship which must be treated with respect if it is to survive.

City and Regional Planning

In American urban history city and regional planning have represented a conscious commitment to coordination and central control. Before 1900 consolidation and annexation often helped cities manage their environs. But since then suburban jurisdictions have increasingly resisted political absorption, and cities have relied more and more on planners to control, even combat, the disorderly dispersal of people and activities from the urban core.

CITY PLANNING

Concern for the city as an organic whole began long before the rapid growth of areas outside its political limits overshadowed that of the city itself. In the 1880s the first city planners emphasized aesthetic and social aims, a balance of priorities which was forgotten by the leaders of the City

Beautiful movement at the beginning of the twentieth century. Support for parks and playgrounds which could be both attractive and useful now gave way to favor for grand boulevards and pretentious public buildings. Among planners urban layout and appearance still remain important considerations, but as long ago as 1909 the participants at the first National Conference on City Planning began to show an awareness of the economic benefits to be gained from directed growth and redevelopment. Although still strongly influenced by the values of the City Beautiful movement, the Chicago plan of the same year stressed the importance of coordinated transportation facilities and the health of the central business district. In the 1920s several cities in the United States prepared or commissioned comprehensive plans which concentrated on matters like streets, zoning, and mass transit. The depression prompted more concern for social and economic planning than ever before, but it also brought local budget cuts which new federal leadership and aid could recover only in part.[25]

In one important respect Philadelphia was planned from the beginning. The street grid approved by William Penn and implemented by his surveyor, Thomas Holme, gave a regular, almost rigid quality to the layout of the city. Nearly 40 years later in 1721 the Pennsylvania Assembly permitted Philadelphia to appoint "surveyors and regulators" who would see that the city maintained orderly street and building lines. When Philadelphia consolidated in 1854, this tradition was upheld through the provision of a Board of Surveyors and Regulators. At the same time by extending the reach of its power over surrounding districts, the city government hoped to control the process of decentralization, and with this goal in mind it established a separate department to prepare a complete plan of the city and recommend future improvements.[26]

Over the next half century the ideal of a regular city was not forgotten in Philadelphia but neither was it vigorously encouraged. A Bureau of Surveys took charge of local development in 1885, and its general plans division, organized eight years later, specialized in streets and traffic. But in a city which still relied heavily on pedestrian travel, the problems of movement were just becoming complex, and few if any Philadelphians worried about the dispersal of population or the decline of the downtown. In fact, the inner city was so crowded that in 1888 the City Parks Association formed to alert the public to the need for more open spaces in congested areas. It also favored opening a direct route between the new City Hall, rising at Centre Square, and Fairmount Park through what was then a densely settled section of the city.[27]

The idea of a street to connect the Park with the downtown did not originate with the City Parks Association. As early as 1871 it was privately proposed that the east side of the Park be linked with Broad Street north of Callowhill Street, and 13 years later Charles K. Landis, the

TABLE 10-1 The 25 Leading Shopping Centers by Sales in the Eight-County Philadelphia SMSA, 1972

County & Facility	1972 Rank	Open (O) or Enclosed (E)	Date Opened
Philadelphia County, Pa.			
Philadelphia CBD	1	dna*	dna*
Roosevelt Mall/Cottman & Bustleton			1961 &
Shopping Center	2	O	1964
Germantown Business District	10	dna	dna
Oregon Avenue Shopping Strip	13	dna	dna
Northeast Shopping Center/			
Blue Grass Plaza	25	O	1959

Total sales, 1972: $893,103,000

County & Facility	1972 Rank	Open (O) or Enclosed (E)	Date Opened
Bucks County, Pa.			
Neshaminy Mall	6	E	1968
Levittown Shopping Center	20	O	1953

Total sales, 1972: $109,292,000

County & Facility	1972 Rank	Open (O) or Enclosed (E)	Date Opened
Montgomery County, Pa.			
King of Prussia Plaza	3	E	1962
Jenkintown Business District	5	dna	dna
Plymouth Meeting Mall	12	E	1966
Cedarbrook Mall	14	E	1964
Abington Shopping Center	16	O	1959
Cheltenham Shopping Center	17	O	1959
Norriton Square Center/Penn Square/			
Swedes Square	21	O	1960
Logan Square	22	O	1954
Bala Cynwyd Center	23	O	1955
Pottstown Business District	24	dna	dna

Total sales, 1972: $468,677,000

County & Facility	1972 Rank	Open (O) or Enclosed (E)	Date Opened
Delaware County, Pa.			
69th Street Business District	8	dna	1927
Baltimore Pike Shopping Strip	11	dna	unknown
Marple Springfield/Springfield			1957 &
Shopping Center	19	0	1964

Total sales, 1972: $166,092,000

County & Facility	1972 Rank	Open (O) or Enclosed (E)	Date Opened
Chester County, Pa.			
none			
Camden County, N.J.			
Cherry Hill Mall	7	E	1961
Black Horse Pike Center	9	0	1961
Echelon Mall	15	E	1970

Total sales, 1972: $175,105,000

County & Facility	1972 Rank	Open (O) or Enclosed (E)	Date Opened
Burlington County, N.J.			
Moorestown Mall	4	E	1963
Willingboro Plaza	18	0	1959

Total sales, 1972: $126,495,000

Gloucester County, N.J.
none

Total Sales, 1972
Philadelphia County: $ 893,103,000
Seven suburban counties combined: $1,045,661,000

SOURCE: *Major Retail Centers in the Philadelphia Metropolitan Area* (Philadelphia: *The Philadelphia Inquirer* and *Daily News,* 1975). Milton A. Paule, ed., *Directory of Shopping Centers in the United States and Canada*, 16th ed. (Burlington, Iowa: National Research Bureau, 1975).

*dna = does not apply.

founder of Vineland, New Jersey, presented a design for a wide boulevard from the Park to City Hall. In the 1890s the city even placed such an avenue on its official plan, but because of opposition the Board of Surveyors removed it in 1895.[28] The setback was only temporary. The area north of Filbert Street and south of Pennsylvania Avenue through which the thoroughfare would pass had been on the decline since being surrounded by railroad tracks in the 1880s. Home buyers and small businessmen shied away, and public action seemed to be required if the neighborhood was not to become an eyesore near the center of town. In the spirit of the City Beautiful movement, in vogue at the time, the Art Federation endorsed the grand development of this part of the downtown. In 1900 it organized a Parkway Association which approved a plan for a museum in the park at the end of a wide boulevard from City Hall via Logan Square. Adopted by the city in 1904, this proposal survived several revisions. It took five years for the route to be finalized, and nearly another decade passed before the French architect Jacques Greber presented a plan for buildings and street decorations which would receive general approval. Like many improvements in other cities in the early twentieth century, the Benjamin Franklin Parkway thus drew its inspiration from that ideal of urban planning which emphasized the monumental enhancement of the city's core, and when it finally opened along its entire length in 1919, Philadelphia proved that it could successfully undertake an experiment in at least one kind of city planning (see Figures 10-1 and 10-2).[29]

Like an arrow pointed from the Schuylkill River, the new avenue clearly directed attention to the downtown. So, too, did Philadelphia's first planning committee created by the city government in February 1912. It appeared because Mayor John Reyburn had appointed several citizens committees in 1909 to develop comprehensive plans for the city, and their work, completed in 1911, faced oblivion without further action by the administration. That politics would conflict with planning immediately became apparent when a new committee authorized by ordinance in 1911 was quickly scuttled because it received full power to alter the city's comprehensive plans at the expense of existing departments.[30] The Permanent Committee on City Plans of 1912 could only advise the mayor and the director of the Department of Public Works, but undaunted, it called for the physical improvement of Philadelphia over a 25- to 35-year span. It strongly supported the development of the Parkway and, in addition, a central traffic circuit to relieve "the congested conditions existing in the business district."[31] But even this committee was not on good terms with most of the city's departments; in 1914 no agreement could be reached with the department of transit about the coordination of the subway's new downtown delivery loop with the central traffic circuit. By 1919 the permanent committee had lost its funding, and although the city charter enacted in that year allowed Philadelphia to establish an advisory commission on planning, no action was taken. In fact, more than 20 years would pass before the city would make a firm commitment to planning.[32]

During the 1920s Philadelphia remained without any agency to coordinate and systematize its development. A separate zoning commission sanctioned by the charter of 1919 also failed to gain a firm foothold, even though laws to regulate land use and building size were becoming popular in many American cities at the same time.[33] But while the city government neglected planning, the same cannot be said for others in the city. In 1920 the Engineers Club of Philadelphia urged the mayor, J. H. Moore, to establish an effective planning commission, and four years later a federation of regional planners, newly organized in the area, called "the need for planning and zoning in the city . . . imperative." High buildings were going up on narrow, congested streets, and there was "evidence that the unplanned growth of the city's early days" was continuing. In 1929 the City Council appropriated funds for a planning commission which formed but did not prosper. After 1933 it was forced to rely on federal money, and as this support was gradually withdrawn, the commission languished.[34] While it survived, the agency took a special interest in the central city, a focus which was indicative of future trends. Aware that suburbanization was draining the city's resources, the commission proposed plans to improve the accessibility and appeal of the central business district. It called for the upgrading of Chestnut Street in the vicinity of Independence Hall and a diagonal northeast-southwest thoroughfare which would feed the downtown and "do more than anything else . . . to bring back real estate values in the area."[35]

Security for city planners in Philadelphia finally arrived in the early 1940s. Despite the demands of the war, leaders in several cities, including Buffalo and Los Angeles as well as Philadelphia, anticipated the need for planning which peace would bring. In Philadelphia an unsuccessful campaign for a new home rule charter first alerted many citizens to the need for foresight. Lacking "authoritative city planning," said the home rule charter commission in 1938, Philadelphia had suffered "untold loss, extravagance, and waste."[36] A strong planning board was in order, and to form one a flurry of organizational activity ensued. Local corporate executives like Walter M. Phillips created the City Policy Committee which in turn spearheaded the formation of the Joint Committee on City Planning. It marshaled business and neighborhood support, and in 1942 the City Council responded by firmly establishing a new city planning commission. Although headed by a blue ribbon panel of nine, the agency was still limited to an advisory role, as the Bureau of Municipal Research had recommended the year before.[37] Nonetheless, it was charged with preparing a six-year plan of public improvements for which it received $149,000 with the promise of $700,000 more. In 1943 a Citizens' Council on City Planning appeared, and led by

Figure 10-1. The Fairmount Neighborhood in 1909. Looking northwest toward Fairmount Park and the Schuylkill River from City Hall Tower, this view shows the neighborhood through which the Benjamin Franklin Parkway was about to be built. The white slash in the center background was deliberately put on the print to indicate where the road would enter the city and the direction it would take. *Courtesy of the Philadelphia City Planning Commission.*

Figure 10-2. The Benjamin Franklin Parkway in 1919. The route of the Benjamin Franklin Parkway was completed, but such public buildings as the Philadelphia Museum of Art which now surround it had yet to be erected. The tower of the Pennsylvania Railroad's Broad Street Station stands in the foreground. *Courtesy of the Philadelphia City Planning Commission.*

Walter Phillips, it encouraged the new commission to address both neighborhood and city-wide needs. When the commission sponsored the Better
Philadelphia Exposition in 1947, it articulated some of these concerns,
stressing the wisdom of downtown renewal and expressways bracketing
the core.[38] It was aware of Philadelphia's reputation as a city of neighborhoods, but in its judgment the most important one was in the heart of town.

Planning in Philadelphia was not the exclusive preserve of the planning
commission. After World War II other public and private bodies made their
presence felt in this field. Chartered in 1946, the Philadelphia Redevelopment Authority controlled renewal and redevelopment, and along with the
planning commission and the Philadelphia Housing Authority, it undertook a housing quality survey in 1947.[39] A creature of the business community,
the Greater Philadelphia Movement began trying to repair the city's economic and political image one year later. It studied a variety of broad problems such as land use in the downtown and supported a new home rule
charter for Philadelphia. When approved in 1951, this document strengthened
the city's government and enhanced the centralization of leadership in
Philadelphia. It enlarged the duties of the planning commission and the
appointive powers of the mayor, and between them they contributed mightily
to the so-called Philadelphia renaissance.[40] Led by reformers Joseph Clark
and Richardson Dilworth, the mayors of the 1950s, the government took a
more active role in the economic and social life of the city and a special
interest in the welfare of the downtown. The planning commission strongly
supported the private construction of Penn Center, a complex of office
buildings on the site of the old Broad Street Station. It drew plans for a mall
north of Independence Hall and even resurrected a proposal, first advanced
in the 1920s, to "relieve traffic congestion" in the central business district
by demolishing all of City Hall save the tower.[41]

Both Joseph Clark and Richardson Dilworth gave practical meaning to
the power prescribed for the mayor by the new charter. Under his authority
Clark appointed several committees within the city to coordinate public
and private policy making on housing, business, and the downtown.[42]
Among others, their members included representatives from several nonprofit
corporations, established in Philadelphia in the 1950s to promote specific
changes in the commercial, industrial, and residential pattern. In 1955 the
Greater Philadelphia Movement and Mayor Clark jointly sponsored the
creation of one of these—the Food Distribution Center Corporation, formed
to move the city's wholesale market to South Philadelphia. The achievement
of this goal in 1959 contributed valuable land to the redevelopment of the
southeast corner of the downtown as an elite residential neighborhood. In fact,
the Old Philadelphia Development Corporation, organized under Dilworth's
aegis in 1956, concentrated on rehabilitating this area without sacrificing its
historic appearance or reputation. Society Hill, as it is now called, has kept

Dilworth's name alive in Philadelphia while acting as a reminder of his preoccupation with "the renewal of the central business district and the Center City historic areas."[43]

Since the consolidation of 1854 no Philadelphia administration has been able to ignore, without peril, the city's outlying districts and, more recently, its suburban hinterland. At first, it was sufficient for the city to provide every neighborhood with such essential services as police and fire protection, but paradoxically perhaps, the social and geographic fragmentation of Philadelphia since the mid-nineteenth century has encouraged a broader perspective. Both Clark and Dilworth understood the value of comprehensive vision; yet, even as they sponsored neighborhood renewal or social and economic studies of the entire city, their commitment to centralization remained in view. The University City Science Center in West Philadelphia dispossessed local residents but would, it was hoped, produce jobs in research and development while insuring that many of the city's medical and educational resources would remain concentrated near the downtown. According to Edmund N. Bacon, the director of the Philadelphia Planning Commission, the layout of the Center would even complement the downtown, uniting Market Street on both sides of the Schuylkill River and revitalizing the renewal area by thrusting "the influence of Center City deep into West Philadelphia."[44]

While the reformers were in office, the city undertook several major studies of its problems and prospects, all of which were supportive of the downtown. Appointed in 1952, the Urban Traffic and Transportation Board reported in 1955 on the need for a regional transportation policy combining rapid transit with automobiles and focusing on communication with the central business district. At the same time the Central Urban Renewal Area Study called for clearance and/or rehabilitation from the center outward, but the city's development coordinator, William L. Rafsky, recommended beginning in more promising neighborhoods farther from the core, and as late as 1967 Philadelphia was still trying to find an effective compromise between inner-city renewal and a more extensive program with wider political appeal.[45]

Federal housing policy helped prepare the way for comprehensive planning in cities like Philadelphia. Legislation passed by Congress in 1949 and 1954 required cities to have general plans before they could qualify for federal aid for urban renewal. In Philadelphia public and private support for a comprehensive plan was widespread. Among others the Urban Traffic and Transportation Board and the Old Philadelphia Development Corporation furnished staff time and ideas while the Citizens' Council on City Planning created a Comprehensive Planning Committee in 1954.[46] The final document as published in 1960 under the supervision of the planning commission's executive director, Edmund Bacon, proved to be one of the most important contributions of the reform era. Unlike earlier efforts, it addressed the future of every section of the city, rethinking both the status of the downtown and the standing of the many residential and industrial neighborhoods away from the core. It justified local facilities for recreation and government business not merely as expedients due to dispersal but as focal points "designed to foster a sense of community identity." According to Bacon, the city should have many "strongly articulated nuclei . . . throughout the residential fabric [to] generate neighborhood identification, loyalty, and pride, and serve as links for identification with the city and the region."[47]

But ultimately Philadelphia's planners believed that it was the central business district which would have to carry the city and hold it together. "Center City," the 1960 plan said, "is now and will continue to be, the most important section of the City economically, in every sense of that term." It deserved special attention in the improvement of Philadelphia's transportation patterns and facilities. Regional and local shopping centers should be satellites of it, and accordingly, in the planning commission's special plan for the downtown released in 1963, it was proposed that Market Street east of Broad be redeveloped to make the area competitive with the suburban shopping plazas and bring residents back into the city. The downtown, the commission said, must be "the principal place for doing business" in the Delaware Valley and a "springboard from which waves of revitalization spread outward as suburban families are attracted to urban living."[48] The commitment to centralization was clear; Philadelphia's comprehensive planning body believed that the future of the city depended on a strong central business district and a redistribution of the region's population into a more compact form.

REGIONAL PLANNING

Someday suburban dwellers may transform Philadelphia once again by resettling in the inner city. But in the 1960s there was little indication that such a shift was even a remote possibility. Census figures showed that at least for the foreseeable future centralization in the region would have to be more political than demographic, and the Delaware Valley Regional Planning Commission, which appeared in 1967, has aimed at this objective. Achieving it, however, has proven to be difficult at best.

Metropolitan planning in the United States dates from the early twentieth century. In major cities like Boston and New York civic leaders discussed its desirability, and in Chicago Daniel Burnham's plan for the city, completed in 1909, addressed many regional needs. Fearing domination by their urban neighbors, rural and suburban leaders opposed such innovations. But because of the growing popularity of the automobile, demographic dispersal accelerated in the 1920s, and at least some Americans became convinced of the wisdom of regional planning. Pioneering efforts were undertaken in cities like Los Angeles and New York where a report, issued in 1929, favored what might be called coordinated decentralization. Prepared by the Committee on the Regional Plan, it accepted that commerce, industry, and residence would be located throughout the metropolitan area but argued that they should be concentrated in separate centers adjacent to one another.[49]

At the beginning of the twentieth century most people in the Delaware Valley lived in Philadelphia, but within its environs there were dozens of large settlements clustered at highway and railroad intersections. In fact, nearly 80 percent of all those in the area lived in communities of more than 5,000, and in 1912 an association was privately organized "to promote cooperation between the towns and boroughs of suburban Philadelphia on town planning mattters."[50] One year later the Pennsylvania legislature authorized the creation of a Metropolitan Planning Commission. It was to prepare comprehensive plans for the region on such physical features as roads, sewage disposal, and parks. But many towns viewed it as an intruder, and the state lawmakers abolished it in 1915. Within Philadelphia there was some awareness that a lack of planning in the suburbs was detrimental to the city. The Permanent Committee on Comprehensive Plans endorsed an extension of the city's boundaries into Delaware County where growth was proceeding in an "unregulated manner," and failing that, it tried, again unsuccessfully, to convince the state legislature to give Philadelphia control over street openings and land subdivisions within three miles of its borders.[51] In 1924 what could have been a major step was taken with the formation of the Regional Planning Federation of the Philadelphia Tri-State District. An offshoot of similar efforts in New York, the Federation supported land use planning on a regional scale and intergovernmental cooperation, but lacking strong business support for such policies, its influence turned out to be largely educational.[52]

In a preliminary survey conducted in the year of its founding the Federation took the decentralization of people and jobs as a given but justified its existence by identifying the need to coordinate such growth within a 30-mile radius of Philadelphia. Both the city and the suburbs stood to gain; the two were becoming increasingly interdependent, and, said the Federation, "the only solution for the common problems of such a metropolitan area, is through . . . the development of a regional plan."[53] When a drive for money to fund further work was undertaken in 1927, outlying communities made it clear that they would lend their support only if it was understood that annexations or regional government were out of the question. The Federation was able to raise $600,000, and its report, published in 1932, stressed the importance of metropolitan cooperation to promote development and combat blight. While preserving open spaces, planning would enable the Philadelphia region to support as many as 15 million inhabitants by 1980.[54] Considering the depressed state of the nation's economy, such expectations must have seemed fantastic to outsiders, but they were not uncommon among planners at this time. The profession believed that planning was not just compatible with phenomenal growth but a prerequisite for it. Both the spirit and policies of the early New Deal encouraged this point of view, and yet in the Delaware Valley there was insufficient support to save the Regional Planning Federation of the Philadelphia Tri-State District. Its recommendations of 1932 were never implemented, and it disappeared seven years later when it merged with the Institute for Local and State Government at the University of Pennsylvania.[55]

By the end of World War II regional planning was neither common nor effective in the United States. Several cities established metropolitan planning boards in the 1940s, but forced to rely mainly on goodwill, they could not really control the suburban growth which spawned them. As a result of the Better Philadelphia Exposition, business leaders formed the Delaware Valley Council in 1949. An enthusiastic advocate of regional planning, it even tried to revive the report of the Regional Federation but abandoned this objective in 1954 because of inadequate support.[56] Meanwhile, four counties in the Philadelphia area (Montgomery, Bucks, and Delaware counties in Pennsylvania and Camden County in New Jersey) organized planning commissions, and in 1952 the three in Pennsylvania joined forces to form the Southeastern Pennsylvania Regional Planning Commission. In addition to being prompted by suburban growth in general, these planning bodies appeared because of the decision to build the Schuylkill Expressway and the construction by United States Steel of a new plant in lower Bucks County. But county commissions in Pennsylvania did not share a common frame of reference about the nature of suburban planning, and their regional offspring suffered accordingly. When they also chose to exclude Philadelphia from their Regional Commission, they revealed their timidity and assured their ineffectiveness.[57]

The need for coordination in the Delaware Valley persisted nonetheless. In the 1950s the Urban Traffic and Transportation Board addressed a regional problem of special magnitude and convinced city and suburban leaders to search together for solutions. One result was the Southeastern Pennsylvania Transportation Authority, established to consolidate under public control all the private rail, surface and underground commuter lines in the area. The widely recognized importance of improved circulation gave rise to further research and, not surprisingly, a greater awareness of the wisdom of intergovernmental cooperation. The directors of the Penn Jersey Transportation Study, commenced in 1959, quickly discovered that without broad political backing they were wasting their time. A regional civic group called Penjerdel (the Pennsylvania-New Jersey-Delaware Metropolitan Project, Inc.) helped them form the Regional Conference of Elected Officials to stimulate voluntary cooperation among governmental units. But lacking universal support, the regional conference was ineffective.[58]

In 1965 Pennsylvania and New Jersey began to explore the possibility of interstate cooperation on matters of mutual interest, and two years later the two states approved a compact which brought the Delaware Valley Regional Planning Commission (DVRPC) into existence. It started by gathering data on topics like housing, employment, and population growth, and viewing these variables as related, it encouraged policy making with this interdependence in mind. Throughout its history the DVRPC has shown no special sympathy for the revitalization of downtown Philadelphia. In fact, in 1970 it concluded that the inner city was oversupplied with retail establishments and recommended public programs to help small businessmen either cluster in the core or relocate in the suburbs.[59] But, no supporter of suburban sprawl, the Commission also favored multipurpose centers for commerce, recreation, and public services to bring focus to outlying areas. In 1967 the DVRPC acquired some power when the federal government made its review an essential prerequisite for grant money to finance recreation, sewage, and transportation improvements of area-wide significance. The Commission has acted as a forum for the discussion of intergovernmental problems, but political centralization on a regional basis has not been achieved.[60] Although integral to the area, the state of Delaware has never joined the partnership, nor has the DVRPC worked closely with the Philadelphia Planning Commission. As an advisory body, it cannot overrule local governments, let alone initiate positive action to coordinate regional development.

A strong desire for planning has existed in some circles in the Delaware Valley since the early 1940s, but its advocates have differed about the meaning of centralization. They have reached no consensus about Philadelphia's proper role in the region and remain divided over the merits of physical and economic as opposed to political centralization. Meanwhile, local loyalties continue, especially among those who live in Philadelphia, the city of neighborhoods. The preoccupation of planners and most municipal officials with metropolitan growth and coordination has been matched in Philadelphia and elsewhere by a countervailing trend to make the residential neighborhood more important in the daily lives of urban Americans. In its many and varied forms this small but basic unit is a familiar feature of the modern metropolis, and given the devotion it inspires, not to mention its vital role in the ecology of the city, it deserves careful scrutiny in Philadelphia.

Local Loyalties: Neighborhoods and Civic Organizations

Most Americans who live in cities know that they reside in two places at once. They tell outsiders that they live and work in Los Angeles, New York, or Philadelphia even though their homes or jobs may be in the suburbs rather than inside the political boundaries of the city itself. But for local friends and relatives urban Americans must be more specific; they must identify the neighborhood where they make their home or do their work.

Since the end of the nineteenth century more and more city dwellers have had to distinguish between where they live and where they work. Increasingly, neighborhood has come to mean that part of the city to which a worker returns at the end of the business day. Where he goes says something about who he is, for neighborhoods have identities. To some extent this image is a reflection of the social and economic characteristics of the people who live there. But what other people think they see may not be accurate, and a neighborhood's reputation, based on rumor, sensationalism, or past events, may be more important in defining its identity than the socioeconomic realities which currently prevail. Physical features like historical landmarks or major thoroughfares also shape our perception of the city and help determine where we divide in our mind one neighborhood from another. Yet geographic as well as social boundaries are not always precise or universally known, and people from different backgrounds and traditions vary in their views about how large their neighborhood really is.[61]

In Philadelphia there are many neighborhoods. According to the city planning commission, in 1976 there were more than 100, and their residents can be very loyal. However, the neighborhoods with which people identify do not invariably coincide with those drawn on a map by politicians and planners. In some working-class districts like South Philadelphia where thousands of eastern European immigrants settled at the beginning of the twentieth century, many people still think of their neighborhood as only three or four blocks. Even in such a small space 70 years ago Italians and Jews, Poles and Irish often lived side by side. These Philadelphians associated largely with their ethnic counterparts, distinguishing between the place where they lived and their own cultural community within it. In the industrial city the shared customs and values of each group were reassuring to its members and even helped indirectly to generate loyalty to the neighborhood itself. Perhaps the greatest inducement for local awareness has been the threat of invasion and settlement by unfamiliar outsiders. At the end of the nineteenth century the Irish reacted defensively when confronted at home by Italian or Polish newcomers, and more recently in inner-city neighborhoods like Kensington the white working class has become more outspoken about the virtues of their area as the black ghetto has moved closer.[62]

Such friction has never been wholly ethnic or racial. Economic competition has often brought groups into conflict in Philadelphia. Artisans and unskilled laborers were at odds in the city before the Civil War as the factory system began to transform the local economy at the expense of independent craftsmen, and in the twentieth century the bureaucratization of business has widened the distance between employers and employees. Mere access to jobs was and still is very important, especially to stable neighborhoods. As late as 1920 an area with enough opportunities for work could be nearly self-sufficient, and despite political centralization, local residents could almost forget that they were part of a larger whole. But whether around the corner or at the other end of an affordable commute, jobs have always been essential to any neighborhood, regardless of its social characteristics.[63]

The Philadelphia suburbs in Pennsylvania and New Jersey have their neighborhoods, too. Like Chestnut Hill, Rhawnhurst, and Fishtown within the city, there are elite, middle-class, and blue-collar areas in the surrounding hinterland. Since the end of the nineteenth century Main Line communities like Radnor and Ardmore have attracted new wealth as well as old. Not far away modest row homes in Upper Darby and Lansdowne testify to the unpretentious stature of these neighborhoods. North of the city Jenkintown remains desirable if not as fashionable as it once aspired to be, while Levittown and Fairless Hills offer a little more space and status than the nearby neighborhoods of Northeast Philadelphia.[64]

On the whole, suburban communities are more extensive than those inside the city limits and less important to their residents as an object of identification and commitment. Many who live there work far away, and being modest in size, local institutions like public schools do not create the illusion of independence from outside influences. Within the city, on the other hand, such a delusion sometimes encourages powerful, even parochial loyalties to agencies like the police or the schools. This is not to say, of course, that the people in the suburbs are indifferent about local autonomy; their opposition to political consolidation and metropolitan government is well documented. But the majority of those who live outside cities like Philadelphia are middle- or upper-class, and they have a broader personal and occupational frame of reference than the blue-collar workers who, more often than not, reside within them.[65]

Spatial specialization by income, occupation, and ethnicity within Philadelphia itself is neither new nor unimportant. As early as the 1810s the elite concentrated below Market Street near Washington Square. Blacks lived to the south and west of this neighborhood. The middle class found housing along the Delaware waterfront from Vine to South Street, and the white poor often settled in the undesirable areas at the edge of the developed city.[66] It should be reemphasized, however, that before 1860 such spatial differentiation was at most incipient, and it was not until the advent of the commuter railroad and the trolley that Philadelphia started to move undeniably toward becoming a truly divided metropolis. The middle class and the elite fanned out of the old city to the north and west. Trade and manufacturing clusters began to emerge, and as Sam Bass Warner has pointed out, by the 1920s land use in Philadelphia was sharply differentiated by ethnicity, class, and function, a condition which continues today.[67]

More land is devoted to housing in Philadelphia than any other purpose, and in its many different residential areas there are numerous organizations. Some are purely private and take no interest in the community, but many others have a public role. Participants in the city's continuing experience with centralization and decentralization, they focus local loyalties and represent the neighborhood in the city as a whole. Their interests are often specialized. The Health and Welfare Council expresses the community's views on the quality of local medical services; the Home and School Association concentrates on educational issues, and the businessmen's league tries to improve the economic climate in the neighborhood. At the same time many of these groups are linked to city-wide or even national organizations devoted to the same concerns. But the neighborhood comes first, and among such groups perhaps the most revealing of the localism in cities like Philadelphia are the neighborhood civic organizations. They are closely identified with their communities. The local community is their *raison d'etre*, and while their array of interests can be impressive, it seldom transcends the social issues commonly associated with home life in a compartmentalized society.

Neighborhood civic organizations first became numerous in Philadelphia after World War II. Before then such groups were largely confined to middle-class neighborhoods and appear to have been modest in their activities and aspirations.[68] More often than today the informal ties of family, religion, and nationality gave mutual support. Immigrants in Philadelphia and other cities reinforced such personal links by forming fraternal and benefit associations. In the nineteenth century the Irish supported one another at the neighborhood level through mutual assistance societies, fire companies, and savings and loan associations. Later, social clubs and neighborhood insurance societies were common among the Poles.[69] Even the native-born elite supplemented family and religious networks by creating formal clubs and organizations. Such venerable institutions as the First City Troop and the Philadelphia Club not only recognized status but also strengthened ties among local aristocrats. In respectable suburbs like Overbrook Farms in upper West Philadelphia social organizations became politically active on occasion, but before 1945 such displays of civic consciousness were not frequent. Meanwhile, the dispersal of population and its increasing differentiation by income in urban space made it more and more difficult for ethnic and religious similarities to act as a basis for mutual support.[70] In addition, the separation of work and play, along with the growth of personal autonomy and the centralization of government since the end of the nineteenth century, has led, according to one sociologist, to "the decline of the neighborhood as a significant unit in both rural and urban areas."[71]

But the specialization of land use by race and social class as well as by social and economic function has fostered local loyalties and encouraged the defense of neighborhood interests. Formal associations among businessmen, the parents of schoolchildren, and other community groups have long been active, and since 1945 neighborhood civic organizations have become commonplace in Philadelphia. Without ethnic or religious affiliations groups like the Paschall Betterment League or the Grays Ferry Community

Council have solicited members solely on the basis of residence within prescribed boundaries. Like other voluntary associations they have provided opportunities for social participation and mutual support which once might have occurred more informally. Following the pattern in other cities, they have been more prevalent in areas where the people are prosperous and well educated. In Philadelphia they have also appeared more frequently in older neighborhoods with a clearly residential character; in such places, whether rich or poor, there was something worth protecting against onrushing change (see Table 10-2).[72]

In many cases Philadelphia's local civic organizations formed to repel a specific threat to the residential integrity or social traditions of their neighborhoods. In 1946 the Center City Residents Association was created to prevent the construction a parking garage under Rittenhouse Square. Such crises increased in the 1960s, and a flurry of organizational foundings followed. In 1963 the people of Queen Village (once known as Southwark) formed an association to deal with housing, zoning, and traffic in their neighborhood. The residents of this increasingly affluent area just south of the old city were concerned about the impact on their community of an interstate highway being built nearby, and two years later in the renewed and upgraded neighborhood of Society Hill to the north a civic association was set up in part to lobby for the construction of a roof over this road to conceal it from view.[73] In outlying neighborhoods like Wynnefield, Overbrook Park, and East Mount Airy civic organizations emerged or matured in response to racial change. A strong voluntary association seemed the best vehicle to stabilize the community and preserve integration.[74]

Throughout the twentieth century but especially since 1945 most neighborhood civic organizations in Philadelphia have addressed themselves only to community matters like housing, zoning, recreation, and education (see Table 10-3). Their approach has been orderly, even bureaucratic, and some have been sensitive to the realities of city politics. Their formalism may be alien to the ideal of neighborliness, but their concerns have been those of residence, a viewpoint which would have seemed too narrow to nineteenth-century Philadelphians whose homes and jobs were usually in close proximity. Modern community organizations like the Northwood Civic Association in northeast Philadelphia want "to preserve the residential nature" of their communities. For more than 30 years the Center City Residents Association has supervised an area which includes some of the central business district, but it has always said that its purpose was to make its part of the city "a better place [in which] to live."[75] In a divided metropolis it is difficult to see that neighborhood welfare is dependent on the city's economic health as a whole.

Local civic organizations in Philadelphia have received occasional support from the city government. Although of different minds on the question of centralization, these organizations and City Hall have cooperated at times,

TABLE 10-2 Neighborhood Civic Organizations in Philadelphia by Location and Decade of Origin, 1950–1968

Section	Population 1950	% Non-White	Orgs. Begun in 1950s	Population 1960	% Non-White	Orgs. Begun in 1960s	Population 1970	% Non-White	Orgs. Active in 1968	Persons Per Org. 1968	Total Orgs., 1950-68	Orgs. 4 or More Years Reporting
Section												
Center City	51,792	23.1	4	38,323	21.6	4	43,465	10.7	4	10,866	8	1
South Phila.	310,144	23.3	15	257,302	26.0	22	231,107	30.5	25	9,244	37	11
So. West Phila.	109,857	8.6	6	100,258	11.0	11	96,440	33.0	10	9,644	17	13
West Phila.	118,276	5.7	2	104,244	43.2	9	99,626	70.4	7	14,232	11	4
Upper West Phila.	212,010	40.6	9	197,588	57.9	17	175,944	67.0	19	9,260	26	19
No. Phila. West	264,041	40.3	10	244,352	72.8	21	206,041	85.4	23	8,958	31	23
No. Phila. East	205,137	30.8	6	156,033	39.2	15	112,361	43.7	12	9,363	21	12
Inner NE Phila.	467,583	1.0	26	481,360	1.3	23	458,706	6.3	33	13,900	49	33
Far NE Phila.	68,980	5.4	13	139,809	3.2	19	237,321	2.2	22	10,787	32	22
Northwest Phila.	226,414	5.9	22	239,661	16.0	31	238,628	47.8	35	6,818	53	12
Roxborough Manayunk	37,371	2.5	5	39,898	2.2	7	48,260	2.6	11	4,387	12	4
Totals	2,071,605	18.3	118	1,998,828	26.7	179	1,947,899	34.4	201	9,691	297*	154

SOURCE: Chamber of Commerce of Philadelphia, Associations of Greater Philadelphia (Philadelphia: 1950). Division of School Extension: School District of Philadelphia, *Community Organizations in Philadelphia (Community Councils, Civic Associations, Improvement Associations, etc.)* (Philadelphia: 1951, 1955, 1958, 1961, 1965, & 1968).

*This list is not comprehensive. It excludes block organizations and other minor civic groups whose active life was short, but the distribution by area indicated here is very probably representative.

and in the mid-1950s the government even encouraged such groups. The inducement was federal money. The Housing Act of 1954 made funds available to combat blight, but to qualify for them cities had to meet several requirements, one of which was providing for the participation of both city-wide and neighborhood associations in urban renewal. Pilot projects were undertaken in four parts of the city with the help of three social settlements and three civic organizations. In upper West Philadelphia a new, more comprehensive civic association emerged during the rehabilitation effort, but in the manner of Mayor Clark, the reformers in office were always more comfortable working with elite groups with a cosmopolitan vision like the Citizens Council on City Planning or the Greater Philadelphia Movement.[76] In 1964 the city considered acting through neighborhood organizations to make available more owner-occupied, low-income housing, but the Philadelphia Housing Development Corporation, established to build such properties or renovate them, bypassed local groups. Instead it sold them directly to individual buyers or to the Philadelphia Housing Authority for subsequent distribution.[77]

Between 1945 and 1970, when city planning was thriving in Philadelphia, the planning commission possessed great potential to strengthen or weaken the city's neighborhoods. Sometimes it blundered in dealing with local problems and needs. In the 1950s it undercut the financing for a neighborhood renewal project by announcing a scheduled street widening in the affected area. When it also recommended that an expressway be built through a black community along the southern border of the central business district, there was so much community opposition that the idea had to be dropped. But the commission also conducted a number of neighborhood studies and often spoke in favor of citizen involvement in the planning process. After consulting five civic organizations in the northeast in 1950, it developed a commercial zoning policy in harmony with "the residential character" of the area.[78] Twenty years later it reported working "closely with many neighborhood groups in setting goals, determining priorities and preparing plans for the future." Such groundwork eased the way for the acceptance of the commission's city-wide plans. At the same time it developed support for the structuring of neighborhoods around "schools or community buildings."[79] Reformers and educators like Jacob Riis, Edward J. Ward, and Clarence A. Perry introduced this planning strategy for the improvement of cities as far back as the first decade of the twentieth century, and the Comprehensive Plan of 1960 elaborated on it, arguing that local centers like shopping plazas or public recreation facilities could "enhance the feeling of community" within the city without sacrificing any of the advantages of metropolitan living.[80] Clearly, the Philadelphia Planning Commission understood the importance of the city's neighborhoods. But even when working within them, it could not suppress the urge to centralize, and overall it has not regarded them as ends in themselves. Unlike some community activists, the

TABLE 10-3 Statements of Purpose by Philadelphia Neighborhood Civic Organizations: A Representative Sample, 1951-1968

Organization	Year of Statement	Location

Carrol Park Community
Improvement Association   1961   Upper West Phila.
"To guide the community in raising its standards and furnishing its needs (Education), (Culture), (Sanitation), (Relationship)."

Chelten Hills Civic League   1955   Northwest Phila.
"To develop the area as a first class residential community, free from commercial activity; secure proper lighting conditions; insure safety for all residents."

Cottage Green Manor Civic
Association   1965   Far Northeast
"To improve health, welfare and moral standards of the community."

Greater Morton Civic
Association   1961   Northwest Phila.
"To involve neighbors in varied kinds of activities which will promote better group and inter-group relationships. To improve and maintain the physical character of the neighborhood. To create more opportunities for cultural development of children."

Greater Olney Civic
Association   1951   Inner Northeast
"Improvement of public services; such as traffic lights, parking facilities, street car services, police protection, and recreation needs."

Harrowgate Park Civic
Association   1958   Inner Northeast
"Community improvement and civic endeavors."

Kingsessing Gardens Association   1965   Southwest Phila.
"Enforce police, zoning, sanitation, community beautification, better school facilities, cooperate with supporting agencies of [sic] community betterment campaigns of all kinds."

Our Neighbors Association   1961   North Phila. West
"Improvement of neighborhoods—education on health programs—beautification of blocks—elimination of fire hazards—development of youth project and leadership of youth and adults."

Rhawnhurst Civic League   1958   Far Northeast
"Protest any changes in zoning; study the public and civic life of the community and render general community services."

Southwark Community Council   1951   South Phila.
"To present a united front in matters of concern to the district."

SOURCE: Community Organizations in Philadelphia, 1951, 1955, 1958, 1961, 1965.

commission has always viewed neighborhoods as part of a larger whole. Since local loyalties remain strong, perhaps only greater dedication to the ideal of a multinucleated yet interdependent metropolis could have made Philadelphia less divided than it is today.

Conclusion: The Persistent Dualism

In the Delaware Valley the long-standing tension between centralization and decentralization shows no signs of abating. Suburban growth is continuing, but the city remains alive in the region. Among urban observers there is an ongoing debate about the nature and meaning of the relationship between Philadelphia and its suburbs. Are the outlying districts merely parasites which exploit the city but give nothing in return? Many subscribe to this view, but others argue that the suburbs not only rely on Philadelphia but also demonstrate its health through the persistence of its powers of attraction.[81] Neither interpretation will be convincing in the future if those living outside the city cease to use it regularly for work or recreation. Such dependence even now is unnecessary; all of life's needs can be satisfied in the suburbs.

But Philadelphia refuses to die. The city's neighborhood associations have not only multiplied but also formed a city-wide coalition to represent them. In more than one neighborhood near the downtown the affluent have reappeared as tenants and home owners. The central business district is attracting new investment, and as the planner August Heckscher has observed, this area is still an essential part of any metropolis. The downtown "today tends to be a center among several lesser centers," he has written, "a dominant node among the nodes that constitute the modern urban complex."[82] In the past 150 years Philadelphia's core has experienced many changes and survived many challenges to its vitality. Technology, social and economic conflict as well as the politics of business and government have divided the city but not broken it apart. What will become of these trends is impossible to say. All that seems certain is that in the Delaware Valley the forces of dispersal and concentration will not soon achieve any permanent equilibrium.

Notes

1. Mel Scott, *American City Planning Since 1890* (Berkeley: University of California Press, 1969), pp. 343-45. For their assistance in the preparation of this chapter special thanks are due to Mark H. Haller, Frederic Miller, Peter Silverman, Sondra Schneider, and Alois K. Strobl.

2. Kenneth T. Jackson, "Metropolitan Government Versus Political Autonomy: Politics on the Crabgrass Frontier," in *Cities in American History,* ed. Kenneth T. Jackson and Stanley K. Schultz (New York: Alfred A. Knopf, 1972), pp. 446, 450-

55, 458; Conrad Weiler, *Philadelphia: Neighborhood, Authority, and the Urban Crisis* (New York: Praeger, 1974), pp. 36-38.

3. Weiler, *Philadelphia: Neighborhood, Authority, and the Urban Crisis,* pp. 39-40; William H. Issel, "Modernization in Philadelphia School Reform, 1882-1905," *The Pennsylvania Magazine of History and Biography* 94 (July 1970): 358-83.

4. Weiler, *Philadelphia: Neighborhood, Authority, and the Urban Crisis,* pp. 40-42, 183.

5. Peter O. Muller, Kenneth C. Meyer, and Roman A. Cybriwsky, *Metropolitan Philadelphia: A Study of Conflicts and Social Cleavages* (Cambridge, Mass.: Ballinger Publishing Co., 1976), pp. 55-56; Jean Gottmann, *Megalopolis: The Urbanized Northeastern Seaboard of the United States* (Cambridge, Mass.: The M.I.T. Press, 1961), pp. 206-7, 516-18, 550, 564, 638-39; Joseph Oberman and Stephen Kozakowski, *History of Development in the Delaware Valley Region* (Philadelphia: Delaware Valley Regional Planning Commission, 1976), p. 61.

6. Allen R. Pred, *The Spatial Dynamics of U.S. Urban-Industrial Growth, 1800-1914: Interpretive and Theoretical Essays* (Cambridge, Mass.: The M.I.T. Press, 1966); Oberman and Kozakowski, *Development in the Delaware Valley,* pp. 40-47, 54-55, 71; Gottmann, *Megalopolis,* p. 201.

7. Kenneth T. Jackson, "Urban Deconcentration in the Nineteenth Century: A Statistical Inquiry," in *The New Urban History: Quantitative Explorations by American Historians,* ed. Leo F. Schnore (Princeton, N.J.: Princeton University Press, 1975), pp. 116-17, 121-24, 129-30, 135-37; E. Digby Baltzell, *Philadelphia Gentlemen: The Making of a National Upper Class* (Chicago: Quadrangle Books, 1971), pp. 181-87.

8. Glen E. Holt, "The Changing Perception of Urban Pathology: An Essay on the Development of Mass Transit in the United States," in *Cities in American History,* ed. Jackson and Schultz, pp. 324-38; Oberman and Kozakowski, *Development in the Delaware Valley,* pp. 45, 50, 61-62.

9. *1855 Annual Report of the Chestnut Hill Railroad* quoted in Willard S. Detweiler, Jr., *Chestnut Hill: An Architectural History* (Philadelphia: Willard S. Detweiler, Jr., Inc., 1969), pp. 21, 26.

10. Detweiler, *Chestnut Hill,* p. 27; Baltzell, *Philadelphia Gentlemen,* pp. 205-6.

11. Detweiler, *Chestnut Hill,* p. 23; Baltzell, *Philadelphia Gentlemen,* pp. 125-26, 210-12; Dick Pothier, "'North Suburbs': Not Main Lane, but they're close," *The Philadelphia Inquirer,* May 15, 1977.

12. Oberman and Kozakowski, *Development in the Delaware Valley,* pp. 59, 62; Detweiler, *Chestnut Hill,* p. 24; Holt, "Changing Perception of Urban Pathology," p. 337; Gottmann, *Megalopolis,* p. 388.

13. Oberman and Kozakowski, *Development in the Delaware Valley,* pp. 65, 78-80; Gottmann, *Megalopolis,* pp. 480, 590; Weiler, *Philadelphia: Neighborhood, Authority, and the Urban Crisis,* pp. 32-33.

14. Oberman and Kozakowski, *Development in the Delaware Valley,* pp. 60, 62, 65, 93-94; Scott, *American City Planning,* pp. 536-41; Victor Gruen, *The Heart of Our Cities. The Urban Crisis: Diagnosis and Cure* (New York: Simon and Schuster, 1964), p. 123.

15. Muller, Meyer, and Cybriwsky, *Metropolitan Philadelphia,* pp. 32-33.

16. Scott, *American City Planning,* p. 185; *Comprehensive Plan: The Physical Development Plan for the City of Philadelphia* (Philadelphia: City Planning Com-

mission, 1960), p. 22; Adam Tait, ed., *1976 Bulletin Almanac* (Philadelphia: *The Evening and Sunday Bulletin*, 1976), pp. 205-6.

17. *Land Use in Philadelphia, 1944-1954* (Philadelphia: City Planning Commission, 1956), p. 6.

18. Weiler, *Philadelphia: Neighborhood, Authority, and the Urban Crisis*, p. 30; Oberman and Kozakowski, *Development in the Delaware Valley*, pp. 86, 96; Gottmann, *Megalopolis*, pp. 210, 461, 464-65, 486-87; Muller, Meyer, and Cybriwsky, *Metropolitan Philadelphia*, pp. 55-56; Herbert J. Gans, *The Levittowners: Ways of Life and Politics in a New Suburban Community* (New York: Random House, 1967), p. 5.

19. Gottmann, *Megalopolis*, pp. 185-86, 390-92.

20. Oberman and Kozakowski, *Development in the Delaware Valley*, p. 60; Gruen, *Heart of Our Cities*, pp. 183-89; Muller, Meyer, and Cybriwsky, *Metropolitan Philadelphia*, pp. 47-48; Scott, *American City Planning*, p. 459; Gottmann, *Megalopolis*, pp. 507-9.

21. Muller, Meyer, and Cybriwsky, *Metropolitan Philadelphia*, pp. 52-54; Milton A. Paule, ed., *Directory of Shopping Centers in the United States and Canada*, 16th ed. (Burlington, Iowa: National Research Bureau, 1975), pp. 1105, 1484.

22. Gurney Breckenfeld, "'Downtown' Has Fled to the Suburbs," *Fortune* 86 (October 1972): 83; Muller, Meyer, and Cybriwsky, *Metropolitan Philadelphia*, pp. 49-50.

23. Paule, ed., *Directory of Shopping Centers*, pp. 2068, 2070-71; Oberman and Kozakowski, *Development in the Delaware Valley*, pp. 79, 84; Gottmann, *Megalopolis*, p. 508; Breckenfeld, "'Downtown' Has Fled to the Suburbs," pp. 158, 162; *The Plan for Center City Philadelphia* (Philadelphia: City Planning Commission, 1963), p. 7.

24. Weiler, *Philadelphia: Neighborhood, Authority, and the Urban Crisis*, pp. 58-59, 66-69; Scott, *American City Planning*, p. 323; Oberman and Kozakowski, *Development in the Delaware Valley*, pp. 77-78, 95; James Coke, "The Southeastern Pennsylvania Regional Planning Commission: A Case Study in Organization for Metropolitan Area Planning," Ph.D. dissertation, University of Minnesota, 1956, pp. 48-49; Gottmann, *Megalopolis*, pp. 743-46. At the end of the nineteenth century many reformers viewed governmental centralization as essential to the future well-being of the city, and it is at least ironic that yesterday's bureaucratization has become a justification, even in part, for today's decentralization.

25. Scott, *American City Planning*, pp. 10-23, 43-46, 95-105, 229-30, 278-83, 301-4, 354.

26. Ibid., pp. 5-6; James W. Follin, "City Planning and Zoning in Philadelphia," *The Journal of the Engineers' Club of Philadelphia* 37 (August 8, 1920): 1.

27. W. Clark Hanna, "Organization and Operation of City Planning Activities in Philadelphia," *Legal Intelligence*, March 28, 1946, p. 3; Follin, "City Planning and Zoning," pp. 2-3; George B. Ford, ed., *City Planning Progress in the United States, 1917* (Washington, D.C.: Journal of the American Institute of Architects, 1917), pp. 136-37; Scott, *American City Planning*, pp. 57-60.

28. W. S. Stanton, "Report: Outline History of the Fairmount Parkway, 1871-1935," The Philadelphia City Planning Commission, unpublished manuscript, March 1935, Philadelphia City Archives, Box A 595, pp. 1-2.

29. Ibid., pp. 2-6; Scott, *American City Planning*, pp. 57-60.

30. Ford, ed., *City Planning Progress,* p. 141; Follin, "City Planning and Zoning," pp. 4, 6.

31. Follin, "City Planning and Zoning," p. 2; *Annual Report of the Permanent Committee on Comprehensive Plans of the City of Philadelphia for the year ending December 31, 1915* (Philadelphia: 1916), pp. 4-6, 12; *Annual Report of the Permanent Committee on Comprehensive Plans for the City of Philadelphia for the year ending December 31, 1916* (Philadelphia: 1917), pp. 6-9.

32. Follin, "City Planning and Zoning," p. 7. First proposed in 1911, the rail-subway loop which was to run under Walnut, Race, 12th, and 16th streets was never fully completed. Lenora Berson, "The South Street Insurrection," *Philadelphia Magazine* 60 (November 1960): 91; Hanna, "Organization and Operation of City Planning Activities," pp. 4-7; "A Regional Plan for the Philadelphia Metropolitan District, 1924" in the papers of the Philadelphia Housing Association, Box 24, Urban Archives, Paley Library, Temple University, pp. 13-14.

33. Hanna, "Organization and Operation of City Planning Activities," p. 4; Scott, *American City Planning,* pp. 237-42. The first zoning commission in Philadelphia was established in 1916, but it passed out of existence three years later with the enactment of the new charter. Follin, "City Planning and Zoning," pp. 3, 8.

34. Follin, "City Planning and Zoning," p. 1; "Regional Plan for the Philadelphia Metropolitan District, 1924," p. 14; Hanna, "Organization and Operation of City Planning Activities," p. 4; Charles L. Crangle, "Philadelphia Tomorrow," *U.S.A. Tomorrow,* October 1954, p. 22, in the papers of the Philadelphia Housing Association, Box 23, Urban Archives, Paley Library, Temple University.

35. Report of the Philadelphia City Planning Commission," November 12, 1930, in the Philadelphia City Archives, pp. 4, 8.

36. Scott, *American City Planning,* p. 397; "Philadelphia Charter Commission Urges Better Planning," *ASPO News Letter* 4 (November 1938): 91, quoted in ibid., p. 354.

37. Hanna, "Organization and Operation of City Planning Activities," pp. 4-5; Kirk R. Petshek, *The Challenge of Urban Reform: Policies & Programs in Philadelphia* (Philadelphia: Temple University Press, 1973), pp. 18-21, 72, 155; Bureau of Municipal Research, "Proposed Reorganization of City Planning in Philadelphia," May 1942, in the papers of the Philadelphia Housing Association, Box 21, Urban Archives, Paley Library, Temple University, pp. 8, 12-14. Phillips later became a member of the Philadelphia Housing Authority and during Mayor Joseph Clark's administration, the city's director of commerce. Petshek, *Challenge of Urban Reform,* pp. 72, 155.

38. Scott, *American City Planning,* p. 401; *Annual Report of the Philadelphia City Planning Commission for 1943* (Philadelphia: 1944), pp. 17-18, 33-34; Petshek, *Challenge of Urban Reform,* p. 25; Weiler, *Philadelphia: Neighborhood, Authority, and the Urban Crisis,* pp. 130-31; Crangle, "Philadelphia Tomorrow," p. 22.

39. Philadelphia City Planning Commission, Philadelphia Redevelopment Authority, and Philadelphia Housing Authority, *Philadelphia Housing Quality Survey* (Philadelphia: 1951), p. 1; Weiler, *Philadelphia: Neighborhood, Authority, and the Urban Crisis,* p. 134.

40. Weiler, *Philadelphia: Neighborhood, Authority, and the Urban Crisis,* pp. 41-42; Petshek, *Challenge of Urban Reform,* pp. 30-32, 34-38, 86-87, 184.

41. Crangle, "Philadelphia Tomorrow," pp. 24-27; Weiler, *Philadelphia: Neighborhood, Authority, and the Urban Crisis*, pp. 134-35; "Report of the Philadelphia City Planning Commission," November 12, 1930, p. 8; *City Planning in Philadelphia: A Record of Progress. City Planning Commission Annual Report, 1952* (Philadelphia: 1953), pp. 9-10.

42. Petshek, *Challenge of Urban Reform*, pp. 89-90.

43. Weiler, *Philadelphia: Neighborhood, Authority, and the Urban Crisis*, pp. 122-33, 141-42; Petshek, *Challenge of Urban Reform*, pp. 86-88, 134, 184-92, 203-4, 220-28.

44. Petshek, *Challenge of Urban Reform*, pp. 250-55; Edmund N. Bacon, *Design of Cities* (New York: Viking Press, 1967), p. 262.

45. Petshek, *Challenge of Urban Reform*, pp. 138-44, 173-81; Weiler, *Philadelphia: Neighborhood, Authority, and the Urban Crisis*, pp. 136-40; Scott, *American City Planning*, pp. 523-24.

46. Scott, *American City Planning*, pp. 493, 501; *Comprehensive Plan . . . for the City of Philadelphia*, p. v.

47. *Comprehensive Plan . . . for the City of Philadelphia*, p. 62; Bacon, *Design of Cities*, p. 277. See also Scott, *American City Planning*, pp. 531-36. According to James Vance, the new interest among planners in the relationship between outlying areas and the downtown has enhanced the planner's role. "Finally," he has written, "the process of segregation begins to produce a city for which planning has meaning. Before separate functional districts came into being, the problems facing downtown areas are primarily architectural but once we begin to deal with large, interacting functional units, architecture becomes derivative and design begins as spatial planning." James E. Vance, Jr., "Focus on Downtown," in *Internal Structure of the City: Readings on Space and Environment,* ed. Larry S. Bourne (New York: Oxford University Press, 1971), p. 116.

48. *Comprehensive Plan . . . for the City of Philadelphia*, pp. 17, 44, 48-54, 94, 98, 100. *Plan for Center City Philadelphia*, pp. 7, 12-13, 22-30.

49. Scott, *American City Planning*, pp. 81-83, 102-4, 110-17, 174-80, 193, 198-203, 261-62, 583.

50. In 1900 Philadelphia accounted for 65 percent of all the people in its nine-county region in Pennsylvania and New Jersey. Oberman and Kozakowski, *Development in the Delaware Valley*, pp. 50-54; "City Planning Progress," p. 142.

51. Follin, "City Planning and Zoning," p. 2; Scott, *American City Planning*, p. 176. *Annual Report of the Permanent Committee on Comprehensive Plans . . . for the year ending December 31, 1916*, pp. 10-11; *Annual Report of the Permanent Committee on Comprehensive Plans of the City of Philadelphia for the year ending December 31, 1917* (Philadelphia: 1918), pp. 11, 13.

52. Scott, *American City Planning*, pp. 216-21.

53. "Regional Plan for the Philadelphia Metropolitan District, 1924," pp. 4, 9-11.

54. *The Regional Plan of the Philadelphia Tri-State District* (Philadelphia: Regional Planning Federation of the Philadelphia Tri-State District, 1932), pp. 2, 4, 10-11, 22, 40-42, 67-68.

55. Scott, *American City Planning*, pp. 251, 301-11; Coke, "Southeastern Pennsylvanian Regional Planning Commission," p. 59.

56. Scott, *American City Planning*, pp. 433-48, 513; Coke, "Southeastern Pennsylvania Regional Planning Commission," pp. 66-69.

57. Philadelphia Conference Committee, *The Greater Philadelphia Story* (Philadelphia: 1954) in the papers of the Philadelphia Housing Association, Box 23, Urban Archives, Paley Library, Temple University, unpaginated; Coke, "Southeastern Pennsylvania Regional Planning Commission," pp. 113-37, 158, 228.

58. Oberman and Kozakowski, *Development in the Delaware Valley*, p. 91; Scott, *American City Planning*, pp. 582-83. Because such services as transportation, water supply, and sewage are essential, some county governments in the Philadelphia area have taken responsibility for their provision, and there has even been some cooperation on these and other matters among the authorities of individual suburbs, especially those which share high socioeconomic status or similar financial resources. But such centralization and coordination have occurred on an item-by-item basis, and this piecemeal response to problems which require some form of collective action has severely limited the willingness of the people in these suburban areas to consider metropolitan government as a whole. Oliver P. Williams, Harold Herman, Charles S. Liebman, and Thomas R. Dye, *Suburban Differences and Metropolitan Policies: A Philadelphia Story* (Philadelphia: University of Pennsylvania Press, 1965), pp. 242-43, 300, 308-9.

59. Scott, *American City Planning*, p. 583; *Annual 1968-1969 Report: Delaware Valley Regional Planning Commission* (Philadelphia: 1969), pp. 1-3; *Retail Development in the Delaware Valley Urban Area: Technical Record* (Philadelphia: Delaware Valley Regional Planning Commission, 1970), pp. 92-97.

60. *Annual 1968-1969 Report: Delaware Valley Regional Planning Commission*, p. 5; Scott, *American City Planning*, p. 528; *12 Facts about the Delaware Valley Regional Planning Commission* (Philadelphia: Delaware Valley Regional Planning Commission, no date), unpaginated.

61. Gerald D. Suttles, *The Social Construction of Communities* (Chicago: University of Chicago Press, 1972), pp. 15, 21-23; Kevin Lynch, *The Image of the City* (Cambridge, Mass.: The M.I.T. Press, 1960), pp. 46-87; Suzanne Keller, *The Urban Neighborhood: A Sociological Perspective* (New York: Random House, 1968), pp. 98-101.

62. Caroline Golab, *Immigrant Destinations* (Philadelphia: Temple University Press, 1977), pp. 112-13, 116, 129-31; Peter Binzen, *Whitetown, U.S.A.* (New York: Random House, 1970), pp. 142-43.

63. Michael Feldberg, *The Philadelphia Riots of 1844: A Study of Ethnic Conflict* (Westport, Conn.: Greenwood Press, 1975), pp. 57-58, 68, 82-85; Golab, *Immigrant Destinations*, p. 134; William L. Yancey and Eugene P. Ericksen, "The Antecedents of Community: The Economic and Institutional Structure of Urban Neighborhoods," unpublished manuscript, Philadelphia, 1977, pp. 8-9, 28; Sam Bass Warner, Jr., *The Private City: Philadelphia in Three Periods of Its Growth* (Philadelphia: University of Pennsylvania Press, 1968), pp. 162-69.

64. Baltzell, *Philadelphia Gentlemen*, pp. 174-81; Muller, Meyer, and Cybriwsky, *Metropolitan Philadelphia*, pp. 35-40; Dick Pothier, "From a City Flat to the Green of Bucks County," *The Philadelphia Inquirer*, May 8, 1977; Dick Pothier, "Delaware Co.: A Crazy-quilt of Development," *The Philadelphia Inquirer*, June 5, 1977.

65. Keller, *Urban Neighborhood*, pp. 103-6; Muller, Meyer, and Cybriwsky, *Metropolitan Philadelphia*, pp. 23, 46-48.

66. Norman J. Johnston, "The Caste and Class of the Urban Form of Historic Philadelphia," *Journal of the American Institute of Planners* 32 (November 1966), pp. 334-50; Oberman and Kozakowski, *Development in the Delaware Valley*, pp. 32-34.

67. Emma Jones Lapsansky, "South Street Philadelphia, 1762-1854: 'A Haven for those Low in the World,' " Ph.D. dissertation, University of Pennsylvania, 1975, pp. 108-55, 264-65; Jackson, "Urban Deconcentration in the Nineteenth Century," pp. 129-37; Oberman and Kozakowski, *Development in the Delaware Valley*, pp. 33-34, 50; Warner, *Private City*, pp. 177-200; Muller, Meyer, and Cybriwsky, *Metropolitan Philadelphia*, pp. 15-16, 19.

68. In the early twentieth century the Philadelphia City Council was petitioned now and then about matters like sanitation and traffic by "improvement associations" from such respectable neighborhoods as Cobbs Creek and Overbrook in West Philadelphia, Olney and Rhawnhurst in the Northeast, and Germantown and Chestnut Hill in the Northwest. *Journal of the Select Council of the City of Philadelphia* (Philadelphia: George F. Lasher, 1907-1909), April 1, 1907-April 1, 1909; *Journal of the City Council of Philadelphia* (Philadelphia: Dunlap Printing Co., 1920-1922), January 5, 1920-December 28, 1922; *Journal of the City Council of Philadelphia* (Philadelphia: Dunlap Printing Co., 1930-1932), January 9, 1930-December 28, 1932.

69. Dennis Clark, *The Irish in Philadelphia: Ten Generations of Urban Experience* (Philadelphia: Temple University Press, 1973), pp. 56-58, 109-111, 115-17; Golab, *Immigrant Destinations*, pp. 143-44.

70. Margaret S. Marsh, "Suburbanization and the Search for Community: Residential Decentralization in Philadelphia, 1880-1900," *Pennsylvania History* 44 (April 1977): 108-110, 112-16; Baltzell, *Philadelphia Gentlemen*, pp. 335-63. Compared to most other ethnic groups the Jews seem to have been better able to preserve ethnic organizational ties despite geographic and demographic deconcentration. William L. Yancey and Eugene P. Ericksen, "The Structure of Pluralism: Sources of Urban Ethnicity," unpublished manuscript, Philadelphia, 1978, p. 23.

71. Roland L. Warren, *The Community in America* (Chicago: Rand McNally & Co., 1963), p. 62. See also Keller, *Urban Neighborhood*, pp. 46-47, 116-17.

72. *Partnership for Renewal: A Working Program* (Philadelphia: Office of the Development Coordinator, City of Philadelphia, 1960), p. 64; Mirra Komarovsky, "The Voluntary Associations of Urban Dwellers," *American Sociological Review* 11 (December 1946): 691-94; Wendell Bell and Maryanne T. Force, "Urban Neighborhood Types and Participation in Formal Associations," *American Sociological Review* 21 (February 1956): 28-31; Warren, *Community in America*, pp. 186-208; Suttles, *Social Construction of Communities*, pp. 264-68.

73. Weiler, *Philadelphia: Neighborhood, Authority, and the Urban Crisis*, pp. 131-32; telephone interview with Roberta Burke, past president of the Center City Residents Association, November 1977; Queen Village Neighbors in the papers of the United Neighbors Association, Box 28, Urban Archives, Paley Library, Temple University; Valerie Sue Halverson Pace, "Society Hill Philadelphia: Historic Preservation and Urban Renewal in Washington Square East," Ph.D. dissertation, University of Minnesota, 1976, pp. 139-41, 281.

74. *EMAN: Making a Good Community Better, 1966-1976* (Philadelphia: East Mount Airy Neighbors, 1976), p. 5; typescript in the papers of the Wynnefield Residents Association, Box 1, Urban Archives, Paley Library, Temple University.

75. Warren, *Community in America*, pp. 270, 327-28, 330-31; Division of School Extension, School District of Philadelphia, *Community Organizations in Philadelphia (Community Councils, Civic Associations, Improvement Associations, etc.)* (Philadelphia: 1965), pp. 7, 36. *See also* Irene S. Jameson, "A Study of the Intended Influences of Neighborhood Associations on the Public Schools of an Urban School District," Ed.D. dissertation, Temple University, 1973, pp. 215-18.

76. Scott, *American City Planning*, p. 501; *Partnership for Renewal*, pp. 8-10, 15, 18, 24, 42, 44, 63-64; Petshek, *Challenge of Urban Reform*, pp. 302-3.

77. Petshek, *Challenge of Urban Reform*, pp. 159-61.

78. *Partnership for Renewal*, p. 19; Berson, "The South Street Insurrection," pp. 86-92, 174-82; *Near Northeast Philadelphia: Proposed Commercial Zoning* (Philadelphia: City Planning Commission, 1951), pp. 1, 3, 10-15.

79. *Annual Report: Philadelphia City Planning Commission, 1970-1971* (Philadelphia: 1971), p. 14; *Annual Report of the Philadelphia City Planning Commission for 1943*, p. 15.

80. Scott, *American City Planning*, p. 72; Clarence A. Perry, *Wider Use of the School Plant* (New York: Russell Sage Foundation, 1910), pp. 4-13, 270-73; *Comprehensive Plan . . . for the City of Philadelphia*, pp. 85-86. See also *Annual Report 1966: Philadelphia City Planning Commission* (Philadelphia: 1967), p. 9.

81. Gottmann, *Megalopolis,* pp. 185-86; Muller, Meyer, and Cybriwsky, *Metropolitan Philadelphia,* pp. 63-64; Weiler, *Philadelphia: Neighborhood, Authority, and the Urban Crisis,* pp. 208-9.

82. August Heckscher, *Open Spaces: The Life of American Cities* (New York: Harper & Row, 1977), p. 245.

Bibliography

Philadelphia Since 1800

This bibliography, organized by topic, is intended to assist and give direction to anyone interested in doing further reading or research on the history of Philadelphia since 1800. It is a select list comprised primarily of secondary works published in the last 20 years. However, some doctoral dissertations have also been included as well as those published primary works which can be regarded as important to the study of the city's history in the nineteenth and twentieth centuries. Manuscript and photograph collections, property atlases, and census documents have been excluded because they are too numerous and varied to describe adequately here. For the serious student such materials and many more besides can be found at the following major research facilities: Free Library of Philadelphia, Logan Square; Historical Society of Pennsylvania, 1300 Locust Street; Library Company of Philadelphia, 1314 Locust Street; Philadelphia City Archives, Room 523, City Hall Annex; Philadelphia Historical Commission, Room 1313, City Hall Annex; Philadelphia Social History Project/Center for Philadelphia Studies, University of Pennsylvania; Urban Archives, Samuel Paley Library, Temple University. In addition, the Social Science Data Library at Temple University has population and industrial data for Philadelphia in machine-readable form drawn from the manuscripts of the United States Census from 1850 to 1880.

ABBREVIATIONS

PH—*Pennsylvania History*
PMHB—*Pennsylvania Magazine of History and Biography*
U of P—University of Pennsylvania

General

Burt, Struthers. *Philadelphia: Holy Experiment.* Garden City, N.Y.: Doubleday, Doran & Co., 1945.

Clark, Dennis J., ed. *Philadelphia, 1776-2076: A Three Hundred Year View.* Port Washington, N.Y.: Kennikat Press, 1975.

Collins, Herman Leroy, and Wilfred Jordan. *Philadelphia: A Story of Progress.* 4 vols. New York: Lewis Historical Publishing Co., 1941.

Federal Writers Project, Pennsylvania. *Philadelphia: A Guide to the Nation's Birthplace.* Harrisburg, Pa.: William Penn Association of Philadelphia, Inc., 1937.

Hershberg, Theodore, ed. *Toward an Interdisciplinary History of the City: Work, Space, Family and Group Experience in Nineteenth-Century Philadelphia.* New York: Oxford University Press, 1980.

Jackson, Joseph. *Encyclopedia of Philadelphia.* 4 vols. Harrisburg, Pa.: National Historical Association, 1931-1933.

Joyce, J. St. George, ed. *Story of Philadelphia.* Philadelphia: Harry B. Joseph, 1919.

Lippincott, Horace M. *Philadelphia.* Philadelphia: Macrae Smith, 1926; reprinted, Port Washington, N.Y.: Kennikat Press, 1970.

Looney, Robert F. *Old Philadelphia in Early Photographs, 1839-1914.* New York: Dover Publications, Inc., 1976.

Morgan, George. *The City of Firsts: A Complete History of the City of Philadelphia.* Philadelphia: The Historical Publication Society in Philadelphia, 1926.

Morley, Christopher. *Travels in Philadelphia.* Philadelphia: David McKay Co., 1920.

Muller, Peter O., Kenneth C. Meyer, and Roman A. Cybriwsky. *Metropolitan Philadelphia: A Study of Conflicts and Social Cleavages.* Cambridge, Mass.: Ballinger Publishing Co., 1976.

Naumes, Margaret. "The Existence and Growth of the Very Large City: The Philadelphia Story," Ph.D. dissertation, Stanford University, 1974.

Oberholtzer, Ellis P. *Philadelphia: A History of the City and Its People, A Record of 225 Years.* 4 vols. Philadelphia: S. J. Clarke, 1912.

Oberman, Joseph, and Stephen F. Kozakowski. *History of Development in the Delaware Valley Region.* Philadelphia: Delaware Valley Regional Planning Commission, 1976.

Scharf, J. Thomas, and Thompson Westcott. *History of Philadelphia, 1609-1884.* 3 vols. Philadelphia: L. H. Everts & Co., 1884.

Shackleton, Robert. *The Book of Philadelphia.* Philadelphia: Penn Publishing Co., 1918.

Walther, Rudolph J. *Happenings in Ye Olde Philadelphia, 1680-1900.* Philadelphia: Walther Printing House, 1925.

Warner, Sam Bass, Jr. *The Private City: Philadelphia in Three Periods of Its Growth.* Philadelphia: U of P Press, 1968.

Watson, John F. *Annals of Philadelphia and Pennsylvania in the Olden Time being a Collection of Memoirs, Anecdotes, and Incidents of the City and Its Inhabitants.* 1st edition, 1830. Enlarged and revised edition, 3 vols., with Willis P. Hazard, Philadelphia: E. S. Stuart, 1897.

Wolf, Edwin, 2nd. *Philadelphia: Portrait of an American City.* Philadelphia: Stackpole Books, 1975.

Young, John R., ed. *Memorial History of the City of Philadelphia: From Its First Settlement to the Year 1895.* 2 vols. New York: New York History Company, 1895-1898.

Architecture, Housing, and Planning

Ames, Kenneth. "Robert Mills and the Philadelphia Row House," *Journal of the Society of Architectural Historians* 27 (May 1968): 140-46.

Bauman, John F. "Black Slums/Black Projects: The New Deal and Negro Housing in Philadelphia," *PH* 41 (July 1974): 311-38.

_____. "Disinfecting the Industrial City: The Philadelphia Housing Commission and Scientific Efficiency, 1909-1916," in *The Age of Urban Reform: New Perspectives on the Progressive Era,* ed. Michael H. Ebner and Eugene M. Tobin, pp. 117-30. Port Washington, N.Y.: Kennikat Press, 1977.

_____. "Safe and Sanitary Without the Costly Frills: The Evolution of Public Housing in Philadelphia, 1929-1941," *PMHB* 101 (January 1977): 114-28.

Coke, James G. "The Southeastern Pennsylvania Regional Planning Commission: A Case Study in Organization for Metropolitan Area Planning," Ph.D. dissertation, University of Minnesota, 1956.

Cooledge, Harold N., Jr. "Samuel Sloan, Architect," Ph.D. dissertation, U of P, 1963.

Detweiler, Willard S., Jr. *Chestnut Hill: An Architectural History.* Philadelphia: Willard S. Detweiler, Jr., Inc., 1969.

Dinwiddie, Emily W. *Housing Conditions in Philadelphia: An Investigation Made Under the Direction of a Committee of the Octavia Hill Association.* Philadelphia: Octavia Hill Association, 1904.

Follin, James W. "City Planning and Zoning in Philadelphia," *The Journal of the Engineers' Club of Philadelphia* 37 (August 8, 1920): 1-11.

Hanna, W. Clark. "Organization and Operation of City Planning Activities in Philadelphia," *Legal Intelligence,* March 28, 1946.

Lee, Antoinette Josephine. "The Rise of the Cast Iron District in Philadelphia," Ph.D. dissertation, The George Washington University, 1975.

Muller, Henry M. *Urban Home Ownership: A Socio-economic Analysis with Emphasis on Philadelphia.* Philadelphia: College Offset Press, 1947.

Murtagh, William J. "The Philadelphia Row House," *Journal of the Society of Architectural Historians* 16 (December 1957): 8-13.

O'Gorman, James F., George E. Thomas, and Hyman Meyers. *The Architecture of Frank Furness.* Philadelphia: Philadelphia Museum of Art, 1973.

Pace, Valerie S. H. "Society Hill Philadelphia: Historic Preservation and Urban Renewal in Washington Square East," Ph.D. dissertation, University of Minnesota, 1976.

Philadelphia City Planning Commission. *Comprehensive Plan: The Physical Development Plan for the City of Philadelphia.* Philadelphia: Philadelphia City Planning Commission, 1960.

_____. *Report of the Physical Survey in the Central City Intensive Area of Philadelphia, Pennsylvania by the Federal Works Progress Administration,* Robert Folson, project director. Report number 4421. Philadelphia: 1937.

Philadelphia Museum of Art. *Philadelphia: Three Centuries of American Art,* ed. Darrell Sewell. Philadelphia: Philadelphia Museum of Art, 1976.

"Philadelphia on the Eve of the Nation's Centennial: A Visitor's Description in 1873-74," edited and translated by Stewart A. Stehlin, *PH* 44 (January 1977): 25-36.

Phillips, Harland B. "A War on Philadelphia's Slums: Walter Vrooman and the Conference of Moral Workers, 1893," *PMHB* 76 (January 1952): 47-62.

Post, Joyce A. *A Consolidated Name Index to the Hexamer General Surveys.* Philadelphia: no publisher, 1974. Available at the Free Library of Philadelphia.

Regional Planning Federation of the Philadelphia Tri-State District. *The Regional Plan of the Philadelphia Tri-State District.* Philadelphia: Regional Planning Federation of the Philadelphia Tri-State District, 1932.

Roach, Hannah B. "The Planting of Philadelphia: A Seventeenth Century Real Estate Development," *PMHB* 92 (January 1968): 3-48, 92; (April 1968):143-94.

Steen, Ivan D. "Philadelphia in the 1850's: As Described by British Travelers," *PH* 33 (January 1966): 30-49.

Sutherland, John F. "The Origins of Philadelphia's Octavia Hill Association: Social Reform in the 'Contented' City," *PMHB* 99 (January 1975): 20-44.

Tatum, George. *Penn's Great Town: 250 Years of Philadelphia Architecture illustrated in prints and drawings.* Philadelphia: U of P Press, 1961.

Teitelman, Edward, and Richard W. Longstreth. *Architecture in Philadelphia: A Guide.* Cambridge, Mass.: MIT Press, 1974.

Webster, Richard. *Philadelphia Preserved.* Philadelphia: Temple University Press, 1976.

White, Theo B., ed. *Philadelphia Architecture in the Nineteenth Century.* Philadelphia: U of P Press, 1953.

Winpenny, Thomas. "The Nefarious Philadelphia Plan and Urban America: A Reconsideration," *PMHB* 101 (January 1977): 103-13.

Yarnall, Elizabeth B. *Addison Hutton: Quaker Architect, 1834-1916.* Philadelphia: Art Alliance Press, 1974.

Business and Transportation

Adams, Donald R., Jr. "Wage Rates in Philadelphia, 1790-1830," Ph.D. dissertation, U of P, 1967.

Appel, Joseph H. *The Business Biography of John Wanamaker . . . 1861-1922 with glimpses of Rodman Wanamaker and Thomas B. Wanamaker.* New York: The Macmillan Co., 1930.

Baldwin-Lima-Hamilton Corporation. *History of the Baldwin Locomotive Works, 1832-1913.* Philadelphia: privately printed, 1913.

Biddle, Cordelia Drexel. *My Philadelphia Father.* Garden City, N.Y.: Doubleday & Co., 1955.

Burgess, George H., and Miles C. Kennedy, *Centennial History of the Pennsylvania Railroad Company, 1846-1946.* Philadelphia: privately printed, 1949.

Cox, Harold E., and John F. Meyers. "The Philadelphia Traction Monopoly and the Pennsylvania Constitution of 1874: The Prostitution of an Ideal," *PH* 35 (October 1968): 406-23.

Fowler, John A. *History of Insurance in Philadelphia for Two Centuries, 1683-1882.* Philadelphia: Review Publishing & Printing Co., 1888.

Freedley, Edwin T. *Philadelphia and Its Manufactures: A Handbook Exhibiting the Development, Variety, and Statistics of the Manufacturing Industry of Philadelphia in 1857.* Philadelphia: Edward Young & Co., 1858.

_____. *Philadelphia and Its Manufactures: A Handbook of the Great Manufactories and Representative Mercantile Houses of Philadelphia in 1867.* Philadelphia: Edward Young & Co., 1867.

Gotwals, Joan I. "Decisions of the Urban Traffic and Transportation Board, 1953-1956," Ph.D. dissertation, U of P, 1963.

Hare, Jay V. *History of the Reading.* Philadelphia: 1909-1919; reprinted, Philadelphia: John H. Strock, 1966.

Lief, Alfred. *Family Business: A Century in the Life and Times of Strawbridge & Clothier.* New York: McGraw Hill, 1968.

Lindstrom, Diane. *Economic Change in the Philadelphia Region, 1810-1850.* New York: Columbia University Press, 1978.

Livingood, James W. *The Philadelphia-Baltimore Trade Rivalry, 1780-1860.* Harrisburg, Pa.: Pennsylvania Historical and Museum Commission, 1947.

Milgram, Grace S. "The City Expands: A Study of the Conversion of Land from Rural to Urban Use, Philadelphia 1945-1962," Ph.D. dissertation, U of P, 1967.

Miller, Roger. "Time-Geographic Assessment of the Impact of Horse-Car Transportation in Philadelphia, 1850-1860," Ph.D. dissertation, University of California, Berkeley, 1979.

Nelson, Daniel. *A Checklist of Writings on the Economic History of the Greater Philadelphia-Wilmington Region.* Wilmington, Del.: Eleutherian Mills Historical Library, 1968.

Peters, William S. "Centralization of Retail Trade in the Philadelphia Standard Metropolitan Area," Ph.D. dissertation, U of P, 1954.

Plummer, Wilbur C. *The Road Policy of Pennsylvania.* Philadelphia: U of P, 1925.

Porter, Patrick G., and Harold Livesay. "The Ante-Bellum Drug Trade: Troth & Company of Philadelphia," *PMHB* 94 (July 1970): 347-57.

Proudfoot, Malcolm J. "City Retail Structure," *Economic Geography* 13 (October 1937): 425-28.

Roberts, Thomas. "A History and Analysis of Labor-Management Relations in the Philadelphia Transit Industry," Ph.D. dissertation, U of P, 1957.

Rosenberger, Homer T. *The Philadelphia and Erie Railroad: Its Place in American Economic History.* Potomac, Md.: The Fox Hills Press, 1975.

Shelling, Richard I. "Philadelphia and the Agitation in 1825 for the Pennsylvania Canal," *PMHB* 62 (April 1938): 175-204.

Sparks, Robert M. "The Motivation of Manufacturing Movement in Southeastern Pennsylvania, 1943 to 1955," Ph.D. dissertation, U of P, 1957.

Speirs, Frederic W. *The Street Railway System of Philadelphia: Its History and Present Condition.* Baltimore: The Johns Hopkins Press, 1897.

Taylor, George R. "The Beginning of Mass Transportation in Urban America," *The Smithsonian Journal of History* 1 (Summer 1966): 35-50; 1 (Autumn 1966): 31-54.

Tooker, Elva. *Nathan Trotter, Philadelphia Merchant, 1787-1853.* Cambridge, Mass.: Harvard University Press, 1955.

Twining, William S. *A Study and Review of the Problem of Passenger Transportation in Philadelphia by a United System of Lines.* Philadelphia: City of Philadelphia, 1916.

Wainwright, Nicholas B. *History of the Philadelphia Electric Company, 1881-1961.* Philadelphia: Philadelphia Electric Company, 1961.

_____. *History of the Philadelphia National Bank: A Century and a Half of Philadelphia Banking 1803-1953.* Philadelphia: Philadelphia National Bank, 1953.

Widener, Peter A. B. II. *Without Drums.* New York: G. P. Putnam's Sons, 1940.

Winkler, Allan M. "The Philadelphia Transit Strike of 1944," *Journal of American History* 59 (June 1972): 73-89.

Winpenny, Thomas. "The Locational Impact of the Motor Truck on the Industrial Structure of Philadelphia, 1900-1930," Ph.D. dissertation, University of Delaware, 1973.

Social and Cultural Life

Bell, Marion L. "Religious Revivalism in Philadelphia: From Finney to Moody," Ph.D. dissertaton, Temple University, 1974.

Bloom, Robert L. "The Philadelphia 'North American': A History, 1839-1925," Ph.D. dissertation, Columbia University, 1952.

Blumberg, Leonard, Thomas E. Shipley, Jr., and Irving W. Shandler, *Skid Row and Its Alternatives: Research and Recommendations from Philadelphia.* Philadelphia: Temple University Press, 1973.

Cornog, William. *School of the Republic: 1893-1943. A Half Century of the Central High School of Philadelphia.* Philadelphia: Rittenhouse Press, 1952.

Costello, William J. "The Chronological Development of the Catholic Secondary School in the Archdiocese of Philadelphia," Ed.D. dissertation, Temple University, 1957.

Custis, John T. *The Public Schools of Philadelphia: Historical, Biographical, Statistical.* Philadelphia: Burk & McFettridge Co., 1897.

Cutler, William W., III. "A Preliminary Look at the Schoolhouse: The Philadelphia Story, 1870-1920," *Urban Education* 8 (January 1974): 381-99.

Ditter, Dorothy E. "The Cultural Climate of the Centennial City: Philadelphia, 1875-1876," Ph.D. dissertation, U of P, 1947.

Doherty, Robert W. "Social Bases for the Presbyterian Schism of 1837-1838: The Philadelphia Case," *Journal of Social History* 2 (Fall 1968): 69-79.

Donaghy, Thomas J. *Philadelphia's Finest: A History of Education in the Archdiocese of Philadelphia.* Philadelphia: American Catholic Historical Society, 1972.

Edmonds, Franklin Spencer. *History of Central High School of Philadelphia.* Philadelphia: J. B. Lippincott Co., 1902.

Fishbane, Richard B. "The Shallow Boast of Cheapness: Public School Teaching as a Profession in Philadelphia, 1865-1890," *PMHB* 103 (January 1979): 66-84.

Franklin, Vincent P. "Educating the Black Community: The Case of Philadelphia, 1900-1950," Ph.D. dissertation, University of Chicago, 1975.

Geffen, Elizabeth M. "Philadelphia Protestantism Reacts to Social Reform Movements Before the Civil War," *PH* 30 (April 1963): 192-202.

Haber, Carol. "The Old Folks Home: The Development of Institutionalized Care for the Aged in Nineteenth Century Philadelphia, *PMHB* 101 (April 1977): 240-57.

Hamlin, Talbot F. *Benjamin Henry Latrobe*. New York: Oxford University Press, 1955.

Issel, William H. "Modernization in Philadelphia School Reform, 1882-1905," *PMHB* 94 (July 1970): 358-83.

James, Reese D. *Cradle of Culture, 1800-1810: The Philadelphia Stage*. Philadelphia: U of P Press, 1957.

Kirlin, Joseph J. J. *Catholicity in Philadelphia from the earliest missionaries down to the present time*. Philadelphia: James McVey, 1909.

Lester, John A., ed. *A Century of Philadelphia Cricket*. Philadelphia: U of P Press, 1957.

Loetscher, Lefferts A. "Presbyterianism and Revivals in Philadelphia since 1875," *PMHB* 68 (January 1944): 54-92.

McCadden, Joseph. *Education in Pennsylvania 1801-1835 and its Debt to Roberts Vaux*. Philadelphia: U of P Press, 1937.

_____. "Joseph Lancaster and the Philadelphia Schools," *PH* 3 (October 1936): 225-39.

Nash, Charles R. "The History of Legislative and Administrative Changes Affecting the Philadelphia Public Schools, 1869-1921," Ed.D. dissertation, Temple University, 1943.

Nash, Gary B. "The Philadelphia Bench and Bar, 1800-1861," *Comparative Studies in Society and History* 7 (January 1965): 203-20.

Neilly, Andrew H. "The Violent Volunteers: A History of the Volunteer Fire Department of Philadelphia, 1736-1871," Ph.D. dissertation, U of P, 1960.

O'Breza, John E. "Philadelphia Parochial School System from 1830 to 1920: Growth and Bureaucratization," Ed.D. dissertation, Temple University, 1979.

O'Hara, Leo J. "An Emerging Profession: Philadelphia Medicine, 1860-1900," Ph.D. dissertation, U of P, 1976.

Pepper, George Wharton. *Philadelphia Lawyer: An Autobiography*. Philadelphia: J. B. Lippincott Co., 1944.

Rauch, Julia B. "Quakers and the Founding of the Philadelphia Society for Organizing Charitable Relief and Repressing Mendicancy," *PMHB* 98 (October 1974): 438-55.

Robinson, Elwyn P. "The Public Ledger: An Independent Newspaper," *PMHB* 64 (January 1940): 43-55.

Rubinstein, Stanley. "The Role of the Trustees and the Librarians in the Development of the Enoch Pratt Free Library and the Free Library of Philadelphia, 1800-1914," Ph.D. dissertation, The George Washington University, 1978.

Schreiber, Lee L. "The Philadelphia Elite in the Development of the Pennsylvania Academy of the Fine Arts, 1805-1842," Ph.D. dissertation, Temple University, 1977.

Silcox, Harry C. "Philadelphia Negro Educator: Jacob C. White, Jr., 1837-1902," *PMHB* 97 (January 1973): 75-98.

Sims, Joseph P., ed. *The Philadelphia Assemblies. An account of the Assemblies printed for the two hundredth anniversary, January 2nd, 1948.* Philadelphia: privately printed, 1947.

Sinclair, Bruce. *Philadelphia's Philosopher Mechanics: A History of the Franklin Institute, 1824-1865.* Baltimore: Johns Hopkins University Press, 1974.

Uberti, John R. "Men, Manners, and Mechanics: The Young Man's Institute in Antebellum Philadelphia," Ph.D. dissertation, U of P, 1977.

Visco, Anthony F., ed. *The Sixty Year History of Frankford High School, 1910-1970.* Philadelphia: Alumni Association of Frankford High School, 1973.

Wainwright, Nicholas B., ed. *A Philadelphia Perspective: The Diary of Sidney George Fisher Covering the Years 1834-1871.* Philadelphia: Historical Society of Pennsylvania, 1967.

Welch, Charles E. *Oh! Dem Golden Slippers.* New York: Thomas Nelson, 1970.

Whiteman, Maxwell. *Gentlemen in Crisis: The First Century of the Union League of Philadelphia, 1862-1962.* Philadelphia: The League, 1975.

Ethnicity, Race, and Social Class

Alexander, John K. "The City of Brotherly Fear: The Poor in Eighteenth Century Philadelphia," in *Cities in American History*, ed. Kenneth T. Jackson and Stanley K. Schultz, pp. 79-97. New York: Alfred A. Knopf, 1972.

Arky, Louis H. "The Mechanics' Union of Trade Associations and the Formation of the Philadelphia Workingmen's Movement," *PMHB* 76 (April 1952): 142-76.

Baltzell, E. Digby. *Philadelphia Gentlemen: The Making of a National Upper Class with a New Afterword by the Author.* Chicago: Quadrangle Books, 1971.

Benjamin, Philip S. "Gentlemen Reformers in the Quaker City, 1870-1912," *Political Science Quarterly* 85 (March 1970): 61-79.

———. *The Philadelphia Quakers in the Industrial Age, 1865-1920.* Philadelphia: Temple University Press, 1976.

Blodget, Lorin. *The Social Condition of the Industrial Classes of Philadelphia.* Philadelphia: Philadelphia Social Science Association, 1883.

Blumin, Stuart. "Mobility and Change in Ante-Bellum Philadelphia," in *Nineteenth Century Cities: Essays in the New Urban History,* ed. Stephan Thernstrom and Richard Sennett, pp. 165-208. New Haven, Conn.: Yale University Press, 1969.

Burstein, Alan N. "Residential Distribution and Mobility of Irish and German Immigrants in Philadelphia, 1850-1880," Ph.D. dissertation, U of P, 1975.

Burt, Struthers. *The Perennial Philadelphians: The Anatomy of an American Aristocracy.* Boston: Little Brown, 1963.

Cale, Edgar B. "The Organization of Labor in Philadelphia," Ph.D. dissertation, U of P, 1940.

Clark, Dennis J. *The Irish in Philadelphia: Ten Generations of Urban Experience.* Philadelphia: Temple University Press, 1973.

———. *Proud Past: Catholic Laypeople of Philadelphia.* Philadelphia: Catholic Philopatrian Literary Society, 1976.

_____. "Babes in Bondage: Indentured Irish Children in Philadelphia in the Nineteenth Century," *PMHB* 101 (October 1977): 475-86.

Commonwealth of Pennsylvania. *The Care of Poor People in Philadelphia from Colonial Times to 1971: An Annotated Bibliography.* Harrisburg, Pa.: Commonwealth of Pennsylvania, Department of Public Welfare, 1972.

Curtis, Julia B. "The Organized Few: Labor in Philadelphia, 1857-1873," Ph.D dissertation, Bryn Mawr College, 1970.

Davis, Allen F., and Mark H. Haller, eds. *The Peoples of Philadelphia: A History of Ethnic Groups and Lower Class Life, 1790-1940.* Philadelphia: Temple University Press, 1973.

Du Bois, W. E. B. *The Philadelphia Negro: A Social Study.* 1899; reprinted New York: Schocken Books, 1967.

Ericksen, Eugene P., and William L. Yancey. "Work and Residence in an Industrial City," *Journal of Urban History*, forthcoming.

Feldberg, Michael. *The Philadelphia Riots of 1844: A Study of Ethnic Conflict.* Westport, Conn.: Greenwood Press, 1975.

Foner, Philip S. "The Battle to End Discrimination Against Negroes on Philadelphia Streetcars: Part I, Background and Beginning of the Battle," *PH* 40 (July 1973): 261-90; and "Part II, The Victory," *PH* 36 (October 1973): 355-79.

Franklin, Vincent P. "The Philadelphia Race Riot of 1918," *PMHB* 99 (July 1975): 336-50.

Freedman, Murray, and Daniel J. Elazar. *Moving Up: Ethnic Succession in the Philadelphia Schools.* Philadelphia: American Jewish Committee, 1976.

Furstenberg, Frank, Jr., Theodore Hershberg, and John Modell. "The Origins of the Female-Headed Black Family; The Impact of the Urban Environment," *Journal of Interdisciplinary History* 6 (September 1975): 211-33.

Geffen, Elizabeth M. "Violence in Philadelphia in the 1840's and 1850's," *PH* 36 (October 1969): 381-410.

Glassberg, Eudice. "Work, Wages and the Cost of Living: Ethnic Differences and the Poverty Line, Philadelphia, 1880," *PH* 46 (January 1979): 17-58.

Golab, Caroline. *Immigrant Destinations.* Philadelphia: Temple University Press, 1977.

Hershberg, Theodore. "Free Blacks in Antebellum Philadelphia: A Study of Ex-Slaves, Freeborn, and Socioeconomic Decline," *The Journal of Social History* 5 (Winter 1971-72): 183-209.

_____. "Freeborn and Slaveborn Blacks in Antebellum Philadelphia," in *Race and Slavery in the Western Hemisphere: Quantitative Studies*, ed. Eugene D. Genovese and Stanley L. Engerman, pp. 395-426. Princeton, N.J.: Princeton University Press, 1975.

_____, Alan N. Burstein, Eugene P. Ericksen, Stephanie Greenberg, and William L. Yancey. "A Tale of Three Cities: Blacks and Immigrants in Philadelphia, 1850-1880, 1930 and 1970," *The Annals of the American Academy of Political and Social Science* 441 (January 1979): 55-81.

_____, Michael B. Katz, Laurence Glasco, Stuart Blumin, and Clyde Griffen. "Occupation and Ethnicity in Five Nineteenth Century Cities: A Collaborative Inquiry," *Historical Methods Newsletter* 7 (June 1974): 174-216.

Houghes, Gwendolyn S. *Mothers in Industry: Wage Earning Mothers in Philadelphia.* New York: New Republic, Inc., 1925.

Johnston, Norman J. "The Caste and Class of the Urban Form of Historic Philadelphia," *Journal of the American Institute of Planners* 32 (November 1966): 334-50.

Juliani, Richard. "The Social Organization of Immigration: The Italians of Philadelphia," Ph.D. dissertation, U of P, 1971.

King, Moses. *Philadelphia and Notable Philadelphians.* New York: Moses King, 1901.

Klaczynska, Barbara M. "Working Women in Philadelphia, 1900-1930," Ph.D. dissertation, Temple University, 1975.

Laurie, Bruce. *Class and Culture: The Working People of Philadelphia, 1800-1851.* Philadelphia: Temple University Press, 1980.

_____. "Nothing on Compulsion: Life Styles of Philadelphia Artisans, 1820-1850," *Labor History* 15 (Summer 1974): 337-66.

_____, Theodore Hershberg, and George Alter. "Immigrants and Industry: The Philadelphia Experience, 1850-1880," *Journal of Social History* 9 (Winter 1975): 219-67.

Lees, Lynn H., and John Modell. "The Irish Countryman Urbanized: A Comparative Perspective on the Famine Migration," *Journal of Urban History* 4 (August 1977): 391-408.

Light, Dale B., Jr. "The Making of an Ethnic Community: Philadelphia's Irish, 1840-1890," Ph.D. dissertation, U of P, 1979.

Mackey, Philip E. "Law and Order, 1877: Philadelphia's Response to the Railroad Riots," *PMHB* 96 (April 1972): 183-202.

McLeod, Richard A. "The Philadelphia Artisan, 1828-1850," Ph.D. dissertation, University of Missouri, 1971.

Montgomery, David. "The Shuttle and the Cross: Weavers and Artisans in the Kensington Riots of 1844," *Journal of Social History* 5 (Summer 1972): 411-46.

Nelson, H. Viscount, Jr. "Race and Class Consciousness of Philadelphia Negroes with Special Emphasis on the Years between 1927 and 1940," Ph.D. dissertation, U of P, 1969.

Pennell, Elizabeth R. *Our Philadelphia.* Philadelphia: J. B. Lippincott, 1914.

Philadelphia and Popular Philadelphians. Philadelphia: The North American, 1891.

Runcie, John. "'Hunting the Nigs' in Philadelphia: The Race Riots of August 1834," *PH* 39 (April 1972): 187-218.

Sears, Irwin. "The Growth of Population in Philadelphia: 1860-1910," Ph.D. dissertation, New York University, 1960.

Seller, Maxine. "Isaac Leeser: A Jewish-Christian Dialogue in Antebellum Philadelphia," *PH* 35 (July 1969): 231-42.

Sheridan, Peter B. "The Immigrant in Philadelphia, 1827-1860: The Contemporary Published Report," Ph.D. dissertation, Georgetown University, 1957.

Silcox, Harry C. "Nineteenth Century Philadelphia Black Militant: Octavius V. Cato (1839-1971)," *PH* 44 (January 1977): 53-76.

_____. "Delay and Neglect: Negro Public Education in Ante-bellum Philadelphia, 1800-1860," *PMHB* 97 (October 1973): 444-64.

Simpson, Henry. *The Lives of Eminent Philadelphians, now deceased collected from original and authentic sources.* Philadelphia: William Brotherhead, 1859.

Society of Friends. *Statistical Inquiry into the Condition of the People of Color of the City and Districts of Philadelphia.* Philadelphia: 1849.

Sullivan, William A. *The Industrial Worker in Pennsylvania, 1800-1840.* Harrisburg, Pa.: Pennsylvania Historical and Museum Commission, 1955.

Varbero, Richard A. "Urbanization and Acculturation: Philadelphia's South Italians, 1918-1932," Ph.D. dissertation, Temple University, 1975.

Whiteman, Maxwell. "The East European Jew Comes to Philadelphia," in *The Ethnic Experience in Pennsylvania,* ed. John E. Bodnar. Lewisburg, Pa.: Bucknell University Press, 1973.

Williams, Henry, and Robert Ulle. "Frankford, Philadelphia: The Development of a Nineteenth-Century Urban Black Community," *Pennsylvania Heritage* 4 (December 1977): 2-8.

Wolf, Edwin, 2d, and Maxwell Whiteman. *The History of the Jews in Philadelphia from Colonial Times to the Age of Jackson.* Philadelphia: Jewish Publication Society of America, 1957.

Zachary, Alan M. "Social Disorder and the Philadelphia Elite Before Jackson," *PMHB* 99 (July 1975): 288-308.

Neighborhoods

Alderfer, E. Gordon. *The Montgomery County Story.* Norristown, Pa.: Commissioners of Montgomery County, 1951.

Bean, Theodore W. *History of Montgomery County, Pennsylvania.* 2 vols. Philadelphia: Everts & Peck, 1884; reprinted Evansville, Ind.: Unigraphic, 1975.

Binzen, Peter. *Whitetown, U.S.A.* New York: Random House, 1970.

Campbell, W. B. *Old Towns and Districts of Philadelphia.* Philadelphia: City History Society of Philadelphia, 1941.

Chestnut Street Philadelphia. Descriptive, Reminiscent, Sentimental. Text by an Ex-Reporter. Philadelphia: Thomson, 1904.

Cohen, Charles J. *Rittenhouse Square: Past and Present.* Philadelphia: privately printed, 1922.

Cybriwsky, Roman A. "Social Relations and the Spatial Order in the Urban Environment: A Study of Life in a Neighborhood in Central Philadelphia," Ph.D. dissertation, The Pennsylvania State University, 1972.

Davis, W. W. H. *The History of Bucks County, Pennsylvania from the Discovery of the Delaware to the Present Time.* 2d ed., revised and enlarged, Warren S. Ely, ed., with John W. Jordan. New York: Lewis Publishing Co., 1905.

Foster, George. "Philadelphia in Slices," *PMHB* 93 (January 1969): 23-72.

Franklin, Leonard. "The Definition and Analysis of Stable Racial Integration: The Case of West Mount Airy," Ph.D. dissertation, U of P, 1973.

Hocker, Edward W. *Germantown, 1683-1933: The Record that a Pennsylvania Community has Achieved in the Course of 250 Years. Being a History of the People of Germantown, Mount Airy and Chestnut Hill.* Philadelphia: by the author, 1933.

_____. *A History of the Township of Abington.* Abington, Pa.: Board of Commissioners of Abington, 1956.

Hotchkin, Rev. S. F. *Ancient and Modern Germantown, Mount Airy and Chestnut Hill.* Philadelphia: P. W. Ziegler & Co., 1889.

Jackson, Joseph. *America's Most Historic Highway, Market Street, Philadelphia.* Philadelphia: John Wanamaker, 1926.

Jackson, Kenneth T. "Urban Deconcentration in the Nineteenth Century: A Statistical Inquiry," in *The New Urban History: Quantitative Explorations by American Historians,* ed. Leo F. Schnore, pp. 110-42. Princeton, N.J.: Princeton University Press, 1975.

Jones, Arthur H. "Cheltenham Township," Ph.D. dissertation, U of P, 1940.

Kensington: A City Within a City, An Historical and Industrial Review. 1891; reprint ed., Philadelphia: Kensington Printing House, 1928.

Keyser, Naaman H., C. Henry Kain, John P. Garber, and Horace F. McCann. *History of Old Germantown.* Germantown, Philadelphia: H. F. McCann, 1907.

Lapsansky, Emma Jones. *Before the Model City: An Historical Exploration of North Philadelphia.* Philadelphia: Philadelphia Historical Commission, 1968.

_____. "South Street Philadelphia, 1762-1854: 'A Haven for Those Low in the World,'" Ph.D. dissertation, U of P, 1975.

Levy, Paul R. *Queen Village: The Eclipse of a Community.* Public Papers in the Humanities No. 2. Philadelphia: Institute for the Study of Civic Values, 1978.

Ley, David F. "The Black Inner City as a Frontier Outpost: Images and Behavior of a Philadelphia Neighborhood," Ph.D. dissertation, The Pennsylvania State University, 1972.

Lippincott, Horace M. *A Narrative of Chestnut Hill, Philadelphia, with some account of Springfield, Whitemarsh, and Cheltenham Townships in Montgomery County, Pennsylvania.* Jenkintown, Pa.: Old York Road Publishing Co., 1948.

Little, Esther J., and William J. H. Cotton. *Budgets of Families and Individuals of Kensington, Philadelphia.* Lancaster, Pa.: Press of the New Era Printing Co., 1920.

Marsh, Margaret S. "Suburbanization and the Search for Community: Residential Decentralization in Philadelphia, 1880-1900," *PH* 44 (April 1977): 99-116.

Martindale, Joseph C. *A History of the Townships of Byberry and Moreland in Philadelphia, Pa.,* rev. ed. by Albert W. Dudley. Philadelphia: George W. Jacobs, n.d.

Miles, Joseph S., and William H. Cooper. *A Historical Sketch of Roxborough, Manayunk, Wissahickon compiled from the records of Joseph S. Miles.* Philadelphia: G. Fein & Co., 1940.

Rosenthal, Leon. *A History of Philadelphia's University City.* Philadelphia: West Philadelphia Corporation, 1963.

Rothschild, Elaine W. *A History of Cheltenham Township.* Cheltenham, Pa.: Cheltenham Township Historical Commission, 1976.

Southwark, Moyamensing, Weccacoe, Dock Ward for Two Hundred and Seventy Years. Philadelphia: Quaker City Publishing Co., 1892.

Weaver, W. W. *West Philadelphia: A Study of Natural Social Areas.* Philadelphia: by the author, 1930.

Politics and Government

Abernethy, Lloyd. "Insurgency in Philadelphia, 1905," *PMHB* 87 (January 1963): 3-20.

Allinson, Edward P., and Boies Penrose. *Philadelphia 1681-1887: A History of Municipal Development.* Philadelphia: Allen, Lane and Scott Publishers, 1887.

Bowden, Robert D. *Boies Penrose: Symbol of an Era.* New York: Greenberg, 1937.

Crumlish, Joseph. "The Philadelphia Home Rule Charter Movement," Ph.D. dissertation, Georgetown University, 1964.

Daly, John, and Allen Weinberg. *Genealogy of Philadelphia County Subdivisions.* 2d ed. Philadelphia: Philadelphia Department of Records, 1966.

Disbrow, Donald W. "Reform in Philadelphia under Mayor Blankenburg, 1912-1916," *PH* 27 (October 1960): 379-96.

Drayer, Robert E. "J. Hampton Moore: An Old Fashioned Republican," Ph.D. dissertation, U of P, 1961.

Dusinberre, William. *Civil War Issues in Philadelphia, 1856-1865.* Philadelphia: U of P Press, 1965.

Ershkowitz, Miriam, and Joseph Zikmund, II, ed. *Black Politics in Philadelphia.* New York: Basic Books, Inc., 1973.

Fink, Joseph R. "Reform in Philadelphia, 1946-1951," Ph.D. dissertation, Rutgers University, 1971.

Fox, Bonnie R. "The Philadelphia Progressives: A Test of the Hofstadter-Hays Thesis," *PH* 34 (October 1967): 372-94.

_____. "Unemployment Relief in Philadelphia, 1930-1932: A Study of the Depression's Impact on Voluntarism," *PMHB* 93 (January 1969): 86-108.

Gillette, Howard, Jr. "Corrupt and Contented: Philadelphia's Political Machine, 1865-1887," Ph.D. dissertation. Yale University, 1970.

_____. "Philadelphia's City Hall: Monument to a New Political Machine," *PMHB* 97 (April 1973): 233-49.

Greenberg, Irwin F. "Philadelphia Democrats Get a New Deal: The Election of 1933," *PMHB* 97 (April 1973): 210-32.

Grove, Stephen B. "The Decline of the Republican Machine in Philadelphia, 1936-1952," Ph.D. dissertation, U of P, 1976.

Kurtzman, David H. "Methods of Controlling Votes in Philadelphia," Ph.D. dissertation, U of P, 1935.

Lewis, Eugene. "Socio-economic Variables with Political Change in Philadelphia, 1950-1965," Ph.D. dissertation, Syracuse University, 1967.

McClure, Alexander K. *Old Time Notes of Pennsylvania.* 2 vols. Philadelphia: John C. Winston & Co., 1905.

Maiale, Hugo V. "The Italian Vote in Philadelphia between 1928 and 1946," Ph.D. dissertation, U of P, 1950.

Petshek, Kirk R. *The Challenge of Urban Reform: Policies & Programs in Philadelphia.* Philadelphia: Temple University Press, 1973.

Pivar, David J. "Theocratic Businessmen and Philadelphia Municipal Reform, 1870-1900," *PH* 33 (July 1966): 289-307.

Price, Eli K. *The History of the Consolidation of the City of Philadelphia.* Philadelphia: J. B. Lippincott Co., 1873.

Quay, William L. "Philadelphia Democrats, 1880-1910," Ph.D. dissertation, Lehigh University, 1969.

Reichley, James. *The Art of Government: Reform and Organization Politics in Philadelphia.* New York: Fund for the Republic, 1959.

Salter, J. T. "The End of Vare," *Political Science Quarterly* 50 (June 1935): 214-35.

Shover, John L. "Ethnicity and Religion in Philadelphia Politics, 1924-1940," *American Quarterly* 25 (December 1973): 499-515.

_____. "The Emergence of a Two-Party System in Republican Philadelphia, 1924-1936," *Journal of American History* 60 (March 1974): 985-1002.

Sprogle, Howard O. *The Philadelphia Police, Past and Present.* Philadelphia: 1887; reprinted, New York: Arno Press, 1971.

Tabachnik, Leonard. "Origins of the Know-Nothing Party: A Study of the Native American Party in Philadelphia, 1844-1852," Ph.D. dissertation, Columbia University, 1973.

Vare, William S. *My Forty Years in Politics.* Philadelphia: Roland Swain, Co., 1933.

Weiler, Conrad. *Philadelphia: Neighborhood, Authority, and the Urban Crisis.* New York: Praeger, 1974.

Williams, Oliver P., Harold Herman, Charles S. Liebman, and Thomas R. Dye. *Suburban Differences and Metropolitan Policies: A Philadelphia Story.* Philadelphia: U of P Press, 1965.

Index

Page numbers in italics indicate illustration

About the Authors

The Editors:

William W. Cutler, III, is Assistant Dean of the Graduate School and Associate Professor of History and Foundations of Education at Temple University. He is a past winner of the *American Quarterly* Award and has published articles in a wide variety of professional journals.

Howard Gillette, Jr., is Associate Professor of American Civilization and director of the American Studies Program at The George Washington University. His previous scholarly articles have appeared in the *Pennsylvania Magazine of History and Biography, American Quarterly,* and *American Studies.*

The Contributors:

Deborah C. Andrews is a member of the Department of Humanities-Communications at Drexel University. She is interested in buildings as cultural artifacts and the impact of technology on social institutions, and she has published articles on technology in the home in nineteenth-century America.

John F. Bauman is a member of the Department of History/Urban Affairs at California State College, California, Pennsylvania. He has published several articles on low-income urban housing and is presently completing a study of the history of public housing in Philadelphia. His book, with Thomas H. Coode, *People, Poverty, and Politics: Pennsylvania in the Great Depression,* will be published by Bucknell University Press.

Dennis J. Clark has published many books and articles on American city life. His book *The Irish in Philadelphia* (1973) deals with the adjustment of immigrants to urban life and is part of a continuing series of studies that he has pursued on ethnic development.

Stephanie W. Greenberg is a Research Sociologist at the center for the Study of Social Behavior of the Research Triangle Institute and a Research Associate at the Philadelphia Social History Project. Her major areas of interest are relationships among urban economic development, socioeconomic attainment, and neighborhood composition and stability. Her chapter in this book is drawn from a larger study of the location of work opportunities and residential patterns in Philadelphia between 1880 and 1930.

Margaret S. Marsh teaches history at Stockton State College in New Jersey. She has published several articles dealing with women in Américan life and with the processes of urbanization and suburbanization in nineteenth- and twentieth-century America.

Jeffrey P. Roberts is a co-owner of Clio Group, Inc., a corporation that provides consulting services in architecture, American history, and land use. Concerned with the evolution of urban land use, he is presently completing a study of Philadelphia's downtown between 1830 and 1900 from which his chapter in this book is taken.

Meredith Savery was Coordinator of Community Studies in the American Studies Program at Temple University. She is currently Executive Director of the Philadelphia Area Cultural Consortium.

George E. Thomas is a member of the Growth and Structure of Cities Department at Bryn Mawr College. He is a co-owner of Clio Group, Inc. and has published numerous studies on the architecture of Philadelphia as well as its seaside resorts, including *Cape May: Queen of the Seaside Resorts* (1976).